# INTERPRETING CHEKHOV

# INTERPRETING CHEKHOV

GEOFFREY BORNY

E PRESS

E PRESS

Published by ANU E Press
The Australian National University
Canberra ACT 0200, Australia
Email: anuepress@anu.edu.au
Web: http://epress.anu.edu.au

National Library of Australia
Cataloguing-in-Publication entry

Borny, Geoffrey, 1942- .
Interpreting Chekhov.

ISBN 1 920942 67 X (pbk.).
ISBN 1 920942 68 8 (online).

1. Chekhov, Anton Pavlovich, 1860-1904 - Criticism and interpretation. I. Title.

891.723

All rights reserved. No part of this publication may be reproduced, stored in a retrieval system or transmitted in any form or by any means, electronic, mechanical, photocopying or otherwise, without the prior permission of the publisher.

Indexed by John Owen
Cover design by ANU E Press
Art work by Geoff Pryor

This edition © 2006 ANU E Press

*For Gabrielle*

# Table of Contents

Preface .................................................................................................... v
Acknowledgements ............................................................................... ix
Introduction ........................................................................................... 1
1. Chekhov's Vision of Reality ............................................................ 21
2. The Search for Form ......................................................................... 57
3. Failed Experiments: The Early Plays ............................................. 93
4. *The Seagull*: From Disaster to Triumph ........................................ 127
5. *Uncle Vanya*: 'A Glimmer of Light Shining in the Distance' ......... 169
6. *Three Sisters*: 'Oh if we could only know!' .................................... 195
7. *The Cherry Orchard*: Complete Synthesis of Vision and Form ..... 225
Conclusion ........................................................................................... 263
Select Bibliography ............................................................................. 267
Index ..................................................................................................... 303

# Preface

It is now common practice for literary texts to be taught in translation at universities. The plays of Chekhov are taught not only by Russian scholars but also by academics trained in such disciplines as English who have little or no knowledge of the Russian language. Understandably, many scholars who are Russian language experts question this practice and imply that critical insight into the works of a writer such as Chekhov can be achieved only by those who have a command of the Russian language. While I have some sympathy for this view, I believe that it is flawed because it fails to take into account the legitimate aims and objectives of disciplines other than the discipline of Russian language and literature.

Apart from his short stories Chekhov wrote plays and these latter works clearly become the legitimate object of investigation by scholars such as myself who teach in the discipline of Drama and Theatre Studies. Having published a translation of Racine's only comedy, *Les Plaideurs*,[1] and written about the nature and process of translation,[2] I realise that a knowledge of the language of the source text is the *sine qua non* of translation. It is true that knowledge of Russian would have been useful to me when writing about Chekhov, as it would have allowed me to read the considerable amount of Russian scholarly work on Chekhov that has not yet been translated into English. However, knowledge of the Russian language is *not* the *sine qua non* of a Theatre Studies analysis of this playwright.

It is the normal function of translation experts such as Ronald Hingley to convert Russian source texts into English target texts. These English versions of the plays then become the source texts used by critics writing about how Chekhov's plays function as pieces of drama and theatre. Similarly, directors of Chekhov's plays in the English-speaking theatre use translations as source texts which they transform into the target texts of theatrical production. Drama and Theatre Studies departments nearly always rely on translations of playtexts and do not require either the teachers or students to have a knowledge of the original language in which the plays were written. If this were not the case, then a course on Modern European Drama and Theatre would require a knowledge of Swedish (Strindberg), Norwegian (Ibsen), German (Brecht), French (Ionesco), Spanish (Lorca), and Russian (Chekhov).

Given that the use of translations for the purpose of critical analysis is normal practice in the discipline of Drama and Theatre Studies, the question of which translation to use remains. Although every translator of Chekhov's plays has a mastery of the Russian language, the translations that they produce vary considerably. Not surprisingly, American translators tend to produce target texts that sound natural when performed by American actors, while English translators such as Ronald Hingley tend to produce target texts that have a noticeably British quality about them. It is quite common for individual directors to commission new translations, or to adapt existing translations, to make them sound more natural and intelligible to their target audience. Provided that the translations being considered are accurate ones, the choice of which one to use in performance becomes a question of personal taste.

I have chosen to use Ronald Hingley's translations in the Oxford University Press edition of Chekhov's works for a number of reasons. In the first place, the OUP edition is the most recent English translation of Chekhov's works to include both the short stories and the plays, all of which I refer to in this study. In addition, Hingley includes important variants and early draft versions of some of the plays that I also wished to refer to in my analysis. Forsås–Scott's notes on *The Cherry Orchard* include laudatory comments about Volume 3 of Hingley's *Oxford Chekhov* translation. Her observations apply with equal validity to the other collections of plays in *The Oxford Chekhov* series:

> Hingley's volume contains a general introduction, but particularly useful are the appendices which accompany each of the plays. In these the translator has gathered Chekhov's comments on the plays, arranging the material under headings such as 'The composition', 'The text', and 'Some further comments by Chekhov'. In Hingley's translation are also included notes on words and phrases, details about the pronunciation of Russian names, and a bibliography.[3]

Hingley's translation is recognised as being accurate, even though it has been criticised by some scholars for being too British in tone. It is perhaps worth noting that, while there will never be general agreement about which English translation is the best, Hingley's version is highly regarded by a number of scholars both for his accuracy and, significantly for my purpose, for his performability. As Lauren Leighton notes in his review of English translations of Chekhov:

> Among modern translations of Chekhov's plays Bristow finds ... that only Tyrone Guthrie's translation done with Leonid Kipnis and Ronald Hingley's Oxford translations serve performance and diction sufficiently well to be recommended.[4]

The question of the transliteration of Russian names is an important one for any translator. In the 1999 *Modern Drama* special issue on Chekhov, the editor, Ralph Lindheim, ensured that there was an overall consistency among the various essays by adopting clear principles of transliteration:

> Throughout these essays on Chekhov I have employed, whenever possible, a modified version of the Library of Congress transliteration schemes that is similar to the system developed by Frank Whitfield for his edition of D. S. Mirsky's *A*

*History of Russian Literature*, which was originally published by Alfred A. Knopf in 1949.[5]

The editors of *The Cambridge Companion to Chekhov* take an altogether different approach from Lindheim. In their Editorial Notes, Gottlieb and Allain state that:

> The editors took the decision *not* to standardize the various systems of transliteration used by contributors from Russia, from the United States, France, the Irish Republic and the UK. In the case of this volume, where there are different scholarly approaches, varied angles, emphases and priorities, one contributor may need one of the four systems of transliteration (American Library of Congress Systems, I, II, III, IV) while another may require either a different system — or none at all, as in the case of chapters 9 and 11, for instance.[6]

Significantly, the chapters referred to were written by two theatre practitioners: the director Trevor Nunn and the actor Ian McKellen. They are less interested in the niceties of translation than in problems involved in interpreting Chekhov for the stage.

In my own study I have not felt the need to utilise any specific system of transliteration. I have chosen particular spellings of Russian names that are generally regarded as acceptable versions. For example, 'Stanislavski' and 'Chekhov' are used throughout my text. Whenever I have quoted from a critic I have followed the practice of Gottlieb and Allain who 'left each contributor free to choose the transliteration system that suits him or her, rather than enforce consistency of any one system.'[7] Consequently, the reader may often find variant versions of names appearing in quotations — 'Stanislavsky' and 'Tchekoff' are two examples. The variants should cause no problem for the reader.

Hingley has taken the unusual course of anglicising the Russian names of the characters. Whenever it seemed necessary to avoid confusion, I have inserted in brackets the names used by Hingley in quotations from critical works which use alternative Russian names — for example, 'Konstantin [Treplev]'. Similarly, wherever there is a possibility of confusion when quoting from Hingley's translation, I have inserted in brackets the Russian version of each name — for example, 'Helen [Yeliena]'.

While I have employed no fixed system of transliteration, I have attempted to ensure that readers are not confused by the complexity of Russian names and titles. This flexible approach may not seem rigorous enough to some scholars but we should keep in mind Michael Frayn's comment on transliteration that 'Rigidity can in any case produce nonsense'.[8]

## ENDNOTES

[1] Borny, G., *Petty Sessions,* a verse translation of Racine's *Les Plaideurs,* University of New England Press, Armidale, 1988.

[2] Borny, G., 'Appropriate Mis/Appropriations: Translating Racine's *Les Plaideurs'*, in *Dis/Orientations Conference Proceedings,* Australasian Drama Studies Association, Centre for Drama and Theatre Studies, Monash University, Melbourne, 1997, pp. 12–19.

[3] Forsås-Scott, H., *The Cherry Orchard: York Notes,* Longman York Press, Beirut, 1983, p. 11.

[4] Leighton, L. G., 'Chekhov in English', in Clyman, T. W., *A Chekhov Companion,* Greenwood Press, Westport, 1985, p. 304.

[5] Lindheim, R., 'A Note on the Transliteration of Russian Names, Words, and Titles', *Modern Drama,* Vol. 42, No. 4, 1999, p. 470.

[6] Gottlieb, V. and Allain, P., 'Editorial Notes', *The Cambridge Companion to Chekhov,* Cambridge University Press, Cambridge, 2000, p. xxvi.

[7] Ibid.

[8] Frayn, M., 'A Note on the Translation' in Frayn, M, trans., *Chekhov Plays,* Methuen, London, 1991, p. 358.

# Acknowledgements

I wish to express my appreciation to both The University of New England and The Australian National University for granting me study leave to carry out much of the research for this book.

More particularly, I am deeply grateful to Barbara Holloway and Maggie Shapley for their painstaking editorial work. Barbara helped me make the first of many much needed pruning operations on the manuscript. Maggie provided me with advice on how to trim and focus the argument even further. In addition, Maggie has been responsible for the copy editing of the book in preparation for publication.

My final word of thanks goes to my wife, Gabrielle Hyslop, who, besides assisting in editing, has had to live with this Chekhov project for a considerable number of years. Her support and belief in the value of this book have sustained me throughout.

# Introduction

*For better or worse, Chekhov's major plays were written at a time when the stage director was becoming a dominant factor in the modern theatre.* (Laurence Senelick)[1]

*It is the total incomprehension of the central themes of Chekhov's plays that explains why directors are so prone to indulge in wild fantasies.* (David Magarshack)[2]

Throughout his life, Anton Chekhov was highly critical of many features of the theatre of his day. His negative attitude towards directors and actors who presented his plays in a manner that displeased him led Chekhov to make the acerbic comment, 'The stage is a scaffold on which the playwright is executed'.[3] Even the director who did the most to establish Chekhov's fame in the theatre, Konstantin Stanislavski, did not escape the playwright's anger. The depth of Chekhov's discontent with theatre artists is well documented. As Philip Callow points out:

> There is no doubt that Chekhov was disillusioned with contemporary theatre from the outset. He commented bitingly, to various correspondents, on the egotism and obtuseness of actors, not to mention their incompetence; on the limitations of the repertoire, the stupidity of directors, the passive acceptance of audiences. He engaged in a war of attrition with the theatre of his day, even when a theatre under Stanislavsky devoted itself to him, and he invariably lost. Stanislavsky, a pioneer of the experimental new drama, was for Chekhov a more complex foe, stubbornly refusing to see that tragedy could be depicted through comedy.[4]

My own study of the playwright and the experience of having acted in and directed several of his plays has led me to the conclusion that Chekhov had valid grounds for his animosity towards interpreters of his plays. From the time when they were written to the present day both critics and theatre directors have regularly misinterpreted Chekhov's plays.

A claim such as this immediately raises the question of what constitutes a valid interpretation. At the beginning of the twenty-first century, with the advent of postmodern theories of literature, it has become increasingly difficult to talk with any sense of authority about a playwright's intentions, or to argue that any particular interpretation of a playwright's work is more accurate than any other interpretation. Thirty years ago, it was not uncommon for critics and directors to confidently assert that their job was to provide an interpretation that would accurately reflect the playwright's intention. Today, many critics and directors not only assume that there is no sense in talking about the author's intention, but also believe there should be no limitation at all on interpretation.

Today there is no generally accepted way to approach the critical and stage interpretation of plays.

The claim that Chekhov's plays are often misinterpreted is clearly not in accord with those postmodern theories that deny the very possibility of valid interpretation. Consequently it is important to outline what the critical assumptions are that underpin this study. This work expresses the view recently voiced by Jonathan Miller, the English director, that there are two extreme critical positions relating to theatrical interpretation that must be avoided:

> At the moment there are two millstones of folly which are threatening to grind the theatre into a state of pulverised idiocy. On the one hand, there is the existing notion that there is some sort of canonical version, the original version, the version which would most have pleased the playwright, the version that most realises the playwright's intention. And on the other, the notion that there is no such thing as the playwright's intention, that there is no such thing as a standard canonical formal meaning in a text, and that actually these texts constantly renew themselves under the pressure of interpretation, which allows there to be almost anything and the text is taken as an unstructured thing altogether. Both of these seem to me to be a misunderstanding of what the nature of a text is.[5]

While there are no definitive versions of Chekhov, there are 'preferred readings' or 'valid interpretations'. Clearly, directors who deny the need for any interpretation and produce what I call 'texts on legs' will reject the idea that a plurality of readings is possible. Equally, the idea that there may be 'invalid interpretations' will have little appeal to postmodern directors who deny that plays have any inherent meaning and choose to create theatrical events that have only a peripheral connection with the author's playtext.

The aim of this study is to provide insights that will help students, directors and actors to 'read' the plays in a manner that will assist in the creation of valid versions. In order to make clear the assumptions that underpin this study of Chekhov, it is necessary to understand that in the field of Theatre Studies a play does not exist as a single text. There are two separate but related texts: the written playtext and the performance playtext. The author's playtext is inevitably mediated in the production of the performance text. There are still critics who argue that such mediation is unwarranted. They argue that playwrights should be allowed to speak for themselves in the performance text without the intrusive mediation of other theatre artists like directors. This critically discredited view has been given a new lease of life recently as a result of its being adopted by conservative critics and audiences as a means to attack more extreme postmodern theatrical interpretations. It is still quite common to hear theatre-goers and critics harking back to some mythical golden age when the director didn't exist and the playwright's play delivered itself to the audience without having to be interpreted. As Jonathan Miller stated in an impromptu talk he gave at the Adelaide Festival in the late 1970s on the topic 'Directing the Classics', certain people still believe that the director "should simply act as a butler ushering the work of the great classic onto the stage and then retire gracefully into the wings".[6]

The desire for an unmediated, uninterpreted performance that will let the playwright speak for himself can never be satisfied, for, as Peter Brook has pointedly asserted, 'if you just let a play speak, it may not make a sound. If what you want is for the play to be heard, then you must conjure its sound from it.'[7] Brook's views are echoed by Miller when he baldly asserts that 'the act of interpretation is absolutely essential ... The so-called pure version of the bard speaking for himself hasn't ever and will never happen.'[8]

Both Miller and Brook are theatre directors and consequently it is not surprising to find them defending the creativity of their task and rejecting the passive 'butler' idea of direction. However, not all playwrights are totally happy about giving directors a free hand when it comes to interpreting their works. Knowing that their plays will inevitably be mediated through the work of directors, actors and designers, many playwrights have commented on the danger that the author's vision may be lost or falsified in production. Chekhov, for instance, constantly expressed deep dissatisfaction with what directors and actors did to his plays. Like his character Treplev, the tortured playwright in *The Seagull*, Chekhov saw much that was wrong with the theatre of his time. His blunt comment on Stanislavski's interpretation of *The Cherry Orchard* clearly expresses his belief that his playtext was not adequately realised in Stanislavski's performance text: 'All I can say is, Stanislavski has wrecked my play.'[9]

If Chekhov was unhappy about the treatment meted out to playwrights in his own time, he would probably be even less contented in today's theatrical milieu where the playwright's status relative to that of the director has diminished. Critics and directors such as Basil Ashton who argue that 'a director is only of any use when he serves the dramatist and allows the public to see and understand what the dramatist intended'[10] have become an endangered species. The artistic 'creativity' of the modern director has become privileged above the contributions of all other theatre artists, including the once dominant playwright. We go to see Brook's *Lear* and Zeffirelli's or Baz Luhrmann's *Romeo and Juliet*, not Shakespeare's plays. The poster for Barry Kosky's Australian production of *King Lear* made no mention of Shakespeare at all.

In the current world in which 'director's theatre' dominates it has become difficult to argue for the primacy of the playwright's play in the complex and composite art of theatre-making. Defenders of the playwright's supreme contribution have come under attack for their failure to accept the implications of postmodern critical theories, particularly deconstruction, which assert that the existence in any meaningful sense of the 'playwright's play' is a fiction.

The decision to privilege the playwright's function over that of the director, or conversely, to privilege the director's function over that of the playwright, radically affects what we are likely to see in the theatre. We need to decide on the relative status of the playtext and the performance text.

This study aims to assist directors and students of theatre to see *what* Chekhov's plays are about, and *how* the playwright provides his interpreters with clues about how to realise the action of his plays on stage. The intention is to stimulate theatre practitioners to create productions that are theatrically rich 'valid versions' of the play. The need to find the right balance between validity and originality in interpretation is the director's constant aim and there is no fixed way of achieving this goal. As Richard Hornby observes: 'although there might be one best way for a particular company to perform a playtext at a particular time, in a particular theatre, and at a particular period in their development, there is obviously more than one way of performing it in general.'[11]

The initial task of this study will be to examine the writings of Chekhov in order to ascertain what vision of reality is embodied in his plays and to elucidate how he dramatised that vision. Evidence will be drawn from Chekhov's plays, short stories and letters, as well as from the vast corpus of Chekhov criticism.

One can safely assume that most playwrights write with performance in mind. They write in a linguistic code, producing strings of words that will eventually be spoken by actors. They sometimes also write stage instructions and notes that suggest, to some degree, how they think their plays should be staged. These words, the literary playtext, are interpreted by a reader, critic, or director. In the case of the director, this interpretation is then re-encoded in terms not of a written code but a performance code involving a plethora of sub-codes including casting, vocal interpretation, facial expression, gesture, make-up, costume and movement within the dramatic space.[12] This total performance code, or performance text, is then interpreted by each member of an audience.

There are two distinct acts of interpretation that are of interest to any critic. The first involves the task of interpretation and translation undertaken by the director. This is a twofold task. Initially, the director analyses a playtext in order to find out what they believe the author's play is about: what constitutes the play's overall action and what vision of reality is expressed in it. Then, having explored these questions of interpretation, the director proceeds to the second task of translating their understanding of the literary playtext into the performance text by utilising the performance codes that are embodied in the work of actors, set and lighting designers, etc. Thus the director has to both interpret the play's meaning and find suitable theatrical means to translate that intellectual and emotional understanding into a 'readable' performance text.

This movement from page to stage involves the director in the difficult task of finding an objective correlative for their understanding of the play.

The second act of interpretation is undertaken by the members of any audience who witness the performance text. Martin Esslin, despite flirting with the view that, since no two audience members will ever interpret a performance in *exactly* the same way, the performance text is 'open to any interpretation that a reader or viewer may bring to it',[13] concedes that a knowledge of how the signifying systems of the performance code work should 'help the director to attain a higher degree of certainty that he will actually convey the meaning he intended, at least to the majority of the audience'.[14] Some consistency of reception is therefore possible in this second act of interpretation which can be suitably characterised as a movement 'from stage to audience'.

The chain of communication from the playwright to the audience has three main links. Firstly, there is the *playwright's playtext*, which is in the form of a written text that contains a series of encoded signals with potential for realisation in performance. The second link we may call the *director's performance text*, which involves the twofold task of a decoding interpretation of the playwright's playtext and a re-encoding of that interpretation in theatrical terms using the services of actors, designers, etc. The third major link in the communication chain is made up of the *audience's decoding* of the director's performance text.

The communication chain is, of course, far more complex than the above model suggests. If, for example, an audience member has studied the playwright's play and decoded or interpreted it in a way that is markedly different from the director's, then that audience member's decoding of the director's performance text may well result in a baffling and possibly irritating experience. These intertextual considerations, while they point out the 'interference' that is involved in the lines of communication between the playwright's play and the audience, mediated as it is through the director's interpretation and its realisation in terms of the various performance codes, should not lead to the conclusion that no communication is possible. A reasonably competent audience member can hear and see productions of plays and distinguish between those which are recognisably intelligible versions of the playwright's play and those which are not. Clearly there is a marked difference between the more direct way an author of a novel communicates with their readers and the ways in which playwrights have to communicate with audience members. The novelist does not have to go through the mediation of directorial interpretation and translation into performance codes which can lead playwrights like Chekhov to suffer the agonies that result from too much 'interference' by directors.

The chain of communication from the playwright to the audience includes reference to the problematic concept of 'the playwright's play' which is rejected in much current literary theory. Attempts to set limits on critical or directorial interpretation through appeals to concepts such as authorial intentions and authorial meanings have been vigorously attacked. So Barthes, in his seminal essay 'The Death of the Author', written in 1968, asserted that individual readers are free to choose any meaning they wish from the text they read.[15] As Selden notes: 'The reader is thus free to enter the text from any direction; there is no correct route.'[16] The logic of such a position in terms of the theatre is that a director can 'read' a play in any way they wish and then, presumably, the audience members can also read the resulting performance in any way they wish. The very idea of a production of, let us say, Chekhov's *Uncle Vanya* as opposed to Brook's *Uncle Vanya*, for instance, becomes unintelligible since the author is no longer to be considered of importance in the determination of the play's possible meanings. Andrei Serban in his production of this play at La Mama in New York in 1983 fully accepted his right to read the play freely. He chose to introduce such 'creative' moments as having 'Vania sitting on the professor's lap and the professor lecherously pawing Elena'.[17] And why not, if anything goes?

It is precisely this totally anarchic view of interpretation that needs to be questioned, for in order to have even the possibility of supplying insights that might help students, directors and actors understand Chekhov's plays, one needs to be convinced that the playwright has *some* authority in the complex process of interpretation. The relationship between authors and their interpreters needs to be further examined.

Both Peter Holland and Michael Quinn[18] have illuminated this problematic relationship. Quinn begins his article with a useful statement about the complex nature of theatrical interpretation as it is perceived today:

> Play production involves the activity of an entire collective, and the relations among the many agents of the theatrical performance often become extremely complex. The relation between the author of the text and the stage director is perhaps the most difficult of these to sort out and understand, for those occupying the roles often claim a kind of primary or founding status.[19]

Arnold Wesker, a playwright who, like Chekhov, felt that his works were often misinterpreted, passionately argues the case for the primacy of the playwright over the director's function. In an article significantly titled 'Interpretation: To Impose or Explain', Wesker puts forward the extreme form of the argument that privileges the playwright over the director:

> Let us remind ourselves of something that is perhaps forgotten. The raw material of the playwright is his individual experience of life. This experience is a kind of chaos into which occasionally there shines a light, a tiny light of meaning. A small part of the chaos is identified, sometimes comprehended. The playwright gives this chaos a shape, an order. He calls it a play ... The original play should

be considered the primary work, the director's production the secondary work. But a strange metamorphosis is taking place: the director is treating the play as *his* primary source, as *his* raw material to do with it how he fancies. The playwright endures the life and from it shapes a play, the director then robs, scavenges, rapes it.[20]

Chekhov felt a similar anguish to Wesker when he saw his own plays misinterpreted. The gap that he perceived between his playtexts and the performance texts that they were transformed into led him to lose some of his initial love of the theatre. In a letter to Suvorin, his friend and publisher, in 1898, Chekhov declared:

> Formerly I had no greater delight than to sit in a theatre, but now I sit there feeling as though at any moment someone in the gallery will shout: 'Fire!' And I don't like actors. The change is due to my being a playwright.[21]

Chekhov became so disillusioned with theatrical misinterpretations of his plays that, at various times, he declared that he would never again write for the stage.

The idea that the director should be privileged over the playwright has been given support by modern deconstructive theory. Gerald Rabkin puts this theoretical position starkly when he claims that:

> Since the director is the main instrument of interpretation in the theatre of our time, the playwright holds no more privilege over the director than literature holds over criticism.[22]

This stretches the idea of 'interpretation' to a point where it loses its primary meaning. The Macquarie Dictionary defines the verb to 'interpret' as: 'to set forth the meaning of; explain or elucidate'. Consequently, to critically interpret a play would mean 'to set forth the meaning of a play; to explain or elucidate a play'. This implies that there is a pre-existing entity to be interpreted. It would more accurately reflect Rabkin's actual argument if he replaced 'interpretation' with the word 'creation' since it is this latter word which best describes what he sees as the actual functional achievement of the modern director. This becomes obvious when one looks at another revealing statement in Rabkin's article entitled 'Is There a Text on This Stage?: Theatre/Authorship/Interpretation':

> If it is as valid to speak of performance text as of written text, the vital theatrical problem is the relationship between the two, for in the dominant hierarchical model in western culture the performance text is offered as an interpretation — a reading — of the dramatic text. The rise of 'director's theatre' mirrors literary criticism's movement from the emphasis upon the immanent 'meaning' of literary texts to the acceptance of the processes of reading and interpretation which determine meaning.[23]

The Macquarie Dictionary provides another definition of 'interpretation' that suggests a much stronger connection between the playtext and the performance text than that put forward by Rabkin. This definition refers specifically to theatrical interpretation. To theatrically interpret a play is 'to bring out the meaning of (a dramatic work, music, etc.)'.

Neither of the two extreme critical positions dealing with the importance placed on the playwright's or the director's contribution to the theatrical event is satisfactory. On the one hand there are those who are convinced that the meaning of any play lies in the literary playtext and that any theatrical interpretation of that text will debase that meaning — a meaning that can only be perceived by an elite! So Harold Goddard gets rid of the thorny problem of the relationship between the literary playtext and the performance text by denying the validity of performance. In what seems to be a perverse sort of bardolatry, he argues that drama:

> ... must make a wide and immediate appeal to a large number of people of ordinary intelligence ... The public does not want the truth. It wants confirmation of its prejudices ... What the poet is seeking, on the other hand, is the secret of life, and, even if he would, he cannot share with a crowd in a theatre, through the distorting medium of actors who are far from sharing his genius, such gleams of it as may have been revealed to him. He can share it only with a few, and with them mostly in solitude ...[24]

One must presume that Goddard sees himself as one of 'the few' with a direct line through to the genius of Shakespeare. By receiving a playwright's work in solitude without the mediation of the theatre and all of its performance codes, a critic like Goddard can deceive himself into thinking that his interpretation of Shakespeare is identical to the meaning intended by Shakespeare. No one will be able to contradict him — Shakespeare is dead and Goddard is in solitude!

It is just this sort of ridiculous search for a single meaning that leads some critics and audience members to seek a 'definitive' production of a play. In effect, what seems to happen is that these particular audience members have in their minds some preconceived image or idea of the play's meaning. This image or idea, which they assume to be the playwright's meaning rather than their own interpretation of the play, is compared with the actual production they are witnessing. If the production mirrors their own idea of the play they regard it as successful while, if it fails to mirror their own idea of the play, they claim that the directors and cast have presented a distortion of the playwright's play.

The fact that no single meaning of a play exists, and consequently no definitive theatrical interpretation of a play is possible, does not imply that plays can mean anything and that *any* theatrical interpretation is acceptable. Even the deconstructionists find this conclusion difficult to accept. Rabkin has tried to extricate the deconstructionists from a critical position that appears to deny the possibility of artistic discrimination. He uses the term 'misreading' to mean any and all interpretations and, in so doing, removes the useful distinction between an acceptable reading or interpretation and a misreading or misinterpretation:

> But how, then, does one avoid excusing weak or banal productions as necessary deconstructive strategies? How does the audience, the critic discern which directorial 'manhandling' is valid, which simplistic reduction or mere caprice? Deconstruction does not assert that anything goes, that all interpretation is equal. The Yale deconstructors have warned against the freedom of mis-reading. All mis-readings are not equally valid. [Hillis] Miller insists that the reader is *not* free to give the narrative any meaning he wishes, but that ... meaning emerges from a reciprocal act in which interpreter and what is interpreted both contribute to the making or the finding of a pattern.[25]

Hillis Miller's comment raises more questions than it answers. Should a director concentrate on 'the finding of a pattern' in the play or focus their activities on 'making a pattern'? The first approach assumes that there is a pattern, presumably created by the playwright, which is to be found in the play, while the second approach effectively makes the director the author of the work. Is the director who 'makes a pattern' interpreting the play or creating it? Interpretation and creativity need not be antithetical. It is important to recognise that some playtexts are more 'open' to the possibility of a range of acceptable readings or interpretations than others. Plays such as *Hamlet* and *The Cherry Orchard* may well have various patterns that can be realised on stage in different productions and thus encourage directorial creativity. A melodrama such as *Lady Audley's Secret* may be more 'closed' in terms of the possible patterns of interpretation. It may not allow for as great a 'plurality of readings'.

Harold Goddard, when assessing the rival claims of the playwright and the director, avoids dealing with the difficult question of the relationship between the literary text and the performance text by simply rejecting the value of the performance text altogether. In a similar manner, those who wish to privilege the performance text tend to regard the literary text as a mere pretext. One can see some validity in such a position when one is dealing with unscripted performance-art creations. Theatrical events such as happenings, much experimental performance art and improvisational theatre allow the directors or performers a free hand in the 'making of a pattern'. This is surely because the performance text is the only text. There is no prior literary text whose pattern a director might try to find. However, the kind of critical stance which claims that plays which have a literary text really exist, or can be understood, *only* in performance leads, as Richard Levin has pointed out, to all sorts of problems:

> If a play really exists only in performance, then, since there would be no way to determine *which* performance (since that would bring us back to the author's

text, and so confer 'reality' upon it as well), it would have to mean *any* performance. This would mean that any alterations made in the text during any performance, even including actors' errors, would become part of the 'real' play. Then there would be no 'real' play, but only the aggregate of all the different performances, which would all be equally legitimate, since the author's text, and hence his meaning, could no longer be relevant, and the sole criterion for judging them would be whether each one 'worked' in its own terms. But then it would make no sense to say that a play can be really understood only in performance, because there would be no independent 'reality' apart from the performance that could be understood. Thus the assertion that a play can be understood only in performance would seem to be either tautological (if the play and the performance are identical) or self-contradictory (if they are not).[26]

There is no way of excluding the author and the literary text when questions of interpretation arise. What needs to be worked out is the precise nature of the relationship between director and playwright in what Hillis Miller called 'the reciprocal act' of theatrical interpretation.

There is in fact no need to privilege either the playwright or the director. Peter Holland has argued that Stanislavski's despotic control over the production of Chekhov's *The Cherry Orchard* privileged the director over the playwright. In order to redress this imbalance he claims that:

> There is of course no reason why the deprivileging of the director should make the writer privileged in turn. If the director no longer has control in an absolute way as in the past, then we should not assume that the writer can therefore choose to fill the vacuum. The writer's reading is only one among competing preferences.[27]

It is now generally, though not universally, conceded that due acknowledgement of the playwright does not involve the consequent downgrading of all of the other theatre artists involved in the group creation of a production. It is difficult to take seriously the idea that the playwright's play has some golden nugget of meaning embedded in it which the director digs out, and hands over to the actors who, in turn, hand the unchanged ore over to an audience to take home and add to their wealth of experience! The meaning of a play is never a stable object that remains unchanged through the mediation and transformation processes that constitute theatrical production. What is actually seen as meaningful in a play varies from director to director, from generation to generation, and from culture to culture. Consequently, the most interesting and enduring plays seem to be those that invite a plurality of readings or interpretations. As Jonathan Miller commented in his Adelaide Festival talk: 'What is so interesting about rich complex works of the imagination is that you can still focus on different levels at different periods.'[28]

Bernard Beckerman makes the additional important point that a variety of possible readings is inevitable regardless of whether we tend to privilege the playwright over the director or vice versa:

> As we become aware of how successive generations have responded to specific plays, we come to see that a text does not have a single ideal manifestation. Instead it experiences a succession of transformations. Whether one chooses to consider these diverse transformations as complementary expressions of a single textual core or to see them as independent reconstructions of a potential but incomplete idea, the existence of valid alternate versions of a text emphasizes our obligation to see a play as a complex of dynamic possibilities.[29]

What is also significant about Beckerman's comment is that he realises that the fact that there will always be differing interpretations does not mean that all interpretations are acceptable. The idea of 'valid alternate versions of a text' not only opens the possibility for an infinite number of possible versions but also implies that there are or can be 'invalid' versions. Possible theatrical interpretations or readings must allow for possible misinterpretations or misreadings. There have been productions of *Hamlet* where Ophelia's madness has been presented in a sadly lyrical manner, others in which her madness has been portrayed in a violent and frightening way. Both of these approaches are possible interpretations and are certainly not contradicted by the text. However, a production in which Ophelia is presented as not being mad at all constitutes a misinterpretation since all the available evidence in the playtext suggests that she goes mad.

Whether Stanislavski's production of Chekhov's *The Cherry Orchard* should be regarded as one valid interpretation amongst the multiplicity of possible interpretations or as a misinterpretation, as Chekhov claimed, is open to debate. If we still wish to distinguish between theatrical interpretations that are valid and those that are not, we need to establish workable criteria to allow us to make such a distinction.

Few critics have written anything that is particularly helpful on this topic. One notable exception is Roger Gross, whose book *Understanding Playscripts: Theory and Method* is both clear and subtle in its explication of the complexities involved in theatrical interpretation. Several of Gross's insights underpin my critical assumptions in this study of Chekhov. Gross uses the twin concepts of 'parameters' and 'tolerances', which he borrows from the fields of mathematics and mechanics, as analytical tools to help directors arrive at a valid, or as he calls it, 'correct' interpretation:

> A 'correct' reading is one which fully rationalizes the playscript so that the performance based on it is coherent and complete without contradicting or omitting any of the requirements of the Commanding Form.[30]

The 'parameter' that any director considers when interpreting a playscript involves asking the question: 'What *must* happen in a production of this play?' As Gross defines it:

> The parameter is that in a variable system which remains constant while other factors change. The playwright may be said to have established a parameter, certain Psychic Events which must occur if the play is to be considered an acceptable version of the playscript.[31]

By 'Psychic Events' Gross means the 'understanding' that an audience has as a result of seeing the 'Physical Events' on the stage:

> Physical Process is pre-verbal, pre-conceptual. It is what is; when it is noticed, the noticing is a Psychic Event. Physical Processes are the 'matter' of drama. Psychic Events are what Physical Processes provoke in our minds, and that is what really counts. Physical Processes are the medium by which Psychic Events are communicated from artist to audience. Only when an appropriate Psychic Event occurs in the mind of the audience or the interpreter has the play 'succeeded'. Only Physical Processes are actually on stage. Psychic Events, Dramatic Actions for example, exist only as mental events in the audience and as sign-potential of the play/script.[32]

Later Gross defines the Aristotelian concept of the overall action of a play in terms of Psychic Event:

> The simplest definition of 'the Action' is 'the Master Psychic Event' of the play. That is, the play as a whole seen as one Psychic Event.[33]

An Ophelia who never goes mad may be considered a misinterpretation if, as a result of omitting the Physical Event of Ophelia's madness specified in the playtext, we destroy the required Psychic Event that constitutes one of the parameters of *Hamlet*.

The 'tolerance' as defined by Gross involves the director asking the question: 'What may *not* happen in a production of this play?':

> The tolerance of a system is the degree to which factors may vary and still perform their functions in the system. The playwright may be said to have established tolerances, certain limits within which Psychic Events must occur if the play is to be considered an acceptable version of the playscript.[34]

The manner in which any given Ophelia goes mad allows for a great range of interpretations that are within the tolerances of the playscript. Serban's decision to have Professor Serebryakov 'lecherously pawing' Helen in his production of *Uncle Vanya* lies outside the tolerances of that playscript and is an example of what the critic Stark Young scathingly described as 'virtuosity':

Directors move more toward virtuosity when they take the play only as material for some idea that they wish to express. They are not concerned with giving us the play's idea so much as their own. An extreme virtuoso in the theatre uses the play as the other sort of director uses the actors or the décor, it does not provide the main idea or the mood of the theatre work but is employed to express his idea. He does not develop the play for what is in it but uses it to create a sort of drama of his own. He distorts the play and forces it to ends not its own but his.[35]

To be sympathetic to Young's viewpoint does not mean that one approves of 'museum theatre' or conservative productions of plays or wishes to deny the creativity of directors, designers and actors. When Peter Brook sets *A Midsummer Night's Dream* in a white box with characters swinging on trapezes, or when Jonathan Miller sets *The Merchant of Venice* in nineteenth-century London, they are not being virtuosi in the sense implied by Stark Young. Rather, they are aware that plays and audiences exist in time and that their task as directors is to make plays from the past speak to an audience of today. They realise that, in order to achieve this goal, plays need to be constantly re-interpreted. The effect of seeing such productions is that, as a result of the directorial transformations made in production, the audience comes away with a clearer and deeper understanding of the play.

This experience is superbly described by Rodney Ackland after witnessing Miller's 1976 production of *Three Sisters*. When he went to see the play, he carried with him his vivid memory of Komisarjevsky's famous 1926 production. Miller's production forced Ackland to see that Komisarjevsky's interpretation was not the only possible way of presenting Chekhov's play:

> ... all these unimaginable years later, I could perceive, quite clearly in my mind's eye, an image of Trixie Thompson [the actress who played Irina in Komisarjevsky's production] as she was in the first act, with her delicate, flower-like beauty and her tremulous hopes of happiness, a perfect paradigm of all Chekhov's young girls, the 'little victims' who, all unconscious of their fourth-act doom, do, in the first act, play. This, surely, was the only possible Irina, the true Irina of Chekhovian intent.

> But here, before my present eyes, was a determined young person in a stiff and starchy high-necked dress, abrasive and unyielding in manner as the material the dress was made of. And she too, according to Dr Miller and Miss Angela Down [the actress who played Irina in Miller's production], was supposed to be Irina. I found this difficult to accept. I resisted it. I hated it! But gradually, reluctantly and fighting every inch of the way, I was won over.

Obliged by this new approach to give a truly 'cool, hard' hearing to Irina's lines, sure enough, they gave little evidence of the tenderness, the sympathy, the delicacy of feeling which I had taken for granted to be hers.[36]

Clearly Miller convinced Ackland that his production was in some sense justified by the text and made sense of the text in 1976. In Gross's terminology, the Physical Events used by Komisarjevsky in 1926 which seemed to produce appropriate Psychic Events in audience members did not seem to Miller to be appropriate to his understanding of the play in 1976. Consequently, Miller required a new set of Physical Events to produce the appropriate Psychic Events. These transformations wrought upon the play by Miller are not pieces of virtuosity but necessary ways of communicating the action of Chekhov's play. Without such transformations of the Physical Events, without re-interpretation, Chekhov's play would not deliver itself to a modern audience.[37]

The general line of argument put forward by the critic and director Jonathan Miller suggests that the relationship between the director and the author is neither one of self-effacing subservience nor of self-aggrandising arrogance. The director in this view is neither 'butler' nor 'virtuoso'. The 'reciprocal act' of theatrical interpretation, while it demands the freedom necessary for the director to find the appropriate Physical Events to realise the play's Psychic Events, necessarily denies the director total freedom to create whatever they wish if the realisation of the play's Psychic Events remains the objective of that director.[38] Where Gross talks of 'parameters' and 'tolerances', Miller talks of 'determinancy' and 'indeterminancy'. Both acknowledge the existence of the playwright's play. There may not be clearly defined 'nuggets' of meaning to be dug out of the playscripts and delivered to audiences, but the playscripts do at least define and limit the possible meanings. We cannot define all of the valid potential meanings of a given playtext, but we can often exclude certain readings as being too far-fetched. Jonathan Miller, when discussing how knowledge of a play's historical context partially determines meanings, wittily illustrates this point:

> That is why, in fact, one speaks of the indeterminancy of works of art and plays in particular. It is not that they are totally undetermined, or undeterminable, because there are certain things that are obviously determined — to a very large extent — by their actual linguistic structure. When Hamlet says 'To be or not to be' it is quite clear that he is not talking about making raspberry jam.[39]

What needs to be established is not some spurious hierarchy that privileges one theatre artist over another in the creation of the theatrical event, but some means of deciding how the various artists are to function creatively in relation to each other. It is here that the idea of 'priority' becomes more important than 'privileging'. The work of the playwright is prior to, though not necessarily more important than, the work of directors and actors. In a production of

Chekhov's *The Seagull*, the work of the director and of the actors is clearly as necessary to a performance of the play as are the playwright's words. All are necessary and none are by themselves sufficient, but there is a sequential order in which work has to be done to produce the play. It is in this 'sequential' rather than any 'privileging' sense that the playwright's play takes priority over the work of the director and of the other theatre artists.

Today, when directorial and critical virtuosity is rampant, it is salutary to be reminded of the importance of priority of the literary text. It is significant that one of the major criticisms made about Stanislavski's productions of Chekhov's plays was that, by privileging the contributions of the director and actor in the theatrical creation, and by failing to accept the importance of the playwright's play, he failed to create the Master Psychic Event of Chekhov's play for the audience.

Necessarily, this study concentrates on examining the literary rather than the performance texts of Chekhov's plays. They will be examined from the point of view of a director, actor or student of theatre who wishes to discover how these plays might be interpreted in production. This study will mainly deal with the *playwright's playtext*, and the *director's performance text*. It will not deal directly with the *audience's decoding* of the *director's performance text*.

The reason for this approach should be fairly clear by now. The overall aim of this work is not to legislate what actual productions of Chekhov should look like but to suggest approaches to interpretation that should produce richer, more valid versions of these plays in production. Jean Howard is correct when she claims that 'there is a crucial difference between examining the plays viewed as blueprints for performance and examining the plays as enacted in *particular performances*'.[40] Actual productions referred to in this study will be used to illustrate the extent to which they failed or succeeded in fulfilling the specifications of the play's 'blueprint'. The precise relationship between the actor's approach to building a character and the director's approach to the communication of the idea of the play, between what Gross calls the 'fictional' and the 'functional' versions of the play, will be dealt with more fully in the chapters that analyse Chekhov's plays. While the two approaches are clearly related, they are not identical.

The emphasis placed on the playtext in this study in no way denies the creativity of a director. Due emphasis needs to be placed on both the author's and the director's artistic input. Tyrone Guthrie is surely correct when he argues, in defence of Stanislavski's and Nemirovich-Danchenko's approach to Chekhov's plays, that 'they were surely entitled to their view of what the script meant to them; and as directors of the production, were not only entitled but bound to interpret it in their way'.[41] Guthrie realises that any interpretation must depend upon the amount of information and knowledge the director has about the play.

He acknowledges that Stanislavski and Nemirovich-Danchenko will no doubt 'have been very much influenced by the author's disagreement and will have made many changes, often against their better judgement; but without their being able to help it, the interpretation will have, in general, been what *they* make of the script'.[42]

The act of 'transposing a written work from the imaginary realm of reading to the concrete realm of the stage'[43] is the director's task but, as the French director, Jean Vilar, has pointed out, that task can be carried out sensitively or stupidly. Vilar's rhetorical question to would-be directors, 'Can one interpret something one doesn't understand?'[44] is clearly to be answered in the negative. He implies that there is a literary text that needs to be understood by the director before they can intelligently transform it into a performance text. Because Vilar felt not enough attention was being paid to the playwright's play he added: 'One can never read the play often enough. Actors never read it often enough.'[45]

Vilar's words echo those of Chekhov who complained that both Stanislavski and Nemirovich-Danchenko did not pay close enough attention to his playscripts. In a letter to his wife Olga Knipper on 10 April 1904, the dying playwright fulminated about the Moscow Art Theatre co-founders for having misinterpreted his last play: 'Nemirovich and Alekseyev positively do not see in my play what I wrote, and I am ready to vouch that neither of them read *The Cherry Orchard* through carefully even once.'[46]

Both Nemirovich-Danchenko and Stanislavski record Chekhov's advice to actors concerning how to play certain roles. Neither director found his advice either clear or helpful. Nemirovich-Danchenko claims that 'Chekhov was incapable of advising actors, even later when he came into contact with the actors of the Art Theatre. Everything appeared so comprehensible to him: "Why, I have written it all down", he would answer.'[47] Stanislavski noted that Chekhov's reticence to talk about his plays was habitual:

> It may seem strange, but he could not talk about his own plays. Feeling as if he were being questioned himself by a judicial examiner, he would grow confused, and in order to find a way out of the strange situation and to get rid of us, he would take advantage of his usual statement: 'Listen, I wrote it down, it is all there.'[48]

Regardless of Chekhov's belief that his dramas were perfectly clear, both critics and directors have interpreted his plays in markedly different ways. My re-examination of Chekhov's plays will concentrate on establishing precisely 'what is there'. We can then discover some of the 'parameters' and 'tolerances' of Chekhov's drama and, as a result, suggest possible valid interpretations of his plays, and in addition explain why some other versions of his dramas are misinterpretations. In particular we should be able to find out why critics and directors alike have arrived at such widely divergent interpretations of his work.

In Chekhov's lifetime there was considerable critical disagreement amongst Russian critics concerning both the nature and value of his literary creations. Since that time the critical fluctuations, both in Russia and abroad, have become polarised into the 'gloomy' and 'positive' schools of Chekhov criticism. It is not surprising to find that Soviet critics have tended 'to find and accentuate optimistic and positive values in Chekhovian drama and to emphasise that the author had a message for the masses',[49] nor is it strange to find many Western critics discovering the 'existential' even 'absurdist' pessimistic Chekhov whose plays show us 'that time cannot be slowed or reversed, that human nature cannot be reformed or revitalised'.[50]

Both Soviet and Western critics necessarily approach Chekhov from their own ideological standpoint and the patronising attitude that is often expressed by Western critics towards the 'optimistic' Soviet reading of Chekhov often stems from a failure to see that we have our own biases. As Tulloch perceptively notes: 'For too long Western critics have pinpointed the value-laden assumptions of Soviet interpretation of Chekhov without equally questioning their own epistemologies.'[51]

Chekhov's complex attitude toward both life and art make any simple pigeonholing of his vision of reality under headings like 'optimistic' or 'pessimistic' wholly unsatisfactory. As Joseph Wood Krutch has pointed out, 'if he had been simply unconcerned with the future and engaged in nothing but a defence of his dying aristocrat, he would merely have been a possibly interesting conservative'.[52] Such 'gloomy' Western interpretations of Chekhov are no more, and no less, satisfactory than the 'uplifting' interpretations of the early Soviet critics who tried to make of Chekhov 'a sort of John the Baptist of the Revolution preparing the way for the appearance of Lenin'.[53]

Even amongst critics who share similar ideologies there is disagreement about the nature of Chekhov's works. Just as critics in the West argue about whether Chekhov's works should be classified as being optimistic or pessimistic, so Marxist critics squabble about the nature of the playwright's vision of reality:

> A.V. Lunacharskii, People's Commissar of Public Education and himself a playwright, was very positive about Chekhov, whom he believes to have been 'in love with life', while the Bolshevik ideologue P. I. Lebedev-Polianskii found only 'hopeless pessimism' in Chekhov.[54]

Depending upon whether directors have been convinced by the 'gloomy' or the 'positive' school of critics, Chekhov's plays have been produced in a manner that emphasises either their tragic potentialities (as Stanislavski insisted) or their comic possibilities (as Chekhov advocated).

It was not simply the 'pessimism/optimism' and the consequent 'tragic/comic' dualism that fascinated Chekhov but also such potentially antithetical pairings as 'science/art', 'ideal/real', 'mask/face', and 'outer life/inner life'. The new form of drama that he devised to express the complex relationship between these various dualities was itself dependent on the formal duality of text/subtext. The examination that follows will demonstrate the ways in which productions of Chekhov's plays that foreground either the tragic or comic elements to the exclusion of the other are misinterpretations. One-sided productions falsify the playwright's vision of reality embodied in the overall action of the plays and affect the manner in which the action is expressed. The form and content of Chekhov's plays depend upon the inter-relationship and tension between the polarities of gloomy negativity and facile optimism. Indeed a central unifying thread that connects all of Chekhov's writings is his attempt to recognise, relate and reconcile a whole series of dualisms.

It is when critics and directors concentrate on one element of these dualisms and ignore the other that one-sided and reductionist readings of Chekhov occur. Productions of Chekhov's plays that over-emphasise either the outer surface reality of the text or the inner hidden reality of the subtext will inevitably be 'thin'. The plays are constructed in such a way that their full complexity and richness can only be realised in performance when emphasis is placed on the dynamic relationship between the outer and inner reality, between the text and the subtext.

Any polarised reading inevitably posits an 'either/or' approach whereas a 'both/and' interpretation of Chekhov more accurately describes both the vision and form of his works. An examination of just *how* Chekhov manages to write in such a way that the 'characters and situations' can be seen simultaneously as both tragic and comic and the play as a whole can be interpreted simultaneously as both pessimistic and optimistic needs to be explored. This study will have achieved its aim if it persuades directors and critics to attempt to create rich, balanced and complex readings of Chekhov's plays by avoiding simplistic polarised readings of these works.

## ENDNOTES

[1] Senelick, L., 'Chekhov on Stage,' in Clyman, T. W., ed., *A Chekhov Companion*, Greenwood Press, Westport, 1985, p. 209.

[2] Magarshack, D., *The Real Chekhov*, George Allen and Unwin, London, 1972, p. 9.

[3] Ibid.

[4] Callow, P., *Chekhov: The Hidden Ground*, Ivan R. Dee, Chicago, 1998, p. 105.

[5] Miller, J., in Delgado, M. M. and Heritage, P., eds, *In Contact with the Gods?: Directors Talk Theatre*, Manchester University Press, Manchester, 1996, p. 163.

[6] Miller, J., 'Directing the Classics', ABC broadcast of Adelaide Festival Talk, n.d.

[7] Brook, P., quoted in Rabkin, G., 'The Play of Misreading: Text/Theatre/Deconstruction', *Performing Arts Journal*, Vol. 7, No. 1, 1983, p. 57.

[8] Miller, J., loc. cit.

Introduction

⁹ Chekhov, A., quoted in Hingley, R., *A New Life of Chekhov*, Oxford University Press, London, 1976, p. 305. Among the more recent playwrights who have complained bitterly about the dire fate of the playwright when placed in the hands of theatre practitioners, we can include such writers as Eugene O'Neill, Tennessee Williams and Arnold Wesker.

¹⁰ Ashton, B., Letter to *New Statesman*, 11 September 1970, quoted in Magarshack, D., op. cit., p. 7.

¹¹ Hornby, R., *Script into Performance: A Structuralist Approach*, Paragon House Publishers, New York, 1987, p. 95.

¹² The multiplicity of signifying systems that operate in any performance may be one of the main reasons why 'the stage, unlike literature, will never be subject to computerized semiotic analysis'. (Quinn, M. L., 'Reading and Directing the Play', *New Theatre Quarterly*, Vol. 3, No. 11, August 1987, p. 221.) This is why Esslin, for all his attraction to semiotics, concedes that, 'it may be an over-ambitious project to reduce the semiotics of dramatic performance to an "exact science"'. (Esslin, M., *The Field of Drama*, Methuen, London, 1987, p. 51.) Chekhov, himself a trained scientist, believed that there are areas of human experience that do not provide fruitful results when subjected to scientific analysis. This study reflects both the playwright's deep respect for scientific method and his awareness of its limitations:

> Anyone who has mastered the wisdom of the scientific method and therefore knows how to think scientifically undergoes any number of delightful temptations ... A physiology of creativity probably does exist in nature, but all dreams of it must be abandoned at the outset. *No good will come of critics taking a scientific stance*: they'll waste ten years, they'll write a lot of ballast and confuse the issue still further — and that's all they'll do. It's always good to think scientifically; the trouble is that thinking scientifically about art will inevitably end up by degenerating into a search for the 'cells' or 'centres' in charge of creative ability, whereupon some dull-witted German will discover them somewhere in the temporal lobes, another will disagree, a third German will agree ... and for three years an epidemic of utter nonsense will hover in the Russian air, providing dullards with earnings and popularity and engendering nothing but irritation among intelligent people. (Chekhov, A., Letter to A. S. Suvorin, 3 November 1888, in Karlinsky, S. and Heim, M. H., *Anton Chekhov's Life and Thought*, University of California Press, Berkeley, 1975, pp. 121–2.)

¹³ Esslin, M., op. cit., p. 156.

¹⁴ Ibid., p. 50.

¹⁵ Barthes, R., 'The Death of the Author', in Rice, P. and Waugh, P., eds, *Modern Literary Theory*, Edward Arnold, London, 1990, pp. 114–18.

¹⁶ Selden, R., *A Reader's Guide to Contemporary Literary Theory*, The Harvester Press, Brighton, 1985, p. 175.

¹⁷ Senelick, L., op. cit., p. 223.

¹⁸ Holland, P., 'The Director and the Playwright: Control over the Means of Production', *New Theatre Quarterly*, Vol. 3, No. 11, August 1987, pp. 207–17, and Quinn, M. L., op. cit., pp. 218–23.

¹⁹ Quinn, M. L., op. cit., p. 218.

²⁰ Wesker, A., 'Interpretation: To Impose or Explain', *Performing Arts Journal*, Vol. 11, No. 2, 1988, pp. 63–4.

²¹ Chekhov, A., Letter to A. S. Suvorin, 13 March 1898, in Yarmolinsky, A., *Letters of Anton Chekhov*, The Viking Press, New York, 1973, p. 308.

²² Rabkin, G., loc. cit.

²³ Rabkin, G., 'Is There a Text on This Stage?: Theatre/Authorship/Interpretation', *Performing Arts Journal*, Vol. 9, Nos 2 and 3, 1985, p. 155.

²⁴ Goddard, H., quoted in Levin, R., 'Performance Critics vs Close Readers in the Study of Renaissance Drama', *Modern Language Review*, Vol. 81, July 1986, p. 547.

²⁵ Rabkin, G., 'The Play of Misreading', p. 59.

²⁶ Levin, R., op. cit., p. 548.

²⁷ Holland, P., op. cit., p. 216.

²⁸ Miller, J., loc. cit.

²⁹ Beckerman, B., in Hobgood, B. M., ed., *Master Teachers of Theatre: Observations on Teaching Theatre by Nine American Masters*, Southern Illinois University Press, Carbondale, 1988, p. 30.

30 Gross, R., *Understanding Playscripts: Theory and Method*, Bowling Green University Press, Bowling Green, 1974, p. 134. 'Commanding form' is a term Gross borrows from Suzanne Langer. 'This "commanding form" established by the script ... does not dictate the precise nature of each textural detail of performance; *it sets limits of purpose and form within which other elements must function or dissipate the unity of the play.* Unity is achieved when each element of production is a response to the commanding form established by the script.' (Gross, R., op. cit., p. 12.) 'The closest the interpreter can hope to come is to construct a play which in no way violates the commanding form conceived by the author, and implied by the playscript.' (Gross, R., op. cit., pp. 133–4.)

31 Ibid., p. 134.

32 Ibid., p. 53.

33 Ibid., pp. 109–10.

34 Ibid., p. 134.

35 Young, S., *The Theater*, Doran, New York, 1927, p. 85.

36 Ackland, R., quoted in Allen, D., 'Jonathan Miller Directs Chekhov', *New Theatre Quarterly*, Vol. 5, No. 17, February 1989, p. 54.

37 The need for directors to constantly find new Physical Events to stimulate appropriate Psychic Events in spectators can be graphically illustrated if we look at one of the more obvious problems associated with a modern production of *Everyman*. Because, in the middle ages, 'mortification of the flesh' was seen as a virtue, a 'good deed', the Physical Event of the self-whipping of the character Everyman was an effective means of eliciting the appropriate Psychic response of approval from an audience. The spectators saw the character Good Deeds rise up refreshed as a result of this beating. A modern audience would probably not regard this self-flagellation as an act that they would consider to be a good deed. A director today may well wish to find some other Physical Event to replace the whipping in order to trigger the Psychic Event of 'approval' in the audience. This sort of transformation is more likely to communicate the meaning implied in the text than any 'museum' reconstruction of the original performance of *Everyman* could possibly hope to do.

38 Significantly, Jonathan Miller dislikes any directorial practice that changes the Psychic Events of a play as this alters the play's implied 'action'. His response to those directors who make Shakespeare's plays relevant by making them speak about today's political and social situation is trenchantly negative. 'What I hate is the vision of Shakespeare frog-marched into the twentieth century and made to, as it were, speak on behalf of twentieth century problems of which he had no knowledge.' (Miller, J., Adelaide Festival Talk, n.d.)

39 Miller, J., *Subsequent Performances*, Faber and Faber, London, 1986, p. 155.

40 Howard, J. E., *Shakespeare's Art of Orchestration*, University of Illinois Press, Urbana, 1984, p. 57.

41 Guthrie, T., 'A Director's View of *The Cherry Orchard*', in Guthrie, T. and Kipnis, L., trans., *The Cherry Orchard*, University of Minnesota Press, Minneapolis, 1965, p. 13.

42 Ibid.

43 Vilar, J., 'Murder of the Director', in Corrigan, R., op. cit., p. 143.

44 Ibid., p. 146.

45 Ibid.

46 Chekhov, A., Letter to O. L. Knipper, 10 April 1904, in Yarmolinsky, A., op. cit., p. 466.

47 Nemirovich-Danchenko, V., *My Life in the Russian Theatre*, Geoffrey Bles, London, 1968, p. 62.

48 Stanislavski, C., *My Life in Art*, Eyre Methuen, London, 1980, p. 361.

49 Moravcevich, N., 'The Dark Side of the Chekhovian Smile', *Drama Survey*, Vol. 15, No. 3, 1966–67, p. 244.

50 Rayfield, D., *Chekhov: The Evolution of His Art*, Paul Elek, London, 1975, pp. 226–7.

51 Tulloch, J., 'Chekhov Abroad: Western Criticism', in Clyman, T. W., op. cit., p. 203.

52 Krutch, J. W., *'Modernism' in Modern Drama*, Russell and Russell Inc., New York, 1962, pp. 71–2.

53 Ibid., p. 72.

54 Terras, V., 'Chekhov at Home: Russian Criticism', in Clyman, T. W., op. cit., pp. 170–1.

# Chapter 1. Chekhov's Vision of Reality

> *... I'm not much interested in such questions as the hereafter or the fate of humanity and I'm not much of a one for flights into the sublime either. What terrifies me most is just ordinary everyday routine, the thing none of us can escape ... My living conditions and upbringing have imprisoned me in a closed circle of lies, I know ... Worrying how to deceive myself and others every day without noticing that I'm doing so ... that's my entire existence, I know that too, and I dread not being rid of this fraud until I'm in my grave.* (Dmitry Silin in *Terror* by Anton Chekhov)[1]

> *I believe that future generations will find things easier and see their way more clearly. They will have our experience to help them. But we do want to be independent of future generations, don't we, we don't want to live just for them? We only have one life, and we should like to live it confidently, rationally and elegantly. We should like to play a prominent, independent, honourable role, we should like to make history so that these same future generations won't have the right to call each one of us a nonentity or worse.* (Vladimir in *An Anonymous Story* by Anton Chekhov)[2]

Some critics have argued that the vision of reality expressed in Chekhov's plays and short stories is deeply pessimistic, others that his view is essentially progressive and optimistic. There have even been critics who deny that Chekhov had any overall vision at all. Maurice Valency, for example, seems to think that a writer can simply describe life without having any world view underpinning that description. According to Valency:

> [Chekhov] had no theory of life to expound, no point to make, no thesis. It is quite unnecessary for the understanding of his drama to discuss his world view. If he had anything of the sort, it was irrelevant to the subject of his art. His great talent lay in his sensitive depiction of life around him, the physical and psychic landscape in which he lived.[3]

When Ronald Hingley raised the question of what 'outlook on life' was expressed in Chekhov's short stories, he warned of the danger of coming up with any simple answer:

> To this question no neat, all-embracing answer will ever be given. Chekhov was no builder of water-tight philosophical systems, but even less was he a pure aesthete indifferent to the ethical or other non-artistic implications of his work.[4]

The danger of arriving at any over-simplified version of Chekhov's vision of reality is not to be discounted. Nevertheless, it is important for critics and directors to decide on the nature of his vision. Some of the more extreme misinterpretations of Chekhov's plays have been the result of directors failing to realise the playwright's world view on stage. The vision of reality expressed in Chekhov's plays is an expression of the whole man, not just the artist. The artist who wrote plays and short stories was also a practising doctor, an environmentalist, a researcher and a philanthropist. It is only when we examine Chekhov's work in the light of the multiplicity of his roles that we can see how important his sense of social responsibility was in his overall vision of reality. Chekhov may not have outlined his world view in the explicit form of a manifesto, but it is nevertheless implied in his works. That world view obviously changed and developed throughout Chekhov's life but to suggest, as Valency does, that he lacked any view, is simply nonsense.

Chekhov vigorously attacked the idea that artists should express no viewpoint in their depictions of life. Chekhov wrote to Suvorin in 1892, pouring scorn on the ideas of Sofya Ivanovna Sazonova, who had written to him claiming that, in order to be a literary artist, it was unnecessary to have a world view:

> If you are looking for insincerity, you will find tons of it in her letter. 'The greatest miracle is man himself and we shall never tire of studying him.' Or: 'The aim of life is life itself.' Or: 'I believe in life, in its bright moments, for the sake of which one *can*, indeed one *must* live; I believe in man, in that part of his soul which is good ...' Can all this be sincere, and does it mean anything? This isn't an outlook, it's caramels.[5]

Sazonova's opinion and, by extension, Valency's, denies the need for the presence in literary works of any authorial 'aim', 'tendency', 'general idea' or 'world view'. Chekhov was quick to attack Sazonova's position which he felt promoted a nihilistic view of life:

> ... in her opinion all our trouble comes from the fact that we keep pursuing lofty and distant aims. If this isn't a country wife's logic, it's the philosophy of despair. He who sincerely believes that man needs lofty and distant aims as little as a cow does, that 'all our trouble' comes from pursuing these aims — has nothing left him but to eat, drink, sleep, or if he is fed up with that, he can take a running start and dash his head against the corner of a chest.[6]

Chekhov's work does not exist in some artistic never-never land where the precise historical situation and the particular values and beliefs of the playwright have no relevance. He knew how important belief systems were to all human beings, including literary artists. In one of his notebook entries he writes: 'Man is what he believes'.[7] It is difficult to see how Valency can acknowledge the greatness of Chekhov as a literary artist, while at the same time suggesting that he has nothing to present beyond the mere 'depiction of life around him'.

At times Chekhov was quite explicit about his artistic purpose. Reacting against the way in which Stanislavski turned his plays into tragedies, he said to the writer Alexander Tikhonov in 1902:

You tell me that people cry at my plays. I've heard others say the same. But that was not why I wrote them. It is Alexeyev [Stanislavski] who made my characters into cry-babies. All I wanted was to say honestly to people: 'Have a look at yourselves and see how bad and dreary your lives are!' The important thing is that people should realize that, for when they do, they will most certainly create another and better life for themselves. I will not live to see it, but I know that it will be quite different, quite unlike our present life. And so long as this different life does not exist, I shall go on saying to people again and again, 'Please, understand that your life is bad and dreary!' What is there in this to cry about?[8]

If we assume that Chekhov knew what his plays were about, then we come to the inescapable conclusion that part of the purpose for which he wrote them was to provide some constructive criticism of the social behaviour of his contemporaries. Seen in this light, his plays conform to the 'social corrective' nature of comedy. Productions which actually deny this positive aspect of his vision of reality seem to me to have gone beyond the 'tolerances' and 'parameters' of interpretation.

If the plays are examined solely from an aesthetic point of view, it is possible to interpret them as expressing either a progressive or a nihilistic world view. We know, for instance, that from the time of Stanislavski to the present Chekhov's plays *can* be read and performed in a way that makes them bleakly pessimistic in outlook. However, if it can be demonstrated that the plays *can* be read and played in a much more positive manner, and also, that the evidence of Chekhov's own beliefs about the plays and about life in general suggest that this positive reading of the central action of his plays is the one he wished to have realised upon the stage, then I think it becomes a clear case of misinterpretation to present the plays in the gloomy manner.[9]

Evidence outside the plays themselves confirms Chekhov's positive views. Gorky recounts how after reading a speech from a play he was writing in which the hero, Vasska, vows that if he had 'more strength and power' he would transform the earth into a beautiful place, Chekhov responded:

'That's very fine indeed! Very true, and very human! In this lies the essence of all philosophy. Man has made the earth habitable – therefore he must also make it comfortable for himself.' He shook his head in obstinate affirmation and repeated: 'He will!'[10]

Chekhov's belief in the possibility of change and progress manifested itself in his general attitude and behaviour. His faith in education and work in general is well documented, but even the relatively trivial fact that he had a great love of gardening is consistent with his overall belief in progress. To cultivate the earth sensibly was for Chekhov a means of closing the gap between humanity and nature. As Ehrenburg perceptively pointed out:

> Gardening was not for him a minor passion like fishing or shooting is for many; in the growth of a shrub or a tree he responded to the thing that moved him most — the affirmation of life. Kuprin has quoted his words: 'Look, every one of the trees you see here was planted under my eyes and of course it is precious to me. But even that isn't what matters, the thing is that before I came this was a wilderness full of idiotic holes and ditches, all stones and weeds ... Do you know, in another three or four hundred years the whole earth will be a flowering garden.'[11]

Gorky's and Kuprin's hearsay evidence concerning the more progressive aspects of Chekhov's vision of reality is supported by statements made by Chekhov in his *Notebooks* and in many of his letters. Again and again the idea of progress occurs, and particularly the idea of progress through work. Sometimes the statement is made explicitly: 'The power and salvation of a people lie in its intelligentsia, in the intellectuals who think honestly, feel, and can work.'[12] At other times Chekhov presents the same idea in a form reminiscent of a parable:

> A Mussulman for the salvation of his soul digs a well. It would be a pleasant thing if each of us left a school, a well, or something like that, so that life should not pass away into eternity without leaving a trace behind it.[13]

Chekhov's certainty that human beings were able to improve the world through work was, according to Gorky, a central part of the playwright's belief system:

> I have never known a man feel the importance of work as the foundation of all culture, so deeply, and for such varied reasons, as did Tchekoff ... He loved to build, plant gardens, ornament the earth; he felt the poetry of labour ... he used to say: 'If every man did all he could on the piece of earth belonging to him, how beautiful would this world be!'[14]

Whether or not Chekhov felt the 'poetry of labour', as Gorky claims, he certainly believed that through hard work, the conditions of life could be improved. His basic belief in the potential of the natural world was expressed in an uncharacteristically effusive manner in a letter which he wrote to his publisher and friend A. S. Suvorin on his return journey from his research trip to Sakhalin. The many letters to Suvorin contain some of the most revealing insights into Chekhov's views about life and art. In this letter, written in late 1890, Chekhov recounts his experiences while travelling through the Middle East. Chekhov, an unbeliever, was so moved by the sight of Mount Sinai that he expressed both his faith in the world's potential and his dismay at how poorly humans exploit that potential:

God's world is good. Only one thing isn't good: ourselves. How little there is in us of justice and humility, how poor is our conception of patriotism! The drunken bedraggled, good for nothing of a husband loves his wife and children, but what's the good of that love? We, so the newspapers say, love our great country, but how is that love expressed? Instead of knowledge — inordinate brazenness and conceit, instead of work — laziness and swinishness; there is no justice; the concept of honor does not go beyond 'the honor of the uniform', the uniform which is the everyday adornment of the prisoners' dock. What is needed is work; everything else can go to the devil. The main thing is to be just — the rest will be added unto us.[15]

The almost religious fervour with which Chekhov advocated the need for 'knowledge', 'justice' and 'work' to improve the quality of life squared with his own behaviour. He was a doer, not just a talker. As Simon Karlinsky has pointed out, Chekhov may not have been a revolutionary, but in both medicine and literature he attempted to bring about change and improvement in life. His scientific research into the physical and social conditions then prevailing in the penal colony on the Island of Sakhalin was only one small part of Chekhov's active approach to alleviating social ills:

His life was one continuous round of alleviating famine, fighting epidemics, building schools and public roads, endowing libraries, helping organize marine biology libraries, giving thousands of needy peasants free medical treatment, planting gardens, helping fledgling writers get published, raising funds for worthwhile causes, and hundreds of other pursuits designed to help his fellow man and improve the general quality of life around him.[16]

Chekhov lived for only forty-four years and for much of that time he suffered from the debilitating disease of tuberculosis, from which he died. Despite the brevity of his life Chekhov managed to achieve an enormous amount. Besides involving himself in all of the activities noted by Karlinsky, he managed to write a large number of short stories, a scientific treatise on prison conditions, and the plays for which he is best known. In doing all of this in so short a time, Chekhov lived up to his own ideals. He is reported to have said, 'I despise laziness, as I despise weakness and inertia in mental activities'.[17]

If the value of work and hatred of laziness was a central part of Chekhov's individual and social morality, the value he placed on the need for education was equally great. 'The Mother of all Russian evils is gross ignorance', he wrote to Suvorin in 1889.[18]

Anyone who doubts that Chekhov believed in change need only read John Tulloch's *Chekhov: A Structuralist Study*. Tulloch undertakes a sociological analysis of Chekhov and his work. He establishes beyond doubt that Chekhov the doctor, with his scientific training, accepted 'the particular social Darwinist belief that by changing the environment one might change people and reform society'.[19] Realising that Chekhov the doctor is not a separate person from Chekhov the literary artist, Tulloch points out that although we know 'that a tragic interpretation of Chekhov has been quite well established in Western culture since his death ... a simple tragic vision seems, *a priori*, unlikely in view of Chekhov's optimism in the potential of science'.[20]

The evidence I have already presented suggests that it is not defensible to interpret Chekhov's writings as expressions of tragic fatalism. Nevertheless, this dark view of Chekhov has been maintained by many important critics and as important a director as Stanislavski. Just how such a reading of Chekhov has come about needs to be explained. It is only by understanding why sensible people might interpret his works in this gloomy way, and by coming to see the validity of alternative readings, that we will avoid perpetuating these depressing and ultimately unsatisfying misinterpretations.

In 1916, twelve years after Chekhov's death, one of the most bleak and, unfortunately, influential interpretations of Chekhov was written by the important Russian émigré critic, Leon Shestov. In his essay titled 'Anton Tchekhov: Creation from the Void', he depicts the playwright as a Job-like proto-absurdist:

> To define his tendency in a word I would say that Tchekhov was the poet of hopelessness. Stubbornly, sadly, monotonously, during all the years of his literary activity, nearly a quarter of a century long, Tchekhov was doing one thing alone: by one means or another he was killing human hopes. Herein, I hold, lies the essence of his creation.[21]

The 'void' — the meaninglessness that lies at the heart of existence — mentioned by Shestov in relation to Chekhov was to be a central concern of the Absurdist dramatists of the nineteen-fifties. Many critics since Shestov have felt a sense of the 'void' in Chekhov's works. As a result, the playwright has been hailed as a forerunner of the Absurdist Movement. Robert Corrigan, for example, asserts that: 'Chekhov ... is the legitimate father of the so-called "absurdist" movement in the theatre.'[22] J. Oates Smith argues that: 'In his philosophical grasp of his material as well as in a number of particular dramatic devices, Chekhov anticipates the contemporary theatre of the absurd.'[23] Walter Stein claims that: 'The Tchekhovian heritage of pseudo-comedy is now being turned inside out in the dustbins of Samuel Beckett.'[24]

More recently, Martin Esslin, who seems to include some extraordinarily diverse dramatists under the classification of 'Absurdist', has argued that:

> There is only a small step from Chekhov's images of a society deprived of purpose and direction to the far more emphatic presentation of a world deprived of its 'metaphysical dimension' in the plays of Beckett, Genet, Adamov or Ionesco ...

Chekhov's determination to look at the world not merely with the cool objectivity of the scientist but also with the courage to confront the world in all its absurdity and infinite suffering (without flinching or self-pity and with a deep compassion for humanity in its ignorance and helplessness) led him to anticipate, far ahead of all of his contemporaries, the mood and climate of our own time.[25]

Unlike Valency, the critics I have just cited acknowledge the importance of Chekhov's world view when they analyse his works. However, the absurdist vision of reality that they ascribe to Chekhov is, according to other important analysts, totally inapplicable to the playwright. These contradictory interpretations of Chekhov's world view are logically incompatible. If Corrigan and Esslin are right when they claim that Chekhov's world view is basically 'absurdist', then Karlinsky and Tulloch are wrong when they argue for a 'progressive' reading of his works. This logical and critical impasse is actually only apparent and not real. By adopting the formal conventions of realism in the dramatisation of his vision of reality, Chekhov created plays which are potentially ambiguous. The same events can be read as part of either an absurdist or a progressive world view.

The essence of an absurdist view of life is contained in the opening line of Beckett's *Waiting for Godot* when Estragon says 'Nothing to be done'. This one line sums up the sense of hopelessness and futility that characterises Beckett's unchanging and unchangeable world. However Chekhov is not Beckett. What he depicts is a world in which 'no one is doing anything'. Far from denying change or hope, his plays embody an attempt to *awaken* an audience to the possibilities of change and improvement. It is not existential angst at the fixed nature of the world that is being expressed by Chekhov, but his sense of humanity's comic and pathetic failure to make the most of the world. It was Chekhov, not Beckett, who could write: 'God's world is good. Only one thing isn't good: ourselves.'[26] It is surprising how few critics and directors acknowledge this positive aspect of Chekhov's vision of reality.[27]

Chekhov depicts a world which has all the appearance of purposeless absurdity because humanity has failed to make life meaningful by refusing to work with nature in the processes of change and evolution. Displaying what Sartre called 'bad faith', those of Chekhov's characters who have let time pass them by bewail the waste of their lives or fantasise about the possibility of escape in the future. They resolutely refuse to face, or attempt to change, present reality.[28] Nyukhin, the comically pathetic 'hero' of *Smoking Is Bad for You*, tells his audience how, when he has given himself some 'dutch courage', he dreams of both the past and the future. All his regrets and aspirations however are seen as ridiculous as he continues in the present to carry out the ludicrous and trivial tasks demanded of him by his gorgon of a wife:

> One glass is enough to make me drunk, I might add. It feels good, but indescribably sad at the same time. Somehow the days of my youth come back to me. I somehow long — more than you can possibly imagine — to escape. [*Carried away.*] To run away, leave everything behind and run away without a backward glance. Where to? Who cares? If only I could escape from this rotten, vulgar, tawdry existence that's turned me into a pathetic old clown and imbecile![29]

The anguish that Chekhov felt about the trivial emptiness of much of life around him has little to do with the quietist pessimism of the 'nothing to be done' school of Absurdists. Chekhov, particularly in his short stories, presents human inactivity not as being inevitable but the result of human lethargy. Actual failure is seen in the light of potential achievement and not as an unavoidable part of the human condition. The difficulty of depicting failure while at the same time communicating the possibility of human achievement became one of the central problems that Chekhov faced.

Chekhov committed himself as an artist to the conventions of realism because he believed that 'literature is called artistic when it depicts life as it is'.[30] Everything in his art had to be true to life. Consequently, he could not show his reader or audience some putative utopian future, since the present life he was depicting was far from utopian. At best, Chekhov could suggest the possibility of such an improved future. As Vladimir Yermilov has pointed out, one of the main techniques that Chekhov employed, particularly in his short stories, was to consistently present a gap between the beauty of nature and the ugliness of human life as it is presently lived:

> The beauty of nature is used as a constant criterion in evaluating a given social reality and as a reminder of what it could and should be like on this lovely earth.[31]

Depicting the gap between human possibility and actuality, between desire and achievement, was a central means that Chekhov employed to show his readers and audiences 'how bad and dreary your lives are!'[32] The idea of presenting a world of wasted opportunities was not something that he thought of 'late in his life', as Valency claims.[33] As early as 1887 we find Chekhov writing about his response to revisiting his birthplace, Taganrog. The criticism of the inhabitants' failure to fulfil their potential and make the most of nature's gifts is clearly stated:

> Sixty thousand inhabitants busy themselves exclusively with eating, drinking, procreating, and they have no other interests, none at all. Wherever you go there are Easter cakes, eggs, local wine in fonts, but no newspapers, no books ... The site of the city is in every respect magnificent, the climate glorious, the fruits of the earth abound, but the people are devilishly apathetic. They are all

musical, endowed with fantasy and wit, high-strung, sensitive, but all this is wasted.[34]

Chekhov's belief in the value of education and knowledge in the battle to improve social conditions led him to endow many libraries. For this action, Tsar Nicholas II granted him 'hereditary nobility' and decorated him as a reward for his 'exemplary zeal and exertions directed towards the education of the people'.[35] Not surprisingly, it was Taganrog library that benefited most from Chekhov's donations.[36]

Chekhov's philanthropy and commitment to social improvement are seldom given the importance they deserve by critics involved in delineating Chekhov's overall vision of reality. Too often critics in the West overemphasise the dark side of the playwright's vision and refuse to see that Chekhov was more progressive than the surface reality of his stories and plays initially suggest. Chekhov, the short-term pessimist, was a long-term optimist. His optimistic long view is denied by critics like Ronald Hingley. Referring to Alexander Kuprin's *Reminiscences of Anton Tchekhov*,[37] Hingley claims that:

> ... Kuprin goes on to evoke a Chekhov spectacularly un-Chekhovian. 'Do you know,' he [Kuprin's Chekhov] suddenly added *with an earnest face and tones of deep faith*. 'Do you know that, within three or four hundred years, the whole earth will be transformed into a blossoming garden? And life will then be remarkably easy and convenient.' Tones of deep faith! How could anyone familiar with Chekhov's work, as Kuprin was, conceivably introduce this of all clichés?[38]

While Hingley may find Kuprin's style too florid for his reserved Anglo-Saxon taste, there is ample evidence that Chekhov did believe in the possibility of a better life and that this evolutionary 'epic vision', as Tulloch calls it, was indeed a 'faith' that was central to Chekhov's vision of reality.

It is because Hingley himself does not accept the possibility of radical change that he cannot accept it in Chekhov. His response to the conversion of Layevsky at the end of *The Duel*, a conversion that reminds one of the Damascan experience of St Paul, is totally negative:

> With regard to the ending of *The Duel*, though it would admittedly be praiseworthy and desirable for a real life Layevsky to take up serious work, pay off his debts and marry his mistress, the standards of real life and art do not always coincide, and the solution offered by Chekhov is an artistic disaster.[39]

Simply because Hingley feels that any kind of conversion that brings about significant change in a character's behaviour is not true to real life is not a reason to assume that Chekhov felt the same. We have evidence that Chekhov, while he believed that humanity was capable of degeneration, also believed in regeneration. Hingley may find the idea of humans changing for the worse more convincing than the idea of their changing for the better but for Chekhov both types of change were possible and neither type of change was inevitable. Ehrenburg claims that Chekhov angrily dismissed all talk about the inevitable degeneration of mankind: 'However great the degeneration, it can always be defeated by will and education.'[40]

Chapter XVII of *The Duel* begins this process of regeneration for Layevsky. He comes to see that many of the awful things that have happened to him have been brought about through his own self-centred inaction and self-deception:

> He had failed to cultivate integrity, having no need for it. His conscience, mesmerized by depravity and pretence, had slept or remained silent. Like some stranger or hireling — like one from another planet — he had shirked collective social life, caring nothing for the sufferings of others, nothing for their ideas or religions, nothing for what they knew, nothing for their quests and struggles ... He had not done a thing for his fellows but eat their bread, drink their wine, steal their wives and borrow their ideas, while seeking to justify his despicable, parasitical existence in the world's eyes and his own by passing himself off as a higher form of life: It was all lies, lies, lies.[41]

The fact that Chekhov wrote a conclusion to the story in which the three main characters are reformed leads Hingley to describe the ending as 'feeble ... unconvincing and banal'.[42] These comments perhaps tell us more about Hingley's world view than they do about that of Chekhov. John Tulloch is surely correct when he claims that Layevsky's 'conversion is potentially "lifelike" within Chekhov's *perceived* concept of reality: he had, after all, his whole medical training to tell him it was so'.[43]

Layevsky comes to see that his life has been 'all lies, lies, lies'. His conversion involves the rejection of lies altogether. By examining the social and environmental causes of his and his mistress Nadezhda's situation, he comes to see that her loose behaviour with Kirilin and Achmianov is to a great degree his own responsibility:

> A weak young woman, who had trusted him more than her own brother — he had taken her from her husband, her circle of friends and her homeland. He had carried her off to this sweltering fever-ridden dump, and day after day she had inevitably come to mirror his own idleness, depravity and spuriousness, the whole of her feeble, listless, wretched existence being utterly abandoned to these things. Then he had wearied of her and come to hate her. But not having the guts to leave her, he had tried to enmesh her even more tightly in the web of his lies. Achmianov and Kirilin had completed the job.[44]

This concern with the need for people to live authentically was a recurring theme in Chekhov's work. Deception, especially self-deception, is constantly shown to be connected with human failure and waste. Again and again Chekhov, through the depiction of what happens to his inauthentic self-deceivers, tried to show his readers and audience that the very possibility of progress is destroyed if reality is not faced. One of his notebook entries is particularly illuminating on this need to reject all forms of deception:

> A clever man says: 'This is a lie, but since the people cannot do without the lie, since it has the sanction of history, it is dangerous to root it out all at once; let it go on for the time being but with certain corrections.' But the genius says: 'This is a lie therefore it must not exist.'[45]

Chapter XVII of *The Duel* begins with a quotation from Pushkin which acts as a pointer to the stage of regeneration that Layevsky has reached:

> Reading, appalled, my life's sad tale, I tremble, curse the waste of days. But naught my bitter tears avail The gloomy record to erase.[46]

The depressing realisation that the past has been wasted and is irremediable is only the beginning for Layevsky. The chapter ends on a more positive note. He goes out to have a duel with Van Koren but only after he has forgiven his mistress and restored his faith in life and the future:

> He stroked her hair, gazing into her face — and knew that this unhappy immoral woman was the one person in his life. She was near to him, dear to him. She was the only one. He left the house and took his seat in the carriage. Now he wanted to come home alive.[47]

Layevsky survives the duel and begins a life of hard work that is part of his redemption. Chekhov's belief in the possibility of change for the better and in progress suffuses *The Duel*. At the end of the story Layevsky, watching the scientist Von Koren's boat battling against the rough seas, sees it as an image of the human quest for truth. Chekhov makes sure that the reader is left with some hope that the object of the quest is attainable:

> When seeking truth, people take two steps forward to one step back. Suffering, mistakes and world weariness throw them back, but passion for truth and stubborn will-power drive them onwards. And — who knows? — perhaps they will reach real truth in the end.[48]

Layevsky's 'conversion' and the restoration of his 'faith' in the future is not a sign that Chekhov had ceased to see life in materialist terms. As a non-believer, Chekhov employed the term 'faith' in a secular sense. However, while the term had no transcendental significance for him, he felt that faith played an important role in the creation of civilised society. 'Faith', he says in his *Notebooks*, 'is a spiritual faculty; animals have not got it; savages and uncivilized people have merely fear and doubt. Only highly developed natures can have faith.'[49] In *The*

*Duel,* Chekhov presents Layevsky's change in a positive light. In the stories and plays in which the characters continue to waste their lives through inaction and refusal to change, they are subject to the author's implied criticism. The underlying vision of reality remains consistent in that all of these works are underpinned by a belief in the possibility of progress.

'The tones of deep faith' perceived by Kuprin are not so 'spectacularly un-Chekhovian' as Hingley maintains. In 1888, only three years before he wrote *The Duel,* Chekhov wrote an obituary for the explorer N. Przevalsky in which his praise for this man of action was couched in terms of an attack on the spineless intelligentsia who lacked any aim or faith in anything.[50] This attack gives us a clear idea of how important it was in Chekhov's overall world view for humans to have some purpose and some degree of social conscience:

> In these morbid times, when European societies are overcome by idleness, boredom with life and lack of faith, ... when even the best of men sit with their arms folded and justify their indolence and depravity by the absence of any definite aim, heroes and ascetics are as vital as the sun ... In themselves they are living documents, showing society that alongside those who argue about pessimism and optimism, ... succumb to debauchery out of nihilism and earn their daily bread by lying, that alongside those sceptics, ... there also exist men of a wholly different kind, heroic men, full of faith, heading towards a clearly determined goal.[51]

In 1890, at the height of his literary career, Chekhov emulated Przevalsky by undertaking an extraordinary journey across the length of Russia to carry out a scientific analysis of the conditions in the penal colony on the island of Sakhalin, which lies just north of Japan. This research trip to Sakhalin may well have been partly motivated by his desire to show his contemporaries that he was not one of the spineless intelligentsia, but a man with a purpose who was capable of social action. As Philip Callow notes:

> It must be remembered ... that the attacks on Chekhov in the Russian critical monthlies for his refusal to concern himself with political and social questions had been mounting in virulence for years. An article in *Russian Thought*, labelling him as one of the priests of 'unprincipled writing', stung him so badly that he felt driven to defend himself for the only time in his life.[52]

Chekhov's anger at the inactivity of his people and their government when faced with the facts of prison life in Russia is further evidence that he did not hold any proto-absurdist view of life where there is nothing to be done. His anger is at those who have done nothing to change conditions and his act of going to Sakhalin himself is his individual proof that something can be done:

> From the books I have been reading it is clear that we have let *millions* of people rot in prison, destroying them carelessly, thoughtlessly, barbarously; we drove

people in chains through the cold across thousands of miles, infected them with syphilis, depraved them, multiplied criminals, and placed the blame for all this on red-nosed prison wardens. All civilized Europe knows now that it is not the wardens who are to blame, but all of us, yet this is no concern of ours, we are not interested. The vaunted 60s did *nothing* for the sick and the prisoners, thus violating the basic commandment of Christian civilization. In our time something is being done for the sick, but for prisoners nothing; prison problems don't interest our jurists at all. No, I assure you, we need Sakhalin, and it is important to us, and the only thing to be regretted is that I am the one to go there and not someone else who is better equipped for the task and is more capable of arousing public interest.[53]

The arduous journey to Sakhalin almost certainly shortened Chekhov's life, but it was important to the writer that he make some useful contribution to his society.[54] Finding a purpose to life through socially useful activity was one of the main themes expressed at the time of the Sakhalin trip. Even though no character in his works is the mouthpiece of Chekhov's views, it is difficult not to see certain affinities between some of the ideas expressed by his characters and Chekhov's own behaviour. For instance, in *An Anonymous Story*, a story that Chekhov wrote soon after he returned from Sakhalin, the narrator, Vladimir, expresses a sense of mission that echoes that of his author:

> I have now really grasped both with my mind and in my tortured heart, that man either hasn't got a destiny, or else it lies exclusively in self-sacrificing love for his neighbour. That's the way we should be going, that's our purpose in life. And that is my faith.[55]

By going to Sakhalin on a mission to help his fellow man, Chekhov acted out in practice what was to become one of the major themes of his writings. Indeed, Sophie Laffitte has argued that this theme 'was to serve as the ulterior basis of all Chekhov's works'. She rightly points out that this theme was 'never explicitly expressed, merely suggested'.[56]

Chekhov's research trip to Sakhalin had been partly motivated by his sense of guilt at having spent too much time on writing literature and not having made enough use of his training as a doctor. The Sakhalin research, Chekhov said, was intended 'to pay off some of my debt to medicine, toward which, as you know, I've behaved like a pig'.[57]

When *The Island: A Journey to Sakhalin* was printed Chekhov wrote to Suvorin expressing the pride he felt in his scientific work:

> My *Sakhalin* is an academic work ... Medicine cannot now accuse me of infidelity ... I rejoice because the rough garb of the convict will also be hanging in my (literary) wardrobe.[58]

The need to see Chekhov's literary career and his practice of medicine as interrelated has now been established.[59] While ever he was physically able to, Chekhov continued to practise medicine and to be a writer. When Suvorin advised him to give up medicine, he replied:

> I feel more alert and more satisfied with myself when I think of myself as having two occupations instead of one. Medicine is my lawful wedded wife, and literature my mistress. When one gets on my nerves, I spend the night with the other.[60]

Chekhov's early belief that literature should simply show life as it is was clearly related to his scientific training as a doctor. Despite being written as a scientific thesis, *The Island* displays several recognisably Chekhovian elements and much of the work is enlivened by anecdotes and descriptions that remind one of scenes in his short stories. Thus what J. L. Conrad calls the 'notable similarities between *The Island* and his more famous literary productions',[61] should make us aware that, for Chekhov, science and literature were not mutually exclusive. Both were attractive bedfellows.

Chekhov strongly believed that progress would be brought about through education and, in particular, through the exploitation of the discoveries of science. His medical training and his faith in the scientific method were of central importance both in the development of his vision of reality and in the development of the artistic means to express that vision. Being a materialist, Chekhov wished in his plays and short stories to analyse human behaviour in a wholly scientific manner.[62] He endeavoured to apply the methods of science to his artistic creations. In particular he strove to employ the concept of scientific objectivity in all of his writing. The need to depict 'life as it actually is' was for Chekhov the *sine qua non* of his artistic and personal credo. Like other naturalistic writers, Chekhov's scientific approach to literature led him to include the seamy side of life in his depictions of real life. When he was attacked for including unpalatable elements in his short story *Mire*, he defended his approach by applying the principles of science:

> For chemists there is nothing unclean on this earth. A writer should be as objective as a chemist; he must give up everyday subjectivity and realize that dunghills play a very respectable role in the landscape and that evil passions belong to life as much as good ones do.[63]

Like Shaw and Molière, Chekhov had a social corrective theory of art. It is encapsulated in one of his *Notebook* entries: 'Man will only become better when you make him see what he is like.'[64] Critics and stage directors should bear this comment in mind when interpreting Chekhov, since, by following its implications, they will avoid producing pessimistic, absurdist misinterpretations of his works.

The most frequently quoted statement of Chekhov's concerning the need for artists to have some overall aim underpinning their work is contained in an important letter to Suvorin written in November 1892. It deserves to be quoted at length because of the light that it throws on what the playwright perceived to be the dual function of the literary artist, and on the failure of his own generation of writers, himself included, to carry out the second function. The first function of the artist, Chekhov claims, is to depict life accurately but the second function he suggests expresses the artist's vision of reality, his attitude towards life. He describes his ideal literary artist as follows:

> The best of them are realistic and describe life as it is, but because each line is saturated with the consciousness of its goal, you feel life as it should be in addition to life as it is, and you are captivated by it.[65]

It was because he felt that writers of his generation lacked any real goals in their work that Chekhov complained of the particular time in which he was living. He claimed that for writers 'this is a precarious, sour, dreary period'. The cause, Chekhov argues, is not lack of talent, but rather 'a malady that for an artist is worse than syphilis or sexual impotence'. That malady is a lack of overall purpose:

> Keep in mind that the writers we call eternal or simply good, the writers who intoxicate us, have one highly important trait in common: they're moving toward something definite and beckon you to follow, and you feel with your entire being, not only with your mind, that they have a certain goal ... Depending on their calibre, some have immediate goals — the abolition of serfdom, the liberation of one country, politics, beauty or simply vodka ... — while the goals of others are more remote — God, life after death, the happiness of mankind, etc.[66]

Chekhov's letters provide evidence of an ongoing interest in the question of the artist's purpose. As early as 1888 he wrote to Suvorin pointing out the necessity for literary artists to have some socio-political aim or goal underpinning their works. For Chekhov, an artist without a purpose was a contradiction in terms:

> The artist observes, selects, guesses and synthesizes. The very fact of these actions pre-supposes a question; if he hadn't asked himself a question at the start, he would have nothing to guess and nothing to select. To put it briefly, I will conclude with some psychiatry: if you deny that creativity involves questions and intent, you have to admit that the artist creates without premeditation or purpose, in a state of unthinking emotionality. And so if any author were to boast to me that he'd written a story from pure inspiration without first having thought over his intentions, I'd call him a mad man.[67]

At that time, Chekhov was aware that he had as yet developed no clearly articulated aim. This had not been a problem when he had regarded his writing as mere hack scribblings. When he came to take his work seriously, he bemoaned this lack of any clear aim or vision of reality. He was aware that without an aim, he could only depict the mere *surface* of life as it is. Chekhov wrote to Grigorovich, who had encouraged him to take more care over his writings:

> As yet I have no political, religious and philosophical view of the universe; I change it every month and will be compelled to limit myself solely to descriptions of how my chief characters make love, get married, give birth, meet death, and how they talk.[68]

Chekhov was aware that *all* artists necessarily express *some* viewpoint in their works. Not surprisingly, he expressed a degree of anguish at the fact that, in 1888, he was unable to articulate any stable vision of reality that could be expressed in his works. Despite the fact that he knew that the literary artist needed to have a viewpoint, his commitment to objectivity meant that Chekhov could not write polemically. As we shall see later when discussing his approach to form, Chekhov did not believe in any sort of judgemental didacticism. He reported to Suvorin in 1890:

> Of course, it would be gratifying to couple art with sermonizing, but personally, I find this exceedingly difficult and, because of conditions imposed by technique, all but impossible.[69]

Chekhov refused to write about areas of experience outside his understanding. Providing answers to questions about whether or not to abolish serfdom, or whether or not God exists, were beyond Chekhov's area of expertise and consequently lay outside his literary purview. As he pointed out to Suvorin:

> ... it's none of the artist's business to solve narrowly specialized problems. It's bad when an artist tackles something that he does not understand.[70]

Unlike Tolstoy or Dostoevsky, he had no knowledge of or belief in God. In 1903, he wrote: 'I long since lost belief and can merely keep glancing in perplexity at every intellectual who is a believer.'[71] Equally, he could not write about 'life after death', as this was a concept he did not understand. Just as he would attack Tolstoy for writing about science, which that author did not understand,[72] so Chekhov himself refrained from writing about spiritual matters, which were Tolstoy's forté. In hospital following a severe tuberculosis attack, Chekhov was visited by Tolstoy who began to discuss 'life after death'. Chekhov's response is revealing:

> We talked about immortality. He takes immortality in the Kantian sense; he holds that all of us (people and animals) will live in a principle (reason, love), the essence and purpose of which is a mystery to us. To me this principle or

force presents itself as a formless jellylike mass, my 'I' — my individuality, my consciousness, will be fused with this mass — such immortality I don't need, I don't understand it, and Lev Nikolayevich [Tolstoy] was astonished that I didn't understand it.[73]

Chekhov felt himself unqualified and uncomfortable dealing with vague philosophical generalities such as 'the happiness of mankind' or 'immortality'. He was committed to depicting 'life as it is' in all of its realistic specificity. This was what he knew and understood. As Gorky remarked:

Nobody understood so clearly and keenly as Anton Chekhov the tragedy of life's banalities, nobody before him could with such merciless truthtelling depict for people the shameful and painful picture of their life in the dreary chaos of petty bourgeois prosiness.[74]

It is hardly surprising that an author whom Gorky characterises as creating his artistic works in order to say to his readers and audiences 'You live abominably, Gentlemen!'[75] should find it impossible to depict 'the happiness of mankind'. Chekhov refused to falsify his depictions by making them more pleasant than life itself. In defence of his realistic approach to his art he wrote to one correspondent:

Literature is called artistic when it depicts life as it actually is. Its purpose is truth, honest and indisputable. To limit its functions to special tasks, such as the finding of 'pearls', does it mortal injury ... I agree that a 'pearl' is a good thing, but a writer is not a confectioner, not a cosmetician, not an entertainer; he is a man with an obligation, under contract to his duty, his conscience; he must do what he has set out to do; he is bound to fight his squeamishness and dirty his imagination with what is dirty in life. He is like an ordinary reporter.[76]

'If you wish to become an optimist and understand life', he wrote in his *Notebooks*, 'stop believing what people say and write; observe and discover for yourself.'[77] Chekhov's own observations led him to believe that literature without any overall goal was essentially trivial, no matter how accurately the writer depicted external reality. In his long letter to Suvorin in November 1892, Chekhov outlined the 'malady' that he believed was crippling the literary artists of his generation and weakening his own work. His comments emphasise just how vital a role artistic goals played in his artistic credo:

But what about us? Us! We describe life as it is and stop dead right there ... We have neither immediate nor remote goals, and there is an emptiness in our soul. We have no politics, we don't believe in revolution, there is no God, we're not afraid of ghosts, and I personally am not even afraid of death or blindness. No one who wants nothing, hopes for nothing, and fears nothing can be an artist.[78]

As we shall see, Chekhov was to develop a means of successfully presenting both 'life as it is' and 'life as it should be' by finding a way to present the second function indirectly, through implication. One of Robert Brustein's many perceptive comments on Chekhov provides a key to the understanding of how the playwright was to go about combining his truthful and realistic depiction of the dreary apathetic life led in the Russia of his time, with his goal of unpolemically suggesting a vision of how good life could and should be. Brustein argues that Chekhov's 'concern with "life as it is" is eventually modified by his growing conviction that "life as it is" is life as it should *not* be'.[79] Brustein does not follow the implications of his own observation, since he sees Chekhov as a deeply pessimistic writer, but his observation in fact allows us to see how it is possible to *show* a bleak life while *suggesting* a brighter possible future alternative. Simply because Chekhov refuses to *overtly* depict 'the happiness of mankind' does not imply that he thinks that such happiness can never be attained. On the contrary, by presenting in his works the banality of 'life as it is' and by suggesting the possibility of change and progress, be it gradual or not, Chekhov presents, *by implication,* 'life as it should be'.

Throughout Chekhov's writings we find implied criticism of inertia, pessimism and lack of aim, vision or goal. At times, aspects of his vision of reality are made explicit. In his *Notebooks* we find him writing: 'We judge human activities by their goal; that activity is great of which the goal is great.'[80] There is an implied criticism of those characters in Chekhov's short stories and plays who commit suicide. Their loss of faith in progress or change results in a complete loss of any goal in life. In his feuilleton, *A Moscow Hamlet*, published in December 1891, Chekhov pillories the world-weary 'superfluous man' who does nothing to improve life, and who, having no aim in life, simply whines about it. Chekhov presents suicide as the logical conclusion to such a life. He ends the self-pitying diatribe of the Moscow Hamlet with a statement that he had already put into the mouth of 'a certain gentleman unknown to me, evidently not a Moscovite', who, when asked what the Moscow Hamlet should do about his constant boredom, replied with irritation: 'Ah, take a piece of telephone wire and hang yourself to the first telegraph pole! There is nothing else left for you to do!'[81]

For some critics, Chekhov's denial of any transcendent purpose to life ultimately suggests to them a pessimistic attitude, but Chekhov's 'epic vision' of the possibility of progress for humanity, while it may look bleak to those who have a Pollyanna view of life, must surely look positively rosy when compared with the nihilistic vision of the Absurdists. As Herbert Müller persuasively argues:

> The question, again, is whether on the conditions of modern knowledge and experience men can still come to satisfactory terms with life. And though Chekhov's terms manifestly cannot satisfy those who require fixities or religious

certainty, there are at least honourable terms, they include Christian ethical values, ... and they represent a positive acceptance. They foster a reverence for life, and for all possibilities of a richer more humane life.[82]

In *A Dreary Story,* Chekhov refused to allow the dying professor to console the one person he loved, Katya, with any false optimism. When the professor is faced with the existential despair of Katya, who has come to ask him to give her a reason for living so that she will not commit suicide, he can only make her the truthful reply: 'But what can I say? I ask in bewilderment. There's nothing I can say.'[83]

Chekhov's sense of purpose is rarely expressed in terms of straightforward optimism. His long-term optimism was almost always balanced by his awareness that in the short term things might not improve. Future generations might have a better life but, being aware of his own failing health, Chekhov knew that there was little hope for himself. Gorky recalls a time when the sick Chekhov expressed his anguish at the thought of his impending premature death: 'One day, lying on a couch, coughing and playing with a thermometer, he said: "To live in order that we may die is not very pleasant, but to live knowing that we shall die before our time is up is profoundly stupid."'[84]

Several of Chekhov's characters face their approaching deaths with a sense of hopelessness. The professor in *A Dreary Story* bemoans the fact that his life has been wasted because he lacked any goal or purpose:

> I'd like to wake up a hundred years from now and cast at least a cursory glance at what's happening in science. I'd like to have lived another ten years or so. And then?
>
> The rest is nothing. I go on thinking — for a long time — but can't hit on anything. And rack my brains as I will, broadcast my thoughts where I may, I clearly see there's something missing in my wishes — something vital, something really basic. My passion for science, my urge to live, my sitting on this strange bed, my urge to know myself, together with all my thoughts and feelings, and conceptions which I form about everything — these things lack any common link capable of bonding them into a single entity. Each sensation, each idea of mine has its own separate being. Neither in my judgements about science, the stage, literature and my pupils, nor in the pictures painted in my imagination could even the most skilful analyst detect any 'general conception', or the God of a live human being. And if one lacks that, one has nothing.[85]

Several of Chekhov's letters written in 1892–93 suggest that he was undergoing some personal crisis which manifested itself in terms of a temporary loss of his positive attitude towards life. In April 1892, when he was only 32, he complained:

> I turned thirty long ago and already feel close to forty. And I've aged in spirit as well as in body. In some silly way I've grown indifferent to everything around me and for some reason the onset of this indifference coincided with my trips abroad. I get up and go to bed with the feeling that my interest in life has dried up.[86]

A similar note of depression is sounded in a letter to Suvorin in October of the same year: 'not only am I bored and dissatisfied, but as a doctor I am cynical enough to be convinced that from this life we can expect only evil errors, losses, illnesses, weakness, and all kinds of dirty tricks.'[87]

However, even in this bleak period of his life, Chekhov did not give up his struggle to find purpose in life. The very next sentence of the letter just quoted, begins with the words: 'Nevertheless, if you only knew how pleasant ...' In another letter to Suvorin written a week earlier, Chekhov responds to life's hardships in a positive life-affirming manner:

> In spite of the cholera turmoil and impecuniousness, which kept me in its paws until fall, I liked life and wanted to live. How many trees I planted![88]

Again, in a letter to L. S. Mizonova, written in August 1893, Chekhov complained of feeling old. He complained that 'life is so empty that one feels only the flies biting — and nothing more'. However, despite this expression of personal depression, he asserted that: 'One must have a purpose in life ...'[89]

Chekhov's own biological clock was running down and he seemed to be well aware of the fact five years before his massive lung haemorrhage in 1897 told him how little time he had left. Writing from his estate at Melikhovo to another friend, I. L. Leontyev-Shcheglov in October 1892, he talks of the advantages of not being in Moscow, but then exclaims:

> ... but, dear captain — there's old age! Old age, or being too lazy to live, I don't know which, but one does not particularly want to live. One does not want to die but living, too, has become a bore somehow. In short, the soul is having a taste of what the cold sleep is like.[90]

When, a month later, Chekhov wrote to Suvorin bemoaning the lack of such an aim or purpose in the work of artists of his time, he accepted that he was also suffering from the same 'disease'. Characteristically, while refusing to console himself with any unfounded optimism, he refrained from giving in to depression and refused to follow the logic of the absurd that leads to suicide. In what appears to be an almost Kierkegaardian leap to faith, Chekhov accepts the idea of the world having some purpose even if that purpose is not directly perceivable:

> I won't throw myself down a stairwell like Garshin,[91] nor shall I delude myself with hopes for a better future. I am not to blame for my illness, and it is not for

me to doctor myself, for the disease, it must be supposed, has ends that are hidden from us and that have not been visited upon us without reason.[92]

Chekhov's 'faith' is not in any transcendental God or afterlife but in progress and evolution, and, as such, it is humanist faith. Chekhov's materialist vision of reality helps us to see why he felt unable to answer any questions about the ultimate meaning of life. Spiritual and metaphysical speculations lie outside the reach of scientific materialism. This belief is expressed in one of his *Notebook* entries: 'There is no single criterion which can serve as the measure of the non-existent, of the non-human.'[93] Chekhov wrote about the future of humanity in terms of evolutionary gradualism incorporating a sense of purpose and belief in progress. However, when he looked at life from his own individual standpoint, he expressed a sense of his own insignificance and mortality. During the late 1880s and early 1890s, Chekhov seems to have suffered great anguish at what seemed to him to be the purposelessness of each individual's life. Probably brought on by his own illness, Chekhov began suffering from depression and panic attacks. Magarshack writes that, though he was no longer being plagued by 'violent convulsions at night', Chekhov's mental and physical health was extremely poor:

> A worse trouble beset him now. In addition to the current symptoms of tuberculosis as well as the constant attacks of haemorrhoids, he was now obsessed by mental terrors, caused chiefly by the suppressed thought of his own illness.[94]

The depression that Chekhov was suffering at this time was translated into his writing. One prime example is the monologue fragment that is one of the earliest entries in his *Notebooks*, which he had started to write in 1892. Chekhov records: 'Solomon made a great mistake when he asked for wisdom.'[95] The nature of that unwelcome 'wisdom' becomes clear when one examines the monologue that was intended to be delivered by the character Solomon:

> SOLOMON. [*Alone.*] Oh! how dark is life! No night, when I was a child, so terrified me by its darkness as does my incomprehensible existence. Lord, to David my father thou gavest only the gift of harmonizing words and sounds, to sing and praise Thee on strings, to lament sweetly, to make people weep, or admire beauty; but why has Thou given me a self-tormenting, sleepless hungry mind? Like an insect born of the dust, I hide in darkness; and in fear and despair, all shaking and shivering, I see and hear in everything an incomprehensible mystery. Why this morning? Why does the sun come from behind the temple and gild the palm tree? Why the beauty of women? Where does the bird hurry; what is the meaning of its flight, if it and its young and the place to which it hastens will, like myself, turn to dust? It were better I had never been born, or were a stone, to which God has given neither eyes nor thoughts. In order to tire

out my body by nightfall, all day yesterday, like a mere workman, I carried marble to the temple; but now the night has come, and I cannot sleep ... I'll go and lie down. Phorses told me that if one imagines a flock of sheep running and fixes one's attention upon it, the mind gets confused and one falls asleep. I'll do it ... [*Exit*.][96]

When we read many of the letters and works produced at this period of Chekhov's life, we can see why some critics have been misled into seeing the playwright as a proto-absurdist. That Chekhov himself suffered a 'dark night of the soul' similar to that endured by his character Solomon seems fairly certain. However, for most of his creative life Chekhov did not view life in a nihilistic manner or concentrate on his own personal problems. His works mainly focus on humanity at large and depict the purposiveness of nature seen from a Darwinian evolutionary viewpoint. Even in 1892, when some of his most pessimistic statements about life were made, we find Chekhov placing individual mortality in the larger context of nature and evolutionary progress. Again, Chekhov supplies no simplistic answers to life's mysteries. Relying on his faith in science and progress, he works on the assumption that, while not everything has been explained, everything on earth is potentially explainable. He writes to Suvorin:

> In central Russia the horses have influenza. They die. If you believe that everything that happens in nature is designed and purposeful, then obviously nature is straining every nerve to get rid of debilitated organisms and those she doesn't need. Famines, cholera, influenza ... only the healthy and strong will remain. But to reject the doctrine that there is purpose in things is impossible. Our starlings, young and old, suddenly flew away somewhere. This was baffling, because the time for the migration of birds was still far off. But unexpectedly we learned the other day that clouds of southern dragonflies, mistaken for locusts, had flown across Moscow. The question arises: how did our starlings learn that on such-and-such a day, miles from Melikhovo, multitudes of insects would be flying? Who informed them? Verily this is a great mystery. But it is a wise mystery. The same wisdom it occurs to one is hidden in famines and the illnesses that succeed them. We and our horses represent the dragonflies and famine and cholera — the starlings.[97]

Chekhov's faith in the possibility of a scientific explanation of nature combined with his essentially humble attitude towards human ignorance of many of nature's mysteries is further evidence of his balanced approach to life and this sense of balance is also evident in his art.

Chekhov appears to have hated extremism of any sort. This rejection of extremes again goes some way to explain why, though he could not believe in God, he nevertheless had faith in humanity. Chekhov believed that those who adopt extreme positions were bound to misunderstand most of life, since it is precisely between extremes that most of life takes place. To argue that Chekhov's plays are either 'comedies' or 'tragedies' without considering what lies between these two genres is to miss most of what Chekhov is about. To argue that he is either a proto-Marxist or a proto-Absurdist can only result in his works being misinterpreted. His vision of reality embodies an outlook that lies between these two polar extremes. This is illustrated in a diary entry for 1897 where he writes about 'faith'. He makes the following illuminating and balanced comment:

> Between 'there is a God' and 'there is no God' lies a vast tract, which the really wise man crosses with great effort. A Russian knows one or other of these two extremes, and the middle track between them does not interest him; and therefore he usually knows nothing or very little.[98]

Chekhov accepted the 'both/and' approach to life and depicted it with all of its inherent contradictions. Late in his life Chekhov wrote to Diaghilev about God. Even though he was a materialist who rejected any conception of the kind of transcendent God conceived of by writers like Tolstoy and Dostoevsky, Chekhov did not reject the idea of a more scientifically based concept of the deity. He wrote of 'discovering' God through evolutionary progress:

> Modern culture is the beginning of an effort that will continue for tens of thousands of years to the end that, if only in the distant future, mankind may know the true, real God, i.e. not conjecturing, not seeking for him in Dostoevsky, but will know Him clearly, know as it knows that two times two is four. Culture today is the beginning of such an effort, but the religious movement about which we talked is a survival, already almost the end of what is dying or dead.[99]

Examining the world from his Darwinian viewpoint, Chekhov saw abundant evidence of change and progress. He knew that any given individual might not see much improvement in his own life, but, with work, future generations of humanity would have a better life. Occasionally, even in an individual's lifetime, change and improvement could be spectacular. The efforts made by Chekhov and his fellow *zemstvo* doctors to control the cholera epidemic of 1892 brought about just such a spectacular improvement in the lives of the peasants. Dr Chekhov was suitably proud of his work:

> In Nizhny at the fair, they are working miracles, which are liable to compel even Tolstoy to adopt an attitude of respect for medicine and, in general, for intervention in life by men of culture. It looks as though cholera has been lassooed ... We have no assistants, we shall have to act simultaneously both as physicians and medical orderlies; the peasants are coarse, unclean, mistrustful, but the reflection that our labours will not go for nought makes all this almost unnoticeable.[100]

The almost euphoric tone of Chekhov's letter is mirrored in those cases in his fiction when a central character like Layevsky in *The Duel* or Vladimir in *An Anonymous Story* discovers a purpose outside their own egocentric concerns. The more optimistic side of Chekhov's world view is to be found in his depictions of characters who, like Layevsky and Vladimir, are sustained by their faith in a brighter future.

Whenever friends expressed totally pessimistic views about life Chekhov, while acknowledging that life at present was bad, would point out that it does improve. Writing to Leontyev-Shcheglov, Chekhov takes him to task for saying 'What a mess modern life is!':

> Your attitude toward our times has always struck me as unfair, always seemed to pass through your art like a morbid shudder ... I am far from enthusiastic about the contemporary scene, yet I think one ought to be objective, as far as possible. If things are not good now, if the present is not to one's liking, the past was simply abominable.[101]

What Chekhov is at pains to criticise is the lack of necessary human action to speed up the processes of improvement in living conditions in the Russia of his day. So his experiences in Hong Kong in 1890 on his return trip from the Island of Sakhalin did not lead him to attack the faults of British colonialism. Instead he criticised the relative lack of activity on the part of his own countrymen in improving life in Russia:

> I rode in jinrickshas, which is to say, in vehicles drawn by men; bought all sorts of rubbish from the Chinese; and waxed indignant as I listened to my Russian fellow travellers upbraiding the English for their exploitation of the natives. Yes, thought I, the Englishman exploits Chinese, Sepoys, Hindus, but he gives them roads, aqueducts, museums, Christianity; you too exploit but what do you give?[102]

Despite his awareness of colonial exploitation, Chekhov believed that people in India had acquired some benefit from the British occupation. In particular, he made it clear that he was in favour of human beings modifying their world and making use of nature's wealth. His one proviso was that this should be done in an environmentally sound manner that took into account the quality of life of future generations as well as that of the present generation. Once we understand this attitude it will be harder for us to interpret a character like Lopakhin in *The Cherry Orchard* as some monster bent on the destruction of all that is beautiful.

In Chekhov's major works the people whom he subtly criticises are those who waste their lives, but his strongest criticisms were kept for those who, like the people of the 'vaunted 60s', hypocritically claimed to be doing something to improve life but in fact did nothing. In his *Notebooks* there are three clear examples of this kind of bad faith, and each foreshadows the sort of inauthentic behaviour that is adopted by so many of the characters in his stories and plays. The first example reads like a small parable:

> The new Governor made a speech to his clerks. He called the merchants together — another speech. At the annual prizegiving of the secondary school for girls a speech on true enlightenment. To the representatives of the press a speech. He called the Jews together: 'Jews, I have summoned you …' A month or two passes – he does nothing. Again he calls the merchants together — a speech. Again the Jews: 'Jews, I have summoned you …' He has wearied them all. At last he says to his Chancellor: 'No, the work is too much for me, I shall have to resign.'[103]

There are many talkers who are not doers in Chekhov's plays. A character like Trofimov in *The Cherry Orchard*, who does nothing and has failed to complete his degree, nevertheless talks a great deal, especially about the value of hard work! The following extract from the *Notebooks* might help us to see how Chekhov wished such characters as Trofimov, or Serebryakov in *Uncle Vanya*, to be interpreted: 'Nowadays when a decent working-man takes himself and his work critically, people call him grumbler, idler, bore; but when an idle scoundrel shouts that it is necessary to work, he is applauded.'[104]

While neither Trofimov nor Serebryakov are 'scoundrels', both are gently satirised by Chekhov. The eternal student becomes an object of fun because his laudable call for people to work is undercut by his own inactivity, while the professor's exhortation that everyone should work is undermined by the fact that his labours have produced little of worth. The comic tactlessness exhibited by both characters is made clear by Chekhov having them make their calls to work in the presence of 'decent' characters, Lopakhin and Vanya, who have worked extremely hard all their lives.

The third example from the *Notebooks* is another example of the talker who does nothing. The consistently critical attitude expressed by Chekhov towards those who claim to have a purpose, but who do nothing to achieve their aims, is worth bearing in mind when we come to interpret similar characters in Chekhov's plays. A character like Vershinin in *Three Sisters* may well mouth laudable sentiments but he is personally satirised for merely philosophising about action. The entry in the *Notebooks* is as follows:

> One remembers the arguments about the brotherhood of man, public good, and work for the people, but really there were no such arguments, one only drank at the University. They write 'one feels ashamed of the men with University degrees who once fought for human rights and freedom of religion and conscience' — but they never fought.[105]

The depiction of 'life as it is' presented as realistically as possible was Chekhov's first artistic objective. The reason he presented a picture of 'life as it should *not* be' was that he hoped to produce a negative response to the spineless behaviour depicted and a positive response to those characters whose behaviour was liable to improve the human lot. As John Hagan puts it:

> Chekhov's ultimate purpose is to communicate an attitude of one kind or another; but his immediate purpose is to create in the reader [or audience] a certain kind of illusion — an illusion that he is holding up for inspection a piece of unmediated reality, a segment of life rendered with matter of fact lucidity in all its circumstantiality, uncolored by the moods or opinions of any observer.[106]

As we have seen, Chekhov's optimism was hard won. Not believing in God or an afterlife, he had to develop a secular faith based on science and, as we shall see, that scientific attitude informed not only his vision of reality, but also the artistic form that he utilised to realise that vision. Any attacks on science and the scientific method were dealt with severely by him. So of the many faults that he found in Bourget's *Disciple*, Chekhov asserted in a letter to Suvorin in 1889 that: 'the main one among them is his pretentious crusade against materialist doctrine'.[107] The importance to Chekhov of a materialist approach to the understanding of life cannot be overemphasised. For the playwright this scientific method of analysis was not an optional way of seeing the world — it was *the* way. Chekhov fulminates against what he sees as Bourget's attacks on materialism:

> To begin with, materialism is not a school or doctrine in the narrow journalistic sense. It is neither chance occurrence nor passing fancy; it is something indispensable and inevitable and beyond human power. Everything that lives on earth is necessarily materialistic ... Prohibiting materialist doctrine is tantamount to preventing man from seeking out the truth.[108]

Even Chekhov's attitude towards psychology depended on a materialist methodology. He attacks Bourget and many other psychologists of his time for their spiritualistic approach to the study of the human mind:

> As for his bookish, learned psychology, he [Bourget] knows about it as little as the best of psychologists. Knowing it is just about the same as not knowing it, since it is more a fiction than a science, a kind of alchemy, and it is high time for it to be filed away in the archives.[109]

Such concepts as the human 'soul' meant little to Chekhov because there could be 'no criterion which could serve as the measure' of such 'fictional' entities. For him human psychology could only be a real science when it was dealt with through an examination of the human organism which, being material, was open to observation. In the same letter to Suvorin, Chekhov notes:

... psychic phenomena are so strikingly similar to physical ones that it is almost impossible to figure out where the former start and the latter end? It seems to me that, when a corpse is being dissected, even the most inveterate spiritualist must *necessarily* come up against the question of where the soul is. And if you know how great the similarity is between mental and physical illnesses and when you know that both one and the other are treated with the very same remedies, you can't help but refuse to separate soul from body.[110]

Such a view of human psychology has far-reaching ramifications for not just the content, but the form of Chekhov's literary works. In particular, the style of acting that Chekhov admired and which is appropriate for the performing of his own plays is one in which, as Chekhov advised Meyerhold: 'Subtle emotion of the spirit ... must be expressed subtly, *through external behaviour.*'[111]

Chekhov's approach to life and to art were inextricably linked together by his scientific materialism. That in literary matters he was drawn to Naturalism was almost inevitable, given his scientific training. The central dogma of Naturalism, that creative writers were to employ the scientific method in their works and were 'to observe and to record as dispassionately and impersonally as the scientist',[112] was not in any way strange to the medically trained Chekhov. This is hardly surprising when one realises that, as Furst and Skrine note, for the Naturalists 'the most common analogy was between the writer and the doctor dissecting the human mind and body'.[113]

As we shall see in the next chapter, Chekhov's commitment to Naturalism led him to confront certain major artistic problems and led, not to any rejection of Naturalism in general, but to the development of his own modified version of that literary movement's platform. Nicholas Moravcevich fairly sums up Chekhov's general position in relation to Naturalism when he notes: 'Zola's demands for a complete surrender of intuition to scientifically collected data were at times too extreme for Chekhov, but in general he at that time [1888] had no quarrel with an artistic method based on faithful reproduction of materialistic phenomena.'[114]

Certainly, as late as 1899, when he was asked to supply an autobiographical sketch for an album to be published of all the alumni of the 1884 class of the Medical School of Moscow University, Chekhov still wished to acknowledge his affiliations with Naturalism. Almost half of his autobiographical sketch is taken up with his explanation of the importance of scientific method in his artistic works. He likewise acknowledged that such a naturalistic approach to creative works was problematic:

> I don't doubt that the study of the medical sciences seriously affected my literary work; they significantly enlarged the field of my observations, enriched me with knowledge, the true value of which for me as a writer can be understood

only by one who is himself a physician; they also had a directive influence and probably because I was close to medicine I avoided many mistakes. Acquaintance with the natural sciences, with scientific method, kept me always on guard and I tried, wherever possible, to bring my writings into harmony with scientific data, and where this was impossible, I preferred not to write at all. Let me observe that creativity in the arts does not always admit total agreement with scientific data; thus it is impossible to represent on the stage death from poisoning as it actually takes place. But agreement with scientific data must be felt in the conventions accepted, that is, it is necessary for the reader or spectator to grasp clearly that these are only conventions, and that he is dealing with an author who knows the true facts. I do not belong to the fiction writers who have a negative attitude toward science ...[115]

As we have seen, the playwright's vision of reality cannot be adequately described in terms of absolutes. Any polarised interpretation of his plays that plumps for 'Chekhov the pessimist' or 'Chekhov the optimist' is bound to be reductionist. His own hatred of pigeonholing and extremes, and his love of honesty and truth, were part of his world view as early as 1888, and remained of central importance to his vision all of his life. Chekhov's attitude toward those critics who insisted on simplistically 'plucking' out his mystery by seeing him in the extreme terms of 'either/or' was entirely negative:

> I am afraid of those who look for a tendency between the lines and insist on seeing me as necessarily either a liberal or a conservative. I am not a liberal, not a conservative, not a gradualist, not a monk, not an indifferentist. I should like to be a free artist and nothing more, ... I regard trademarks and labels as prejudicial. My holy of holies is the human body, health, intelligence, talent, inspiration, love and absolute freedom — freedom from force and falsehood, no matter how the last two manifest themselves. This is the program I would follow if I were a great artist.[116]

Even calling Chekhov a follower of Naturalism would seem to run the risk of 'labelling' him. The term can be accurately applied to him only in the general sense of his being committed to a materialist view of life, and to a scientifically based view of literary creation. Naturalism was never monolithically absolute itself, and many of the dualistic 'both/and' elements to be found in Chekhov were already part of the literary movement itself. When Furst and Skrine claim: 'that the scientific discoveries of the nineteenth century and the introduction of the scientific method in the arts were fundamental factors in shaping Naturalism',[117] we may be tempted to see this movement in unambiguous terms. However, as they proceed to point out, Naturalism as a movement:

> ... was never as rational or as logically consistent as it may first seem. The second half of the nineteenth century was a time of bewildering contradictions, of

which Naturalism had its fair share. It was ... torn between its theory and practice, between materialism and optimism. On the one hand it faced the iniquities of a rapidly industrialized (polluted) world while on the other it placed boundless faith in the future progress of that world with the help of scientific advance. The Naturalists did not go as far as the Marxists in reviling the present and nurturing Messianic hopes for the future, but they did try to combine high-minded idealism with the sobriety of detached observers. Looking at the world and at man, they despaired and hoped at one and the same time. This underlying dualism helps to account for some of the apparent inconsistencies within Naturalism and it also invests the movements with a certain dialectical tension. In this respect too Naturalism is as much an expression of its age as the socio-political system of Marx and the philosophy of Nietzsche. Each represents an attempt to make a reckoning with a drastically changed universe.[118]

Chekhov's work displays all the ambiguities and 'apparent inconsistencies' of the Naturalist movement as a whole and I will argue that much of the power of Chekhov's work is generated precisely out of the 'dialectical tension' that characterised the ideology of Naturalism.

Neither a social revolutionary nor an absurdist, Chekhov, with his faith in science and the future of humanity (if not in God and the afterlife), presents a world as it is, which is, at the same time, a world as it should not be. What Chekhov's plays and short stories explore, though solely by implication, is a picture of the world as it should be. The world of boredom and apathy which he presented in his works, and which he felt had to be changed, is described perfectly in another entry in his *Notebooks:* 'In the life of our towns there is no pessimism, no Marxism, and no movements, but there is stagnation, stupidity and mediocrity.'[119]

Chekhov's aim was to make his readers and spectators aware of the stagnant, stupid and mediocre lives they all lived and, by doing so, make them aware that this was not the inevitable fate of humanity. He felt that work, education and business would help speed up the improvement of life. Even though Chekhov was faced with the fact that, for the most part, there were largely untrained teachers in poor quality schools and considerable resistance to education on the part of the peasants themselves, he retained his faith in education and applied science as means to improve living conditions:

> For one sensible person there are a thousand fools ... the thousands overwhelm the one and that is why cities and villages progress so slowly. The majority, the mass, always remains stupid; it will always overwhelm, the sensible man should give up hope of educating and lifting it up to himself; he had better call in the assistance of material force, build railways, telegraphs, telephones — in that way he will conquer and help life forward.[120]

Chekhov understood clearly how difficult a task changing people's consciousness actually was in practice. Thinking for oneself, making authentic decisions and refusing to live a lie were all infinitely harder to achieve in the deeply authoritarian bureaucratic world of Tsarist Russia than in other, more democratic societies. As Chekhov noted, 'nowhere else does the authority of a name weigh so heavily as with us Russians, who have been obsessed by centuries of slavery and fear freedom'.[121]

Making his readers and audience aware that they could in fact be free and masters of their fate was of crucial significance for Chekhov. The ludicrous picture of the clerk in *The Sneeze*, who is so upset at having sneezed over the back of one of his social superiors in the theatre that he eventually goes home and dies, is just one example of Chekhov using the classic scourge of ridicule to point out the absurdity of such servile behaviour. He believed that a 'sense of personal freedom' was 'indispensable',[122] not just for the creative artist, but also for humans wishing to change their world. He saw his own life in terms of acquiring that sense of freedom. In Chekhov's works, the characters who behave inauthentically by denying their freedom to act are laughed at and criticised. It is a gross misinterpretation of his plays to present the inactivity of his characters as though such behaviour were inevitable. Chekhov's characters operate in a fictional world in which personal and social development is possible. Chekhov's vivid description of his own hard-won emancipation attests to his belief in the possibility of such achievement:

> Write a story, do, about a young man, the son of a serf, a former grocery boy, a choir singer, a high school pupil and university student, brought up to respect rank, to kiss the hands of priests, to truckle to the ideas of others — a young man who expressed thanks for every piece of bread, who was whipped many times, who went out without galoshes to do his tutoring, who used his fists, tortured animals, was fond of dining with rich relatives, was a hypocrite in his dealings with God and men, needlessly, solely out of a realization of his own insignificance — write how this young man squeezes the slave out of himself, drop by drop, and how, on awaking one fine morning, he feels that the blood coursing through his veins is no longer that of a slave but that of a real human being.[123]

One of the more sensitive summations of Chekhov's aims in life and art was made, not by a professional critic or theatre director, but by the Russian cosmonaut, Vitali Sevastyanov. Perhaps this is not as surprising as it might first appear. Critics and directors from Chekhov's own day to the present have tended to present polarised pictures of the writer that I have argued are one-sided misinterpretations. Sevastyanov's response to Chekhov, coloured as it inevitably is by his own belief in the positive value of the Russian revolution, nevertheless eschews such one-sided readings. Despite the simplicity of his response, he captures the sense of dualistic balance that I believe lies at the heart of Chekhov's vision:

> I think Chekhov loved his people and his country very much. He saw how pitiful man could be and was aware of his potential greatness. To me, Chekhov's writings are full of torment over life's rough handling of man, who often — contrary to his own interests — helps life in demeaning human dignity. I reject the view that Chekhov lacked social commitment. That notion was thought up by his narrow-minded admirers, or is just a plain myth. He portrayed the life of society in a way that left no doubt in the reader's mind that such a life had to be changed. And he depicted individual lives so that every man could understand that only he himself was capable of changing his own life. Chekhov, of course, is not a 'propagandist' or an 'activist'. Chekhov is not a political writer. Even so, he played an enormous role in preparing public opinion for the revolution.[124]

The central elements of Chekhov's vision of reality should now be clear. A critic or director should now be able to recognise the 'parameters' and 'tolerances' that would define what constitutes a valid interpretation of the vision of reality expressed in his plays. The discussion so far has only attempted to clarify the 'parameters' and 'tolerances' of *what* Chekhov was trying to portray in his works. Before we can go on to examine the individual plays we need to examine *how* Chekhov sought to communicate his vision. Finding the appropriate dramatic form to act as the objective correlative of his vision was to be one of Chekhov's major achievements.

## ENDNOTES

[1] Chekhov, A., *Terror*, in Hingley, R., *The Oxford Chekhov*, Vol. 6, Oxford University Press, London, 1971, p. 174.

[2] Chekhov, A., *An Anonymous Story*, in Hingley, R., op. cit., p. 250.

[3] Valency, M., *The Breaking String*, Oxford University Press, London, 1966, p. 184.

[4] Hingley, R., 'Introduction', in Chekhov, A., *Ward Number Six and Other Stories*, World's Classics, Oxford University Press, Oxford, 1992, p. xiv.

[5] Chekhov, A., Letter to A. S. Suvorin, 3 December 1892, in Yarmolinsky, A., *Letters of Anton Chekhov*, The Viking Press, New York, 1973, p. 227.

[6] Ibid., p. 228.

[7] Koteliansky, S. S. and Woolf, L., trans., *The Notebooks of Anton Tchekhov*, The Hogarth Press, London, 1967, p. 60.

[8] Chekhov, A., Comments recorded by A. Tikhonov, 1902, quoted in Magarshack, D., *Chekhov the Dramatist*, Eyre Methuen, London, 1980, pp. 13–14.

[9] I think it is clear that what follows from my line of argument is that it is quite possible to have theatrically successful and popular 'misinterpretations' of any given play. The casting of Marlon Brando in the role of Stanley Kowalski, according to many critics, myself included, distorted the meaning of Tennessee Williams' *A Streetcar Named Desire*, yet the production was extremely successful in the theatre.

[10] Chekhov, A., quoted in Gorky, M., *Fragments from My Diary*, Penguin, Harmondsworth, 1940, p. 173.

[11] Ehrenburg, I., *Chekhov, Stendhal and Other Essays,* Macgibbon and Kee, London, 1962, pp. 65–6. The Soviet critic, A. P. Chudakov, is another writer who persuasively argues that Chekhov felt there was a need for a symbiotic connection between human beings and their environment, and that material and spiritual progress were dependent on this connection. Chudakov argues that, while Chekhov avoided dogmatism at all times, he 'clearly sympathises with those remarks by his heroes in which the appraisal of man's attitude to nature is placed on the same level as the value of spiritual phenomena. In his nocturnal reflections before the duel, Laevsky counts among his moral crimes not only his lies and indifference to people's sufferings, ideas, searchings and struggles, but also the fact that he does not love nature and that "in his own garden he has never planted a single tree or grown a single blade of grass".' (Chudakov, A. P., 'The Poetics of Chekhov: The Sphere of Ideas', *New Literary History*, Vol. 9, Winter 1978, p. 374.)

[12] Koteliansky, S. S. and Woolf, L., op. cit., p. 15.

[13] Ibid., p. 29. Amongst the things Chekhov left behind him after his death were three schools.

[14] Gorky, M., op. cit., p. 172.

[15] Chekhov, A., Letter to A. S. Suvorin, 9 December 1890, in Yarmolinsky, A., op. cit., p. 170.

[16] Karlinsky, S., 'The Gentle Subversive', Introduction to Karlinsky, S. and Heim, M. H., trans., *Anton Chekhov's Life and Thought*, University of California Press, Berkeley, 1975, p. 26.

[17] Chekhov, A., quoted in Shakh-Azizova, T., 'A Russian *Hamlet*', *Soviet Literature,* Vol. 1, January 1980, p. 162.

[18] Chekhov, A., Letter to A. S. Suvorin, 28 October 1889, in Yarmolinsky, A., op. cit., p. 122.

[19] Tulloch, J., 'Chekhov Abroad: Western Criticism', in Clyman, T. W., ed., *A Chekhov Companion,* Greenwood Press, Westport, 1985, p. 198.

[20] Tulloch, J., *Chekhov: A Structuralist Study,* Macmillan Press, London, 1980, pp. 100–1. When Chekhov wrote to Suvorin in 1894 outlining his reasons for rejecting Tolstoy's anti-scientific philosophy of life, his belief in the idea of progress through science was prominent. 'I have peasant blood flowing in my veins and I'm not one to be impressed with peasant virtues. I acquired my belief in progress when still a child; I couldn't help believing in it because the difference between the period when they flogged me and the period when they stopped flogging me was enormous ... Prudence and justice tell me there is more love for mankind in electricity and steam than in chastity and abstention from meat.' (Chekhov, A., Letter to A. S. Suvorin, 27 March 1894, in Karlinsky, S., op. cit., p. 261.)

[21] Shestov, L., *Chekhov and Other Essays,* University of Michigan Press, Ann Arbor, 1966, pp. 4–5.

[22] Corrigan, R., 'The Plays of Chekhov', in Corrigan, R. and Rosenberg, J. L., eds, *The Context and Craft of Drama*, Chandler Publishing Co., Scranton, 1964, p. 145.

[23] Smith, J. O., 'Chekhov and the "Theatre of the Absurd"', *Bucknell Review*, Vol. 14, December 1966, p. 45.

[24] Stein, W., 'Tragedy and the Absurd', *The Dublin Review,* Vol. 233, Winter 1959–60, p. 381.

[25] Esslin, M., 'Chekhov and the Modern Drama', in Clyman, T. W., op. cit., pp. 143, 145.

[26] Chekhov, A., Letter to A. S. Suvorin, 9 December 1890, in Yarmolinsky, A., op. cit., p. 170.

[27] Unlike many of our current critics, M. Robinson, writing in 1927, was able to avoid seeing Chekhov's plays through an absurdist lens. He perceived that Chekhov rejected any sense of inevitability about the fate of his characters.
> But conceding, for the sake of argument, that Chekhov does write of people who are conquered by life, what does that prove about his view of the universe? It only proves something about his attitude towards his fellow-man. Not, though, that he regarded man as a being who must inevitably be conquered by life; but that there was in him as a root quality that profound pity which can only be felt by a character at once strong and balanced ... When Chekhov presents such [defeated] characters, he is not trying to rouse us into a state of false indignation against life and fate; he did not intend to put the blame for anything that is wrong in the world of men upon those vague and convenient scapegoats; he wanted us to put the blame where it belongs: on ourselves. (Robinson, M., 'M. Robinson Replies to the Notion that Chekhov's Characters "Are Forever Conquered by Life"', *Adelphi,* May 1927, in Emeljanow, V., ed., *Chekhov: The Critical Heritage,* Routledge and Kegan Paul, London, 1981, pp. 318–19.)

[28] Chekhov's depiction of a generation whose avoidance of any social responsibility and refusal to face reality reduced their lives to absurdity was a major influence on George Bernard Shaw when he wrote *Heartbreak House*, significantly subtitled 'A Fantasy in the Russian Manner'. Both dramatists believed

in the idea of progress and both, in their differing ways, were critical of the refusal by many of their countrymen to help effect change.

[29] Chekhov, A., *Smoking Is Bad for You*, in Hingley, R., *The Oxford Chekhov*, Vol. 1, Oxford University Press, London, 1968, p. 157.

[30] Chekhov, A., Letter to M. V. Kiseleva, 14 January 1887, in Yarmolinsky, A., op. cit., p. 41.

[31] Yermilov, V., 'A Great Artist and Innovator', in Katzer, J., ed., *A. P. Chekhov: 1860–1960*, Foreign Languages Publishing House, Moscow, 1960, p. 126.

[32] Chekhov, A., Letter to A. Tikhonov, 1902, quoted in Magarshack, D., op. cit., p. 14.

[33] Valency, M., op. cit., p. 298.

[34] Chekhov, A., Letter to N. A. Leykin, 7 April 1887, in Yarmolinsky, A., op. cit., p. 46.

[35] Laffitte, S., *Chekhov,* Angus and Robertson, London, 1974, p. 175.

[36] Ibid.

[37] Kuprin, A., 'Reminiscences of Anton Tchekhov' in Koteliansky, S. S., ed., *Anton Tchekhov: Literary and Theatrical Reminiscences*, Haskell House Publishers, New York, 1974, pp. 49–85.

[38] Hingley, R., *A New Life of Chekhov*, Oxford University Press, London, 1976, p. 277.

[39] Hingley, R., 'Introduction', in Hingley, R., *The Oxford Chekhov,* Vol. 5, Oxford University Press, London, 1970, p. 11.

[40] Ehrenburg, I., op. cit., p. 73.

[41] Chekhov, A., *The Duel*, in Hingley, R., *The Oxford Chekhov*, Vol. 5, p. 207.

[42] Hingley, R., 'Introduction', in Chekhov, A., *The Russian Master and Other Stories*, World's Classics, Oxford University Press, Oxford, 1992, p. ix.

[43] Tulloch, J., op. cit., p. 131.

[44] Chekhov, A., *The Duel*, pp. 207–8.

[45] Koteliansky, S. S. and Woolf, L., op. cit., p. 41.

[46] Chekhov, A., *The Duel*, p. 205.

[47] Ibid., p. 209.

[48] Ibid., p. 224.

[49] Koteliansky, S. S. and Woolf, L., op. cit., p. 26.

[50] Philip Callow, in his biography of Chekhov, quotes from a letter to Suvorin written in 1889 in which Chekhov's hatred of the aimless inertia of the intelligentsia was powerfully expressed: '[Chekhov] launched an attack on the "wood lice and molluscs we call the intelligentsia", a lazy, cold, philosophizing species who spent their time blithely negating everything, "since it is easier for a lazy brain to deny than assert".' (Callow, P., *Chekhov: The Hidden Ground*, Ivan R. Dee, Chicago, 1998, p. 137.)

[51] Chekhov, A., 'Obituary for N. Przevalsky', 1888, quoted in Laffitte, S., op. cit., p. 113.

[52] Callow, P., op. cit., p. 138.

[53] Chekhov, A., Letter to A. S. Suvorin, 9 March 1890, in Yarmolinsky, A., op. cit., p. 129.

[54] There is clear evidence of how seriously Chekhov approached his research and of his belief that his medical census would be of social use. While on his return trip from Sakhalin he wrote to Suvorin: 'By the way, I had the patience to take a census of the entire population of Sakhalin. I went around to each of the settlements, stopped at each hut and talked with each person. I used a filing-card system for purposes of the census, and have records of about ten thousand convicts and settlers by now. In other words, there's not a single convict or settler in Sakhalin who hasn't talked to me. I was particularly successful in the children's census and I place great hopes in it.' (Chekhov, A., Letter to A. S. Suvorin, 11 September 1890, in Karlinsky, S., op. cit., p. 171.)

[55] Chekhov, A., *An Anonymous Story*, p. 245.

[56] Laffitte, S., op. cit., p. 135.

[57] Chekhov, A., Letter to A. S. Suvorin, 9 March 1890, in Karlinsky, S., op. cit., p. 159.

[58] Chekhov, A., Letter to A. S. Suvorin, 2 January 1894, in Yarmolinsky, A., op. cit., p. 243. I have included the word 'literary', as this word or the word 'fictional' appears in other translations of this letter, but has been inadvertently omitted by Yarmolinsky.

[59] See in particular Tulloch, J., op. cit.

[60] Chekhov, A., Letter to A. S. Suvorin, 11 September 1888, in Karlinsky, S., op. cit., p. 107.

[61] Conrad, J., 'Chekhov as Social Observer: *The Island of Sakhalin*', in Clyman, T. W., op. cit., p. 284.

[62] In a letter to Suvorin in 1889, Chekhov voiced his total commitment to a materialist view of the world. He wrote: 'To begin with, materialism is not a school or a doctrine in the narrow journalistic sense. It is neither chance occurrence nor passing fancy; it is something indispensable and inevitable and beyond human power. Everything that lives on earth is necessarily materialistic ... thinking humans, are also necessarily materialists. They search for truth in matter because there is nowhere else for them to search: all they see, hear and feel is matter. They can necessarily seek out truth only where their microscopes, probes and knives are effective. Prohibiting materialist doctrine is tantamount to preventing man from seeking out the truth. Outside of matter there is no experience or knowledge, and consequently no truth.' (Chekhov, A., Letter to A. S. Suvorin, 15 May 1889, in Karlinsky, S., op. cit., pp. 143–4.)

[63] Chekhov, A., Letter to M. V. Kiseleva, 14 January 1887, in Yarmolinsky, A., op. cit., p. 42.

[64] Koteliansky, S. S. and Woolf, L., op. cit., p. 55.

[65] Chekhov, A., Letter to A. S. Suvorin, 25 November 1892, in Karlinsky, S., op. cit., p. 243.

[66] Ibid.

[67] Chekhov, A., Letter to A. S. Suvorin, 27 October 1888, in Karlinsky, S., op. cit., p. 117.

[68] Chekhov, A., Letter to D. V. Grigorovich, 9 October 1888, in Yarmolinsky, A., op. cit., p. 84.

[69] Chekhov, A., Letter to A. S. Suvorin, 1 April 1890, in Yarmolinsky, A., op. cit., p. 133.

[70] Chekhov, A., Letter to A. S. Suvorin, 27 October 1888, in Yarmolinsky, A., op. cit., p. 88.

[71] Chekhov, A., Letter to S. P. Diaghilev, 12 July 1903, in Yarmolinsky, A., op. cit., p. 453.

[72] Chekhov wrote to Pleshcheyev in 1890: 'one doesn't feel like forgiving the author — to be precise, the audacity with which Tolstoy discourses on what he knows nothing about and what, out of stubbornness, he does not want to understand. Thus his judgements on syphilis, on founding asylums, on women's abhorrence of copulation, etc., not only can be controverted but also are a direct exposure of a man who is ignorant, who throughout the course of his long life had never gone to the trouble of reading two or three books written by specialists.' (Chekhov, A., Letter to A. N. Pleshcheyev, 15 February 1890, in Yarmolinsky, A., op. cit., p. 125.)

[73] Chekhov, A., Letter to O. P. Menshikov, 16 April 1897, in Yarmolinsky, A., op. cit., p. 286.

[74] Gorky, M., 'Fragment from Reminiscences', in Jackson, R. L., ed., *Chekhov*, Prentice-Hall, New Jersey, 1967, p. 203.

[75] Ibid., p. 205.

[76] Chekhov, A., Letter to M. V. Kiseleva, 14 January 1887, in Yarmolinsky, A., op. cit., p. 40.

[77] Koteliansky, S. S. and Woolf, L., op. cit., p. 27.

[78] Chekhov, A., Letter to A. S. Suvorin, 25 November 1892, in Karlinsky, S., op. cit., p. 243.

[79] Brustein, R., *The Theatre of Revolt*, Little, Brown and Company, Boston, 1964, p. 139.

[80] Koteliansky, S. S. and Woolf, L., op. cit., p. 6.

[81] Chekhov, A., 'A Moscow Hamlet', in Josephson, M., ed., *The Personal Papers of Anton Chekhov*, Lear, New York, 1948, p. 213.

[82] Müller, H. J., *The Spirit of Tragedy*, Alfred A. Knopf, New York, 1956, p. 290.

[83] Chekhov, A., *A Dreary Story*, in Hingley, R., *The Oxford Chekhov*, Vol. 5, p. 81.

[84] Gorky, M., *Fragments from My Diary*, p. 174.

[85] Chekhov, A., *A Dreary Story*, p. 80.

[86] Chekhov, A., Letter to A. S. Suvorin, 8 April 1892, in Karlinsky, S., op. cit., p. 221.

[87] Chekhov, A., Letter to A. S. Suvorin, 18 October 1892, in Yarmolinsky, A., op. cit., p. 223.

[88] Chekhov, A., Letter to A. S. Suvorin, 10 October 1892, in Yarmolinsky, A., op. cit., p. 223.

[89] Chekhov, A., Letter to L. S. Mizonova, 13 August 1893, in Yarmolinsky, A., op. cit., p. 237.

[90] Chekhov, A., Letter to I. L. Leontyev-Shcheglov, 24 October 1892, in Yarmolinsky, A., op. cit., p. 225.

[91] The writer Vsevolod Garshin, who was an admirer of Chekhov's work, had succumbed to depression and hopelessness and committed suicide in 1888. Chekhov contributed a short story, *A Nervous Breakdown*, to an anthology honouring the memory of Garshin.

[92] Chekhov, A., Letter to A. S. Suvorin, 25 November 1892, in Yarmolinsky, A., op. cit., p. 227.

[93] Koteliansky, S. S. and Woolf, L., op. cit., p. 71.

[94] Magarshack, D., *Chekhov: A Life*, Greenwood Press, Westport, 1970, p. 139.

[95] Koteliansky, S. S. and Woolf, L., op. cit., p. 1.

96 Koteliansky, S. S. and Woolf, L., op. cit., pp. 1–2.
97 Chekhov, A., Letter to A. S. Suvorin, 28 May 1892, in Yarmolinsky, A., op. cit., p. 212.
98 Josephson, M., ed., *The Personal Papers of Anton Chekhov*, Lear, New York, 1948, p. 231.
99 Chekhov, A., Letter to S. P. Diaghilev, 30 December 1902, in Yarmolinsky, A., op. cit., p. 438.
100 Chekhov, A., Letter to A. S. Suvorin, 1 August 1892, in Yarmolinsky, A., op. cit., pp. 218–19.
101 Chekhov, A., Letter to I. L. Leontyev-Shcheglov, 20 January 1899, in Yarmolinsky, A., op. cit., p. 329.
102 Chekhov, A., Letter to A. S. Suvorin, 9 December 1890, in Yarmolinsky, A., op. cit., p. 169.
103 Koteliansky, S. S. and Woolf, L., op. cit., p. 11.
104 Ibid., p. 72.
105 Ibid., p. 54.
106 Hagan, J., 'Chekhov's Fiction and the Ideal of "Objectivity"', *Proceedings of the Modern Language Association*, Vol. 81, October 1966, p. 417.
107 Chekhov, A., Letter to A. S. Suvorin, 7 May 1889, in Karlinsky, S., op. cit., p. 143.
108 Ibid., pp. 143–4.
109 Ibid., p. 143.
110 Ibid., p. 144.
111 Chekhov, A., Letter to O. L. Knipper, 2 January 1900, quoted in Tulloch, J., op. cit., p. 107.
112 Furst, L. and Skrine, P., *Naturalism*, Methuen, London, 1971, p. 21.
113 Ibid.
114 Moravcevich, N., 'Chekhov and Naturalism: From Affinity to Divergence', *Comparative Drama*, Vol. 4, No. 4, Winter 1970–71, p. 221.
115 Chekhov, A., Letter to G. I. Rossolimo, 11 October 1889, in Yarmolinsky, A., op. cit., pp. 352–3.
116 Chekhov, A., Letter to A. N. Pleshcheyev, 4 October 1888, in Yarmolinsky, A., op. cit., p. 81.
117 Furst, L. and Skrine, P., op. cit., p. 22.
118 Ibid., pp. 22–3.
119 Koteliansky, S. S. and Woolf, L., op. cit., p. 89.
120 Ibid., p. 16.
121 Ibid., p. 28.
122 Chekhov, A., Letter to A. S. Suvorin, 7 January 1889, in Yarmolinsky, A., op. cit., p. 107.
123 Ibid.
124 Sevastyanov, V., 'Tribute to Chekhov', *Soviet Literature*, Vol. 1, January 1980, p. 191.

# Chapter 2. The Search for Form

*That the theatre should attempt to present a picture of the world as it really is never occurred to the theoreticians or practitioners of pre-modern drama. The theatre was an art — and art was artifice.* (Martin Esslin)[1]

*They act too much. It would be better if they acted a little more as in life.* (Anton Chekhov)[2]

If the first task of any director of Chekhov is to interpret the vision of reality expressed in his plays, then the second task is to come to an understanding of the particular form that Chekhov developed to express that vision. The distinction between form and content is difficult to make in Chekhov's case since both the manner and the matter of Chekhov's dramaturgy are determined by the playwright's belief that dramatic art should be true to life.

Chekhov was quite certain that literary artists should depict 'life as it is'. In 1887, in the much quoted letter to M. V. Kiseleva in which he defended the right and duty of the literary artist to depict the seamier side of life, he enunciated the cornerstone belief of his artistic credo: 'Literature is called artistic when it depicts life as it actually is. Its purpose is truth, honest and indisputable.'[3] Chekhov was equally certain that:

> ... writers whom we call eternal, or simply good and who intoxicate us have one very important characteristic in common: they move in a certain direction ... they have a goal ... because every line is permeated, as with sap, by the consciousness of a purpose, you are aware not only of life as it is, but of life as it ought to be.[4]

What Chekhov was not immediately clear about was how to achieve this aim himself. He felt that the forms of drama and theatre that were popular in Russia when he was writing could not be used successfully to dramatise his vision. The conventions of such dramatic forms as romantic drama, melodrama or the well-made play militated against any attempt to truly show 'life as it is'. Chekhov was thus faced with the initial problem of creating an appropriate set of conventions that would allow him to depict life truthfully.

Having been trained as a doctor, he was conversant with the scientific method and, like other writers of the Naturalistic movement, he applied this method to his creative writing. This helped him to find a way of providing truthful depictions of 'life as it is', but created further problems for him, especially when it came to the question of depicting 'life as it ought to be'. His relatively short career as a playwright was spent searching for an appropriate dramatic and theatrical form to realise his vision of reality. We need to examine the precise nature of the artistic problems faced by Chekhov in his quest to match form with content and outline the steps he took in his search to find the answers to these problems.

Chekhov lived at a time of enormous social, political and scientific change. Living as he was at a time of transition when Modernism was displacing Romanticism, the problem of matching vision and form was acute for him. The sets of conventions that go to make up a literary movement like Modernism are attempts to find appropriate forms in which to express a changed view of the nature of the world. Naturalism, with its emphasis on empiricism and positivism, and the new ideas promulgated by scientists like Darwin and Compte, were fast replacing the outdated idealism of the romantic vision as the accepted world view.

Ronald Gaskell has outlined the effects of this shift in sensibility on drama as follows:

> The significance of this for drama soon becomes evident. For what were the older methods of investigating man that must be discarded or modernized? Theology, ethical and political speculations had all worked deductively. Starting from assumed (a priori) axioms about the soul, the will or the rights of man, they had elaborated systems of thought that led nowhere, or at all events did nothing to explain the way men are shaped by their inheritance and by the world they live in. As for poets and dramatists, where they had not viewed man through the distorting lens of religion or metaphysics, they had worked from a purely subjective standpoint, from the vagaries of personal emotion and sensibility or from an intuitive awareness that could be neither ratified nor disproved. [In response to this, drama] ... might adopt the account of reality assumed and apparently proved by the sciences: an account which their overwhelming success had established so securely that it seemed by now, as the Christian vision had seemed to the medieval dramatist, not to be one interpretation of the world but the world as in fact it is.[5]

Given Chekhov's materialist vision of reality, and his respect for many of the central tenets of Naturalism, we can see why he found many of the 'idealist' assumptions in the work of both Tolstoy and Dostoevsky so repugnant. Chekhov's central artistic problem in dramatising his vision of reality during this time of cultural upheaval was to find artistic means that were consistent with his science-based world view. His refusal to see science and art as antithetical explains why there is a strong literary element in his scientific work. More significantly, this balanced and inclusive approach has meant that there is a strong scientific element in all of his literary works. It is in this sense that one can call Chekhov a Naturalist.[6] As Furst and Skrine have noted:

> This affinity to science was explicitly emphasized by the Naturalists ... The Naturalists believed that the truthfulness for which they aimed could be gained only from a painstaking observation of reality and a careful notation of fact.[7]

Chekhov employed a similar 'painstaking observation of reality and a careful notation of fact' in his depiction of characters in his literary works. The clinical observation of people's behaviour that is evident in his literary works is perhaps what we might expect from a writer who once told a friend: 'If I had not become a writer, I would probably have become a psychiatrist.'[8]

Since in real life one cannot accurately know what people are thinking, Chekhov came to the conclusion that, in describing people in literature, 'It is better to avoid descriptions of the mental states of your heroes; the effort should be made to make these clear from their actions.'[9] This advice to his brother Alexander concerned the writing of short stories, but Chekhov felt that the same technical approach was appropriate to the writing of drama as well. Even more significantly, Chekhov's comments have far-reaching implications for the performance of his plays.

In a letter he wrote to Meyerhold advising him on his role in Hauptmann's *Lonely Lives* which Stanislavski was directing, Chekhov went into considerable detail concerning the character Johannes' 'neuropathological nature'. After giving Meyerhold precise medical and sociological reasons why he should not overplay the character's nervousness, Chekhov warned the actor of the likelihood that Stanislavski would put pressure on him to adopt some cheap theatrical effect. Chekhov encouraged Meyerhold to base his characterisation on scientific truth:

> Don't stress his nervousness ... Project a lonely man, and show his nervousness only in so far as the script indicates ... I know Konstantin Sergeyevich [Stanislavski] will insist on playing up his excessive nervousness; he'll take an exaggerated view of it. But don't give in, don't sacrifice the beauty and power of your voice and delivery for something as trivial as a highlight.[10]

A few months later, Chekhov wrote to his wife, the actress Olga Knipper, and referred to the advice he had given Meyerhold. Once again he suggested that this actor should model his stage performance on the behaviour of human beings in real life. Rather than present conventional stage types, Chekhov advocated that actors should base their creation of stage roles on scientific observation of actual behaviour:

> Suffering should be presented as it is expressed in life: not via arms and legs but through tone and expression; and subtly, not through gesticulations. Subtle emotions of the spirit, as experienced by people of education, must be expressed subtly, through external behaviour. You will argue about stage conditions but no conditions can excuse inaccuracy.[11]

The pride which Chekhov expressed whenever he felt that he had successfully depicted human behaviour with scientific accuracy was evident throughout his creative life. In a letter to Pleshcheyev, written twelve years earlier, he refers to his short story, *A Nervous Breakdown*. The story deals with the traumatic experience suffered by a sensitive student when he visits a series of Moscow brothels. Chekhov proudly wrote: 'It seems to me, as a medico, that I described the psychic pain correctly, according to all the rules of the science of psychiatry.'[12]

The description of the miscarriage in his story *The Party* was likewise defended by Chekhov on the grounds of its accuracy. Replying to Pleshcheyev's query about why he had included the conversation between Olga and the peasant women prior to Olga's miscarriage Chekhov explained that:

> ... [the] conversation is unimportant; I wedged it in only so the miscarriage wouldn't seem *ex abrupto*. I'm a doctor, and so as not to disgrace myself, I must motivate everything in my stories that has to do with medicine.[13]

One of the major reasons for Chekhov's lack of enchantment with the romantic melodramas and well-made plays being presented in Moscow, even in the days just before he had established himself as a dramatist, was their failure to present scientifically accurate depictions of reality. Everything he saw seemed to the young writer to be stale and lacking in any substance. The subtext of his 1885 diatribe against the state of the theatre is loud and clear: 'we need new forms':

> At the Bolshoy Theatre we have opera and ballet. Nothing new. The actors are the old ones and their manner of singing is the old one: not according to the notes, but according to official circulars. In the ballet the ballerinas have been recently joined by Noah's aunt and Methuselah's sister-in-law ... [at the Moscow Imperial Dramatic Theatre, the Maly Theatre] ... Again nothing new ... the same mediocre acting and the same traditional ensemble, inherited from our ancestors. [The Korsh Theatre bears] ... a striking resemblance to a mixed salad: there is everything there except the most important thing of all — meat.[14]

While one should not confuse Chekhov with his own characters, it does not seem far-fetched to suggest that much of the material that he used in his depiction of the old academic who is the narrator 'hero' of *A Dreary Story* (1889) was drawn from his own experience of theatre-going. Chekhov's ambivalent attitude toward the theatre is clearly represented in the short story through the opposing views of his two central characters. On the one hand, the professor dislikes the theatre so much that he feels that 'if a play's any good one can gain a true impression without troubling actors. I think one only needs to read it. And if the play's bad, no acting will make it good'.[15] On the other hand, Katya believes 'that the theatre — even in its present form — was superior to lecture rooms, books and anything else on earth'.[16]

From the professor's point of view — and one suspects Chekhov sympathises with his views — the theatre 'in its present form' needs radical change to bring it up to date and to make it the useful social institution that Katya claims it to be. The professor, like Chekhov, rejects the claim that the theatre of his day had an effective educative function:

> You may convince the sentimental, gullible rabble that the theatre as at present constituted is a school, but that lure won't work on anyone who knows what a school really is. What may happen in fifty or a hundred years, I can't say, but the theatre can only be a form of entertainment under present conditions.[17]

On the one hand, the professor's negative assertions reflect Chekhov's own views about the theatre 'as it is' and 'as it should *not* be'. On the other hand, Katya's faith in theatre's social and aesthetic value corresponds to Chekhov's own desires for a future purposeful theatre. In a letter to Suvorin, written in the same year that *A Dreary Story* was published, Chekhov asserted that the theatre of his day had failed to fulfil its educative function. It was, he complained, 'nothing but a sport'.[18] Chekhov was so disillusioned with contemporary Russian theatre that he advised a fellow playwright Ivan Shcheglov to give up writing for this medium:

> I implore you, please turn from the stage. The good things are lauded to the skies, but the bad are covered up and condoned ... The contemporary theatre — it is an eruption, a nasty disease of the cities. This disease must be pursued with the broom, but to like it — that is not wholesome. You will begin to quarrel with me, to use the old phrase: the theatre is a school; it educates, etc. ... And I state in answer that which I see: the contemporary theatre is not higher than the crowd, but, on the contrary, the life of the masses is higher and cleverer than the theatre. This means that it is not a school but something quite different.[19]

On the same day that he wrote this letter to Shcheglov, Chekhov also wrote to Suvorin and quite clearly laid the blame for the current state of the theatre, not on the low tastes of the audiences, but on the theatre professionals:

> It is not the public which is to blame for the atrocious state of our theaters. The public is always and everywhere the same: intelligent and foolish, cordial and pitiless — depending upon its mood. It always was a herd which needed good shepherds and dogs, and it has always gone wherever it was led by the shepherds and the dogs ... As a general thing the public, for all its foolishness, is nevertheless more intelligent, sincere, and good humored than Korsh,[20] the actors, and the playwrights, who imagine themselves more intelligent.[21]

What Chekhov most objected to about late nineteenth-century theatre was its triviality. Neither vision nor form seemed to Chekhov to have any connection with real life. His angry reaction to Karpov's play *Crocodile Tears* was typical of how he felt whenever he saw stagey nonsense that in no way depicted 'life as it is':

> The whole play, even if one overlooks its wooden naivety, is an utter lie and travesty of life. A dishonest headman of a village gets a young landowner, a permanent member of the local agricultural board, into his power and wants him to marry his daughter, who is in love with a clerk who writes poetry. Before the marriage a young, honest land-surveyor opens the eyes of the landowner, who exposes his would-be father-in-law's crimes, the crocodile, i.e. the headman of the village, weeps, and one of the heroines exclaims: 'And so virtue is triumphant and vice is punished!' which brings the play to an end ... If ever I say or write anything of the kind, I hope that you will hate me and have nothing to do with me any more.[22]

Laurence Senelick has convincingly shown how resilient melodrama was in nineteenth-century Russia. He points out that, while several major writers before Chekhov, including Pushkin and Gogol, had rejected this sentimental and sensational form, the influence of foreign writers like Walter Scott, Guilbert de Pixérécourt and particularly August Kotzebue remained strong. Consequently, Senelick claims that:

> ... although an indigenous melodrama did not evolve, melodramatic devices and coups de théâtre infested Russian social and historical plays of the mid century and lingered until Chekhov's day.[23]

Chekhov had ridiculed and parodied these 'heightened' forms in several pieces that he wrote when he was twenty years old. His technique involves a *reductio ad absurdum* which, as Rayfield points out in the case of Chekhov's *A Thousand and One Passions*, involves 'a condensation of an imaginary Victor Hugo novel so violent as to collapse the romantic novel into a surrealist joke'.[24] At its climax, Chekhov with characteristic irony comments:

> A powerful man, hurling his enemy down the crater of a volcano because of a beautiful woman's eyes, is a magnificent, grandiose and edifying picture! All it needed was lava![25]

His parodies of the theatrical equivalent of the romantic novel are equally hilarious in their pushing of the logic of melodrama to its ludicrous extreme. In *Dishonourable Tragedians and Leprous Dramatists: A Terrible — Awful — Disgraceful Desperate Trrragedy* (1884), the 'hero' Tarnovsky, 'a heart rending male' is desperately trying to write a play that will satisfy the demands of the theatrical impresario, Lentovsky.[26] Chekhov's description of the setting and the staging effects to be used in this skit is not only an extremely funny indication of the sort of theatrical nonsense that still prevailed in late nineteenth-century Russia, but also reminds us why Chekhov made so many objections to Stanislavski's overly theatricalist presentation of his own plays. The setting includes that cliché of nineteenth-century melodrama, the erupting volcano:

> The crater of a volcano. Tarnovsky sits at his desk covered in blood; instead of a head on his shoulders, he has a skull: brimstone burns in his mouth; green little devils, smiling disdainfully, jump from his nostrils. He dips his pen not into the inkstand, but into lava which witches keep stirring. It is frightening. The air trembles with cold shivers. At the back of the stage, shaking knees hang on red hot hooks. Thunder and lightning ... chaos, horror, fear ... The rest may be embellished by the reader's imagination.[27]

The mixture of sentimental nonsense and extravagant stage effects that Chekhov wished to avoid in his serious plays is superbly captured in the speech providing advice to playwrights that Lentovsky declaims in *The Epilogue* which *begins* the play:

> LENTOVSKY. ... what we need is more gunpowder, Bengal lights, and more ringing monologues, that's all! So there should be frequent costume changes, the dddevil take it! Make it broader ... Treachery ... the prison ... the prisoner's sweetheart is made to marry the villain ... And then, the flight from prison ... shots ... I shall not spare the gunpowder ... Further on, a child whose noble origin is only subsequently discovered ... Finally shots again; again a girl, and virtue triumphs ... In a word, concoct it according to cliché, the same way Rocambole and the Counts of Monte-Cristo are concocted ... *[Thunder, lightning, hoar-frost, dew. The volcano erupts. Lentovsky is thrown out.]* [28]

Chekhov's parodies were apparently not far removed from actuality. In 1883, referring to Lentovsky's production of *The Forest Tramp*, Chekhov asserted that: 'Thanks to this new, bitter-sweet, German Liebergottic rubbish all Moscow smells of gunpowder.'[29]

The theatricalist forms parodied by Chekhov were totally unsuitable means to express his vision of 'life as it is'. However, it was not only the totally unlifelike plays with their exaggerated sentiments, elaborate plots and overblown staging that Chekhov objected to. Equally worthy of derision, from his viewpoint, was the style of acting that accompanied this sort of drama. Again, the main criterion for rejecting the highly histrionic style of performance suitable to melodrama and romantic tragedy was that it failed to be lifelike. Chekhov's major criticism of Sarah Bernhardt's acting in the play *Adrienne Lecouvreur* was that it was too obviously technical and not close enough to actual behaviour:

> Every sigh Sarah Bernhardt sighs, every tear she sheds, every antemortem convulsion she makes, every bit of her acting is nothing more than an impeccably and intelligently learned lesson. A lesson, reader, and nothing more! ... She

very deftly performs all those stunts that, every so often, at fate's behest, occur in the human soul. Every step she takes is profoundly thought out, a stunt underscored a hundred times over ... In her acting, she goes in pursuit not of the natural, but of the extraordinary.[30]

This desire for a more realistic acting style, based on observation of how people actually behave, led Chekhov as early as 1889 to make remarks that anticipate many of the ideas on actor-training that Stanislavski was to formulate later as part of his 'system'. Stanislavski has rightly been credited with developing a system of acting that is realistic in that it is based on the way people behave in real life. However, Stanislavski could never totally abandon the use of many of the staging conventions of melodrama and romantic tragedy. Chekhov was to quarrel with Stanislavski over the latter's tendency to employ the excessive theatricality of these earlier dramatic forms in productions of his plays. In many ways, Chekhov's commitment to realism, both in terms of dramatic form and acting technique, was more consistent than Stanislavski's. Chekhov knew that a realistic form of acting was needed in order to achieve the realistic form of drama he was writing. With this in mind, he argued that actors who, of necessity, play a large range of roles should have observed a wide range of people. Chekhov's training in scientific observation, so important for a doctor called on to make diagnosis of ailments, was now applied to the performing art of acting:

> Actors never observe ordinary people. They know neither landowners, nor merchants, nor priests, nor officials. On the other hand, they can represent to the life kept mistresses, empty sharpers, and, in general, all those individuals whom they observe by chance roaming about the eating houses and in bachelor companies. Their ignorance is astounding.[31]

The disastrous first performance of *The Seagull* at the Alexandrinsky Theatre, Petersburg, 17 October 1896, under the direction of E. M. Karpov, himself a writer of melodramas, revealed to Chekhov the ignorance and conservatism of the acting profession in Russia at that time. Simmons' account of the fiasco captures perfectly what happens when a new form of play, needing a new form of acting to realise its meaning, is performed by actors using an earlier form of acting that had been suitable for earlier forms of drama:

> At the sixth rehearsal Chekhov observed with dismay that several of the cast were absent, a few still read their lines from scripts and only an assistant director was present to guide the actors ... Shocked by the stilted, traditional intonation of the actors, their false emphasis in reading lines, and their lack of comprehension of the roles they were portraying, Chekhov frequently interrupted the rehearsal to explain the significance of a phrase or discuss the

real essence of a characterization. 'The chief thing, my dears, is that theatricality is unnecessary. It is entirely simple. They are all simple ordinary people.'[32]

Mundane and apparently trivial events presented in an ordinary true-to-life manner became the trademark of mature Chekhovian drama. The form of acting that Chekhov required had to avoid histrionic exhibitionism. What we might call 'ham' acting today was the heightened style that was eminently appropriate to the dramas that Chekhov was rebelling against. The new form of drama that Chekhov developed and the new form of acting developed by Stanislavski both aimed to be realistic, and both were based on scientific principles.

Chekhov's decision to apply the scientific method to his literary work initially led him to adopt the conventions of what has sometimes been called 'naive realism': 'The naive realist ... imagines that the world is susceptible of representation in words or in some other medium.'[33]

In his early days as a dramatist, Chekhov seems to have thought that the only way to communicate his essentially naturalistic vision was to utilise the formal conventions of realism.[34] He was in total sympathy with Zola's assertion that 'the time has come to produce plays of reality'.[35] In order to satisfy his desire to depict 'life as it is', Chekhov adopted what Gaskell calls 'representational form'. Using this form, the play presents 'an action in which the setting of the play, the characters and their way of speaking, remind us at every moment of daily life'.[36] Chekhov followed the example of those Naturalists who believed that 'the truthfulness for which they aimed could be gained only from a painstaking observation of reality and a careful notation of fact'.[37] He believed that depicting characters and events realistically was the way to provide the appropriate 'Physical Events' that would trigger the particular 'Psychic Events' that he wished his audience to experience in performance. In common with other naturalistic writers like Zola, Chekhov saw a direct correspondence between the naturalistic vision and the realistic form:

> The correspondence theory is empirical and epistemological. It involves a naive or commonsense realist belief in the reality of the external world ... and supposes that we may come to know this world by observation and comparison. The truth it proposes is the truth that corresponds, approximates to the predicated reality, *renders* it with fidelity and accuracy; ... the correspondence theory defers automatically to the fact, and requires the truth to be verified by reference to it. It is democratic; it takes its confidence from the substantial agreement of the majority in its description of reality, which it therefore calls objective.[38]

Chekhov was to discover some of the limitations of the representational form when he attempted to realise his vision in practice. Long before he came to write his four dramatic masterpieces his radically realistic theory of dramaturgy was well-developed. At the time when he was writing *The Wood Demon* he asserted that plays should be 'lifelike' and not 'theatrical' or 'dramatic':

> In real life people don't spend every minute shooting each other, hanging themselves, or making declarations of love. They don't dedicate their time to saying intelligent things. They spend much more of it eating, drinking, flirting, and saying foolish things — and that is what should happen on the stage. Someone should write a play in which people come and go, eat, talk about the weather, and play cards. Life should be exactly as it is, and people should be exactly as complicated and at the same time exactly as simple as they are in life. People eat a meal, and at the same time their happiness is made or their lives are ruined.[39]

Chekhov's statement accurately describes what happens in his mature dramas beginning with *The Seagull*. What is fascinating about this lucid theoretical articulation of the form of drama he wished to write is that Chekhov was unable to put his theory immediately into practice. Early plays like *Platonov*, *Ivanov* and *The Wood Demon*, though written at a time when Chekhov had fully articulated his theory of drama, failed to realise that theory. Like Treplev in *The Seagull*, Chekhov's theoretical position on drama was well worked out, but his practice was inadequate. It took Chekhov another fifteen years before he developed the means to realise his vision in the truthful lifelike form that he desired. *Platonov*, for instance, is far from being a depiction of 'real life'. It is in fact an example of the melodramatic dramas that were the object of Chekhov's scorn. Ronald Hingley's description of the multiplicity of events that occur in this sprawling drama accurately brings out the almost comic overabundance of melodramatic incidents in the play:

> *Platonov* may not be exactly packed with thrills, possessing as it does more than its share of garrulous characters. But it does have its moments. It is, at least, the only play by Chekhov in which a heroine tries to throw herself under a train on stage and is prevented from doing so by a horse-thief who is later lynched by infuriated peasants. The same heroine also saves her husband from being knifed on stage and later attempts to poison herself by eating matches, all this while remaining the most phlegmatic character in the play. Apart from these excitements, *Platonov* is full of quarrels, denunciations and confessions of love or hatred ... *Platonov* ends with a murder, a crime of passion in which the hero is shot by one of three discarded or would-be mistresses.[40]

The melodramatic elements in plays such as *Platonov* and *Ivanov* would eventually be discarded in favour of realism but this new form created new problems for the playwright. The adoption of realism and representational form did not immediately provide Chekhov with the formal objective correlative of his vision. Chekhov was to spend several years working out means to overcome the particular 'limitations' associated with the use of realism and representational form. It was the modifications he made to that realistic form and the dramatic techniques he devised to expand its expressive powers that constitute the distinctive nature of his dramaturgy. As Raymond Williams points out: 'What Chekhov does then, in effect, is to invent a dramatic form which contradicts most of the available conventions of dramatic production.'[41]

By rejecting the sets of conventions that were used by earlier dramatists and adopting the conventions of realism, Chekhov was to encounter major problems that inevitably follow from the 'limitations' inherent in that form of expression. As Una Ellis-Fermor has claimed:

> One of the primary technical characteristics of the dramatic form is the presentation of fact and event through the medium of words spoken by the agents themselves ... But this instrument of direct speech, cogent and powerful as it can be, imposes no less surely its own limitations on the content.[42]

Since realism involves an attempt to present 'life as it is', in a literal sense, anything which does not occur in life must be removed. One of the central conventions of nineteenth-century fiction which has remained a central feature of most narrative fiction today involves the manipulation of the reader's responses through authorial intervention. Without authorial intervention the reader is given little guidance on how to interpret what is being said. This can be illustrated by showing what happens when we remove authorial interventions from a narrative. The following excerpt taken from the Harold Robbins novel, *The Dream Merchants,* will serve as an example. One section of the novel includes the following dialogue:

> JOHNNY. He's been working pretty hard lately. It isn't the easiest thing in the world trying to run two businesses at once.
> ESTHER. Don't tell me that, Johnny. I know better. Since you came back he hasn't had to do a thing at the nickelodeon.
> JOHNNY. But the responsibility is his.
> ESTHER. You're a good boy to say so, Johnny, but you're not fooling anybody.

The dialogue is presented here as it might be in a play. In the full excerpt from the novel, Robbins guides the reader's responses to a significant extent by including explicit authorial commentary:

> Johnny shifted uncomfortably in his seat. He was embarrassed by the sudden flood of her confidence. 'He's been working pretty hard lately,' he said, trying to comfort her. 'It isn't the easiest thing in the world trying to run two businesses at once.'

> A sudden smile at his poor attempt to console her broke through her tears. 'Don't tell me that, Johnny,' she said softly. 'I know better. Since you came back he hasn't had to do a thing at the nickelodeon.'
>
> Johnny's face grew red. 'But the responsibility is his,' he replied lamely.
>
> She took his hand, still smiling. 'You're a good boy to say so Johnny, but you're not fooling anybody.'[43]

Perhaps the most obvious 'limitation' of the realistic dramatic form is the fact that, unlike in the short story or novel, authorial interventions are only to be found in the stage directions. In performance such authorial intrusion can never be justified. The realistic dramatic conventions adopted by Chekhov make authorial interventions of the type employed by Robbins unacceptable because they are not true to life. In life, people exist and events occur without authorial commentary and, consequently, Chekhov argued that the writer's task was to depict the event or character objectively and without making any subjective authorial judgement on that character or event. He defended this form of objectivity on the grounds that: 'The artist ought not to judge his characters or what they say, but be only an unbiased witness.'[44] What is extraordinary about Chekhov's commitment to objectivity was that he applied this criterion not just to his plays but also to his prose fiction. When Suvorin accused him of taking an amoral position in relation to his characters in his story *The Horse Stealers* Chekhov replied:

> You upbraid me about objectivity, styling it indifference to good and evil, absence of ideals and ideas, etc. You would have me say, in depicting horse thieves, that stealing horses is an evil. But then, that has been known a long while, even without me. Let jurors judge them, for my business is only to show them as they are.[45]

In opting to express his vision of reality in realistic form Chekhov, as John Hagan has pointed out, was binding himself to the elimination of:

> ... authorial editorializing of all sorts (overt expressions of his personal feelings, explicit directives to the reader, definitive interpretations of the characters and events, and the like) ... [because Chekhov's] immediate purpose is to create in the reader a certain kind of illusion — an illusion that he is holding up for inspection a piece of unmediated reality, a segment of life rendered with matter of fact lucidity in all its circumstantiality, uncolored by the moods or opinions of any observer.[46]

The adoption of the conventions of realism led Chekhov to move away from overt author intrusion even in his narrative fiction. In his short stories he concentrated on presenting his characters' 'actions' and 'external behaviour' and avoided passing judgement on them.[47]

Andrew Durkin, in his analysis of the narrative techniques employed in Chekhov's two short stories, *A Nervous Breakdown* (1888) and *Dreams* (1886), notes that:

> In both, only brief statements describe the characters' physical actions. The one verb dealing with inner experience — 'he thought' — does not specify the content of that thought. Adjectives and adverbs, which might provide clues to authorial attitude toward the events described, are practically non-existent. In both endings, the reader may infer the inner state of the characters from the events of the preceding narrative, but this can only be conjecture, perhaps differing slightly in the mind of each individual reader. We are not told, we are shown, and we must draw our conclusions, tentative as they may be.[48]

The technique of 'showing' not 'telling' is one of the defining features of drama as a generic form.[49] While a writer such as Brecht may use the device of 'telling' in his plays, it is more normal to confine the technique to narrative fiction.

Chekhov's desire to employ the conventions of realism in which a supposedly 'unmediated reality' is presented on the stage in order to show his audience 'life as it is' created great difficulties for him as a dramatist. The difficulties arose because not only did he wish to convey life's surface appearance, but he also wanted each of his plays to embody a significant action. The conventions of realism enabled the first aim to be achieved, but these same conventions militated against the achievement of his second more important artistic goal. One of the central problems that faces any director of Chekhov is how to find the theatrical means to communicate the significant action of the plays and avoid merely presenting their trivial surface reality. We need to examine the nature of the expressive problems that arise with the adoption of the realistic dramatic form with its demand that art be literally true to life, before proceeding to show how Chekhov found ways of overcoming these problems. A knowledge of Chekhov's solution to these problems provides directors of his plays with clues about how to create both significant action and trivial reality.

One of the limitations of drama cited by Ellis-Fermor, which is of particular relevance to Chekhov's writing difficulties, is 'the problem of conveying to an audience thought which cannot naturally form part of the dialogue'.[50] Chekhov was committed, as Ibsen put it, to 'the very much more difficult art of writing the genuine plain language spoken in real life'.[51]

The problem with attempting to depict how people behave in real life is that such behaviour can be, indeed often is, peculiarly undemonstrative. In real life, as W. B. Yeats noted, people under emotional stress are likely to say very little and are far more likely to be seen 'staring out of the window, or looking into the drawing room fire'.[52] A similar observation has been made by Harold Pinter in a speech entitled 'Writing for the Theatre' which he made at the National Student Drama Festival in Bristol in 1962. Pinter observed that, in life, 'the more acute the experience the less articulate its expression'.[53] People in real life contemplating suicide may well show very few outward signs of their anguish or their intentions, while a character like Hamlet, in an extremely 'artificial' way, may inform an audience of the pros and cons of suicide in heightened poetic language that is both aesthetically pleasing and highly articulate.

Chekhov's theory of drama seems to deny the validity of the features that are normally assumed to distinguish dramatic art from life. His advice to would-be writers again and again advocates the rejection of the depiction of 'theatrical' types and 'theatrical' situations. The reason that Chekhov gives for such a rejection is always the same. Anything that is 'theatrical' is by definition not lifelike.

At the time that he was writing *Ivanov*, Chekhov wrote to his brother Alexander:

> Modern playwrights stuff their work with saints, scoundrels and comic types to the exclusion of everything else. But you can search Russia high and low without finding these things — that is, you may find some, but not in the extreme form required by playwrights ... I wanted to be original, so I haven't brought on one villain or saint (though I haven't managed to keep out the comic types).[54]

Whether giving advice on characterisation for short stories or plays, Chekhov always attacked clichéd literary stereotypes. He was aware that he himself was occasionally given to such unlifelike character depiction. He wrote to Suvorin in March 1884 that he was attempting to write a novel and discussed some of the features of this proposed work:

> Unfaithful wives, suicides, tight-fisted peasants who exploit their fellows, virtuous muzhiks, devoted slaves, argumentative little old ladies, kind old nurses, country wits, red-nosed army captains, and 'new' people — all of those I'll try to avoid, although in places I display a strong tendency toward stereotypes.[55]

Two months later Chekhov wrote to his brother Alexander and advised him:

> Beware of highflown language. Flunkeys must not use vulgar solecisms. Red-nosed retired captains, drunken reporters, starving writers, consumptive working wives, honest, immaculate youths, high-minded virgins, good-natured nurses — all those have already been described and must be avoided like the pit.[56]

Not only did Chekhov believe that literary artists should avoid creating unlifelike characters, he also believed that fanciful situations in which these characters found themselves should also be avoided. As part of his advice to Alexander on how not to write a play, he declared: 'Keep in mind that declarations of love, infidelities of husbands and wives, the tears of widows and orphans and all other kinds of tears have long since been described.'[57]

Alexander Kuprin remembers Chekhov fulminating against the high-flown artificiality of much contemporary writing. Kuprin claimed that Chekhov:

> ... demanded that writers should choose ordinary, everyday themes, simplicity of treatment and absence of showy tricks. 'Why write,' he [Chekhov] wondered, 'about a man getting into a submarine and going to the North Pole to reconcile himself to the world, while his beloved at that moment throws herself with a hysterical shriek from the belfry? All this is untrue and does not happen in real life. One must write about simple things: how Peter Semionovich married Marie Ivanovna. That is all.[58]

There can be no doubt then that at least part of Chekhov's artistic aim was totally in accord with Jean Jullien's famous dictum that: 'A play is a slice of life artistically put on the boards.'[59] Chekhov's early commitment to this extreme form of literal realism inevitably meant that he would have to reject many of the established conventions, not just of melodrama or the well-made play, but of all Western drama since the time of Aeschylus. In a letter written in the late 1880s, Chekhov specifically rejected several of the popular theatrical conventions of his day. He wrote:

> The demand is made that the hero and the heroine should be dramatically effective. But in real life, people do not shoot themselves, or hang themselves, or make confessions of love every minute. Nor do they go around all the time making clever remarks ... Life on the stage should be as it really is and the people, too, should be as they are, and not stilted.[60]

The implications of such a total acceptance of the ideal of fidelity to life were far-reaching for Chekhov. He found that the adoption of realistic conventions cut him off from many of the conventional devices that had been available to earlier playwrights. As Raymond Williams pointed out:

> The naturalist however insisted on representation and accepted the limitations of normal expression. For those of them who were concerned with surface emotions, these limitations presented no difficulty: conversational resources for the discussion of food or money or bedrooms remained adequate. But the more important naturalist writers were fully serious artists, and wanted to be able to express the whole range of human experience, even while committed to the limitations of probable conversation.[61]

Earlier forms of non-realistic drama had no such problems of expression because the conventions that defined them were more flexible than those of realism. A dramatist such as Sophocles who wished 'to convey to his audience any considerable part of his own understanding of his character's experience … [had at hand] some further means of communicating with that audience, more rapid and direct than the medium of strict dramatic dialogue'.[62]

Chekhov certainly 'wanted to express the whole range of human experience', but had no recourse to devices such as Greek choruses or Elizabethan soliloquies to help indicate the significance of events being dramatised. Realism specifically barred the use of these devices since, in real life, there is no such speaking entity as a chorus with its community consciousness, nor do people normally speak their thoughts aloud in soliloquy. It is mainly because of the restrictions imposed by these conventions that many critics have regarded realism as an essentially trivial form of theatre. They argue that only the surface of reality is presented, while the inner meaning of reality, its significance, cannot be communicated.

Chekhov's commitment to depicting 'life as it is' not only cut him off from the use of such devices as the chorus and the soliloquy, but also led him to reject forms of drama which, while they might allow for realistic staging and acting, were nevertheless non-realistic and untrue to life in their overall structure and purpose. As far as Chekhov was concerned, the well-made play (*pièce bien faite*) and the thesis play (*pièce à thèse*) both imposed artificial constructions on life.

Ibsen, whom Chekhov did not think a very good dramatist, had tried to adopt the conventions of realism.[63] Despite all of his efforts to liberate himself from the formal techniques of the Scribean well-made play, Ibsen, who had directed many of Scribe's plays, could not totally rid himself of those theatrical conventions. As Esslin observed:

> Although Ibsen did away with the soliloquy and the 'aside', although he tried to create, in his socially oriented drama, stage environments of the greatest possible realism — rooms with the fourth wall removed — structurally, he tended to adhere to the convention of the well-made play.[64]

The splendidly theatrical curtain lines that end each of the acts of Ibsen's *Ghosts* were unacceptable to Chekhov precisely because of their theatricality. The attempts to combine realism with the well-made play, which Ibsen valiantly attempted to do, was, as John Elsom correctly says 'fraught with difficulties', and was ultimately 'illogical and provided self-contradictions at almost every technical level'.[65]

The problems Ibsen faced were eventually to be solved by Chekhov when he learnt how to do without the well-made play structure. Given his demand for a literal representation of life on stage, Chekhov had no choice. As Elsom perceptively argues:

If you set out to imitate life, it is almost impossible to obey the Unities. Life does not fall easily into syllogistic structures, helping to preserve the Unity of Action. If you try to keep the dramatic events all in one place or one short span of time, you either have to make your characters unconvincingly knowledgeable and lucid about what is happening elsewhere or you have to forget about the pattern of surrounding events which gives the particular situation its wider significance.[66]

Chekhov then, as someone who 'seldom wrote of important people or world-shattering events', and who always associated 'the heroic gesture with the idiotic',[67] could hardly fail to recognise the inadequacy of the well-made play as an appropriate dramatic form to express his vision of reality.

The thesis play was likewise unacceptable to Chekhov because it was equally unrealistic. The naturalist in Chekhov could see that life simply existed and had no thesis to put forward, so, in 1888, he wrote Suvorin that:

> ... it is not the task of fiction writers to solve such problems as God, pessimism, etc. The writer's business is to depict only who spoke or thought about God or pessimism, and how and under what circumstances. The artist ought not to judge his characters or what they say, but be only an unbiased witness.[68]

Five months later Chekhov again took Suvorin to task for having suggested that the playwright should have some sort of thesis in his work:

> In demanding from an artist a conscious attitude toward his work you are right, but you are confusing two concepts: *the solution of a problem* and *the correct posing of a question*. Only the second is obligatory for an artist. Not a single problem is solved in *Anna Karenina* and in *Eugene Onegin*, but you will find these works quite satisfactory only because all the questions in them are correctly posed. The court is obliged to pose the questions correctly, but it's up to the jurors to answer them, each juror according to his own taste.[69]

Early in 1890, Chekhov wrote to Suvorin in response to a letter in which the publisher had criticised him for failing to pass judgement explicitly on the horse-thief in his short story *Thieves* (1890). Chekhov's response is interesting, because it not only reiterates his idea that there is an implied judgement that he assumes will be made by the reader, but also points out that the conventions of realism that he had adopted militate against any authorial comment:

> Of course it would be gratifying to couple art with sermonizing, but, personally, I find this exceedingly difficult and, because of conditions imposed by technique, all but impossible ... when I write, I rely fully on the reader, on the assumption that he himself will add the subjective elements that are lacking in the story.[70]

Nowhere is Chekhov more explicitly non-judgemental than in his correspondence with the writer Yelena Shavrova, who had written to Chekhov for literary advice. Shavrova had written a story in which a character appears who suffers from syphilis. Chekhov's advice is essentially that she make sure that her descriptions of the nature of the malady are factually accurate, and that sermonising judgements be avoided at all costs:

> In order to settle such problems as degeneration psychosis, etc., one must have scientific knowledge of them. The importance of the meaning of the disease (let us call it by the letter S, out of modesty) you exaggerate. In the first place S is curable ... And besides S, there are other diseases no less serious. For instance, tuberculosis. It seems to me, too, that it isn't the business of the artist to lash out at people because they are ill. Is it my fault if I have Migraine? Is it Sidor's fault that he has S? ... No one is guilty, and if there are guilty ones, it concerns the board of health, not the artist.[71]

In the same year in which he gave this advice to Shavrova, Chekhov published a short story entitled *Three Years* in which he clearly suggests that, when questions of how to solve social problems are raised, one should have recourse to the kind of knowledge provided by medical science rather than literary art:

> 'If poetry doesn't solve the problems you think important, then refer to technical works,' said Yartsev. 'Look up your criminal and financial law, read scientific articles. Why should *Romeo and Juliet* discuss educational freedom, say, or prison hygiene, instead of love, when you can find all that stuff in specialist articles and reference works?'[72]

Chekhov rejected the didactic view of art put forward in *Three Years* by Kostya who claims that: 'A work of art is significant and useful only when its theme embraces a serious social problem.'[73] For Chekhov, the central problem with polemical writing was that it ceased to be objective and often became unjust and moralistic. In his letter to Shavrova he criticised her for her one-sided depiction of the gynaecologist and professor in her story: 'I do not venture to ask you to love the gynaecologist and the professor, but I venture to remind you of the justice which for an objective writer is more precious than the air he breathes.'[74]

A sense of justice was for Chekhov the very opposite of making judgements on characters. Neither the horse-thief in *Thieves* (1890), nor the peasant woman who kills a baby by pouring boiling water on it in *In the Hollow* (1900), are overtly judged by Chekhov. Even the depiction of sexually transmitted diseases cannot bring out the moralist in Chekhov. Paradoxically, Chekhov argued that the truly moral, and at the same time aesthetically correct, course of action was for the writer to abstain from making any judgement of characters. Chekhov was quite happy however to make an artistic judgement of Shavrova's literary work:

> ... the lady in your story treats S as a bugaboo. That's wrong. S is not a vice, not the product of evil will, but a disease, and the patients who suffer from it need warm cordial treatment as much as any others. It's wrong for a wife to abandon her sick husband because his illness is infectious or foul. Whatever her attitude toward S, the author must be humane to his fingernails.[75]

The so-called objectivity of Chekhov's writing was determined by his choice of the set of conventions that I have called realism. In his own life Chekhov was certainly not indifferent to moral and social questions, but the adoption of the conventions of realism meant that no overt moral judgement or polemical grandstanding was aesthetically acceptable. Certainly, until the mid eighteen-eighties, all of Chekhov's statements on art show him trying to maintain artistic objectivity. As John Hagan explains, while Chekhov 'was plainly the determined enemy of all that he found mediocre, or stupid or evil in the society around him, particularly Czarist autocracy ... [he nevertheless] was content to diagnose, not prescribe a cure'.[76]

Chekhov's realistic presentation of 'life as it is', that avoided the artificiality inherent in the well-made play or the subjective polemicism to be found in the thesis play, at first sight seems to involve a confusion of art with life. Having created plays in which lifelike people actually do 'come and go, eat, talk about the weather and play cards',[77] it is perhaps not surprising that some critics, who had been accustomed to the overt theatricality of most nineteenth-century drama, regarded Chekhov as being totally incapable of writing plays.

Tolstoy was utterly appalled at Chekhov's anti-theatricalist approach to dramaturgy. He is reported to have complained to the playwright that his plays lacked overt action and that his characters failed to exhibit purposeful behaviour. The exasperated Tolstoy is reported as having said to Chekhov: 'And where does one get with your heroes? From the sofa to the privy and from the privy back to the sofa?'[78] Tolstoy, who hated Shakespeare, was even more disparaging about Chekhov's dramas. Having kissed Chekhov goodbye after the playwright had paid him a visit, Tolstoy could not resist saying, 'But I still can't stand your plays. Shakespeare's are terrible, but yours are even worse.'[79]

Tolstoy's main objection to Chekhov's plays was that they were not dramatic or theatrical enough. Being much more used to plays in which there was a plot full of intrigue, Tolstoy thought that Chekhov's plays were pointless. This led him to state:

> I could not force myself to read his *Three Sisters* to the end — where does it all lead us to? Generally speaking our modern writers seem to have lost the idea of what drama is.[80]

For Tolstoy, the supreme example of dramatic method was the 'problem' play with all its complex intrigues and overt action. All he saw in Chekhov was the creation of 'mood', which he argued was more suitable in a lyric poem:

> Dramatic forms serve, and ought to serve, quite different aims. In a dramatic work the author ought to deal with some problem that has yet to be solved and every character in the play ought to solve it according to the idiosyncrasies of his own character. It is like a laboratory experiment. But you won't find anything of the kind in Chekhov.[81]

Tolstoy's objections to Chekhov's major plays should not be rejected out of hand, for they contain a partial truth. That the great Russian novelist did not really understand how Chekhov's plays worked is true, but the lack of problem-solving and general plot interest, or theatrical pyrotechnics in the mature Chekhov play, are accurately described by Tolstoy. Anyone who has had to sit through a production of a Chekhov play where *only* the surface realism is evident will know how boringly untheatrical Chekhov can be. R. E. C. Long's 1902 description of what he perceived to be the weakness of Chekhov's approach to drama echoes Tolstoy's and highlights the resistance that Chekhov faced when he finally developed his new form of drama:

> The effective drama is based too much upon great motives and sharp contrasts of character and interest to be in consonance with Chekhov's talent. Frivolity has made successful plays, but a continued exposition of the banal never did. Trivial motives, monotonous backgrounds, and the fundamental lack of the heroic, which increase their interest in the dissecting-room of the analytical novelist, in the drama are merely meaningless. In Chekhov's dramas his peculiar genius is obscured, the subjective element, generally suppressed, becomes apparent, and there is no compensatory element of ingenuity of plot or delineation of character.[82]

As far as playwriting was concerned, Chekhov advocated the same rejection of artificial characters and situations. Kuprin reports that he attacked the clichéd conventions of the drama of his day and the conservatism that allowed those conventions to continue:

> In life there are no clear cut consequences or reasons; in it everything is mixed up together; the important and the paltry, the great and the base, the tragic and the ridiculous. One is hypnotized and enslaved by routine and cannot manage to break away from it. What are needed are new forms, new ones.[83]

The type of play that Chekhov was to develop rejected much that previously had been regarded as essential to drama and theatre in terms of both form and content. The radical nature of Chekhov's project of creating a form appropriate to his vision was not achieved without difficulty. Certainly Chekhov's early full-length dramas are not successful applications of his realistic theories.

Prior to writing *The Seagull*, Chekhov made several abortive attempts to develop a form that would act as the objective correlative of his vision. The realistic form that he had chosen for *Platonov*, *The Wood Demon* and *Ivanov*, combined with the scientific objectivity that he employed, allowed him to realise his first aim, to show 'life as it is'. The real problem he faced was how to find adequate ways of expressing the artist's vision of 'life as it ought to be', while avoiding being overtly judgemental or polemical. To achieve this Chekhov had to develop a second subtextual level of meaning in his plays. The text of his plays depicted realistically 'life as it is' in all its banality and failure, while the implied subtext, which dealt with the hopes, fears and aspirations of the characters, was to be created by the actors. Chekhov's problem, and that of any director of his plays, is to find means to make perceptible to an audience the yawning gap between the text and the subtext, between actuality and aspiration, between 'life as it is' and 'life as it ought to be' and thus to communicate Chekhov's vision of reality.

Chekhov's characteristic method of creating a subtext is to suggest that his characters live two lives. One is the external life presented in the text which includes the characters' actions, their environment, and how they appear objectively to other characters. The other life is an internal one which includes the characters' hopes, beliefs and aspirations, as well as their subjective view of themselves and of life. In order to bring this subtext into being and make it perceptible to audiences, Chekhov had to develop several dramatic techniques that extended the expressive range of realism. Having achieved this, by means that we will examine later, Chekhov proceeded to create a perceptible gap between the subjective and objective lives of his characters.

In his short stories, Chekhov often depicted characters who exhibit a rift between their public and private selves; between the mask presented objectively and the face that is known subjectively. In this non-dramatic form the inner and outer lives could both be easily revealed to the reader through the use of narrative commentary. In *The Party* (1888) the public world of the name-day party reveals to the central character, Olga, that she and her husband are living a life of lies and deception publicly, even if they are people of integrity in their private lives. One of the important implications of 'living a lie' that is explored by Chekhov in this story stems from what Karl Kramer has called 'the logic of the lie in the public world'. That logic leads a reader or audience member to doubt the veracity of public statements and to seek for the truth in a subtext that lies behind these statements and which may even contradict them. As Kramer says, this kind of logic means that 'if one seeks the truth, he [sic] must assume that the opposite of what is said represents the real feeling'.[84]

In one exchange between the husband and wife, in which Olga is trying to break down the public masks that separate her 'true' inner self from her husband's 'true' inner self, Chekhov concludes the incident with clear proof that Olga has failed to achieve her aim since her husband refuses to communicate in the level of the text. He will not *say* what he means, but leaves Olga to read the subtext of his mock congratulations:

> 'What are you thinking about, Peter?' she asked.
> 'Oh, nothing,' replied her husband.
> 'You've started having secrets from me lately. That's wrong.'
> 'What's wrong about it?' Peter answered dryly, after a pause. 'We all have our own personal lives, so we're bound to have our own secrets.'
> 'Personal lives, own secrets — that's just words. Can't you see how much you're hurting me?' She sat up in bed. 'If you're worried, why hide it from me? And why do you think fit to confide in strange women rather than your own wife? Oh yes, I heard you by the bee-hives this afternoon, pouring your heart out to Lyubochka.'
> 'My congratulations, I'm glad you did hear it.'
> This meant: 'Leave me alone, and don't bother me when I'm thinking.'[85]

While the discussion between Peter and Olga is, for the most part, written in the form of dramatic dialogue, it is the narrative comment in the final line that explains the subtextual meaning of that dialogue. In a play, the meaning that is stated in a story would have to be made clear to an audience through the actor's tone of voice and manner of delivery.[86]

In *A Dreary Story* (1889), Chekhov's concern with the gap that often exists between the public and private selves is again a central concern of the story. The dying professor's sense of alienation is depicted in terms of his having lost the ability to contact anything but the exterior public selves of his family:

> I watch them both, and only now at lunch does it dawn on me that their inner life has long since vanished from my field of vision. Once I lived at home with a real family, I feel, but now I'm just the lunch-guest of a spurious wife, looking at a spurious Lika.[87]

Chekhov does not imply that this failure to communicate with the inner selves of other people is existentially inevitable. At one time the professor had been able to communicate with his family. His alienated condition is man-made and so is potentially curable. In *The Duel* (1891), Layevsky is redeemed from just such a condition of alienation. He comes to realise that, not only has he deceived others with his mask, he has also deceived himself:

> He had not done a thing for his fellows but eat their bread, drink their wine, steal their wives and borrow their ideas, while seeking to justify his despicable,

parasitical existence in the world's eyes and his own by passing himself off as a higher form of life. It was all lies, lies, lies.[88]

In *Ariadne* (1895) Chekhov once again returns to the idea of the two lives that people lead and the harm that is caused by the lack of correspondence between the two. The landowner, Ivan Shamokin, tells the story of his disastrous relationship with Ariadne, whose real nature he fails to see having been blinded by her beautiful public self: 'To me her lovely face and figure were pledges of her inner self.'[89] It does not take long, however, for Shamokin to become disillusioned with Ariadne. He soon comes to see the yawning gap between her public and private selves:

> When I watched her sleeping, eating or trying to look innocent, I often wondered why God had given her such outstanding beauty, grace and intelligence. Could it really be just for lolling in bed, eating and telling lies, lies, lies?[90]

The almost schizophrenic split between the self that people present to others in public situations and the self they present in more private situations was to be a major preoccupation in Chekhov's mature dramas.

Of all the many depictions made by Chekhov of the dualistic lives lived by his characters, none is more clear or more instructive than the one that appears in his story *A Lady with a Dog* (1899). Gurov, the 'hero' of *A Lady with a Dog*, is taking his daughter to school before meeting up with his mistress, Anne. Like many characters in Chekhov's plays, who talk about the weather in order to hide what they really feel, Gurov ostensibly carries on a conversation with his daughter, but his real self is elsewhere:

> 'It's three degrees above zero, yet look at the sleet,' said Gurov to his daughter. 'But it's only the ground which is warm, you see — the temperature in the upper strata of the atmosphere is quite different.'
>
> 'Why doesn't it thunder in winter, Daddy?' He explained this too, reflecting as he spoke that he was on his way to an assignation. Not a soul knew about it — or ever would know, probably. He was living two lives. One of them was open to view by — and known to — the people concerned. The other life proceeded in secret. Through some strange and possibly arbitrary chain of coincidences everything vital, interesting and crucial to him, everything which called his sincerity and integrity into play, everything which made up the core of his life … all that took place in complete secrecy, whereas everything false about him, the facade behind which he hid to conceal the truth — his work at the bank, say, his arguments at the club, that 'inferior species' stuff, attending anniversary celebrations with his wife — all that was in the open. He judged others by himself, believing the evidence of his eyes, and attributing to everyone a real, fascinating life lived under the cloak of secrecy as in the darkness of the night.[91]

This single quotation should, I believe, be given to every director and actor of Chekhov's plays, since it provides a key to the understanding of the method of characterisation that Chekhov developed in his four major plays. Chekhov's vision of reality which depicts 'life as it is' and implies 'life as it should be' is communicated through the interaction of the text and subtext, the outer and inner lives of his characters. Chekhov systematically creates a gap between his characters' two lives. The gap between the inner world of his characters' private beliefs, aims and hopes, and the outer world of their public actions and relationship with other characters is presented in terms of their failure to realise their aspirations. Productions that allow audiences to become aware of the characters' wasted potential assist in the achievement of Chekhov's central strategy of showing what silly trivial lives these characters lead at present. The sense of waste is felt precisely because Chekhov suggests the possibility of a better life that can be achieved through human action. Chekhov, by implication, encourages his audiences to see that they need to improve their own lives.

The innovative nature of Chekhov's use of subtext is sometimes overlooked now that it has become a commonplace in dramaturgy. We joyfully respond to struggles for dominance and possession which subtextually fester under the civilised text in a play like Pinter's *Old Times*, but we do this primarily because we have learnt the rules of the game from Chekhov. Prior to Chekhov, the actor's subtext would emotionally underpin and align itself with the text's stated meaning. The characters meant what they said, and said what they meant. When Brutus in *Julius Caesar* says of Caesar, 'I know no personal cause to spurn at him',[92] we believe him because the accepted convention of Elizabethan drama was that the soliloquy revealed truthfully what the character believes. In a Chekhov play, text and subtext are split asunder and often contradict each other. A Chekhov character may say one thing but mean another.

It was as a consequence of this radical innovation that, when his plays were first performed, many actors found it difficult to portray this double life. Being used to performing in plays in which characters say what they mean and mean what they say, many early performers of Chekhov's plays, particularly those who had no knowledge of the acting system developed by Stanislavski, were unaware of the implied subtextual inner life of his characters. Certainly, few early performers had the acting technique to play such a subtext. Brooks Atkinson, reviewing the Fagan Company's production of *The Cherry Orchard* in New York in 1928, complained that the actors and the production had only managed to communicate the objective surface of reality that exists in the text, and went on to point out the difficulties facing actors performing in Chekhov's plays:

> At the Bijou Theatre we are drenched in the boredom, but we do not perceive its subtle meaning. It is the cadaver of *The Cherry Orchard* from which the breath

of life has departed. And that is disheartening, since Chekhov radiated life through every word he wrote ... Nothing is more difficult to act on the stage than Chekhovian drama ... As playgoers we hear and see only the exterior impulses. In consequence the essence of the characters, the essence of the story, lie between the lines or rise above the performance as overtones.[93]

Charles Timmer has noted that the effects of this dislocation of the text and subtext in a Chekhov play can lead to events occurring which appear to be bizarre in that they seem to have little or no dramatic relevance.[94] In *Uncle Vanya*, when Astrov is reluctantly about to leave and is trying to put off the moment of departure, he turns to the map of Africa which, as Chekhov's stage instructions point out, 'is obviously quite out of place here'.[95] Astrov makes the bizarre comment that: 'Down there in Africa the heat must be quite something. Terrific!'[96]

The denotational meaning of the line is irrelevant in this context. By this point in the play, the audience's knowledge of Astrov allows them to 'read' his wish to stay on at the estate where he has spent some of his happiest moments. The point is that Astrov's statement is only bizarre in the text, but the actor must make the subtext clear to his audience. When Timmer defines 'bizarre' as 'a statement, or a situation, which has no logical place in the context or in the sequence of events, the resulting effect being one of sudden bewilderment',[97] he is correct only insofar as the text is concerned. In fact, it would be more accurate to say that the bizarre in Chekhov is that 'which has no *apparent* place in the context or in the sequence of events'. Even the scene in Act One of *The Cherry Orchard* in which Lopakhin interrupts the conversation of Anya and Varya by making an animal noise that is variously translated as either mooing or bleating, a scene that Timmer cites as the *locus classicus* of the bizarre; even this scene has a perfectly logical and realistically justified subtextual meaning. As we will see later, Chekhov has provided the textual signals to the actor playing Lopakhin that allows him to know what he means when he makes this apparently meaningless sound. In many cases in Chekhov's plays spoken words no longer have a one-to-one correspondence with their dictionary meanings. Bert O. States is surely correct when he sees how, in this respect, Chekhov is different from a writer like Ibsen. In Chekhov:

> ... there is an immediacy ... which suggests the absence of an author or a clear signal of meaning: there is nothing at any rate that we can trust half as well as Mrs Alving's 'I almost think, Pastor Manders, we are all of us ghosts', or Mrs Helseth's pat summing up of the disaster at Rommersholm: 'The dead wife has taken them!' In other words, the *utile* function is nearly gone ...[98]

These innovations not only provide a difficult creative problem for actors but have, at times, been treated by critics as insurmountable problems. Because the true meaning of Chekhov's lines are not always clearly expressed in the denotational meanings of the text, a critic such as Harvey Pitcher is led to what I believe is an untenable position which suggests that, because Chekhov's meanings are not overtly stated, and are culturally bound in any case, it is unlikely that the playwright's meanings can be communicated. Consequently, Pitcher falls back on a variant of the reader response theory where the audience makes up its own mind about what the play means. Having claimed that Chekhov's 'pauses and stage directions, however subtle, can only take us so far', Pitcher continues:

> There remain vast areas in the Chekhov play where the audience is bound to rely on its own intuition. And this raises one of the trickiest problems in Chekhov interpretations. Chekhov's method of emotional suggestion and implication is necessarily elusive. Whereas qualities like courage and cowardice, being directly linked to human actions, can be demonstrated without difficulty on the stage and are likely to be universally recognised and agreed upon, emotional yearnings or regrets are by their nature obscure and intangible, often they can only be hinted at, and these limits may be interpreted differently by different members of the audience. It is this situation which helps to explain why there is so much diversity in the interpretation of Chekhov's plays.[99]

What Pitcher fails to mention in his essentially literary analysis is that the plays are mediated by the director and actors who determine to a large degree how an audience will interpret the play. No two members of an audience seeing the same production will have an identical interpretation, but they are very likely to have similar ones. Certainly their interpretations are likely to be more alike than would be the interpretations made by two audience members seeing two different productions. Directors, actors and set designers know that, if they are skilled in their various arts, they will communicate *their* interpretation of the play to the audience. Chekhov certainly knew this, and knew that even the denotationally empty utterances, like the following exchange between Masha and Vershinin in *Three Sisters*, has to have an extremely clear subtextual meaning provided by the actors after they have discovered in rehearsal what it does, in fact, mean:

> MASHA. Ti tum ti tu ti –
> VERSHININ. Tum tum tum –
> MASHA. Tara tarara
> VERSHININ. Tum ti tum. [*Laughs.*][100]

Chekhov's care about stage instructions and, in particular, sound effects attests to his concern for communicating meaning other than through the literal meaning of the words in the text. His arguments with Stanislavski about the director's overuse of sound effects were motivated by the fact that Chekhov intended all of his theatrical effects to have a meaning that went beyond the simple fact that those effects were real. In an important article by Nils Ake Nilsson, entitled 'Intonation and Rhythm in Cechov's Plays', the Scandinavian scholar highlights the kinds of interpretative limits that Chekhov gave to the actors of his plays both in actual rehearsal and, more importantly, in the playtext itself. These performance-oriented signals overcome many of the so-called problems of interpretation cited by Pitcher.

Nilsson argues that, while Chekhov may have been influenced by Turgenev in terms of the external realism of his plays, he is closer in spirit to Nemirovich-Danchenko, whose theatrical sense gave Chekhov knowledge of the way in which levels of meaning are created by *how* something is said rather than simply by *what* is said. So a character in one of Nemirovich-Danchenko's plays says:

> To be quite honest the words don't exist for me. I disown them completely. They never show me what the human soul in reality wants. But the sounds — they affect me. Do you follow me? The sounds of the voice. By them I am always able, like a prophet, to discern whether a man is happy at heart or not.[101]

The modern actor, especially one trained in the Stanislavski system, has learnt how to present clear meanings through a subtext which is created by means of such elements as intonation, pitch, pace, stress, gesture and body language. Chekhov, for all his criticisms of some of Stanislavski's excesses, was extremely fortunate that the director was helping to train actors who could adequately present the double life of his characters. Here was the *significant* realism that Chekhov had aspired to in his theories about the drama that depicted the ordinary incidents of life while communicating his own attitude toward that kind of life.

Chekhov's achievement was to overcome a whole series of problems that face any dramatist committed to realism. He was to answer the sorts of questions raised more recently by Nilsson:

> How to combine scenic realism with 'the drama of souls'? How is the realistic playwright to reproduce feeling, the innermost thoughts of man on the stage? How much can words express? How far can he use everyday words without their losing their dramatic tension and — on the other hand — how far can he 'dramatise' words without their ceasing to be natural?[102]

Practically every character in a Chekhov play has a life story full of incidents which the writer of a well-made play would insist on putting on stage but which Chekhov keeps off stage so as not to disturb the gentle flow of everyday life. However, little by little, details of each character's lives are communicated to the audience. The two main devices that Chekhov uses are what I shall call the 'disguised soliloquy' and, borrowing the term from David Magarshack, the 'messenger element'.

The 'disguised soliloquy' occurs in Chekhov's mature plays whenever characters are so moved by the situation they find themselves in that they feel the need to express their innermost thoughts. Magarshack rather misleadingly calls this technique a chorus element, but the term 'disguised soliloquy' more accurately describes Chekhov's technique. Be that as it may, Magarshack's description of what is involved in this technique is essentially correct. He says that Chekhov's characters:

> assume the mantle of the chorus whenever their inner life bursts through the outer shell of their everyday appearance and overflows into a torrent of words. It is this spontaneous and almost palpable transmutation into speech of hidden thoughts and deeply buried emotions that is perhaps the most subtle expression of dramatic action in a Chekhov play.[103]

An obvious example of this sort of disguised soliloquy occurs at the beginning of Act II of *The Cherry Orchard*, when Charlotte talks about her life in front of a group of bystanders. Indeed, Chekhov's use of this technique of establishing the existence of an inner life is pervasive. *Uncle Vanya* has hardly begun before Astrov, using Marina as his sounding board, launches into a long speech about the nature of his life and his attitude towards himself and existence in general. *Three Sisters* opens with Olga's barely disguised soliloquy, as does *The Cherry Orchard* where Lopakhin bares his soul. Indeed, it is only in Chekhov's earliest masterpiece, *The Seagull*, that a disguised soliloquy does not appear almost immediately. In this play we have to wait for the second scene, admittedly only two pages into the play, before Treplev begins his 'soliloquy' with Sorin as silent partner. All of the disguised soliloquies are realistically motivated and arise quite naturally out of the situations in which the characters find themselves. The speaker is not alone, though the other people on stage are often practically silent or not paying much attention to the speaker. Whenever these kind of speeches occur in the plays the audience is allowed to perceive something that is normally part of the private inner life of the characters. Normally this inner life remains in the subtext. However, when under the stress of a particular situation this subtext bubbles up into the text in the form of a disguised soliloquy, the audience obtains privileged knowledge of the character which can be used later in the play. Once this subjective subtextual life has been made objectively textual, the audience knows, firstly, that there is such an inner life and, secondly, that it can use that knowledge when evaluating the character's subsequent overt behaviour. They can perceive whether or not a gap exists between the character's two lives and understand the particular nature of that gap and its effect on the character.

The messenger element is a second technique for providing an audience with privileged information about the inner lives of the characters in a play. When two characters discuss and give information about a third character we have the 'messenger element'. As Magarshack states, the function of this element 'is to keep the audience informed about the chief dramatic incidents, which take place off stage'.[104] Obviously this hearsay information is less reliable than the disguised soliloquy for providing information about the beliefs and aspirations of the character talked about, but it can supply the audience with useful factual information that again modifies its responses to that third character when they next appear. Varya's conversation with Anya in Act One of *The Cherry Orchard* gives us, amongst other things, several crucial pieces of information about Mrs Ranevsky.

To show how these two devices work together and help to guide audience responses, I will outline a simplified model of these techniques in action. Imagine that you are at a circus. A particularly funny clown is making you laugh with his absurd antics. A person next to you begins to talk to you about this clown and says something like: 'Isn't that clown an extraordinary fellow — I heard this morning that his wife had just been killed in a plane crash yesterday — but being the theatrical trouper that he is, he insisted on appearing today — he said that the show must go on.' Assuming that you believe the person next to you, this 'messenger element' cannot help but modify your response to the hilarious antics of the clown. You look closer at this performer doing all of his ludicrous pratfalls and you notice a tear appear and run down his cheek. He quickly wipes the tear away and goes on with his routine. The tear is the clown's disguised soliloquy and his subjective pain has, for a brief moment, bubbled up from its subtextual life into the objective life of his comic performance. Through the use of techniques such as these, Chekhov developed a way to realise his vision of life in all its tragi-comic jumble. Paradoxically, as spectators who have learnt about the clown through the two devices of the 'disguised soliloquy' and the 'messenger element', we are placed in a position where the funnier his behaviour, the more we feel for him.

One final element of Chekhov's approach to form needs to be briefly looked at, before beginning a more detailed examination of the development of his dramatic techniques in the individual plays. This element concerns the playwright's use of symbolism. On the face of it, symbolism would appear to be incompatible with realism, yet we know that Chekhov was attracted to certain aspects of symbolist form. James McFarlane expresses a commonly held view that, though Chekhov concentrated more on the short story during the early eighteen-nineties, 'he nevertheless continued to brood on problems of dramatic composition, especially those bearing on the communication of unspoken thought which (it is reported) he hoped to solve by combining a basic realism with a controlled use of symbols'.[105]

Often when we talk of 'symbolism' we think of something that is essentially non-realistic. The little drama written by Treplev in *The Seagull* is a symbolist play in this non-realistic sense. With this sort of symbolism we recognise, as Wimsatt notes, that the order of images presented to us 'openly prefers the norms of symbolic meaning to those of representation. Then we move off through varying shades of romance, allegory, myth and surrealism.'[106] Chekhov's approach to the use of symbolism was quite different from this. Just as he had adapted devices like the soliloquy and the messenger element from earlier non-realistic forms of drama and made them serve, in modified form, his realistic dramaturgy, so Chekhov utilised symbolism in the same way. It was not a case of *either* symbolism *or* realism but 'both/and'. However paradoxical the term may seem, Chekhov fits the description that Wimsatt gives of 'poetic-realist'. As Wimsatt explains:

> Sometimes the order of images in a story follows or apparently follows the lines of representational necessity or probability, though at the same time a symbolic significance is managed. Then we have realism, though realism of a superior sort, the poetic sort.[107]

The trees that are chopped down at the end of *The Cherry Orchard* certainly function as a symbol of the end of the era of landed gentry, but they also function as real trees being chopped down! Even the breaking string, which is often used as an example of a 'pure' symbol, has its realistic counterpart, for, as I argued elsewhere: 'The breaking string must surely be one of Yepikhodov's guitar strings.'[108] Laurence Senelick likewise sees that Chekhov refused to abandon realism in this instance. Writing of the 'uncanny sound' of the breaking string Senelick comments:

> But even then, Chekhov does not forgo a realistic pretext for the inexplicable. Shortly before the moment, Yepikhodov crosses upstage, strumming his guitar. Might not the snapped string be one broken by the faltering bookkeeper? At the play's end, before we hear the sound dying away, we are told by Lopakhin that he has left Yepikhodov on the grounds as a caretaker. Chekhov always overlays any symbolic inference with a patina of irreproachable reality.[109]

With the writing of *The Seagull*, Chekhov successfully achieved the formal means to communicate his vision of reality. Before he wrote that play, however, he made a number of less successful attempts to match vision with form. As we have already seen, *Platonov*, although not meant for publication, showed Chekhov to be still unable to break away from the conventions of romantic melodrama. In *Platonov*, *The Wood Demon* and *Ivanov*, the old forms of theatre work against the vision that Chekhov is attempting to dramatise.

An examination of a selection of Chekhov's early plays, and of *Ivanov* in particular, will help us to see the difficulties that Chekhov faced in attempting to use the conventions of realism to convey what he perceived to be the action of his play. The partial failure of *Ivanov* stemmed mainly from the limitations inherent in the adoption of the conventions of literal realism and was to lead Chekhov to find ways of modifying and enlarging the expressive possibilities of this representational form. At the time of writing *Ivanov*, Chekhov had not yet developed his method of juxtaposing text with subtext to create the gap between aspiration and achievement, nor had he developed his technique of using the expressive power of symbolism while retaining his adherence to the conventions of realism. Only when Chekhov mastered these techniques could he extend the expressive possibilities of realism to the point where they became capable of depicting accurately 'life as it is' in all of its triviality, while simultaneously implying that this depiction was in fact 'life as it should not be'.

## ENDNOTES

[1] Esslin, M., 'Chekhov and the Modern Drama' in Clyman, T. W., ed., *A Chekhov Companion*, Greenwood Press, Westport, 1985, p. 136.

[2] Chekhov, A., quoted in Nemirovich-Danchenko, V., *My Life in the Russian Theatre*, Geoffrey Bles, London, 1968, p. 160.

[3] Chekhov, A., Letter to M. V. Kiseleva, 14 January 1887, in Yarmolinsky, A., *Letters of Anton Chekhov*, The Viking Press, New York, 1973, p. 41.

[4] Chekhov, A., Letter to A. S. Suvorin, 25 November 1892, in Yarmolinsky, A., op. cit., p. 226.

[5] Gaskell, R., *Drama and Reality: The European Theatre since Ibsen*, Routledge and Kegan Paul, London, 1972, pp. 15 and 18.

[6] There is enormous confusion in the use of such terms as 'Naturalism' and 'Realism'. As Furst and Skrine have argued, Naturalism 'was tied to the apron strings of "Realism" from its first appearance, from Zola's tacit assumption in his art criticism that the terms were virtually identical'. (Furst, L. and Skrine, P., *Naturalism*, Methuen, London, 1971, p. 5.) I intend to use the term 'Naturalism' in much the same way as Furst and Skrine do when they state that 'one of the briefest, though necessarily incomplete, definitions of Naturalism is as an attempt to apply to literature the discoveries and methods of nineteenth-century science'. (Furst, L. and Skrine, P., op. cit., p. 9.) Though Naturalism is historically situated as being related to a specific movement, using the methods of 'nineteenth-century' science, I believe that it is of use to criticism to use the term 'naturalism' to refer to the application of science and scientific method to the arts in any period. The term 'realism' I wish to use in describing the attempts to make art literally imitate life. The movement from poetry to prose in drama, the development of the box set, the removal of footlights, etc., all become, in my definition, examples of increasing 'realism'. The terms now no longer overlap and while someone like Chekhov can be described as both a naturalist and a realist it is possible to be one without being the other. Zolaist naturalism tended to utilise insights drawn from the new science of sociology and therefore was attracted to realism which could effectively show the environment at work. When Strindberg however began to concentrate more on the new science of psychology, his 'super-naturalism', as he called it, led him towards non-realistic methods of writing and presentation. Similarly, Brecht can be termed a naturalist in that he utilises scientific and political analysis of society in his plays. However, Brecht's plays are non-realistic in form. One final example should make my usage of these two terms clear. Stanislavski developed a system of acting based on the current psychological researches of scientists such as Ribot. His system is thus naturalistic, but it can be utilised in ways that are suitable for the performing of either realistic or non-realistic dramas.

[7] Furst, L. and Skrine, P., op. cit., pp. 9 and 13.

[8] Chekhov, A., quoted in Yarmolinsky, A., op. cit., p. 244.

[9] Chekhov, A., Letter to A. P. Chekhov, 10 May 1886, in Yarmolinsky, A., op. cit., p. 37.

[10] Chekhov, A., Letter to V. Meyerhold, October 1889, in Karlinsky, S. and Heim, M. H., *Anton Chekhov's Life and Thought*, University of California Press, Berkeley, 1975, p. 368.

[11] Chekhov, A., Letter to O. L. Knipper, 2 January 1900, quoted in Tulloch, J., *Chekhov: A Structuralist Study*, Macmillan Press, London, 1980, p. 107.

[12] Chekhov, A., Letter to A. N. Pleshcheyev, 13 November 1888, in Yarmolinsky, A., op. cit., p. 92.

[13] Chekhov, A., Letter to A. N. Pleshcheyev, 9 October 1888, in Karlinsky, S., op. cit., p. 112.

[14] Chekhov, A., 'Fragments', 1885, quoted in Magarshack, D., *Chekhov the Dramatist*, Methuen, London, 1980, p. 23.

[15] Chekhov, A., *A Dreary Story*, in Hingley, R., *The Oxford Chekhov*, Vol. 5, Oxford University Press, London, 1970, p. 48. One opinion that Chekhov did not share with the professor was that plays need not be acted to be appreciated. In 1903 he wrote: 'As a rule I cannot understand plays except on the boards, and therefore I do not like to read plays.' (Chekhov, A., Letter to E. N. Chirikov, 7 October 1903, in Friedland, L. S., *Letters on the Short Story, the Drama, and Other Literary Topics by Anton Chekhov*, Dover Publications, New York, 1966, p. 202.)

[16] Chekhov, A., *A Dreary Story*, p. 49.

[17] Ibid., p. 48.

[18] Chekhov, A., Letter to A. S. Suvorin, 14 February 1889, quoted in Magarshack, D., op. cit., p. 23.

[19] Chekhov, A., Letter to I. L. Leontyev-Shcheglov, 7 November 1888, in Friedland, L. S., op. cit., p. 169.

[20] Fyodor Korsh was a theatrical impresario who ran his own professional theatre and was to stage the first production of Chekhov's *Ivanov*.

[21] Chekhov, A., Letter to A. S. Suvorin, 7 November 1888, in Yarmolinsky, A., op. cit., p. 91.

[22] Chekhov, A., Letter to A. S. Suvorin, 11 November 1888, quoted in Magarshack, D., op. cit., pp. 31–2.

[23] Senelick, L., *Russian Dramatic Theory from Pushkin to the Symbolists: An Anthology*, University of Texas Press, Austin, 1981, p. xxiv.

[24] Rayfield, D., *Chekhov: The Evolution of His Art*, Paul Elek, London, 1975, p. 20.

[25] Chekhov, A., quoted in Rayfield, D., loc. cit.

[26] Mikhail Lentovsky was not a fictional creation. He founded the Mountebank Theatre in Moscow. While his aims had originally been to mount important plays, the theatre's repertory gradually degenerated until nearly all plays presented were 'translated farces, melodramas and *féeries* ... Lentovsky's productions abounded in pyrotechnical displays, explosions, fires, collapsing bridges, and the whole impedimenta of sensationalism'. (Senelick, L., *Anton Chekhov*, Methuen, London, 1985, p. 19.)

[27] Chekhov, A., *Dishonourable Tragedians and Leprous Dramatists*, in Gottlieb, V., *Chekhov and the Vaudeville: A Study of Chekhov's One Act Plays*, Cambridge University Press, Cambridge, 1982, p. 193.

[28] Ibid., p. 194.

[29] Chekhov, A., quoted in Senelick, L., *Anton Chekhov*, p. 19.

[30] Chekhov, A., 'More about Sarah Bernhardt', *Spectator*, 6 December 1881, in Senelick, L., *Russian Dramatic Theory*, p. 86.

[31] Chekhov, A., Letter to A. S. Suvorin, 25 November 1889, in Friedland, L. S., op. cit., p. 193.

[32] Simmons, E. J., *Chekhov: A Biography*, Jonathan Cape, London, 1963, pp. 366–7.

[33] Grant, D., *Realism*, Methuen, London, 1970, p. 64

[34] I have argued that there is no logically necessary link between 'Naturalism' and 'Realism' in the sense in which I have defined the two terms (see this chapter, footnote 6), but, as Gaskell correctly points out, the majority of Naturalistic writers tended to adopt the formal conventions of Realism: 'Does a naturalistic vision of the world entail (it certainly encourages) representational form? Were it not for Brecht we might suppose so ... The naturalistic vision, roughly that of nineteenth-century science, was held, though of course not in quite the same way, by Chekhov, Shaw, Brecht, and in a large part Ibsen. In Brecht alone of these four writers we find it supporting non-representational forms.' (Gaskell, R., op. cit., p. 63.)

[35] Zola, E., quoted in Gaskell, R., op. cit., p. 14.

[36] Gaskell, R., op. cit., p. 60.

[37] Furst, L. and Skrine, P., op. cit., p. 13.

[38] Grant, D., op. cit., p. 9.

[39] Chekhov, A., quoted in Melchinger, S., *Anton Chekhov*, Frederick Ungar, New York, 1972, pp. 74–5.

[40] Hingley, R., *The Oxford Chekhov*, Vol. 2, Oxford University Press, London, 1967, pp. 1–2.

[41] Williams, R., *Drama from Ibsen to Brecht*, Penguin, Harmondsworth, 1968, p. 120.

[42] Ellis-Fermor, U., *The Frontiers of Drama*, Methuen, London, 1964, p. 96.

[43] Robbins, H., *The Dream Merchants*, New English Library, London, 1980, p. 54.
[44] Chekhov, A., Letter to A. S. Suvorin, 30 May 1888, in Yarmolinsky, A., op. cit., p. 71.
[45] Chekhov, A., Letter to A. S. Suvorin, 1 April 1890, in Yarmolinsky, A., op. cit., p. 133.
[46] Hagan, J., 'Chekhov's Fiction and the Idea of "Objectivity"', *Proceedings of the Modern Language Association*, Vol. 81, October 1966, pp. 415 and 417.
[47] Instead of using colourful authorial intrusion like that found in the Harold Robbins example, Chekhov moved to a type of writing that foreshadows that of writers like Robbe-Grillet. H. P. Stowell points out: 'What is immediately striking about the prose of Chekhov and Robbe-Grillet is that they both are drawn to the restraint, precision and laconic flatness of what Roland Barthes has called "zero degree writing". This is neutral colorless prose or what Sartre called *l'ecriture blanche*.' (Stowell, H. P., 'Chekhov and the *nouveau roman*: Subjective Objectivism', in Debreczeny, P. and Eekman, T., eds, *Chekhov's Art of Writing: A Collection of Critical Essays*, Slavica Publishers Inc., Columbus, 1977, p. 184.)
[48] Durkin, A. R., 'Chekhov's Narrative Technique', in Clyman, T. W., op. cit., p. 124.
[49] John Hagan notes that: 'It has become common to speak of this as the technique of the "effaced", "invisible" or "disappearing" narrator, or perhaps even more often, since this is inevitably the procedure of the playwright, as the "dramatic" method.' (Hagan, J., op. cit.)
[50] Ellis-Fermor, U., loc. cit. Ellis-Fermor's use of 'naturally' suggests a weakness in her argument in that she is covertly working on the mistaken assumption that *all* dramatists wish to convey thought 'naturally', that is, as in real life. She is apparently approaching drama with a bias towards realism. This weakness does not affect my argument here, in that Chekhov was one of those writers who *did* wish to express thought 'naturally'.
[51] Ibsen, H., quoted in Williams, R., *Drama from Ibsen to Brecht*, Penguin, Harmondsworth, 1976, p. 40.
[52] Yeats, W. B., quoted in Williams, R., *Drama from Ibsen to Eliot*, Penguin, Harmondsworth, 1964, p. 26.
[53] Pinter, H., 'Writing for the Theatre', in *Pinter Plays*, Vol. 1, Methuen, London, 1976, p. 11.
[54] Chekhov, A., Letter to Alexander Chekhov, 24 October 1887, quoted in Hingley, R., *The Oxford Chekhov*, Vol. 2, p. 285.
[55] Chekhov, A., Letter to A. S. Suvorin, 11 March 1889, in Yarmolinsky, A., op. cit., p. 111.
[56] Chekhov, A., Letter to A. P. Chekhov, 8 May 1889, in Yarmolinsky, A., op. cit., p. 117.
[57] Chekhov, A., Letter to A. P. Chekhov, 11 April 1889, in Karlinsky, S., op. cit., p. 142.
[58] Kuprin, A., 'Reminiscences of Anton Tchekhov', in Koteliansky, S. S., ed., *Anton Tchekhov: Literary and Theatrical Reminiscences*, Benjamin Blom, New York, 1965, p. 80. Ilya Ehrenburg records how Chekhov's almost obsessional demand for the depiction of the simple and ordinary became legendary. 'His fellow writers used to joke: When Chekhov revises a story, he cuts out everything; all that's left is that he and she were young, fell in love, got married and then were unhappy. Chekhov used to reply: But listen, that's just what happens in real life ...' (Ehrenburg, I, *Chekhov, Stendhal and Other Essays*, Macgibbon and Kee, London, 1962, pp. 61–2.)
[59] Jullien, J., quoted in Bentley, E., *The Playwright as Thinker*, Meridian Books, New York, 1960, p. 1.
[60] Chekhov, A., quoted in Melchinger, S., op. cit., p. 75.
[61] Williams, R., *Drama from Ibsen to Eliot*, p. 27.
[62] Ellis-Fermor, U., op. cit., p. 97.
[63] Despite Valency's claim that 'Chekhov's debt to Ibsen was incalculable', (Valency, M., *The Breaking String*, Oxford University Press, London, 1966, p. 143.) there is much evidence that Chekhov disliked Ibsen's approach to drama. He described *Ghosts* as 'a trashy play'. (Magarshack, D., *Chekhov: A Life*, Greenwood Press, Westport, 1970, p. 383.) He failed to watch all of the Moscow Art Theatre's production of *Hedda Gabler* and is reported to have said that 'he did not regard Ibsen as a dramatist'. (Magarshack, D., *Chekhov: A Life*, p. 351.) Nicholas Moravcevich is correct, I believe, in claiming that Chekhov was clearly being ironical when, after a lifetime of criticism of the Norwegian, he wrote to A. L. Vishnevsky, 7 November 1903, asking for tickets for *Pillars of Society* saying, 'I want to have a look at this amazing Norwegian play and will even pay for the privilege. Ibsen is my favourite author, you know.' (Chekhov, A., Letter to A. L. Vishnevsky, 7 November 1903, quoted in Moravcevich, N., 'Chekhov and Naturalism: From Affinity to Divergence', *Comparative Drama*, Vol. 4, No. 4., Winter 1970–71, p. 239.) As Magarshack notes, Chekhov's 'chief criticism of Ibsen ... was that the characters in the great Norwegian's plays did not behave as people do "in life"'. (Magarshack, D., *Chekhov the Dramatist*, pp. 83–4.)

64 Esslin, M., loc. cit.
65 Elsom, J., *Post-war British Theatre*, Routledge and Kegan Paul, London, 1979, pp. 40–1.
66 Ibid., p. 40.
67 Rayfield, D., loc. cit.
68 Chekhov, A., Letter to A. S. Suvorin, 30 May 1888, in Yarmolinsky, A., op. cit., p. 71.
69 Chekhov, A., Letter to A. S. Suvorin, 27 October 1888, in Yarmolinsky, A., op. cit., p. 88.
70 Chekhov, A., Letter to A. S. Suvorin, 1 April 1890, in Yarmolinsky, A., op. cit., p. 133.
71 Chekhov, A., Letter to Ye. M. Shavrova, 28 February 1895, in Yarmolinsky, A., op. cit., pp. 256–7.
72 Chekhov, A., *Three Years* (1895), in Hingley, R., *The Oxford Chekhov*, Vol. 7, Oxford University Press, London, 1978, p. 193.
73 Ibid., p. 192.
74 Chekhov, A., Letter to Ye. M. Shavrova, 16 September 1891, in Friedland, L. S., op. cit., p. 17.
75 Chekhov, A., Letter to Ye. M. Shavrova, 28 February 1895, in Yarmolinsky, A., op. cit., p. 257.
76 Hagan, J., op. cit., p. 414.
77 Chekhov, A., quoted in Melchinger, S., op. cit., p. 75.
78 Tolstoy, L., recalled by Gnedich, P. P., quoted in Pitcher, H., *The Chekhov Play*, Chatto and Windus, London, 1973, p. 1.
79 Tolstoy, L., recalled by Bunin, I., quoted in Pitcher, H., loc. cit.
80 Tolstoy, L., recalled by Gnedich, P. P., quoted in Magarshack, D., *Chekhov the Dramatist*, p. 15.
81 Tolstoy, L., quoted in Magarshack, D., *Chekhov the Dramatist*, p. 16.
82 Long, R. E. C., *Fortnightly Review*, July–December 1902, quoted in Emeljanow, V., ed., *Chekhov: The Critical Heritage*, Routledge and Kegan Paul, London, 1981, p. 67.
83 Chekhov, A., recalled by Kuprin, A., quoted in Laffitte, S., *Chekhov*, Angus and Robertson, London, 1974, p. 16.
84 Kramer, K. D., 'Chekhov at the End of the Eighties: The Question of Identity,' *Études Slaves et Est-Européennes*, Vol. 2, 1966, p. 8.
85 Chekhov, A., *The Party*, in Hingley, R., *The Oxford Chekhov*, Vol. 4, Oxford University Press, London, 1980, pp. 149–50.
86 Chekhov seems to have felt it quite natural to write dialogue which can only be 'read' if a subtextual through-line is supplied. Being an author who was 'paid by the line', Chekhov showed how one could make money from this method of payment. He wrote a piece of dialogue that had only ten words — one to each line! In order to make sense of this dialogue, the reader/spectator must supply a coherent subtext. The dialogue that Chekhov wrote is remarkably similar to the kind of dialogue employed today in exercises used to help train actors to establish a clear and readable subtext (the exercise is called 'interpretations'). Chekhov's dialogue is as follows:
'Listen!'
'What?'
'Native?'
'Who?'
'You.'
'I?'
'Yes!'
'No.'
'Pity!'
'H'm.'
(Chekhov, A., quoted in Nemirovich-Danchenko, V., op. cit., p. 17.)
87 Chekhov, A., *A Dreary Story*, in Hingley, R., *The Oxford Chekhov*, Vol. 5, Oxford University Press, London, 1970, p. 55.
88 Chekhov, A., *The Duel*, in Hingley, R., *The Oxford Chekhov*, Vol. 5, p. 207.
89 Chekhov, A., *Ariadne*, in Hingley, R., *The Oxford Chekhov*, Vol. 8, Oxford University Press, London, 1965, p. 76.
90 Ibid., p. 91.
91 Chekhov, A., *A Lady with a Dog*, in Hingley, R., *The Oxford Chekhov*, Vol. 9, Oxford University Press, London, 1975, p. 139.

92 Shakespeare, W., *Julius Caesar*, Act II, Scene i, 10.
93 Atkinson, B., *New York Times*, 11 March 1928, quoted in Emeljanow, V., op. cit., p. 326.
94 See Timmer, C. B., 'The Bizarre Elements in Chekhov's Art', in Eekman, T., ed., *Anton Cechow, 1860–1960: Some Essays*, E. J. Brill, Leiden, 1960, pp. 277–92.
95 Chekhov, A., *Uncle Vanya*, in Hingley, R., *The Oxford Chekhov*, Vol. 3, Oxford University Press, London, 1964, p. 58.
96 Ibid., p. 66.
97 Timmer, C. B., op. cit., p. 278.
98 States, B. O., *Irony and Drama: A Poetics*, Cornell University Press, Ithaca, 1971, p. 71.
99 Pitcher, H., op. cit., pp. 24–5.
100 Chekhov, A., *Three Sisters*, in Hingley, R., *The Oxford Chekhov*, Vol. 3, p. 116.
101 Nemirovich-Danchenko, V., quoted in Nilsson, N. A., 'Intonation and Rhythm in Cechov's Plays', in Eekman, T., op. cit., p. 170.
102 Nilsson, N. A., op. cit., p. 171.
103 Magarshack, D., *Chekhov the Dramatist*, p. 169.
104 Ibid., p. 164.
105 McFarlane, J., 'Intimate Theatre: Maeterlinck to Strindberg', in Bradbury, M. and McFarlane, J., eds, *Modernism*, Penguin, Harmondsworth, 1981, p. 518.
106 Wimsatt, W. K., 'The Two Meanings of Symbolism', *Hateful Contraries*, Kentucky University Press, Kentucky, 1965, p. 53.
107 Ibid.
108 Borny, G. J., 'The Subjective and Objective Levels of Reality in Chekhov's *Ivanov* and *The Cherry Orchard*: A Study in Dramatic Technique', unpublished honours thesis, University of New South Wales, 1969, p. 58.
109 Senelick, L., *Anton Chekhov*, p. 128.

# Chapter 3. Failed Experiments: The Early Plays

*Literature, like art, serves one constructive aim and function: to reproduce the world outside, though it is not of course to be a carbon copy; the creative intelligence must not only render the truth of reality but also interpret and evaluate it.* (Charles I. Glicksberg)[1]

*... it has been thought possible to create a new drama by filling the old forms with the contents of the newer age; but ... we have not got the new form for the contents, and the new wine has burst the old bottles.* (August Strindberg)[2]

Chekhov did not immediately find the dramatic form that would function as the perfect objective correlative of his vision of reality. He began his career as a playwright by adopting the conventions of earlier well-established dramatic genres. As with his short-story writing, Chekhov underwent a period of literary apprenticeship before he was able to free himself from the use of these outdated and inappropriate techniques. As Simon Karlinsky points out: 'It was in *The Seagull* that this liberation first occurred, the creative breakthrough which made Chekhov as much an innovator in the field of drama as he already was in the art of prose narrative.'[3]

As Karlinsky suggests, Chekhov developed new formal techniques appropriate to convey his vision in the two quite different genres of the short story and the drama. Chekhov's fame as a playwright today has partially obscured the fact that, for most of his literary career, he was better known as a prolific short-story writer.[4] Chekhov applied many of the techniques he had developed for the short story to the writing of his later plays, and, in particular, he carried over into his later dramatic technique an avoidance of overt theatricality. As Joseph Wood Krutch correctly notes: 'The very soul of his method [in short story writing] had always been the avoidance of anything artificially 'dramatic' and he was wise enough not to alter it when he came to write drama.'[5]

In an attempt to emphasise the fact that Chekhov was a man of the theatre whose 'only reason for writing a play was the likelihood of its being performed on the stage',[6] David Magarshack undervalues the importance of Chekhov's short-story techniques in the development of his dramatic techniques. He incorrectly suggests that Chekhov did not have to learn his craft as a dramatist:

> Chekhov was not, as is generally supposed, a great short-story writer who took up drama seriously only during the last seven or eight years of his all too short life. He was a born dramatist whose first works of importance were three

full-length plays, two written in his late teens and the third in his early twenties.[7]

Magarshack is correct in his observation that many critics of Chekhov's day regarded him primarily as a writer of narrative fiction. Despite having written several highly successful vaudevilles and three full-length dramas, *Platonov, Ivanov,* and *The Wood Demon,* an early version of *Uncle Vanya,* Chekhov had become so associated with the genre of the short story that, when *The Seagull* was first produced in 1896, he was still not thought of as being primarily a playwright. A disgruntled spectator at the first performance of *The Seagull* is reported to have muttered, 'Why doesn't he stick to short stories?'[8]

Magarshack is also right to emphasise Chekhov's early interest in the theatre. We know that when he was a schoolboy in Taganrog, he had gone to the theatre regularly and that he wrote the early plays that Magarshack refers to. However, it was not until he wrote *The Seagull* that Chekhov developed the dramatic techniques that could adequately express his vision, and this occurred *after* he had mastered the narrative techniques appropriate for his short stories and utilised several of them in his evolving dramatic form.

Chekhov's earliest theatrical efforts, which have not survived, were parodies of the theatrical fare that he had witnessed in Taganrog, and reflect his dissatisfaction with many of these offerings. According to Donald Rayfield, Chekhov saw a wide range of mainly European drama when he was a schoolboy and he 'reacted in his first letters and parodies against the spectacular histrionics of Hugo's drama or Italian opera'.[9] Despite this early manifestation of his dislike of overt theatricality, Chekhov did not avoid this same fault in his first plays. His initial dramatic successes were 'vaudevilles', which employed precisely the kind of theatrical clichés and superficial characterisation that he supposedly despised. Chekhov was aware that his theatrical practice did not match his ideal of theatrical realism. Consequently, it is not surprising that he regarded his vaudevilles simply as lucrative potboilers with little artistic merit. Just as he was scornful of many of his early short stories, regarding them as superficial and derivative, for the same reasons, he regarded much of his early dramatic writing as worthless. Ronald Hingley succinctly outlines Chekhov's attitude to these comic one-acters:

> As was his way, Chekhov disparaged his vaudevilles. He called *The Proposal* 'a wretched, vulgar, boring little skit … a lousy little farce'; and referred to *A Tragic Role* as 'a stale farce which falls flat', being based on 'a stale hackneyed joke'. Still, he appreciated the boost to his income. He was 'living on my dole from *The Bear*', he wrote; it was his 'milch cow'. Any author of ten tolerable vaudevilles could regard his future as assured, he said, for they were as profitable as sixty acres of land. He planned to write a hundred such farces a year, 'vaudeville subjects gush out of me like oil from the Baku wells'.[10]

One vaudeville, whose title is variously translated as *Smoking Is Bad for You* or *On the Harmfulness of Tobacco*, is of particular interest because we have several different versions of the play which demonstrate Chekhov's growing control of the dramatic techniques he was to use in his last four tragi-comedies. Taking only two and a half hours to write, *Smoking Is Bad for You* originally appeared in print in 1886, but, as Hingley recounts: 'it underwent a series of six recensions spread over sixteen years, only attaining its final form in September 1902'.[11]

The original version was regarded by Chekhov as a worthless piece of juvenilia, but his final revision pleased the author enough for him to write to A. F. Marks, the publisher of his *Complete Collected Works*, suggesting that the monologue be included in that edition:

> Among works of mine transmitted to you is the farce *Smoking Is Bad for You*, which is one of the items that I asked you to exclude from my *Complete Collected Works* and never print ... Now I have written a completely new play with the same title, *Smoking Is Bad for You*, keeping only the surname of the *dramatis personae*, and I send it to you for inclusion in volume vii.[12]

Commenting on his original version of the play published in the *Petersburg Gazette* in 1886, Chekhov wrote: 'I have made a mess of this monologue ... My intentions were good, but the execution was execrable.'[13] Clearly, his statement to his publisher that his final version was 'a completely new play' suggests that he felt that there was a radical difference between the various versions. Presumably he felt that both his intentions and his execution were satisfactory in the last version.

An overall description of the nature of this comic monologue and the principal changes that Chekhov undertook is given by Ernest Simmons in his biography of the writer:

> The changes between the first and last version of this slight sketch admirably illustrate the transformation that had taken place in Chekhov's approach to the revelation of character on the stage. In the first version Nyukhin's monologue before the club audience on the harmfulness of tobacco, which his tyrant of a wife compels him to deliver for the purpose of advertising the girls' school she runs, is designed solely to amuse the audience by external comic effects which derive from the oddities, vagaries, and rambling speech of this pathetic old man who is lecturing on a subject which he knows nothing about. In the final version the emphasis has entirely changed. Most of the external comic effects have vanished. Here, Nyukhin's monologue amounts to a subtle psychological analysis of the inner man. He reveals himself, not as he appears in real life, which had been the emphasis in the first version, but as he really is – a man whose fine qualities have been distorted and wantonly destroyed over the years by an insensitive, selfish, and dominating wife.[14]

The significance of the changes has been noted by several critics. Magarshack has argued that:

> It is, indeed, highly probable that Chekhov used this play ... for his experiments in the new method of writing dramatic dialogue which depends for its main effect on inner rather than outer action.[15]

In the final version, Magarshack argues, 'what matters is a character's inward reaction to the circumstances of his life and not the circumstances themselves'.[16] Vera Gottlieb likewise recognises the radical nature of Chekhov's revisions. She argues that:

> As a result of these ... alterations, the emphasis of the play shifts increasingly from the 'comic scene' of a man giving a lecture on a subject that he clearly knows nothing about, to a tragi-comic emphasis on the man himself ...[17]

Chekhov was justified in referring to his final version of *Smoking Is Bad for You* as a new play for, in the course of rewriting, he radically transformed the play's form from a farce to a tragi-comedy.

In the 1889 version, Nyukhin is a stereotypical character, the hen-pecked husband, who is presented as an object of fun, to be laughed at for his comic pratfalls. Even his asthma attack, which potentially could arouse audience sympathy, is treated in a manner that forces an audience to focus on the character's ludicrous behaviour rather than on his suffering:

> NYUKHIN. ... Give me air! [*Balances with his arms and legs to stop himself falling over.*] Whew! Just a moment! Let me get my breath back! Just a moment. One minute. I shall stop this attack by sheer will-power. [*Beats his chest with his fist.*] That will do. Gosh! [*A minute's pause, during which* NYUKHIN *walks up and down the stage panting.*][18]

This early version contains many physical jokes that remind one of the *lazzi* of commedia dell'arte. In the version written a year later, in 1890, much of the physicality is toned down or omitted. Nyukhin's medical complaint is changed from asthma to hiccups. While 'business' still plays an important part in the play, the onset of hiccups is less of a physical tour de force than the asthma attack:

> NYUKHIN. ... Tobacco is, mainly, a plant. [*Hiccups.*] I've got hiccups. A most convenient thing to have too, I might add. It makes you hold your breath and wait a bit. [*A pause of one minute during which* NYUKHIN *stands motionless.*][19]

Even the difference between the 1889 stage direction in which Nyukhin 'walks up and down' and the 1890 stage direction which states that the character 'stands motionless' suggests that Chekhov was moving away from overt histrionics towards a more subtle and realistic presentation of character and situation.

The kind of acting required for the 1902 version of *Smoking Is Bad for You* is essentially realistic and reflects Chekhov's increasing 'avoidance of anything artificially "dramatic"'. As Magarshack says:

> The acting he had in mind for his plays, Chekhov made it clear, did not mean rushing about the stage and expressing emotions by means of gestures. Strong emotion, he pointed out, should be expressed on the stage as it is expressed in life by cultured people, that is to say, not with one's hands and feet, but with the tone of one's voice and with one's eyes, not by gesticulating but by always keeping one's poise.[20]

In effect, the final version of this comic monologue requires the kind of realistic acting technique that was being systematised by Stanislavski; a technique that required the actor to play not simply the text, but also to present an implied subtext. A simple but useful definition of 'subtext' and its relationship to the 'text' is provided by I. Rapaport: 'The written words of the role constitute the text. But *the purpose for which the words are spoken, their inner meaning, we call the "sub-text"*.'[21] What Chekhov had learned by the time he made his final revision of *Smoking Is Bad for You* was how to create characters who had two lives. One life was the externalised objective life that was presented in the text, and the other was the secret subjective inner life that was presented in an implied subtext. The creation of this double life was what enabled audiences to perceive the gap that exists between his characters' subjective and often tragic lives and their objective and often comic behaviour. Through this formal device Chekhov was able to communicate his vision of reality.

In the 1890 version of *Smoking Is Bad for You*, Chekhov attempted to move away from the depiction of Nyukhin's character simply through the presentation of his overt comic behaviour. Chekhov wished to create a subtextual existence for his character but, as yet, he was only able to *state* rather than *imply* that Nyukhin has two lives:

> NYUKHIN. ... 'Children,' I always tell my wife's daughters, 'don't laugh at me. After all, you don't know what's going on inside me.'[22]

Nyukhin tells us that: 'it's better not to get married'.[23] This insight is something that we are left to deduce for ourselves in the final 1903 version. Again, in this 1890 version, the pathetic Nyukhin tells us: 'I've meekly accepted the punishment which she has inflicted on me.'[24] In the final version no such explicit judgement about the character's spineless behaviour is made. It is left to the audience to pass judgement on Nyukhin's pathetic abdication of responsibility for his wasted life.

## Interpreting Chekhov

Finding ways to let an audience know what was going on inside his characters without having them tell the audience directly was a problem Chekhov found difficult to solve in his early plays. The 1903 version of *Smoking Is Bad for You* illustrates how he came to solve this problem.

In this final version Nyukhin does not suffer either from asthma or the hiccups. Instead, Chekhov gives the character a nervous twitch. While asthma, hiccupping and twitching all manifest themselves in a physically comic manner in the text, it is only twitching that implies that there is some subtextual psychological cause. This particular physical behaviour immediately suggests the existence of an inner life. We witness a human being undergoing a breakdown in front of our eyes. Nyukhin desperately and ludicrously attempts to present only the outer life where he pretends to be happy about giving a lecture on the harmfulness of tobacco. As his twitching gets worse, so the happy facade he tries to present crumbles and elements from his tragic subtextual life bubble up and break into the text for all of us to see. Here is a man who, like Andrew [Andrey] in *Three Sisters* and Vanya in *Uncle Vanya*, has wasted his life and, what is more important, knows it.

The moment of recognition arrives for Nyukhin towards the end of the play when he talks about the effect that alcohol has on him. The very mention of the subject causes all of his defences against facing the truth to fall and his subtextually implied tragic inner life can no longer be hidden. His unhappiness becomes overtly presented in the text. What Nyukhin describes as the effects of drink precisely describe the dual experience of Chekhovian tragi-comedy. As audience members we have laughed at the stereotypical hen-pecked male, but now we are forced to see the pathos of Nyukhin's situation and experience Chekhov's implied criticism of this character for wasting his potential:

> One glass is enough to make me drunk, I might add. It feels good, but indescribably sad at the same time. Somehow the days of my youth come back to me, I somehow long — more than you can possibly imagine — to escape. [*Carried away.*] To run away, leave everything behind and run away without a backward glance. Where to? Who cares? If only I could escape from this rotten, vulgar, tawdry existence that's turned me into a pathetic old clown and imbecile! Escape from this stupid, petty, vicious, nasty, spiteful, mean old cow of a wife who's made my life a misery for thirty-three years! Escape from the music, the kitchen, my wife's money and all those vulgar trivialities ... I don't need anything. I'm above all these low, dirty things. Once I was young and clever and went to college. I had dreams and I felt like a human being. Now I want nothing — nothing but a bit of peace and quiet.[25]

Gottlieb is surely correct in her analysis of how this sort of recognition scene is intended to function in this and the four major plays. It is not simply Nyukhin who is intended to see that he has wasted his life. In Chekhov's plays, including the 1903 version of *Smoking Is Bad for You*:

> ... the characters are brought to a point of recognition; and with the characters, so an audience is brought to a similar point of recognition and realisation not to wallow in sad resignation, but — held at a distance — to observe that things need not be so: in Gorky's quotation of Chekhov's words, 'You live badly, my friends. It is shameful to live like that.'[26]

Increasingly, Chekhov came to share Strindberg's belief that expressing a new vision of reality through the use of outdated dramatic conventions was like trying to put new wine into old bottles. Several of his early plays, including *Platonov*, *Ivanov* and *The Wood Demon*, were frustrating attempts at 'filling the old forms with the contents of a newer age'. All of these plays utilised the stock characters and situations of romantic melodrama, and the early versions of *Smoking Is Bad for You* likewise followed the tried and true conventions of vaudeville. The various versions of *Smoking Is Bad for You* clearly illustrate Chekhov's struggle to find a new form and involve him in a movement away from what Magarshack calls plays of 'direct action' to those of 'indirect action'. Increasingly, he sought to present the actuality of life.

What Gottlieb says of the revisional process employed in the multiple versions of *Smoking Is Bad for You* applies equally to the method that Chekhov adopted when he transformed his early melodramatic full-length play, *The Wood Demon*, into the tragi-comedy *Uncle Vanya*. In both cases the 'theatrical' was replaced by the 'realistic':

> Out of the conventional laughing-stock of the hen-pecked husband Chekhov creates a character who is completely three-dimensional, and the balance between the pathetic and the comic is seen very clearly in the characterisation.[27]

It is quite easy for us today to fail to see just how radical Chekhov's innovations were in terms of playwrighting technique. His highly realistic approach to writing, combined with the Stanislavski-inspired realistic approach to acting, has become the theatrical norm of twentieth-century Western theatre practice. At the time when he wrote, however, overt theatricality was the norm in both dramatic writing and acting style. One look at the plot of *Platonov* immediately shows us that realism was not the natural idiom of this fledgling playwright, who initially adopted many of the conventions of late nineteenth-century romantic melodrama.

*Platonov* is almost certainly the play that Chekhov's brother, Mikhail, refers to in his introduction to the second volume of *Letters of A. P. Chekhov*, when he wrote that: 'While he was a student he wrote a long play with the ardent hope of having it presented on the stage of the Maly Theatre, Moscow.'[28] In this elephantine play, which runs to one hundred and thirty-four pages in the original manuscript, exciting theatricality overpowers any sense of human reality. The depiction of sensational events takes precedence over any attempt at psychological consistency in characterisation. Donald Rayfield's outline of some of the main features of the plot clearly illustrates how much the student Chekhov's dramatic technique owed to the histrionic tradition of melodrama:

> In the course of the play, he [Platonov] arranges to elope with his best friend's wife, Sophia, for a 'new life', but he almost succumbs to the best friend's stepmother, the young widow Anna Petrovna Voynitseva, and he flirts with and assaults the rich and eligible Grekova. He is a catastrophic disrupter: his wife, Sasha, tries to kill herself by throwing herself on the railway line (on stage) and then by eating matches (off stage); the horse-thief, Osip, in the nature of familiar spirit to other characters, tries to murder Platonov; his friend, Sergey Voynitsev, nearly dies of despair; Sophia is so angered by Platonov's betrayal that she kills him ... *Platonov* reads like an abandoned and hastily dramatised novel. It makes incredible demands on stage effects ...[29]

*Platonov* was never performed in Chekhov's lifetime. Its main interest lies in its evidence of Chekhov's experimentation with dramatic form. The subtle blending of tragedy with comedy, the hallmark of Chekhov's four mature plays, is nowhere evident in *Platonov*. The play swings wildly between a number of generic forms, and the tone is equally variable. Rayfield notes that in this play, Chekhov mixes 'the tragedy of Platonov with the melodrama of the horse-thief Osip, the comedy of the intriguing guests plotting profitable marriages, and the sheer farce of the hero's incompetent handling of four infatuated women.'[30]

In his mature plays, instead of alternating wildly between different genres, Chekhov developed a technique for creating synthetic tragi-comedy. In these later plays, events are both tragic and comic at the same time, and the audience's response is made to oscillate between laughter and tears. In these late plays melodrama and farce are not given equal status with tragedy and comedy, as they are in *Platonov*, but are employed in a parodic manner that does not upset the overall tragi-comic tone.

The first full-length play by Chekhov to be performed was *Ivanov*. He had been asked by a Moscow theatre owner, Fyodor Korsh, to write a play for production at his theatre. Despite frequently denying that he would take on such a task, Chekhov quickly wrote *Ivanov* in October 1887. This play, which is still performed today, is a transitional piece showing features that we recognise as typical of the late realistic tragi-comedies, combined with the continuing legacy of the 'theatrics' that are so evident in *Platonov*.

At the time when Chekhov wrote *Ivanov* he had already worked out in theory what he wished to achieve with his writings. Certainly at the time when he was completing a revised version of the play to be performed in 1889, Chekhov was able to articulate his artistic aims with great clarity. In a letter to A. N. Pleshcheyev, Chekhov outlined a dual artistic aim that remained of central importance to him throughout his career: 'My goal is to kill two birds with one stone: to paint life in its true aspects, and to show how far this life falls short of the ideal life.'[31]

*Ivanov* failed to achieve the lifelike realism Chekhov sought, though it was certainly much closer to life than *Platonov* had been. However, much to Chekhov's frustration, the second part of his artistic aim continued to elude him.

Several critics have suggested that prior to the late eighteen-eighties, Chekhov had simply wished to depict life as it is, with total objectivity, and that the introduction of the second subjective element that expressed his attitude towards such a life was a major change in his artistic aims. Nicholas Moravcevich writes of Chekhov's 'mellowing' in his views. He claims that he underwent an 'aesthetic transformation' that involved the rejection of his 'youthful aesthetic creed' which had been based on 'his commitment to strict objectivity, which condemned concern with a "message", and denied any usefulness of a didactic stance in the presentation of reality'.[32]

Similarly, Magarshack argues that a radical change occurred in Chekhov's artistic credo and asserts that Chekhov's letter to Suvorin written on 25 November 1892, 're-defined his position as a writer by finally relinquishing his stand-point of strict objectivity and placing the 'aim' of a work of art, i.e. its moral purpose, at the head of all its other distinguishing marks.'[33]

In fact, Chekhov did not abandon his views about the need for the artist to be objective in his writing, nor did he suddenly undergo some Damascan experience which caused him to see the light and be converted into a socially committed writer. John Hagan is essentially correct when he claimed of Chekhov that: 'After 1888, nothing could be clearer of course than his insistence that the artist's work exhibit a distinct "aim" or "intention" by which he meant not only an aesthetic purpose, but a philosophic and moral one.'[34]

Where I believe critics like Hagan, Moravcevich and Magarshack are misleading is in their assertion that Chekhov's aesthetic creed had radically changed. Chekhov's greater volubility in the late eighteen-eighties concerning his artistic aims resulted less from any changes in his artistic creed than from a growing sense of frustration with the realistic form he had employed in writing his plays. Increasingly, this form was proving inadequate to communicate his vision of reality. The world view, which he had hoped was being expressed in his works, was constantly being either overlooked or misinterpreted by readers, audiences and critics.

Chekhov came to realise that his use of the conventions of realism and his objective non-judgemental character depiction were adequate means to communicate a picture of 'life as it is' in all its triviality. However, these same means were not proving adequate to communicate the playwright's criticism of such a life. The critical attitude that he expected his readers and audiences to have in response to the waste of human potential being depicted in his plays did not occur. Both critics and audiences misinterpreted what he was trying to say. The critical reaction to *Ivanov* was to make Chekhov aware that he had not yet created the form needed to communicate his vision.

Chekhov wrote the first draft of *Ivanov* in two weeks. In October 1887, having read and discussed his play with V. N. Davydov who was to play the title role and who loved the play, Chekhov wrote to his novelist friend Yezhov:

> If I am to believe such judges as Davydov, then I know how to write plays. It seems that instinctively, because of some kind of flair, and without being aware of [it] myself, I have written an entirely finished piece and not made a single stage error.[35]

At about the same time, he wrote to his brother Alexander and recounted a similarly enthusiastic response to his play by Korsh who was to present the first production of *Ivanov* at his theatre. Significantly Chekhov's pleasure at the uncritical gushing praise he was receiving from these theatre luminaries was tempered by his own gently sceptical attitude toward his work:

> It took two weeks, or rather ten days, as I had some days off or wrote other things. I can't tell how good it is ... Everybody likes it. Korsh hasn't found anything wrong or unstageworthy in it — which shows what fine, sensitive judges I have. It's my first play, so there are bound to be some mistakes.[36]

In November of the same year we find Chekhov writing to his brother about *Ivanov* in a far less happy fashion: 'You'll never guess what happened. This play ... this wretched piece of crap — it's got completely out of hand.'[37]

This change in Chekhov's attitude was partly due to the fact that rehearsals had gone badly, but the main reason for the playwright's anguish was the reaction of the Moscow press after the first performance at Korsh's Theatre. As far as Chekhov was concerned, they had totally misinterpreted his play. One reviewer described *Ivanov* as being 'essentially immoral and repulsive, a highly cynical libel on contemporary life and people'.[38]

Chekhov should not have believed 'such judges as Davydov'. Both Davydov and Korsh had been brought up in a theatrical milieu that thrived on melodrama and the cheap theatricality that Chekhov was trying to break away from. Davydov was not equipped to act, nor Korsh to direct, in the style suitable for Chekhovian drama. It seems, at first sight, surprising that these two theatre people should have liked *Ivanov* at all. However, a closer examination of *Ivanov* provides us with a reason for their positive response.

Chekhov had failed to write the realistic play that he thought he had written. What Korsh and Davydov had responded to in *Ivanov* were the theatrical elements that they recognised. They felt comfortable with the play's melodramatic *coups de théatre*. Perhaps unconsciously, Chekhov had largely conformed to the rules of the Scribean well-made play. It was the inherent 'Sardoodledom' which Korsh and Davydov had joyfully recognised. The ending of Act II in which Ivanov is caught by his wife Sarah in the act of kissing Sasha could hardly be more clichéd:

> SASHA. ... I love you Nicholas. I'll follow you to the ends of the earth, I'll go wherever you like, I'll die if need be, only for God's sake let it be soon, or I shall choke.
> IVANOV. [*With a peal of happy laughter.*] What does all this mean? Can I start a new life then Sasha? My happiness! [*Draws her to him.*] My youth, my innocence! [ANNA comes in from the garden, sees her husband and SASHA, and stands rooted to the spot.]
> IVANOV. So I'm to live, then, am I? And start work again? [They kiss. After the kiss IVANOV and SASHA look round and see ANNA.]
> IVANOV. [*In horror.*] Sarah!
>
> CURTAIN.[39]

There is no detectable irony or humour in this scene. In *Uncle Vanya* the equivalent situation where Vanya comes across Helen being kissed by Astrov is treated as being ludicrous rather than straining for dramatic effect as in *Ivanov*. In the early play the cliché is simply a cliché while in *Uncle Vanya* it is given new life by being comically subverted.

The old-fashioned and derivative form of *Ivanov* is apparent in the original ending that Chekhov wrote for the play. Just as the grotesque melodramatic events and heightened rhetorical language found in *Platonov* contradict Chekhov's stated aims of putting life as it is on the stage, so the original finale of *Ivanov* shows Chekhov's failure to jettison the clichéd techniques that were inappropriate to the achievement of his aim. The hustle and bustle of the external action copiously specified in the stage instructions may well have been happily accepted by Korsh and Davydov, who would almost certainly have had little difficulty in playing this nonsense.

*Ivanov* ends with Dr Lvov entering and 'unmasking' Ivanov on the day that the latter has just married Sasha. In the middle of the celebration Lvov bursts in and proclaims loudly 'Nicholas Ivanov, I want everyone to hear. You are the most unmitigated swine!' The stage instruction, reminiscent of the *consternation générale* so admired by French melodramatists, is predictably '[*Hubbub in the Ballroom*]'. The final scene of the play then follows:

## SCENE IX

[LVOV, IVANOV, SHABELSKY, LEBEDEV, BORKIN *and* KOSYKH, *followed by* SASHA. IVANOV *runs in from the ballroom, clutching his head. He is followed by the others.*]

IVANOV. What's that for? Tell me why? [*Collapses on the sofa.*]

ALL. Why? What for?

LEBEDEV. [*To* LVOV.] For Christ's sake, why did you insult him? [*Clutches his head and walks about in agitation.*]

SHABELSKY. [*To* IVANOV.] Nicholas, Nicholas! For God's sake — pay no attention. Show yourself above it all.

BORKIN. That was a rotten thing to say, sir. I challenge you to a duel.

LVOV. Mr Borkin, I consider it degrading even to exchange words with you, let alone fight a duel. As for Mr Ivanov, he can receive satisfaction any moment if he wishes.

SASHA. [*Comes in from the ballroom, staggering.*] Why? Why did you insult my husband? … [*To her husband.*] Let's get out of here, Nicholas. [*Takes his arm.*]

LEBEDEV. [*To* LVOV.] As head of the household, as father of my son-in-law — that is of my daughter, sir –

[SASHA *shrieks and falls on her husband. Everyone runs up to* IVANOV.]

LEBEDEV. God, he's dead! Get some water! Fetch a doctor.

[SHABELSKY *weeps.*]

ALL. Fetch water, a doctor, he's dead.

CURTAIN.[40]

The first two acts of *Ivanov* are equally 'theatrical' in the Scribean sense. It is true that in this play people do 'come and go, eat, … and play cards'. There is a great deal of 'eating, drinking, flirting, and saying foolish things', but instead of all this replacing the intrigue-based plots of the well-made play, the trivial day-to-day incidents are additional to the plethora of 'theatrical' events that occur in the play.

Eventually Chekhov did revise *Ivanov* and removed the unacceptable ending where Ivanov literally dies of shame. He replaced this unconvincing ending by having the 'hero' shoot himself. The problem with such a change was that, while it was less ludicrous than the original ending, it conformed even more obviously to the type of 'direct action' drama that Chekhov wished to avoid. The more 'theatrically' acceptable his changes were, the less they fitted his aim to put life on the stage.

It is not only the mechanical plot structure and the theatrical incidents that make *Ivanov* unlifelike. The characterisation itself is often lifeless and two-dimensional. The most theatrically alive characters are creations like Kosykh who is forever talking about his disastrous hands of bridge. This card-playing fanatic is drawn not from life but from the tried and true tradition of the comic vaudeville plays of which Chekhov was a master. While Chekhov was to make use of such comic types in his later plays, he was to transform them into three-dimensional characters with an inner life. The one-dimensionality of the Nyukhin character in the original version of *Smoking Is Bad for You* is also characteristic of Kosykh, who has no dialogue or existence that does not relate to his comic obsession with bridge:

> KOSYKH. [*Tearfully.*] Look here everyone. I held a run — the ace, king, queen and seven small diamonds, the ace of spades and one small heart, see? And she couldn't declare a little slam, damn it! I bid no trumps.[41]

A similar lack of realistic three-dimensionality is to be found in even the main characters in *Ivanov*. Dr Lvov's constant harping on the subject of honesty and Ivanov's whining guilt both have a fixed and wooden quality that remind one of the characters that Strindberg attacked in his Foreword to *Miss Julie:*

> A character came to signify a man fixed and finished: one who invariably appeared either drunk or jocular or melancholy, and characterisation required nothing more than a physical defect such as a club foot, a wooden leg, a red nose; or the fellow might be made to repeat some such phrase as 'that's capital!' or 'Barkis is willing'.[42]

Chekhov, who inveighed against this type of clichéd characterisation whenever he was advising friends or relatives on how to write, was unable to avoid using these clichés himself.

We are fortunate that the normally reticent Chekhov has left behind a considerable amount of detailed information in his letters concerning the problems with *Ivanov*. The first time he became aware that all was not well was during early rehearsals for the play's first production. In a letter to his brother Alexander in which he stated that he 'wanted to be original' by avoiding the depiction of clichéd stereotypes, Chekhov expressed his concerns about whether he had achieved this aim:

> I don't know if I've succeeded. Korsh and the actors are certain it will come off, but I'm not sure. The actors don't understand, they bungle things, they take wrong parts — while I struggle on thinking the play's doomed if they don't keep my casting. If they don't do it my way I'll have to withdraw it, or we'll have a fiasco on our hands.[43]

Almost immediately Chekhov was aware that his play was likely to be misinterpreted. Korsh's and Davydov's initial enthusiasm for the play seems to have misled the young playwright. He assumed that their enthusiasm was based on an understanding of how his play worked. What these two practitioners understood and responded to was the play's old-fashioned theatricality. Chekhov knew that there were stale elements in his play, but he was not concerned about this. What pleased him most was the characterisation of Ivanov which he felt was innovative in an important way:

> The plot's involved and rather clever. I finish each act like my short stories, conducting it quietly and peacefully, but with a pinch on the nose for the audience at the end. I've put my entire energy into a few really powerful, vivid scenes, but the linking passages are weak, feeble and hackneyed. Still I'm pleased. Bad as the play may be, I've created an important literary type and a part that only an actor as good as Davydov would take, a part for the actor to expand in and show his paces ...[44]

The whole experience of rehearsals was traumatic for Chekhov. He thought the production was severely under-rehearsed and complained to his brother Alexander that:

> Korsh promised ten rehearsals, but had only four, and only two of those can really be called rehearsals because the other two were just occasions for the distinguished cast to indulge in slanging matches with each other. Only Davydov [Ivanov] and Glama [Anna] knew their parts. The others got by with the aid of the prompter and their own inspiration.[45]

To another friend he expressed his disillusionment with the production process:

> Unexpectedly my damn play has taken so much out of me that I've lost track of time. I've gone off the rails and I'm heading for a nervous breakdown. It was easy enough to write, but staging it means a lot of nervous strain ...[46]

The anguish of the self-styled '"aspiring" playwright who suddenly finds himself a square peg in a round hole',[47] was expressed in the letter to Nikolai Leykin in which he listed eight complaints. These eight Chekhov felt highlighted only the most glaring concerns. He asserted that: 'There's material enough for another twenty items.'[48]

Korsh is described in complaint number three as 'a business man who just wants a full house and doesn't care about the success of actors and play'.[49] Chekhov found the actors, as a group, to be 'spoilt, selfish, semi-educated and opinionated. They loathe each other and some of them would sell their souls to the devil to stop a colleague getting a good part'.[50] The despairing playwright felt that: 'the one consolation is that Davydov and Kiselevsky will be brilliant'.[51] Even that hope was dashed. After the first performance, Chekhov wrote to his brother Alexander:

> ... I fail to recognise my own play right from the start. Kiselevsky [Shabelsky], of whom I was hoping a lot, did not get one sentence right — literally *not one*, he was ad-libbing ... [In Act IV] Kiselevsky came on. It's a poetic, soul-stirring passage, but friend Kiselevsky doesn't know his lines and is drunk as a lord.

## Failed Experiments: The Early Plays

So a short, poetic dialogue turns into something sluggish and off-putting. The audience is baffled. At the end of the play the hero dies as the result of an insult too great for him to bear. The audience, bored and tired by this time, doesn't understand why he dies.[52]

At the time of the first performance of *Ivanov*, Chekhov was so close to his own play that he could not see that its failure was due not only to the poor acting, but also to his own inexperience as a playwright. He was later to acknowledge his own share in the play's failure to communicate his vision. At the time, however, the painful experience of this initial production led Chekhov to articulate what amounts to a Bill of Rights for playwrights. He was never to relinquish his belief that ultimately the role of theatre artists was to serve the playwright by working within the parameters and tolerances determined by the 'commanding form' of the play. Only nine months before he died, he wrote to Nemirovich-Danchenko, the co-founder of the Moscow Art Theatre, that 'the important thing is to have a play in which one can feel the author's shaping idea'.[53]

Feeling that Korsh and the actors were missing his 'shaping idea', Chekhov had attempted to give them advice at rehearsals. Soon after being advised by Nikolai Leykin that such involvement by the playwright was inappropriate, Chekhov replied with his playwright's Bill of Rights:

> Your lines about production of plays puzzle me. You write that the author only gets in the production's way, makes the actors uncomfortable, and more often than not contributes only the most inane comments. Let me answer you thusly: (1) the play is the author's property, not the actors'; (2) where the author is present, casting the play is his responsibility; (3) *all* my comments to date have improved the production, and they have all been put into practice, as I indicated; (4) the actors themselves ask for my comments; ... If you reduce author participation to a naught, what the hell will you come up with? Remember how Gogol raged when they put on his play! [First production of *The Inspector General*] And wasn't he right?[54]

In the following month Chekhov wrote to Davydov and recounted the critical responses that the play had elicited. Amongst these was the view that 'the ending isn't untrue to life, but is untrue to the stage. It can only satisfy the audience if played superlatively well.'[55] It is difficult to imagine how the playwright could have justified having Ivanov literally die from shame as being true to life.[56]

That Chekhov had not yet learned how to employ representational realism to express his ideas is further shown by his response to one of Suvorin's criticisms of the play. Suvorin had rightly seen that an audience would have difficulty in correctly interpreting the central character. Suvorin's suggested solution to this problem was to advocate that Chekhov adopt dramatic conventions that were alien to dramatic realism. In a letter to Davydov, Chekhov recounted Suvorin's advice:

> Ivanov is *sufficiently characterised* — no need to add or subtract anything. But Suvorin has his own ideas on this: 'I can make sense of Ivanov because I think I *am* an Ivanov. But the general public, which every author must keep in mind, won't understand. Why not give him a soliloquy?'[57]

Given Chekhov's theoretical commitment to realism, we might have expected him to reject Suvorin's suggestion. But when he came to make his first revision of the play later in 1888 in preparation for its St Petersburg revival he wrote to Suvorin saying that he had followed his advice:

> I've radically changed Acts Two and Four of *Ivanov*. I've given Ivanov a soliloquy, touched up Sasha and so on. If people don't understand *Ivanov* even now, I'll chuck it on the fire and write a story called *I've had enough*.[58]

Chekhov had not objected to incorporating a soliloquy for *Ivanov* because he had not yet fully realised the conventional implication of adopting thorough-going realism. The result is that the plays that precede *The Seagull* are part of a mongrel genre with features of realism uneasily mixed up with the conventions of earlier dramatic forms. The addition of a soliloquy for Ivanov did not violate the conventions of Chekhov's play, because the play, especially in its first draft, already had several soliloquies.

Direct address to an audience, while it may well have been one of the central features of the performance of earlier drama, sounds awkward in a play that claims to be realistic. Modern directors, who know the techniques Chekhov used to overcome this awkwardness in his later plays, have used his later techniques retroactively to overcome the difficulty inherent in the use of soliloquies in a play such as *Ivanov* which aspires to be realistic.

David Jones, in his 1976 production of *Ivanov*, did not follow Chekhov's stage direction that Dr Lvov enter and be '*alone*'. Rather than have Lvov embark on a soliloquy in which he debates whether or not to challenge Ivanov to a duel and follow this with Kosykh entering and talking as usual about cards, as Chekhov specified, Jones had Kosykh on stage with Lvov from the beginning. The result was that the awkwardness of the non-realistic convention of soliloquy was replaced by the realistically justified use of 'disguised soliloquy'. Instead of Lvov talking to himself or to the audience, Jones, without changing a line of dialogue, lets Lvov outline his plan to Kosykh. This character is, as usual, obsessed with his constant misfortune at cards and, ignoring Lvov, launches into yet another diatribe against his bridge partner's lack of card sense. Realism is thus maintained by 'disguising' Lvov's soliloquy. As Jones says: 'Lvov *thinks* he's talking to him — but he is not.'[59]

One has only to think of the opening of Act I of *The Cherry Orchard*, where Lopakhin 'soliloquises' in the presence of Dunyasha, who is not listening to him, or the opening of Act II of the same play, where Charlotte is on a crowded stage and 'soliloquises' to a void, in order to realise that Jones got this idea of how to play Lvov's soliloquy from his knowledge of Chekhov's mature dramatic technique. This retroactive application of the Chekhovian technique of disguised soliloquy is completely in tune with Chekhov's stated aim of showing 'life as it is'. In effect, Jones has let the mature Chekhov assist the fledgling playwright.

David Jones later had doubts about trying to 'disguise' the play's soliloquies. He admitted that, under his direction, John Wood was not fully successful in realising Ivanov's monologue in Act III:

> In hindsight, I feel our problem was a technical one. There are moments in the play, and this is one, when a character almost steps out of the scene and addresses the audience. I think that if I was directing the play now, I would encourage John to try to share the speech with the audience, in the Shakespearean manner. The effect, I feel, would be both funnier, and more touching. As it was John was torn between thinking the speech through to himself, and playing it out to the audience.[60]

Jones' earlier solution to the problem of presenting Lvov's soliloquies was closer to Chekhov's stated intention of making his dramas as lifelike and non-theatrical as possible. The director's later idea of having John Wood break the fourth-wall convention by having him direct his soliloquies to an audience fails to accord with the conventions of representational realism. *Ivanov* poses difficulties for directors because Chekhov had not yet solved what Una Ellis-Fermor calls 'the problem of conveying to the audience thought which cannot naturally form part of the dialogue'.[61]

Chekhov considered that both Ivanov's character and the central action of the whole play had been misunderstood. As far as he was concerned, his 'intended' play had not communicated itself to either audiences or critics. In a letter to Michael Chekhov, soon after the first production of *Ivanov*, Chekhov commented:

> Suvorin's excited about the play. The funny thing is that after Korsh's production no one in the audience understood *Ivanov* — they blamed me and pitied me.[62]

Chekhov was able to explain clearly what he intended *Ivanov* to be about. He was equally perceptive about why his artistic intention had not been realised:

> I cherished the audacious dream of summing up everything written thus far about wincing despondent people and of having my *Ivanov* put a stop to this

sort of writing ... My basic conception of the work came close to the mark, but the realisation isn't worth a damn. I should have waited!⁶³

Despite admitting that he had not found the form to realise his vision, Chekhov expressed his satisfaction with what he was trying to depict. It is no wonder that he should have been so upset by the critical misinterpretation of his play. He had intended *Ivanov* to be a play about wasted potential. In particular, Chekhov wished to suggest an implied criticism of his central character. Ivanov was meant to be seen as an example of a literary type well-known in Russia in the late nineteenth-century called the 'superfluous man'. Chekhov had already attacked this type in his feuilleton entitled *A Moscow Hamlet*. The 'superfluous man' was a Russian mixture of the Byronic hero and Hamlet. He was a type who was desirable to women and talented, but who could find no satisfactory goal in life and tended to become over-talkative, indecisive and introspective. Karlinsky points out that: 'Chekhov had hoped finally to put to rest that tired old commonplace of the Russian critical tradition (still with us today, alas): the superfluous man, that sensitive and bright nobleman, unable to find the proper use for his talents.'⁶⁴

Simmons supplies a useful historical contextualisation of this type. He writes that:

> Ivanov was intended to symbolise those people among the educated class who, disillusioned by the repressive political and social conditions that followed the assassination of Alexander II, had fallen into dejection and despair. Chekhov wished to debunk this type, to unmask the futility of the intellectual who dreams pleasantly about his past accomplishments but quails before the abuses of the present, then experiences a vague sense of guilt over them, and ends with unstrung nerves among the 'shattered' and 'misunderstood' people of society.⁶⁵

Chekhov had intended to expose the pretentious nature of this stereotypical character type. In particular, he wished to ridicule their failure to accept responsibility for their own lack of purposeful action. As Karlinsky correctly claims:

> With his habit of breaking through stereotypes, Chekhov wanted to show that for men of this ilk disappointment and frustration spring not so much from immutable social reality as from their own inability to translate their idealism into a meaningful program of action because their interest in any project or undertaking fades so quickly.⁶⁶

This may indeed have been what Chekhov 'wanted to show', but the response of the critics and the public clearly suggests that his intentions were not realised in practice. What his readers and audience read was something entirely different. Karlinsky accurately describes how Chekhov *intended* Ivanov's personality and the situation to be assessed. Karlinsky writes:

Failed Experiments: The Early Plays

> With all his faults and shortcomings, the weak and ineffectual Ivanov (his ordinary name was meant to be symbolic) was contrasted in the play on the one hand with a group of provincial bores and gossips, everyone of them far less attractive than he, and on the other hand with the humourless radical fanatic Dr Lvov, who passes judgement on him for all the wrong reasons and reduces Ivanov's complex predicament to simple-minded sociological clichés.[67]

Far from seeing *Ivanov* as a play debunking the 'superfluous man', the responses of critics oscillated between describing the central characters as yet another appealing example of this sensitive and sympathetic type and seeing him as the melodramatic villain of the piece. Chekhov was equally unhappy about the way that Dr Lvov had been interpreted. Having completed a rewrite of the play, which he now jokingly referred to as *Bolvanov*, in preparation for its St Petersburg production, Chekhov wrote to Suvorin about his attempts to make Ivanov and the play clearer. In this long letter, Chekhov outlined the ways in which he felt the critics and the public had misinterpreted his play. He provided Suvorin with an extraordinarily detailed and precise analysis of his main characters. He explained clearly what he had intended to write. This letter provides documentary evidence of Chekhov's aims, and when these are compared with the play itself we can see how and why his aims and intentions were not met by his achievements. Chekhov explained to Suvorin that, as a result of the revisions he had made:

> Master Ivanov's now much easier to understand. The ending doesn't satisfy me at all — it's too feeble, apart from the revolver shot — but I take comfort in thinking that it's not in its final form yet ...[68]

Chekhov's hope that he had at last clarified Ivanov's character was dashed when the play went into rehearsal. No one seemed to understand his play, least of all Suvorin. The frustrated playwright set out to explain his play:

> The director sees Ivanov as a superfluous man in the Turgenev manner. Savina [Sasha] asks why Ivanov is such a blackguard. You write that 'Ivanov must be given something that makes it clear why two women throw themselves at him and why he is a blackguard while the doctor is a great man.' If all three of you have understood me this way, it means my *Ivanov* is a failure. I must have lost my mind and written something entirely different from what I had intended. If my Ivanov comes across as a blackguard or superfluous man and the doctor as a great man, if no one knows why Sarah and Sasha love Ivanov, then my play has evidently failed to pan out, and there can be no question of having it produced.[69]

Chekhov had hoped to avoid the black-and-white characterisation found in melodramas. He had hoped to depict complex human beings. His Ivanov he saw as someone who exhibited both the attractive features of the 'superfluous man' and the weaknesses inherent in such a type. Simon Karlinsky blames Suvorin and the production team for their melodramatic reading of the characters of *Ivanov*.[70] It might be fairer to say that audiences at the St Petersburg production had responded to the well-made play elements that were plainly evident in the play.

After giving a detailed analysis of his *intended* characterisation, Chekhov reiterated the possibility that the misinterpretation of *Ivanov* was his own fault:

> If nothing I've described above is in the play, there can be no question of having it produced. It must mean I didn't write what I intended. Have the play withdrawn. I don't mean to preach heresy from the stage. If the audience leaves the theatre thinking all Ivanovs are blackguards and Doctor Lvovs are great men, I might as well go into retirement and give up my pen.[71]

In a postscript to that same letter Chekhov again expresses his sense of puzzlement that something that was so clear to himself should have been so difficult for audiences and readers to interpret correctly:

> I'd hoped that the reader and the spectator would be attentive and not need a sign saying, 'This is a plum, not a pumpkin.' I have tried to express myself simply ... I failed in my attempt to write a play. It's a pity, of course. Ivanov and Lvov seemed so alive in my imagination. I'm telling you the whole truth when I say that they weren't born in my head out of sea foam or pre-conceived notions or intellectual pretensions or by accident. They are the result of observing and studying life. They are still there in my mind, and I feel I haven't lied a bit or exaggerated an iota. And if they came out lifeless and blurred on paper, the fault lies not in them, but in my inability to convey my thoughts. Apparently it's too early for me to undertake playwriting.[72]

Chekhov was his own toughest and, in this case, best critic. He gave plenty of evidence that his characters were indeed drawn from life. The medical scientist in Chekhov resulted in the playwright delineating with naturalistic objectivity the way in which a neurasthenic personality such as Ivanov actually behaves in real life. He supplied Suvorin with pages of information, both psychological and sociological, about the type of person Ivanov was. Chekhov, who once admitted to being deeply interested in psychiatry, backed up his analysis with evidence drawn from current medical research. Ivanov is practically psychoanalysed in Chekhov's letter to Suvorin. So Ivanov's bouts of world-weariness are explained as follows:

> This susceptibility to weariness (as Dr Bertenson will confirm) finds expression in more than merely whining or feeling bored. The life of the weary man cannot be represented like this:

## Failed Experiments: The Early Plays

It is not particularly even. The weary do not lose their ability to work up a high pitch of excitement but their excitement lasts for a very short time and is followed by an even greater sense of apathy. Graphically we can represent this as follows:

As you can see, the descent forms something rather different from a gradual inclined plane. Sasha declares her love. Ivanov shouts in ecstasy: 'A new life!' But the next morning he has as much faith in that life as he does in ghosts (see his third act soliloquy).[73]

It was Davydov's inability to oscillate between the moods of ecstasy and depression that led Chekhov to adjust his high opinion of the talents of this actor. He wrote to Suvorin:

> If a skilful, energetic actor were to play Ivanov I would have a free hand. But, alas! Davydov plays the part. This means that one must write concisely, in a grayer tone, keeping in mind that all delicate shadings and 'nuances' will be mingled in one grey monotone, and that they will be dull. Can Davydov be tender and also wrathful? When he plays serious parts it is as if a mill were in his throat, a feebly-turning monotonous mill that acts instead of him.[74]

Chekhov was well aware that correct casting was important in order to achieve a proper stage realisation of his vision. He even did some rewriting of the role of Sasha because he admired the abilities of Savina the actress playing the role:

> Savina has agreed to play Sasha, but Sasha's part's very weak and pretty poor theatre. When I wrote it eighteen months ago I didn't attach special importance to it. But now the honour done to the play by Savina has decided me to alter her part radically. I've already done it in places, in so far as the play's general structure permitted.[75]

Chekhov eventually came to have a mixed opinion about the worth of *Ivanov*. Though he claimed that his 'characters live and aren't artificial',[76] he also came to believe that: 'The play's faults are beyond repair.'[77] In a letter to Suvorin, he had to agree with his friend's criticism of the play: 'You're quite right —

Ivanov probably is clearer in my letter than on the stage.'[78] Chekhov knew that something was not right with the characterisation of his protagonist.

If we examine *Ivanov* without knowing from other sources what Chekhov intended, it becomes difficult to see in what ways Chekhov's character is actually different from the literary stereotype of the 'superfluous man' that he claimed to be attacking. As Hingley wryly comments: 'One could wish that Chekhov had expounded the differences between Ivanov and the superfluous man at greater length.'[79]

Chekhov's claim that Ivanov's acknowledgement of his own responsibility for his behaviour shows that there is a central difference between his character and the literary type, hardly seems to be justified. Most of the objective evidence for such a reading is to be found, not in the play, but in the letter to Suvorin in which he explained what he *intended* his character to be like. So Chekhov's letter clearly states:

> ... when narrow-minded, dishonest people get into a situation like this, they usually place all the blame on their environment or join the ranks of the Hamlets and superfluous men, and let it go at that. The straightforward Ivanov, however, openly admits to the doctor and the audience that he doesn't understand himself.[80]

In *The Duel* (1891), Chekhov has the zoologist, Von Koren, characterise Layevsky as a superfluous man who, characteristically, blames everyone but himself for his lack of drive:

> Why didn't he do anything? Or read anything? Why was he so uncultured, such an ignoramus? At every question I asked he would give a bitter smile and sigh. 'I'm a failure,' he'd say. 'I'm a Superfluous Man' ... Why is he so utterly degenerate, so repulsive? The reason isn't in himself, see — it's somewhere outside him in space. And then — and this is the cunning of it — he's not the only one who's debauched, bogus and odious. There is always *We*. 'We men of the eighties.' 'We, the debilitated, neurotic offspring of the serf system'. 'Civilisation has crippled us.'[81]

Having been enlightened by Von Koren's verbal attack on him, Layevsky undergoes a regeneration process. Ivanov's 'enlightenment' brings about no such transformation but instead leads to his suicide.

It is clear that Chekhov intended Ivanov to be, unlike the 'superfluous man', a person of real integrity. The problem that faces an audience, however, is that this supposed integrity is not made manifest in Ivanov's behaviour. While he takes Chekhov's word that Ivanov has integrity, the Soviet critic G. Berdnikov realises that there is still a major problem of dramatic communication that Chekhov has not solved in this play. Any audience member necessarily interprets

Ivanov on the basis of the character's behaviour and not on some putative subjective integrity whose existence cannot be verified:

> Chekhov decided to make Ivanov precisely this subjectively honest person who tragically survives his downfall. The complexity of the task rested in the fact that this subjective honesty, while it remained unquestionably a real attribute of the hero, could not and did not change his highly unattractive life.[82]

The problem with trying to create a 'subjectively honest person' is that, in order for spectators to see the character in this light, they must have objective evidence of the existence of this subjective honesty. Chekhov had to convince his audience that Ivanov did indeed have an authentic inner life, and the only way the playwright could do this, while continuing to maintain his ideal of objectivity, was to 'show' rather than 'tell' his audience about this so-called authentic self.

The materialist Chekhov, who refused 'to separate soul from body', and who claimed that 'outside of matter there is no experience of knowledge and consequently of truth',[83] was committed to an essentially behaviouristic representation of inner states. His advice to his brother Alexander written in 1886 is typical of the conventional limits Chekhov set himself in his writing of either stories or plays:

> In the area of mental states there are also particulars. May God save you from generalities. It is best to avoid descriptions of the mental states of your heroes; the effort should be made to make these clear from their actions.[84]

In Y. Sobolev's reminiscences entitled 'Tchekhov's Creative Method', he lays great stress on the importance of Chekhov's behaviourist approach to characterisation:

> And this has to be pointed out with particular emphasis, for such also is Tchekhov's creative method: *from the outward to the inward* ... From details, particulars, objects of the external world — to generalizations, to the most important and typical — to the inward, the spiritual.[85]

Chekhov knew, like Freud, that much of what is important in people's lives is hidden from others. It was not just the unconscious that was important to Chekhov. He realised that the inner lives of his characters were rich with conscious, but unspoken, thoughts and beliefs. The problem he faced as a dramatist was that, unless he could discover a way to communicate these inner happenings, audience members would not be aware that this inner life existed at all. Chekhov's recourse to soliloquies in *Ivanov* attests to the difficulties he was having in communicating his central character's subjective honesty through purely objective behavioural means. All the audience could see objectively was Ivanov's 'highly unattractive life'. Much as one may dislike the moralistic Dr

Lvov as a personality, it is difficult not to feel that much of his criticism of Ivanov is justified, since the 'hero's' behaviour toward his wife, for example, *appears* indefensible. The soliloquies introduced to clarify Ivanov's character by revealing his innermost thoughts in the text did not adequately serve Chekhov's purpose. In the first place, they broke realism's fourth-wall convention. The conventional strength of soliloquies had been weakened by the rise of dramatic realism and, just as significantly, by the application of the new science of psychology to the art of characterisation. As Esslin has pointed out, there had been a 'basic assumption that underlay all language used in drama' prior to that of the late nineteenth century. That previously unquestioned assumption was 'that what a character said was not only what he or she meant to say, but that he or she was expressing it as clearly and eloquently as possible'.[86]

Once the conventions of realism are applied, such an assumption is immediately questioned. We don't automatically accept that what Ivanov has to say about himself is the truth. We are forced to evaluate him simply in terms of his behaviour and that behaviour contradicts his claims about his 'integrity'. Interestingly, Tolstoy made a similar, though less justified, criticism of *Uncle Vanya*. He commented that Chekhov, when depicting both Vanya and Astrov:

> ... makes them say that once upon a time they were the best people in the district, but he does not show us in what way they were good. I cannot help feeling that they have always been worthless creatures and that their suffering cannot therefore be worthy of our attention.[87]

In *Ivanov* we find an isolated reference to the hero's integrity in Act I when his wife Anna is talking to Lvov:

> ANNA. ... He's a wonderful man, Doctor, and I'm only sorry you didn't know him a year ago ...[88]

In terms of realistic drama, an audience may well not accept Anna's assessment unequivocally because, in the context in which she makes this statement, she may be simply defending her husband out of love for him rather than out of objective honesty. The only other assertions about Ivanov's integrity are made by Sasha, who also loves him. Her comments can be interpreted as stemming from her 'love' for him rather than any adherence to the truth. Chekhov did not believe that Sasha was truly in love with Ivanov. Rather she is shown to be in love with the idea of rescuing him. Even if one accepts this reading of Sasha, her comments about Ivanov cannot be regarded as being 'objective'.

On the evidence of statements made by two emotionally involved people and a number of self-justifying soliloquies, critics such as Berdnikov accept the truth of Chekhov's statement that this character is a subjectively honest person. However, as any reading or performance of the play illustrates, practically everything that Ivanov does in the play contradicts the high claims made for him. Indeed, Chekhov depicts Ivanov as being unsure about whether or not he has any integrity. At one stage, he says that he is uncertain about whether or not he married Anna for her money.

At the time of writing *Ivanov*, Chekhov had understood in theory the idea of a subtext, but he had not yet discovered the theatrical means to put that theory into effective practice. That the play enjoyed some success was mainly due to its conventionality. It is a theatrically viable treatment of a love triangle and the external events of the play are at times exciting. What Chekhov had not yet developed was a technique whereby the implied subtext could be communicated to an audience. By discovering the ways in which actors could communicate this subtext, Chekhov was to solve the central problem of literal realism and representational form. With the actors using the realistic acting system devised by Stanislavski in the performance of his plays, the problem of expressing 'thought which cannot naturally be expressed through dialogue' was solved. By creating plays with an implied subtext, Chekhov was to rescue his drama from the fate of merely depicting the surface triviality of life.

Throughout his literary career, Chekhov continued to accept the conventions of realism. These conventions allowed him to depict life objectively. The texts of even his last four masterpieces still present the surface triviality of life in a realistic fashion. The subjective or psychic reality of his characters was suggested implicitly through the subtext. Chekhov's objective depiction of life is not compromised by his subjective aim or purpose in writing. John Hagan accurately describes how Chekhov was able to combine objectivity and subjectivity in his mature work. Hagan argues that the playwright:

> ... presents his characters and their behaviour so as to convey their meanings by implication alone ... Chekhov's espousal of this technique in no way implies that he was indifferent to all values but aesthetic ones. There has been a great deal of confusion on this point. It means only that he preferred to communicate his judgements and attitudes implicitly rather than explicitly, with the ultimate purpose of producing only an illusion of unmediated reality. The crucial principle is that of inference: the writer, instead of spelling out and formulating on an intellectual level the interpretations and evaluations which he wants the reader to make, presents him with suggestive particulars and external signs from which he can draw conclusions of his own.[89]

Progressively, from *The Seagull* through to *The Cherry Orchard*, Chekhov made his texts more and more lifelike, as he abandoned many of the mechanical theatrical devices of the well-made play that he had used in earlier plays like *Ivanov*. After *Ivanov*, Chekhov's practice was to begin to match his theory of drama in which life should be presented on stage 'exactly as it is, and people should be exactly as simple as they are in life'.[90]

By the time he wrote *The Cherry Orchard*, Chekhov had managed to remove so much of what was previously regarded as theatrically necessary from his play that, as far as the objectively presented text is concerned, almost nothing happens. Skaftymov aptly describes this development towards what Magarshack calls the plays of indirect action:

> One of the salient features of pre-Chekhovian drama is that everyday life is absorbed into, and overshadowed by, events. The humdrum — that which is most permanent, normal, customary, and habitual — is almost absent from these plays. Moments of the even flow of life appear at the beginning of the play, as an exposition and a starting point, but subsequently the entire play, the entire fabric of dialogue is taken up with events; the daily flow of life recedes into the background and is merely mentioned and implied in places ... In Chekhov it is entirely different.[91]

Chekhov seems to have agreed with the narrator of his short story *Gooseberries* (1898) who asserts that: 'Life's real tragedies are enacted off-stage.'[92] In all of Chekhov's major plays there are several potentially theatrical dramas which never reach the stage. In *The Cherry Orchard*, for example, Mrs Ranevsky's love affair, the drowning of her son and her attempted suicide would all provide incidents suitable for a Scribean melodrama. In *Three Sisters* we learn about, but never see, Vershinin's mad suicidal wife. This sort of detail, the centre of a 'Gothic' novel such as *Jane Eyre*, is kept totally in the background in the play. Likewise, in *Three Sisters*, the duel in which Tuzenbach is killed occurs off-stage. The triviality of the events that occur on-stage gain in significance when read by an audience that is made aware of the dramatic events occurring off-stage. As Skaftymov notes:

> Chekhov moves events to the periphery as if they were details; and all that is ordinary, constant, recurring, and habitual constitutes the main mass, the basic ground of the play.[93]

Chekhov did not do this simply because he wished to present life 'realistically'. If this had been all he wished to achieve, he would simply have been a kind of photographic realist. Chekhov knew perfectly well the difference between life and art. His objections to Stanislavski's attempts to justify the use of several sound effects not specified in his script of *The Seagull* is clear evidence that he wished to use realism with an artistic purpose. Meyerhold recounts the incident as follows:

> Chekhov had come for the second time to visit a rehearsal of *The Seagull* (September 11, 1898) in the Moscow Art Theater. One of the actors told him that during the play, frogs croaked backstage, dragonflies hummed, and dogs howled.
> 'What for?' asked Anton Pavlovich, sounding dissatisfied.

'It's realistic,' said the actor.

'Realistic,' Anton Pavlovich repeated with a laugh. And then after a brief pause, he remarked: '...The stage demands certain conventions ... You have no fourth wall. Besides the stage is art; theatre expresses the quintessence of life. There is no need to introduce anything superfluous onto the stage.'[94]

The achievement of verisimilitude on-stage was not an end in itself for Chekhov. However, living when he did, he felt bound to use the artistic conventions of realism to express his vision of reality. This is hardly surprising since, as Bernard Beckerman notes: '[ever] since "reality" became synonymous with "realism" in the course of the nineteenth century, we find it exceptionally difficult to disassociate the idea of "reality" from that of verisimilitude'.[95] As Skaftymov rightly claims, 'for Chekhov in his excursions into drama, some sort of reproduction of everyday life was an indispensable condition'.[96]

Chekhov however saw that the conventions of realism were artistic customs that were not to be confused with life itself. He knew perfectly well that the conventions of realism were just as 'artificial' as the non-realistic conventions employed by symbolists like Maeterlinck. Chekhov would no doubt have agreed with Raymond Williams, who wrote about the importance of distinguishing between art and life when evaluating a work of art:

> The action of a play ... is often only incidentally important in itself. Its interestingness, its truth, cannot be judged as if it were an action in real life. Similarly, with characters, the important dramatist is concerned, not necessarily to simulate 'real, live people', but rather to embody in his personages certain aspects of experience. That this will frequently result in the creation of characters which we feel we can accept as 'from life itself' is certain, but the result will not always be so, and we must be careful that our judgement depends not on whether the characters are lifelike, but on whether they serve to embody experience which the author has shown to be true.[97]

When we look at his plays as a whole we can see a clear movement from the depiction of external action to that of internal action juxtaposed with external inaction. What Magarshack called the movement from plays of 'direct action' to plays of 'indirect action' may best be illustrated by a look at the decreasing use Chekhov made of violence in his plays. Ronald Hingley provides the following illuminating chart:[98]

| Date | Title of Play | Items |
| --- | --- | --- |
| ?1880–1 | Platonov | Two attempted suicides — one on, one off stage; an attempted knifing; a lynching off stage; murder by shooting. |
| 1887–9 | Ivanov | Suicide by shooting (on stage). |
| 1889–90 | The Wood Demon | Suicide by shooting (off stage, shot not heard by audience). |
| ?1890–96 | Uncle Vanya | Attempted murder by shooting on stage. |

Interpreting Chekhov

| 1896 | *The Seagull* | Attempted suicide; an actual suicide (off stage, shot heard by audience). |
|---|---|---|
| 1900–01 | *Three Sisters* | Death by shooting (off stage in duel; shot heard in distance by audience). |
| 1903–04 | *The Cherry Orchard* | No shooting (but Yepikhodov carries a revolver so that he can commit suicide if necessary). |

From the time when he wrote *The Seagull*, Chekhov was able to dispense with much of the theatrical machinery of the well-made play and develop the dramatic techniques that involved an interplay between an often comic text and implied tragic subtext.

The two levels of text and subtext are reflected in Chekhov's dualistic tragi-comic vision of reality. Chekhov was always aware that life could not be regarded as either totally tragic or totally comic. Kuprin's memory of Chekhov saying that in life 'everything is mixed up together, the important and the paltry, the great and the base, the tragic and the ridiculous'[99] is supported by various statements in the playwright's letters, in which he acknowledges that his particular vision of reality, and, consequently, the generic form needed to express that vision, could never be either pure tragedy or pure comedy. Chekhov's plays combine both tragedy and comedy.

Even an early play such as *Platonov*, which dramatises highly serious issues, is infused with comedy. The English director and actor, George Devine, who has directed this play, stressed the importance of the 'humorous aspect of the young Chekhov's work'. He noted that:

> ... when the play was produced at the Royal Court in 1960, an extraordinary idea was put about with considerable vehemence that the play was meant to be entirely serious. A study of the text and stage directions will prove this contention to be entirely fallacious. Even in the near tragic last moments after Platonov has been shot, the Doctor shouts for water, presumably for the patient, and is handed a decanter. 'The doctor drinks the water and throws the decanter aside', says Chekhov's stage direction. If this is not *intended* by the dramatist to be funny, in the midst of tragedy, I'll be confounded.[100]

In a letter to the poet Yakov Polonsky in 1888, Chekhov wrote about how he found it impossible to write 'seriously' all of the time:

> What am I to do if my fingers are itching and simply force me to commit some tra-la-la? However much I try to be serious, nothing comes of it, and always the serious alternates with the vulgar with me. I suppose that's fate.[101]

The comic gestures that Chekhov's characters make in their inept attempts to realise their dreams are juxtaposed with the seriousness of those aspirations for a better life. The failure of Chekhov's characters to achieve their aims or to live up to their potential is often presented in a comic manner, but their failure is not in any sense inevitable. Part of what makes some of the behaviour of

Chekhov's characters ludicrous is the fact that they could have done better but instead have wasted their lives. If there is a 'tragic' aspect to the lives of Chekhov's characters, it is not because of the existence of any 'tragic inevitability'. As R. L. Jackson has convincingly argued: 'Man's tragedy for Chekhov, lies primarily not in any absolute helplessness before his fate, but in the fact that he is continuously affirming fate's autonomy through abdication of his own responsibility.'[102]

As we shall see, one of the major problems that has beset productions of Chekhov has been the tendency of directors to direct his plays either as gloomy tragedies or, more recently, as hilarious comedies. Chekhov complained about Stanislavski's over-gloomy productions of his plays. He would only have to look at a production like Robert Sturua's Bakhtin-inspired postmodern deconstruction of *Three Sisters* to see how productions have been pushed to the opposite pole. It is an understatement to say that Sturua's *Three Sisters* was an over-funny production:

> It was, wrote Sheridan Morley, theatre critic of the New York *Herald Tribune* 'a knockabout farce ... forever trying on a new emotion as though it were just another funny hat' (19.12.90), while the *Mail on Sunday* noted that the production was 'not short on high jinks, low jinks or even funny noses' ... Masha could be seen at one point in Act Two twanging an elastic band on her comic false nose and there was, declared the *Sunday Telegraph*, 'a great deal of horse-play, and by-play, and just about every play apart from Chekhov's play (16.12.90).[103]

Neither the totally tragic nor the totally comic versions of Chekhov remain within the parameters and tolerances defined by Chekhov's playtexts.[104] Nick Worrall may 'not have been in the least perturbed by the lack of psychological realism' in the Georgian director's production, nor worried about 'his eschewal of emotional empathy in this deliberately stylised conception of *Three Sisters*'.[105] However, I find myself deeply concerned about a production that actively goes against the playwright's specific demands. Consequently, when Worrall states that: 'Sturua's theatre is not one of emotional identification, but one in which a notion of the "theatre theatrical" is deliberately foregrounded',[106] I vividly recall Chekhov's desperate pleas to the actors at the Moscow Arts Theatre to be more lifelike and less theatrical.

No other playwright has been more realistic in form and, at the same time, been able to express truthfully the tragi-comic complexity of life. Even Ibsen preferred to use the basic form of the well-made play in many of his so-called realistic dramas. Chekhov was the first and possibly the writer most thoroughly committed to the realistic depiction of both the surface and inner reality of life. Chekhov's extensions of the expressive possibilities of realism are well described by John Gassner and illustrate just how important his innovations were for generations of later dramatists:

> For plumbing the depths of the individual psyche, realism was of little avail because the realistic technique, with its 'fourth wall' convention and its absence of poetic dialogue and soliloquy, could present our experience and feeling only on one plane; it could let audiences see only the surfaces that any outsider sees. Realistic drama is pre-eminently logical, but the inner self is not logical. The realist cannot allow the individual character to expose his inner processes by means of soliloquies and asides, nor is he free to shape the play to suit the character's state of mind. The ordinary conventional realist is in the position of the diver whose hands and feet are bound, and who is deprived of a pipe line through which he can inhale oxygen and communicate with the surface.[107]

Chekhov was no 'ordinary conventional realist'. We have seen how through the creation of a perceptible subtext he created a 'pipe line' which supplied the necessary life-giving properties that allowed for the communication of the playwright's own vision of reality and all this was achieved while still remaining within the bounds of realistic conventions.

In the next chapter we will examine *The Seagull*, in particular, its two markedly different productions by Evtikhy Karpov in St Petersburg in 1896 and by Konstantin Stanislavski in Moscow in 1898. Chekhov was to see his first masterpiece interpreted in ways that caused him considerable anguish. Chekhov's response to these two productions reveals much about his own views about how the play ought to be performed. Despite Chekhov's reservations, Stanislavski's production proved to be such a theatrical success that the survival of the Moscow Art Theatre was ensured.

## ENDNOTES

[1] Glicksberg, C. I., *Modern Literary Perspectivism*, Southern Methodist University Press, Dallas, 1970, p. 78.

[2] Strindberg, A., 'Foreword to *Miss Julie*', quoted in Williams, R., *Drama from Ibsen to Brecht*, Penguin, Harmondsworth, 1968, pp. 81–2.

[3] Karlinsky, S. and Heim, M. H., trans., *Anton Chekhov's Life and Thought*, University of California Press, Berkeley, 1975, p. 280.

[4] When he was a medical student, Chekhov earned money to support himself and his family by churning out farcical short stories for a variety of comic journals. Almost as if he felt ashamed to acknowledge these hurriedly-written works, Chekhov distanced himself from them by employing a variety of pseudonyms, the most common one being 'Chekhonte'. In 1889, Chekhov received a letter from the then-famous writer, Dmitry Grigorovich, who encouraged him to take his writing talent more seriously. Partly as a result of this recognition, Chekhov began to work on his writing technique and took much greater care with his writing. The result was increasing fame for his expertise in this literary genre.

[5] Krutch, J. W., *Nation*, 31 October 1928, in Emeljanow, V., ed., *Chekhov: The Critical Heritage*, Routledge and Kegan Paul, London, 1981, pp. 338–9.

[6] Magarshack, D., *Chekhov the Dramatist*, Eyre Methuen, London, 1980, p. 21.

[7] Ibid., pp. 19–20.

[8] Avilova, L., *Chekhov in My Life: A Love Story*, Methuen, London, 1989, p. 89.

[9] Rayfield, D., *Chekhov: The Evolution of His Art*, Paul Elek, London, 1975, p. 15.
[10] Hingley, R., *A New Life of Chekhov*, Oxford University Press, London, 1976, p. 108.
[11] Ibid., p. 88.
[12] Chekhov, A., Letter to A. F. Marks, 1 October 1902, quoted in Hingley, R., *The Oxford Chekhov*, Vol. 1, Oxford University Press, London, 1968, p. 189.
[13] Chekhov, A., Letter to V. Bibilin, 14 February 1886, quoted in Magarshack, D., op. cit., p. 151.
[14] Simmons, E. J., *Chekhov: A Biography*, Jonathan Cape, London, 1963, pp. 579–80.
[15] Magarshack, D., op. cit., pp. 150–1.
[16] Ibid., p. 151.
[17] Gottlieb, V., *Chekhov and the Vaudeville*, Cambridge University Press, Cambridge, 1982, p. 187.
[18] Chekhov, A., *Smoking Is Bad for You* (1889), in Hingley, R., *The Oxford Chekhov*, Vol. 1, Oxford University Press, London, 1968, p. 191.
[19] Chekhov, A., *Smoking Is Bad for You* (1890), in Hingley, R., *The Oxford Chekhov*, Vol. 1, p. 197.
[20] Magarshack, D., op. cit., p. 152.
[21] Rapaport, I., *Acting: A Handbook of the Stanislavski Method*, Crown Publishers, New York, 1955, p. 62. I use the term subtext in a wider sense than Rapaport to include not only motivation, but all ideas, values and beliefs that are part of the inner life of a character.
[22] Chekhov, A., *Smoking Is Bad for You* (1890), p. 199.
[23] Ibid.
[24] Ibid.
[25] Chekhov, A., *Smoking is Bad for You* (1903), in Hingley, R., *The Oxford Chekhov*, Vol. 1, pp. 157–8.
[26] Gottlieb, V., op. cit., p. 178.
[27] Ibid., p. 182.
[28] Chekhov, M., quoted in Makaroff, D., 'Notes on the Play', in Chekhov, A., *Platonov*, Methuen, London, 1961, p. 7. The manuscript of this unpublished and untitled play was only discovered in 1920. It has been performed in various cut versions and is usually called *Platonov*. Possibly the most successful version of this play is Michael Frayn's adaptation, entitled *Wild Honey*.
[29] Rayfield, D., op. cit., pp. 96–7.
[30] Ibid., p. 99.
[31] Chekhov, A., Letter to A. N. Pleshcheyev, 9 April 1889, in Josephson, M., ed., *The Personal Papers of Anton Chekhov*, Lear, New York, 1948, p. 150.
[32] Moravcevich, N., 'Chekhov and Naturalism: From Affinity to Divergence', *Comparative Drama*, Vol. 4, No. 4, Winter 1970–71, p. 224.
[33] Magarshack, D., op. cit., p. 40.
[34] Hagan, J., 'Chekhov's Fiction and the Idea of "Objectivity"', *Proceedings of the Modern Language Association*, Vol. 81, October 1966, p. 414.
[35] Chekhov, A., Letter to N. M. Yezhov, 27 October 1887, quoted in Simmons, E. J., op. cit., p. 136.
[36] Chekhov, A., Letter to A. Chekhov between 10 and 12 October 1887, quoted in Hingley, R., *The Oxford Chekhov*, Vol. 2, Oxford University Press, London, 1967, pp. 284–5.
[37] Chekhov, A., Letter to A. Chekhov, 24 November 1887, quoted in Hingley, R., *The Oxford Chekhov*, Vol. 2, p. 287.
[38] Anonymous reviewer, quoted in Valency, M., *The Breaking String*, Oxford University Press, Oxford, 1966, p. 86.
[39] Chekhov, A., *Ivanov*, in Hingley, R., *The Oxford Chekhov*, Vol. 2, p. 197.
[40] Chekhov, A., First draft ending of *Ivanov*, in Hingley, R., *The Oxford Chekhov*, Vol. 2, pp. 325–6.
[41] Chekhov, A., *Ivanov*, p. 183.
[42] Strindberg, A., 'Author's Foreword to *Miss Julie*', in Sprigge, E., ed., *Six Plays of Strindberg*, Doubleday Anchor Books, New York, 1955, p. 64.
[43] Chekhov, A., Letter to A. Chekhov, 24 October 1887, quoted in Hingley, R., *The Oxford Chekhov*, Vol. 2, p. 285.
[44] Chekhov, A., Letter to A. Chekhov, between 10 and 12 October 1887, quoted in Hingley, R., *The Oxford Chekhov*, Vol. 2, p. 285.

45 Chekhov, A., Letter to A. Chekhov, 20 November 1887, quoted in Hingley, R., *The Oxford Chekhov*, Vol. 2, p. 286.

46 Chekhov, A., Letter to N. A. Leykin, 4 November 1887, quoted in Hingley, R., *The Oxford Chekhov*, Vol. 2, p. 285.

47 Ibid., p. 286.

48 Ibid.

49 Ibid., p. 285.

50 Ibid.

51 Ibid., p. 286.

52 Chekhov, A., Letter to A. Chekhov, 20 November 1887, quoted in Hingley, R., *The Oxford Chekhov*, Vol. 2, pp. 286–7.

53 Chekhov, A., Letter to V. Nemirovich-Danchenko, 2 September 1903, in Friedland, L. S., *Letters on the Short Story, the Drama, and Other Literary Topics by Anton Chekhov*, Dover Publications, New York, 1966, p. 201.

54 Chekhov, A., Letter to N. Leykin, 15 November 1887, in Karlinsky, S., op. cit., pp. 70–1.

55 Chekhov, A., Letter to V. N. Davydov, 1 December 1887, quoted in Hingley, R., *The Oxford Chekhov*, Vol. 2, p. 288.

56 One is reminded of melodramas like Hazlewood's *Lady Audley's Secret*, where the lead character conveniently 'goes mad and dies' at the end of the play!

57 Chekhov, A., Letter to V. N. Davydov, 1 December 1887, in Hingley, R., *The Oxford Chekhov*, Vol. 2, p. 288.

58 Chekhov, A., Letter to A. S. Suvorin between 4 and 6 October 1888, quoted in Hingley, R., *The Oxford Chekhov*, Vol. 2, p. 289.

59 Jones, D., quoted in Allen, D., 'David Jones Directs Chekhov's *Ivanov*', *New Theatre Quarterly*, Vol. 4, No. 15, August 1988, p. 246. According to Motowo Kobatake, Chekhov's characters 'often give voice to their feelings and the other characters on the stage are uncertain whether they ought to listen or not'. (Kobatake, M., 'Soliloquy and Modern Drama', *Theatre Annual*, Vol. 18, 1961, p. 22.) Rather than being embarrassed at another character's expression of feelings, it is more accurate to say that Chekhov's characters are usually unaware of other's feelings, being bound up with their own inner lives.

60 Ibid., p. 243.

61 Ellis-Fermor, U., *The Frontiers of Drama*, Methuen, London, 1964, p. 96.

62 Chekhov, A., Letter to M. Chekhov, 3 December 1887, quoted in Hingley, R., *The Oxford Chekhov*, Vol. 2, p. 289.

63 Chekhov, A., Letter to A. S. Suvorin, 7 January 1889, in Karlinsky, S., op. cit., p. 84.

64 Karlinsky, S., op. cit., p. 69.

65 Simmons, E. J., op. cit., p. 138.

66 Karlinsky, S., op. cit., p. 69.

67 Ibid.

68 Chekhov, A., Letter to A. S. Suvorin, 19 December 1888, quoted in Hingley, R., *The Oxford Chekhov*, Vol. 2, p. 290.

69 Chekhov, A., Letter to A. S. Suvorin, 30 December 1888, in Karlinsky, S., op. cit., p. 76.

70 See Karlinsky, S., op. cit., p. 69.

71 Chekhov, A., Letter to A. S. Suvorin, 30 December 1888, in Karlinsky, S., op. cit., p. 80.

72 Ibid., pp. 81–2.

73 Ibid., pp. 78–9.

74 Chekhov, A., Letter to A. S. Suvorin, 7 January 1889, in Friedland, L. S., op. cit., p. 142.

75 Chekhov, A., Letter to F. A. Fyodorov-Yurkowsky, 8 January 1889, in Hingley, R., *The Oxford Chekhov*, Vol. 2, p. 296.

76 Chekhov, A., Letter to A. N. Pleshcheyev, 2 January 1889, in Hingley, R., *The Oxford Chekhov*, Vol. 2, p. 295.

77 Chekhov, A., Letter to I. L. Leontyev-Shcheglov, 31 December 1888, in Hingley, R., *The Oxford Chekhov*, Vol. 2, p. 295.

78 Chekhov, A., Letter to A. S. Suvorin, 6 February 1889, in Hingley, R., *The Oxford Chekhov*, Vol. 2, p. 297.
79 Hingley, R., *The Oxford Chekhov*, Vol. 2, p. 297.
80 Chekhov, A., Letter to A. S. Suvorin, 30 December 1888, in Karlinsky, S., op. cit., p. 77.
81 Chekhov, A., *The Duel*, in Hingley, R., *The Oxford Chekhov*, Oxford University Press, London, 1970, Vol. 5. p. 147.
82 Berdnikov, G., '*Ivanov*: An Analysis', in Jackson, R. L., ed., *Chekhov*, Prentice-Hall, New Jersey, 1967, p. 90.
83 Chekhov, A., Letter to A. S. Suvorin, 7 May 1889, in Karlinsky, S., op. cit., p. 144.
84 Chekhov, A., Letter to A. Chekhov, 10 May 1886, in Yarmolinsky, A., op. cit., p. 37.
85 Sobolev, Y., 'Tchekhov's Creative Method', in Koteliansky, S. S., ed., *Anton Tchekhov: Literary and Theatrical Reminiscences*, Benjamin Blom, New York, 1965, p. 11. For a similar argument see Hagan, J., op. cit., p. 417.
86 Esslin, M., 'Chekhov and the Modern Drama', in Clyman, T. W., ed., *A Chekhov Companion*, Greenwood Press, Westport, 1985, pp. 135–6.
87 Tolstoy, L., quoted in Magarshack, D., op. cit., p. 16.
88 Chekhov, A., *Ivanov*, p. 179.
89 Hagan, J., op. cit., p. 415.
90 Chekhov, A., quoted in Melchinger, S., op. cit., p. 75.
91 Skaftymov, A., 'Principles of Structure in Chekhov's Plays', in Jackson, R. L., op. cit., pp. 74–5.
92 Chekhov, A., *Gooseberries*, in Hingley, R., *The Oxford Chekhov*, Vol. 9, Oxford University Press, London, 1975, p. 35.
93 Skaftymov, A., op. cit., p. 75.
94 Meyerhold, V., 'Naturalistic Theater and the Theater of Mood', in Jackson, R. L., op. cit., pp. 65–6.
95 Beckerman, B., 'The Artifice of "Reality" in Chekhov and Pinter', *Modern Drama*, Vol. 21, 1978, p. 154.
96 Skaftymov, A., op. cit., p. 73.
97 Williams, R., *Drama from Ibsen to Eliot*, Penguin, Harmondsworth, 1953, p. 21.
98 Hingley, R., 'Introduction' to Hingley, R., *The Oxford Chekhov*, Vol. 2, p. 2.
99 Chekhov, A., recalled by Kuprin, A., in Laffitte, S., *Chekhov*, Angus and Robertson, London, 1974, p. 16.
100 Devine, G., 'Introduction', in Chekhov, A., *Platonov*, Methuen, London, 1961, p. 7.
101 Chekhov, A., Letter to Yakov Polonsky, 22 February 1888, quoted in Magarshack, D., *Chekhov: A Life*, Greenwood Press, Westport, 1970, p. 144.
102 Jackson, R. L., 'Perspectives on Chekhov', in Jackson, R. L., op. cit., p. 12.
103 Worrall, N., 'Robert Sturua's Interpretation of Chekhov's *Three Sisters*: An Experiment in Post-modern Theatre', in Clayton, J. D., ed., *Chekhov Then and Now: The Reception of Chekhov in World Culture*, Peter Lang, New York, 1997, p. 79.
104 When Laurence Senelick claims that: 'Sturua's energetic and exuberant prodding unblocked the constipation of the English approach to Chekhov' (Senelick, L., *The Chekhov Theatre*, Cambridge University Press, Cambridge, 1997, p. 348.), or when Nick Worrall states that: 'The critics who complained that the production left them "unmoved" were demanding sentimental productions of a categorically preordained type, based on established traditions' (Worrall, N., op. cit., p. 82), they both imply that it is incorrect to think that there could be 'preferred readings' of Chekhov's works. It may well be that Sturua's unblocking of the constipation of the English approach to Chekhov resulted only in his producing his own diarrhoea. One wonders if Worrall has considered the possibility that being 'unmoved' by a performance of a Chekhov play is a sure sign that the production is an inadequate realisation of the work.
105 Worrall, N., op. cit., p. 82.
106 Ibid., pp. 82–3.
107 Gassner, J., *The Theatre in Our Times*, Crown Publishers, New York, 1963, p. 16.

# Chapter 4. *The Seagull*: From Disaster to Triumph

> *I really do believe that no play can be set up by even the most talented producer without the author's personal guidance and directions ... There are different interpretations, but the author has the right to demand that his play is performed and the parts played wholly according to his own interpretation ... It is necessary that the particular atmosphere intended by the author is created.* (Anton Chekhov)[1]

> *A conductor is entitled to his own interpretation of a score; a director is entitled to his own interpretation of a play. The question is, at what point does leeway become licence?* (Michael Heim)[2]

Despite the fact that he felt that *Ivanov* (1887) had not been interpreted correctly by critics and theatrical practitioners alike, Chekhov had scored a minor theatrical success with that play. He was to endure the pain of seeing his next play, *The Wood Demon* (1889), fail miserably in its Moscow production. J. L. Styan is probably correct when he asserts that:

> The former was a success with the public because it was more closely modelled after the kind of melodrama which was common throughout Europe at that time; the latter was a failure because Chekhov had discarded too many of those theatrical conventions the audience expected.[3]

Chekhov was to wait six years before he again risked presenting a new play for production. *The Seagull* (1896) is a transitional play that only partially achieves his aim of showing 'life as it is' in a realistic manner. The playwright did not totally avoid employing the dramatic clichés that he had inherited from the theatrical tradition of his day. Alan Seymour is quite correct when he points to the exaggerated claims that are made about *The Seagull* in terms of its new 'realistic' dramaturgy and contrasts them with what Chekhov actually achieved:

> The author is ... quoted as the great master of natural dialogue, seemingly casual conversations which reveal character and atmosphere indirectly. How is this for indirect revelation? Medvedenko (Act 1, *The Seagull*): 'Nina Mikhailovna [Zaryechnaia] is to act in a play written by Konstantin Gavrilovich [Treplev]. They are in love with each other' ... and this to Masha who has lived in the house all her life and may be presumed to be already in possession of this information.[4]

This rather clumsy exposition scene is symptomatic of the work of a writer who was still learning his trade as a dramatist. Possibly the most awkward hangover from the earlier non-realistic dramaturgical practices that Chekhov seems to have inherited was the use of the aside and soliloquy. These conventions are unsuitable in a drama that is aiming to be lifelike. Direct address to an audience has a long tradition in theatre, but it feels appropriate only in the type of drama that acknowledges its own theatricality.

Chekhov, at the time of writing *The Seagull*, could not avoid including many asides and soliloquies in the play. These pre-realistic conventions can create difficulties for directors attempting to achieve the level of dramatic realism that Chekhov desired. Irina's aside in Act Three – 'Now he's mine' – that marks her triumphant reassertion of power over her lover, Trigorin, reminds one of the heavily whispered asides of gloating melodrama villains and can easily produce a cheap laugh.[5] Treplev's long soliloquy towards the end of Act Four, in which he talks about his insoluble writing problems, is difficult to perform in the realistic manner that Chekhov desired. Michael Frayn found Chekhov's use of soliloquy in *The Seagull* so awkward that he 'was tempted to reorganise the scenes a little to avoid the need for soliloquy'.[6] While Chekhov may not have totally emancipated himself from the dramaturgy of melodrama and the well-made play, nevertheless, *The Seagull* is vastly more natural and less overtly theatrical than his earlier full-length plays.[7]

The initial reception of the play was not favourable. In fact, *The Seagull* had such a disastrous premiere at the Alexandrinsky Theatre in St Petersburg on 17 October 1896 that the author vowed: 'I shall *never* either write plays or have them acted.'[8] In fact, the catastrophe that occurred on opening night had more to do with factors outside the artistic strengths or weaknesses of the production. The evening's entertainment had been chosen as part of a benefit performance for the well-known performer, E. I. Levkeyeva, whom Heim describes as 'a fat, mustachioed comic actress popular for her comic roles'.[9] Presumably the audience expected something in keeping with the particular talents of this entertainer and was unlikely to appreciate the subtle nuances of this new type of drama. The audience may well have known that Chekhov had described *The Seagull* as a comedy and consequently were bemused and upset by what they witnessed:

> Although there was no part for her in the play, her faithful audience filled the theater expecting to be entertained — if not the way she entertained them, then at least with broad theatrical effects. (*Pashenka*, the play immediately preceding *The Seagull*, had been applauded wildly by the same kind of audience. It told the story of a cafe singer who marries into an aristocratic family, then escapes back to her former life and shoots herself when her husband comes after her.) Looking forward to an evening of either farce or melodrama, they made vociferous fun of Masha's snuff, Treplev's bandage, and could only have been bitterly disappointed when Treplev's suicide took place offstage. Chekhov forced himself to sit through two acts, but finally he fled — first the theater, then St Petersburg.[10]

Lydia Avilova, an admirer of Chekhov, was present at that first performance and has left us a fascinating eyewitness description of what occurred on that occasion. She, like many others in the audience, appears to have found the play difficult to understand. Her comments are useful insofar as they help us to gain some idea of how the play was theatrically interpreted in its initial production. In particular, Avilova describes the manner in which the actress playing Nina performed Treplev's play. As we shall see, the way in which this symbolist playlet is interpreted by directors and actors largely determines how the play as a whole is interpreted and defines the parameters within which any audience makes its own reading. It is clear from Avilova's description of the audience response to Act One of *The Seagull* that the first audience found Treplev's play laughable:

> The play seemed to have no meaning for me. It seemed to get entirely lost. I strained my ears to catch every word of every character who might be speaking. I listened with the greatest possible attention. But I could not make anything out of the play and it left no impression on me. When Nina Zarechnaya began her monologue, 'People, lions, eagles ...' I heard a curious noise in the stalls and I seemed to come to with a start. What was the matter? It seemed to me that suppressed laughter passed over the rows of people below; or wasn't it laughter, but an indignant murmur? Whatever it was, it was something unpleasant, something hostile ... The curtain came down, and suddenly something indescribable happened: the applause was drowned by boos, and the more people applauded, the louder was the booing. And it was then that I could clearly hear the people laugh. And they did not just laugh: they roared with laughter. The audience began to come out into the corridors and the foyer, and I heard how some of them were highly indignant, while others gave vent to their disapproval in bitter and venomous words. 'Some symbolic trash!' 'Why doesn't he stick to his short stories?'[11]

Avilova's description of the response to Act Four conjures up a scene in which the St Petersburg audience destroyed Chekhov's play even more ruthlessly than Irina Arkadina had demolished her son's symbolist drama. The first-night audience and the 'star' actress had something in common in terms of their theatrical tastes. Both appear to have had little sympathy with the 'new forms' of drama being offered them:

> In the last act, which I liked very much and which for a time even made me forget the failure of the play, Kommissarzhevskaya (Nina), recalling Treplyov's [Treplev's] play in which she had acted the World Soul in the first act, suddenly tore off a sheet from the sofa, wrapped it round herself, and again began her monologue, 'People, lions, eagles ...' But she had barely time to start when the whole theatre began to roar with laughter. And that in the most dramatic and moving place in the play which should have made everyone cry! They laughed

at the sheet, ... everyone roared with laughter, the entire theatre laughed, and the end of the play was completely ruined. No one was moved by the shot that put an end to Treplyov's life and the curtain came down to the accompaniment of the same boos and jeers which had drowned the few timid claps at the end of the first act.[12]

It was not just the thwarted expectations of an audience hungry for an evening of light entertainment that provoked the failure of the first production of *The Seagull*. It is generally argued that 'the main reason for its early failure was that Chekhov's artistic intention was not understood by the performers'.[13] Most accounts of this first production judge it solely in terms of what occurred on the disastrous first night. Daniel Gillès' description of the rehearsals that Chekhov attended, and which supposedly gave him nightmares, is fairly typical of this kind of totally negative approach to the St Petersburg production:

> Under bad direction the actors, many of whom had not yet learned their parts, understood nothing of the characters they were playing or of the poetry of the play itself, and they performed with the bombast and grandiloquence that were mandatory on Russian stages in those days. They seemed not to understand what Chekhov meant when he often interrupted them to repeat: 'The main thing, my children, is that it's absolutely unnecessary to make *theatre* of it. The characters are simple, ordinary people.'[14]

The implication that the St Petersburg production had involved directorial misinterpretation and actor incompetence was certainly the argument put forward by the co-founder of the Moscow Art Theatre, Nemirovich-Danchenko, when trying to convince Chekhov that his company should be allowed to produce the Moscow premiere of the play. He wrote encouragingly to the reluctant dramatist:

> Rest assured that everything will be done to assure the play's success ... I am sure that you won't experience anything with us similar to what happened in the Petersburg production. I will consider the 'rehabilitation' of this play one of my greatest achievements.[15]

The closer one looks at the available evidence, the more it becomes clear that the production in St Petersburg was not quite the debacle that both Nemirovich-Danchenko and Stanislavski were happy to assume it had been. Subsequent performances appear to have been received with less hilarity than occurred on the first-night fiasco. Simon Karlinsky has argued that eye-witness evidence suggests that Yevtikhy Karpov's St Petersburg production, 'while under-rehearsed and by no means ideal, was not as bad as subsequent legend made it out to be'.[16] The young and largely unknown actress, Vera Kommissarzhevskaya, who took over the role of Nina from the famous actress Mariya Savina five days before opening, wrote to Chekhov four days after that eventful night, claiming that subsequent performances had been theatrical triumphs. 'Victory is ours,' she effusively wrote, 'the play is a complete, unanimous success, just as it ought to be, just as it had to be. How I'd like to see you now, but what I'd like even more is for you to be present and hear the unanimous cry of "Author".'[17]

Chekhov may have been partially convinced by the reassurances provided by this actress whose talent he admired, but he nevertheless could not forget how poorly the actors had performed on the opening night. He wrote to his brother Mikhail on the following day that the actors 'acted as if they were ashamed to be in the theatre. The performances were vile and stupid. The moral of the story is: I shouldn't write plays.'[18] On 22 October, Chekhov wrote to Suvorin saying that he had recovered from his gruelling theatrical experience to the extent that now he 'wouldn't even mind doing another play', but he could not resist describing the conditions under which his play had been produced. 'Actually there was only one genuine rehearsal, at which it was impossible to tell what was going on; the play was completely lost in a fog of vile acting.'[19] Even Kommissarzhevskaya, who had impressed Chekhov in rehearsal to such an extent that he wrote to his brother Mikhail on 15 October saying that she 'acts amazingly',[20] had proved to be disappointing. 'Kommissarjevskaya is a marvellous actress ... but at the performance she too succumbed to the prevailing mood of hostility toward my *Seagull* and was intimidated by it, as it were, and her voice failed her.'[21]

Chekhov, ever the realist, thanked one of the first-night audience who had written to 'pour healing balm on the author's wounds', but refused to deny the harsh reality of his own experience:

> I did not see everything at the first performance, but what I did see was vague, dingy, dreary, and wooden. I had no hand in assigning the parts, I wasn't given any new scenery, there were only two rehearsals, the actors didn't know their parts — and the result was general panic, utter depression of spirit; even Kommissarjevskaya's performance was nothing much, though her playing at one of the rehearsals was so prodigious that people in the orchestra wept and blew their noses.[22]

It is important not to confuse the first-night performance with the production as a whole. Chekhov had expressed only minor dissatisfaction with Kommissarzhevskaya's interpretation of the role of Nina during rehearsals. He had asked her to tone down her performance of Treplev's play, since, as he pointed out to her, 'Nina is a young girl brought up in the country ... she finds herself on a stage for the first time ... she suffers from stage-fright, she is very nervous'.[23]

When he saw the play, Chekhov was disappointed with the performance, and even with the playing of Kommissarzhevskaya. However, it is clear that this negative reaction was exacerbated by the fact that she had not done herself or the role justice on opening night as a result of having been 'thrown' by the bizarre behaviour of the audience. Chekhov's disappointment may well have been heightened by the fact that he felt that the role of Nina was of central importance in the play. He is reported to have told Karpov, the director of the production, that 'this part means *everything* to me in this play'.[24]

Chekhov was clearly impressed by Kommissarzhevskaya's overall interpretation of the role. Clara Hollosi provides evidence of how enthusiastic the playwright was about the performance of this actress:

> Despite his reaction to this fated premiere, Chekhov maintained a correspondence with Kommissarzhevskaya until the end of his life, and he always remembered her and her performance fondly. For instance, Efros gives his account of a conversation with Chekhov on the occasion of the Alexandrine Theatre's revival of *The Seagull* in 1902: 'We recalled the first *Seagull* in Petersburg. A cheerful smile appeared on Chekhov's sullen visage when he remembered Kommissarzhevskaya's Nina. I don't remember the exact words, only the tone — a tone of delight.' Even a year before his death, when the Moscow Art Theatre was preparing a guest performance in St Petersburg of *The Seagull*, Chekhov suggested that they invite Kommissarzhevskaya to play the role of Nina.[25]

Hollosi's article examines and compares the performance of Kommissarzhevskaya in Karpov's St Petersburg production, with that of Roxonova in Stanislavski's Moscow Art Theatre production in 1898. Having shown that Chekhov obviously preferred the earlier interpretation of Nina's role, Hollosi nevertheless refuses to acknowledge that Roxonova's interpretation of the role was in any way inferior to that of Kommissarzhevskaya. Hollosi states that her article:

> ... does not intend to suggest that either of the two Nina interpretations discussed ... is 'correct' or 'incorrect' in accordance with Chekhov's likes or dislikes: since Stanislavski the director-oriented theatre has long won its right for independent interpretations of the classics.[26]

Hollosi's genuflection to the concept of director's theatre denies the real value of her research. By accepting the idea that there is no necessary nexus between the playwright's play and the director's interpretation of it, she allows for no possibility of directorial misinterpretation. She concludes by making the trivial claim that her study 'simply wishes to throw light on Chekhov's reactions to some early stage interpretations of one of his fascinating ambiguous characters'.[27] What Hollosi's research has achieved, I believe, is much more significant than she claims.

If one does not accept the highly questionable claim that directors have a 'right' to 'independent' interpretations, in which their directorial decisions need bear no relation to what Susanne Langer has called the 'immanent form' of the play; if we can accept that some productions are better than others, on the ground that they more fully realise the action of the play; and if, in fact, we accept that a play can be misinterpreted, then we can learn from Hollosi's article the extent to which Stanislavski misinterpreted the role of Nina and distorted the significance of Treplev's symbolist play. Ultimately, the information supplied in Hollosi's article helps greatly to explain why Chekhov felt Stanislavski did not understand his plays.

We need to examine the ways in which Stanislavski failed to realise on stage the vision of reality expressed in Chekhov's playscript and provide some explanation why this director, despite having misinterpreted *The Seagull*, nevertheless had such a success with this production that the Moscow Art Theatre adopted an image of a seagull as its emblem.

Stanislavski was honest enough to admit in his later writings that he found *The Seagull* 'strange and monotonous after its first reading' and, even after having listened to Nemirovich-Danchenko explain the play and having grown to like the characters, he confessed that 'as soon as I remained alone with the script of the play, I ceased to like it and was bored with it'.[28] Despite his misgivings, Stanislavski set about preparing a detailed *mise-en-scène* for the play in the manner of the autocratic director. As he himself put it: 'At that time, while our actors were yet untrained, the despotic methods of the stage director were in full force. The stage director of necessity became the only creator of the play.'[29]

An examination of Stanislavski's prompt-book for this production reveals his obsession with making the stage 'lifelike' and provides evidence that helps us to understand why this auteur director often missed the artistic point of Chekhov's understated dramaturgy. In his writings on the theatre, Meyerhold, who played Treplev in this production, recalled a typical case of Stanislavskian overkill. The director's love of literal realism was combined with his love of melodrama to produce the kind of 'theatricality' that Chekhov was specifically trying to avoid:

> One of the actors proudly told Chekhov that the director intended to bring the entire household, including a woman with a child crying, on to the stage at the close of the third act of *The Seagull*. Chekhov said: 'He mustn't. It would be like playing pianissimo on the piano and having the lid suddenly crash down.' 'But in life it often happens that the pianissimo is interrupted quite unexpectedly by the forte,' reported one of the actors. 'Yes, but the stage demands a degree of artifice,' said A. P. 'You have no fourth wall. Besides, the stage is art, the stage reflects the quintessence of life and there is no need to introduce anything superfluous on to it.'[30]

Chekhov was too ill to leave Yalta and come up to Moscow to see the Moscow Art Theatre's 'successful' production of *The Seagull*, but he begged to see a special performance of the play when he had recovered enough to travel to Moscow early in 1899. Chekhov had explained to Stanislavski why it was vital for him to see the production: 'Listen, it is necessary for me. I am its author. How can I write anything else until I have seen it?'[31] Stanislavski staged a special performance, without the use of sets, for Chekhov's benefit. Being able to concentrate on the actors' interpretations of their roles, Chekhov soon made it clear to Stanislavski that he disliked the dandified manner in which the director played the role of the writer, Trigorin, but his most scathing criticism was aimed at the actress Roxonova for what he felt was her inept portrayal of the role of Nina. Writing to Maxim Gorky soon after he had seen this performance, he conceded that it 'wasn't bad on the whole', but was deeply distressed by several performances: 'I can't judge the play with equanimity, because the seagull herself gave such an abominable performance — she blubbered loudly throughout.'[32]

Stanislavski's own account of Chekhov's reaction reveals just how upset the playwright was at Roxonova's depiction of Nina as a weeping neurotic. During the act breaks in the performance of the play the director observed Chekhov and noted that 'his face bore no signs of inner joy'. At the conclusion of the play he delivered his critique of the acting:

> Chekhov praised some of the actors, others received their full meed of blame. This was true of one actress especially, with whose work Chekhov was completely dissatisfied. 'Listen,' he said, 'she can't act in my play. You have another actress who could be much finer in the part, who is a much better actress.'[33]

When Stanislavski pointed out that to replace Roxonova in the role would be tantamount to firing her, Chekhov appears to have been so upset by her interpretation that, in his desire to have her replaced, he even went as far as to threaten the director. 'Listen,' Stanislavski reports him saying, 'I will take the play away from you.' Despite hoping that Chekhov would calm down and forget about the idea of replacing Roxonova, Stanislavski was surprised when he kept repeating: 'Listen, she can't act in my play.'[34]

The fact that Chekhov was 'appalled' by 'the hysterical interpretation of Nina'[35] has been noted by many critics, and most assume that the actress was to blame for this depiction. However, evidence cited in Hollosi's article suggests that Roxonova was attempting an interpretation of the role that was uncongenial to her but which had been foisted on her by Stanislavski. As Braun has pointed out, the autocratic approach that characterised Stanislavski's directing style at this stage of his career meant that he controlled every element of the production. 'Every detail of the production was prescribed, including the actor's every move, gesture, and vocal inflection.'[36] Apparently Nemirovich-Danchenko, who was in charge of the 'literary' interpretation of the play's 'content', had interpreted Nina in a positive manner. However, Stanislavski, whose assigned task was the 'formal' stage realisation of that interpretation, disagreed with his partner's view of Nina's character.[37]

Essentially, Stanislavski regarded Nina as a failure in both her life and her art. He had, as Magarshack points out in his biography of the director, 'entirely misunderstood the character of Nina and in doing so distorted the ruling idea of the play'.[38] That ruling idea was bound up with Nina, and in particular with her ability to grow, suffer and ultimately to endure the painful vicissitudes of living a life without illusions. She embodies the hopeful aspects of Chekhov's overall vision of reality. Unless she is interpreted in a positive manner, this 'comedy' becomes a forlorn elegy celebrating the absurdity of the human condition. *The Seagull* becomes the play described by Gillès, namely, 'the drama — or the comedy, according to the author's self-effacing and dishonest subtitle — of ambitions that will never be realised, of inevitably doomed ambitions'.[39]

If, as I have argued, Chekhov is demonstrably not an absurdist, but rather a cautious optimist — 'a believer in a brighter future for the human race', as Magarshack puts it — then, in order to allow this play to 'imperceptibly [force] the spectator to identify himself with this belief',[40] Nina's speeches to Treplev near the end of Act Four must be performed in a manner that suggests that she is not deluding herself:

> NINA. ... Constantine [Treplev], I know now, I've come to see, that in our work — no matter whether we're actors or writers — the great thing isn't fame or glory, it isn't what I used to dream of, but simply stamina. You must know how to bear your cross and have faith. I have faith and things don't hurt me so much now. And when I think of my vocation I'm not afraid of life.[41]

Nemirovich-Danchenko, who had a high regard for the actress Roxonova, even telling Chekhov that this 'spirited young actress' had been described by the painter Ivanov as 'A little Duse',[42] felt moved to tell Chekhov that her performance had not been up to the standard of the other performers in the otherwise highly successful first-night performance of the play in Moscow. The reasons that Nemirovich cites for this relative failure are revealing. Having given a detailed description of the wonderful reception given to the performance, he comments on the acting:

> Weakest of all was Roksanova who was confused by Alekseiev [Stanislavski], who directed her to play like some idiot. I got angry with her and demanded that she go back to the earlier lyrical tone. That confused her.[43]

Any actor who has ever been simultaneously directed by two directors with very different ideas about the same show will appreciate why Roxonova had every right to be 'confused'. Chekhov had seen two rehearsals on 9 and 11

September 1898 and, presumably, the actress playing Nina had been following Nemirovich-Danchenko's 'lyrical' interpretation of the role, which seems to have accorded with Chekhov's own conception. He wrote to the writer Yezhov: 'I saw two rehearsals; I like it. Roxanova is quite good.'[44] He received news in Yalta however which suggested that something was wrong with Roxonova's performance by the time the play actually opened. Chekhov had asked Yezhov to write and give him his impressions of the performance. Yezhov replied:

> Seagull-Zarechnaya — Mme Roxonova was over-anxious to act well, but she couldn't even give a glimpse of the gentle Nina. Her attitude was all wrong, it was as if she were groping blindly, and in each monologue she was searching for the correct path, but alas, could not find it.[45]

Chekhov's anger at the way Nina had been turned into a sobbing wreck under Stanislavski's direction is recorded vividly in Olga Knipper's memoirs. In particular Chekhov was furious at the way Act Four — the Act in which Nina was supposed to face the world's hardships with 'faith' — had been totally misinterpreted:

> Chekhov, the mild-mannered Chekhov, walked on the stage with his watch in his hand, looking grave and pale, and declared in a very determined voice that everything was excellent, 'but,' he continued, 'I suggest that my play should end with the Third Act: I shall not permit you to play the Fourth Act.' He was dissatisfied with many things, chiefly with the tempo of the play. He was very excited, and told us that the Fourth Act was not from his play.[46]

Stanislavski had not simply indulged his penchant for making the stage 'lifelike' by including what was to become his trademark — the use of a multiplicity of naturalistic sound effects and attenuated pregnant pauses — he had transformed the action of Chekhov's play to such an extent that, far from being a drama in which inauthentic and spineless behaviour is shown to reduce life to absurdity, and courageous endurance and work is seen as the hope for improving the conditions of life, it became a self-pitying depiction of *fin-de-siècle* gloom and despair. The play for Stanislavski was about the romantic tragedy of the misunderstood and undervalued artist, and this interpretation was pushed by the director with all of the sentimentality that he used so effectively on his productions of melodramas. 'The tragedy,' he claimed, 'is self-evident. Can the provincial mother understand the complex longings of her talented son?'[47] Once having decided that Treplev was some sort of genius 'with the soul of Chekhov and a true comprehension of art',[48] Stanislavski had to find an explanation why this great talent wasn't immediately recognised when Treplev's symbolist playlet was performed. The scapegoat was near at hand. 'Nina Zarechnaya is the cause of the failure of Treplev's talented play.'[49]

In *My Life in Art* Stanislavski outlines the reading of Nina that he tried to impose on Roxonova. It bears little resemblance to the 'lyrical' interpretation suggested by Nemirovich-Danchenko and lacks any of the maturity and resilience that is implied in Chekhov's script, and which was such an important aspect of the vision of reality that he wished to depict. Writing in the overblown florid style that was so congenial to him, Stanislavski creates the melodrama replete with villains and heroes in which *his* Nina can function:

> She is not an actress, although she dreams of being one so as to earn the love of the worthless Trigorin. She does not understand what she is playing. She is too young to understand the deep gloom of the soul of Treplev. She has not yet suffered enough to perceive the eternal tragedy of the world. She must first fall in love with the scoundrelly Lovelace Trigorin and give him all that is beautiful in woman, give it to him in vain, at an accidental meeting in some low inn. The young and beautiful life is deformed and killed just as meaninglessly as the beautiful white seagull was killed by Treplev because of nothing to do. Poor Nina, before understanding the depth of what she is playing, must bear a child in secret, must suffer hunger and privation many years, dragging herself through the lower depths of all the provincial theatres, must come to know the scoundrelly attentions of merchants to a young actress, must come to know her own giftlessness, in order to be able in her last farewell meeting with Treplev in the fourth act of the play to feel at last all the eternal and tragic depth of Treplev's monologue, and perhaps for the last and only time say it like a true actress and force Treplev and the spectators in the theatre to shed holy tears called forth by the power of art.[50]

Here we have the perfect example of the limitations of Stanislavski as a director of Chekhov's plays. While not being politically radical, the playwright's social ideas were far more progressive than the conservative Stanislavski, whose attitude towards Nina reveals how little he understood this 'new woman'. Stanislavski's strength lay in his ability to create exciting theatre. Nemirovich-Danchenko's own criticisms of Stanislavski's approach are extremely perceptive and highlight both the director's strengths and weaknesses:

> You are an exceptional *regisseur*, but so far only for melodrama or for farce, for productions full of dazzling stage effects, but which bind you neither to psychological nor to verbal demands. You trample upon every creative production. Sometimes you have the good fortune to fuse with it; in such an instance the result is excellent, but more often after the first two acts the author, if he happens to be a great poet or a great playwright, begins to call you to account for your inattention to his play's deepest and most significant inner movements. And that is why with the third act your performances begin their downward turn.[51]

We now have evidence concerning the ways in which Stanislavski changed the meaning of the play. The Russian critic, M. Stroyeva, noted how Nina was encouraged to present herself as a failure, an image of 'ruined illusions'. This critic's description of what Roxonova actually did in performance in order to carry out Stanislavski's wishes is included in Hollosi's article on the two interpretations of Nina. It goes some way to explain why the critic N. Ye. Efros, who was otherwise deeply impressed by *The Seagull*, should have found Roxonova's Nina unsatisfactory, and why Chekhov should have reacted so negatively to this characterisation:

> The actress, writes Stroyeva, emphasised mainly the fall of a human being broken by life's vicissitudes. The figures of Nina and Treplyov were associated in this performance with motifs of despondency, nervous agitation, sharp collisions, and half-hysterical sobbings. To underscore the theme of defeat, Stanislavski omitted this line from the last scene: 'I am a seagull ... No, that's not it. I'm an actress. Oh well.' The whole monologue was presented in 'a single stiff pose', she was 'exhausted', 'leaning her tired head on her hand', and only straightened herself in the end. The recollection of Treplyov's play was accompanied by the endless roar of the wind and the sound of rain through the open door. Nina's exit was prepared by the director so as not to leave any doubt in the spectator about Nina's gloomy, or rather tragic, future.[52]

When we look back at the description by the actress M. Chitau-Karmina, who played the role of Masha in the earlier St Petersburg production, of the way Kommissarzhevskaya attempted to play Nina, we can see how much closer she was to Chekhov's own conception of the role than Roxonova's tearful failure was to be. Apparently the original intention in the first production was to ridicule Treplev's play by staging it 'in a comic vein of old-fashioned taste and spirit'.[53] That plan was abandoned when Kommissarzhevskaya played the role in a non-burlesque manner. This 'serious' playing of the symbolist playlet made it possible for Dorn, the doctor in the play, to praise both the playlet and Nina's performance in it, without appearing to be a complete fool. If Treplev's drama is played in such a way that *both* the on-stage and off-stage audiences are forced to judge it as laughable balderdash, then Dorn must appear to the off-stage audience as a character who is incapable of discriminating between dramatic art and dramatic rubbish. Left alone after the play, Dorn soliloquises:

> Well, I don't know. Perhaps it's all rather beyond me, perhaps I've gone mad, but I liked the play. It has something. When that child spoke about loneliness, and then afterwards when the Devil's red eyes appeared, my hands shook with excitement. It was all so fresh and innocent. Look, I think he's coming. I want to be as nice about it as I can.[54]

Even though Chekhov's use of the non-realistic theatrical convention of the soliloquy fits uneasily into the new kind of realistic drama he was attempting to write, it does suggest that an audience is supposed to interpret Dorn's account of his response to Treplev's play as an honest one. His being alone on stage when he relates his experience ensures the veracity of his comments since he can have no reason to lie to the audience about his positive reaction to Treplev's and Nina's efforts. Chitau's description of Kommissarzhevskaya's performance would certainly suggest that Dorn's favourable response to Nina's acting and to Treplev's play was not ludicrously inappropriate:

> She started the monologue in a low tone of her wonderful voice gradually raising it and engrossing all the attention to its modulations. Then she gradually lowered her voice as if extinguishing a fire, and pronouncing the last words 'and earth will all have been gradually turned to dust' it almost died down.[55]

While some of the audience responded negatively to the play, Kommissarzhevskaya's individual performance elicited rapturous praise. Chitau records that 'everybody felt that the brightness that emanated from the playing of this actress, kept radiating in the theatre. When she came out to bow alone, the audience cheered her with enthusiasm.'[56] Kommissarzhevskaya played the role of Nina in several later productions and, according to contemporary accounts, she always managed to convince the audience that Nina was talented. Indeed, Hollosi points out that Kommissarzhevskaya's playing of Nina was in line with Chekhov's unsentimental view of women. Stanislavski may have held the old-fashioned melodramatic view that to lose her virginity to Trigorin was for Nina to 'give him all that was beautiful in woman', but nowhere in his writings does Chekhov proclaim this antiquated sexist standpoint. Kommissarzhevskaya even felt that Chekhov in *The Seagull* had:

> ... enriched the portrayals of Russian women with a new facet: that of an awakening creative personality. An unhappy love affair no longer destroys such a woman, but activates her to find her true vocation.[57]

Hollosi recounts the story of Kommissarzhevskaya sending a friend a photograph, presumably of herself, on which she had written a quotation from *The Seagull*: 'When I think of my vocation, I am not afraid of life.' The strength of character implicit in this quotation was totally lacking in Stanislavski's interpretation. Roxonova's Nina 'in the first act ... imitated naivete and in the final scene wavered between tearful melodrama and pathological contrivances'.[58] As Hollosi accurately points out:

> The essence of Komissarzhevskaya's portrayal of Nina is this active acceptance of life together with all its hardships. This theme returns repeatedly in Chekhov's later works, and it seems it is not a coincidence that Kommissarzhevskaya's interpretation and performance captivated the author so much.[59]

I have dealt with the markedly divergent directorial interpretations evident in the St Petersburg and Moscow productions not in order to belittle Stanislavski, but rather to suggest that it is possible to misinterpret a play and still produce a resounding success. More importantly, I wish to argue that it is never justifiable for a director to be totally 'independent' of the 'literary text' when preparing the 'performance text'. Finding the means to communicate Chekhov's play is surely more likely to produce a rich theatrical experience than simply relying on a director's 'whims of temperament and chance outbursts of fancy'.[60]

Raymond Williams has suggested that a major problem faced by directors of Chekhov has arisen because of the playwright's adoption of the conventions of realism. Williams argues that the realistic form militates against the possibility of a director achieving any realisation of the play's action, since the more complete the achievement of verisimilitude, the less visible the action becomes. If Harold Pinter is correct in his observation that in our day-to-day living, 'The more acute the experience the less articulate its expression',[61] then a form of drama that attempts to be lifelike will only be able to express the banal surface of life, while the important inner experience remains hidden. In effect the dramatic 'text' that utilises the conventions of realism is, as Williams describes it, 'incomplete', and the play can only be fleshed out through the imaginative interpolations suggested by the director and embodied in the *mise-en-scène* and the actors' 'subtext'.

Williams sums up what he sees as the major problem of Chekhovian dramaturgy and the limitations of the conventions of realism in the following way:

> The representation of appearances, of what is external and on the surface, can be directly dramatized, in that patient stage dressing and carpentry. In Chekhov or Ibsen, on the other hand, what is visible and directly expressible, is no more than a counterpoint to the unrealized life — the inner and common desires, fears, possibilities — which struggles to find itself in just this solidly staged world. When we speak of naturalism, we must distinguish between this passion for the whole truth, for the liberation of what cannot yet be said or done, and the confident and even complacent representation of things as they are, that things are what they seem. This latter convention of the naturalist habit, has been surprisingly durable; it still supports a majority of our dramas, in all forms. But the serious and exploring drama, from Ibsen and Chekhov and Strindberg to Brecht and Beckett, was faced always with a contradiction: that which it seemed to make real, in theatrical terms, was what it wished to show as a limited reality, in dramatic terms. All the difficulties of performing Chekhov come from this contradiction.[62]

Notwithstanding Williams' arguments, it is clear that Chekhov does, in fact, provide the necessary encoded signals in the texts of his plays that allow a director who is willing to seek them out to decipher them and thus to be in a position to theatrically realise the action of Chekhov's plays without having to resort to the 'whims' and 'fancies' that Nemirovich-Danchenko felt Stanislavski employed. Chekhov, of course, was committed to a form of art which aimed, as part of its project, to hide its own artifice, but even though he wished his plays to simulate real life, he always remained an artist who never confused art with life. His artistry involved using the conventions of prosaic realism and transcending the limitations that Williams thought were inherent in that form. So successful was he in doing this that T. S. Eliot was grudgingly led to say that Chekhov did things of which he, Eliot, would not otherwise have thought prose to be capable.

One of Chekhov's earliest references to *The Seagull* shows that he was consciously trying to create a 'new form' of drama that would replace the cheap theatricality of melodrama and the mechanical structure of the well-made play. 'I am writing a play, ... I am writing it with considerable pleasure, though I sin frightfully against the conventions of the stage.'[63] The main convention of the stage that Chekhov was sinning against was the requirement that plays be full of external or what Magarshack calls direct action. Instead of producing exciting on-stage events, Chekhov was attempting to write a work of indirect action, where the main events of the drama take place off-stage and the text reflects only the trivial surface of life. This playtext, however, incorporated sufficient readable signals to the director, and ultimately the actor, to imply a coherent and rich subtext that could be communicated to an audience in performance. Chekhov wished to show his spectators images of people very like themselves who waste their potential by living 'silly trivial lives'. Consequently, he depicted his characters in a way that showed them doing very little that is significant in terms of overt action — indeed, often doing things that are amusing in their banality. It is the task of the actors to make the audience aware of the characters' subtextual desire to be more significant and effective than they actually are. The tragic subtext of unfulfilled desires is juxtaposed with the comic text of silly trivial behaviour and the audience's perception of the gap between the characters' external and internal lives produces the kind of synthetic tragi-comedy that we now recognise as Chekhovian.

In a letter to Suvorin, Chekhov points out the trivial elements that he intended to use for the surface action of *The Seagull*: 'It is a comedy with three female parts, six male, four acts, a landscape (view of a lake), lots of talk on literature, little action and tons of love.'[64] The 'tons of love' does not produce the kind of romantic comedy in which every Jack gets his Jill. That would be the dramatisation of the successful achievement of desire. In *The Seagull*, and in various ways in Chekhov's later plays, the presentation of relationships involves a whole daisy-chain of unrequited lovers, all of whom seem to choose the wrong potential mate to dote on. Each would-be lover is attracted to another person, but seems to be aware only of that person's outer life. This trivial outer life is evident in the text. If these lovers were to pay attention to the signs that periodically surface from the subtextual inner life of the characters they are attracted to, they would realise how unreciprocated and pointless their love is. This lack of awareness of the other is not presented as some existential malaise that is an inevitable part of the human condition, but is simply one of the means that Chekhov employs to show that self-centred behaviour makes human beings ridiculous. The characters in the chain are always so acutely aware of their own anguish and desires that they are unaware of, or ignore the suffering of the other characters who love them.

Brooks and Heilman accurately describe the chain of lovers who are unloved, but fail to note that much of the pain experienced by these characters is self-inflicted, resulting from their own hopelessly egocentric behaviour:

> Medevenko is in love with Masha, who is in love with Treplev, who is in love with Nina, who is in love with Trigorin, who is in love (at least in his own way) with Madame Arcadin, who is in love with herself.[65]

All of the characters in the chain at some time in the play become self-obsessed; some of them never acquire the necessary objectivity to see themselves and others clearly. The opening dialogue of the play presents a perfect example of this self-obsession:

> MEDVEDENKO. Why do you wear black all the time?
> MASHA. I'm in mourning for my life, I'm unhappy.
> MEDVEDENKO. Why? [*Reflects.*] I don't understand. You're healthy and your father's quite well off, even if he's not rich. I'm much worse off than you — I'm only paid twenty-three roubles a month, and what with pension deductions I don't even get that. But I don't go round like someone at a funeral. [*They sit down.*]
> MASHA. Money doesn't matter, even a poor man can be happy.
> MEDVEDENKO. Yes — in theory. But look how it works out. There's me, my mother, my two sisters and my young brother. But I only earn twenty-three roubles and we need food and drink, don't we? Tea and sugar? And tobacco? We can hardly make ends meet.
> MASHA. [*Looking back at the stage.*] The play will be on soon.[66]

Masha, as we will soon learn, is not in mourning for anyone who has died, she is simply in love with Treplev, who does not love her. Both her costume and her speech are excessive responses to what is a sad but hardly extraordinary occurrence. Steiner justly observed that 'melodrama', in its pejorative sense, occurs when 'the effect is invariably in gross excess of the cause'.[67] Masha's behaviour is ludicrously melodramatic for this very reason. Quoting a line from a short story written by the bleakly pessimistic Maupassant and trailing around 'like Niobe, all tears', can be seen as the silly pose that it is, only if the director encourages the actor playing the role to suggest to an audience that Masha's behaviour is excessive. In the script, Chekhov provides clear signals to the director to indicate that Masha is indeed over-dramatising her situation. He has her almost instantaneously drop the pose of suffering tragic heroine and adopt a much more pragmatic and down-to-earth manner. Masha refuses to put up with any romantic nonsense from Medvedenko when he whines about his unrequited love for her. Far from treating him like some tragic lover who, like herself, 'is in mourning for his life', Masha's response is brutally realistic. She is blithely unaware of the gap between her melodramatically excessive response to her own unloved situation and her realistically hardheaded response to Medvedenko's similar loveless condition. What she says to Medvedenko applies with equal validity to her own situation:

> MASHA. What rubbish. [*Takes snuff.*] Your loving me is all very touching, but I can't love you back and that's that. [*Offers him her snuffbox.*] Have some.[68]

Masha's abrupt shift from the world of romantic melodrama to that of modern realism should alert directors to the fact that the audience is not meant to take her grandiose behaviour too seriously. It is peculiarly appropriate that Medvedenko is so bound up with his own problems, especially his obsession with money, he totally fails to respond to Masha's 'tragic' behaviour. He is also completely unaware of the real reason for Masha's unhappiness. At the end of the first act Masha brings her subtextual anguish into the text when she voices her problems to Dr Dorn. He replies in an understanding manner but his comments have a meaning similar to Masha's statement to Medvedenko earlier in the act when she recognised the situation but accepts that 'that's that':

> MASHA. I'm so unhappy. No one, no one knows how I suffer. [*Lays her head on his breast, softly.*] I love Constantine.
> DORN. What a state they're all in. And what a lot of loving. Oh, magic lake! [*Tenderly.*] But what can I do, my child? What can I do?
>
> CURTAIN.[69]

Chekhov has written Masha's confession of her secret love in the language of romantic melodrama, and it was just this kind of sentimental drama that he was trying to avoid writing. Having unquestioningly employed many of the techniques of melodrama in plays like *Platonov* and *Ivanov*, Chekhov increasingly used these outdated techniques ironically and even parodically in *The Seagull* and the plays that followed.

Dr. Dorn plays the role of *raisonneur* in *The Seagull*. He refuses to treat Masha's dramatic confession as if it were some tragic revelation. Dorn's amused response provides the norm by which an audience is encouraged to judge the appropriateness or otherwise of Masha's behaviour. If a director has the actor play Dorn in a manner that emphasises both his warmth and his wisdom, as Chekhov's text implies, then an audience will be more likely to see Masha from his point of view. She is a child in matters of the heart and has yet to learn that life must go on even if romance is not fulfilled.[70]

During the two years that separate Acts III and IV Masha has made an unhappy marriage with the boring schoolteacher, Medvedenko, and, although she still loves Treplev, she appears to have acquired a more realistic view of her situation than she had at the beginning of the play. It is her mother, Polina, who remains the incurable romantic. She is still hopelessly in love with Dr Dorn and, despite his rather cool response to her, she continues to behave like some lovesick heroine in a work of romantic fiction. When Polina attempts to encourage Treplev to 'be a bit nicer' to her 'poor Masha', the daughter's response is evidence that she at least has ceased to live her life in the over-dramatised world of romantic melodrama. Like Nina, she learns how to endure in the prosaic real world:

> POLINA. ... Please be a bit nicer to my poor Masha, dear.
> MASHA. [*Making up the bed*.] Leave him alone, Mother.
> POLINA. [*To* TREPLEV.] She's such a nice girl. [*Pause*.] A woman needs nothing, Constantine, just a few kind looks. I've learnt that.
> [TREPLEV *gets up from the desk and goes out without speaking*.]
> MASHA. Now you've annoyed him. Why go on at him?
> POLINA. I'm sorry for you, Masha.
> MASHA. A lot of use that is!
> POLINA. My heart aches for you. I see everything, you know, I understand.
> MASHA. Don't be so silly. Unhappy love affairs are only found in novels. What nonsense! The thing is, don't give way to it, and don't moon around waiting for the tide to turn. If love enters your heart, get rid of it. My husband's been promised a job in another part of the country. I'm going to forget all this when we move. I'll tear it from my heart.
> [*A melancholy waltz is playing in the next room but one*.]
> POLINA. That's Constantine playing, he must be depressed.
> MASHA. [*Silently does two or three waltz steps*.] The thing is not to keep seeing him, Mother. If only Simon gets that new job, I'll be over this in a month, take it from me. It's all so silly.[71]

The production notes that Stanislavski made for his production of *The Seagull* clearly show that he did not discern any of the gentle irony that underlies Chekhov's use of melodramatic excess. Stanislavski's own love of theatricality and melodrama led him to see characters like Masha as wholly tragic and consequently lines like, 'I'm in mourning for my life, I'm unhappy', are taken seriously and underscored with a battery of staging effects that are not specified by Chekhov. The comic irony implied in Chekhov's script is submerged in the doom-laden *mise-en-scène* provided by the director:

The play starts in darkness, an (August) evening. The dim light of a lantern on top of a lamp-post, distant sounds of a drunkard's song, distant howling of a dog, the croaking of frogs, ... the slow tolling of a distant church-bell — help the audience to get the feel of the sad, monotonous life of the characters.[72]

Just in case the audience might still miss the point that the drama that is to follow is of a portentous and gloomy nature, he includes 'Flashes of lightning, faint rumbling of *thunder* in the distance'.[73] Against such a background, it is hardly surprising that Masha's opening line should have been delivered without any comic irony. Peter Holland is surely correct however, when he observes that Masha's 'comment, viewed by Stanislavski as an expression of an essentially tragic attitude, seems rather to be so off-hand as to be mocking'.[74] In Stanislavski's interpretation, there is no perceivable gap between a 'tragic subtext' and a 'comic text'. Instead, Stanislavski provides stage-business for the actor playing Masha that makes her outer life as tragic as her inner life.

In the scene in Act Four where she talks with Polina about how 'silly' and pointless her love for Treplev is, Stanislavski tries to ensure that his audience is in no doubt that it will be tragically impossible for Masha 'to forget all this' and not to 'give way to it'. Masha's resolve is undercut by several 'sighs', and her statement, 'I'll be over this in a month', is accompanied by the following business:

> Masha sighs again, waltzes to the window, stops beside it, looking out into the darkness, and taking out a handkerchief stealthily, wipes the few tears that roll down her cheeks.[75]

As Holland points out: 'The stealthiness is the cover for the revelation of the 'truth' of her feelings. Stanislavski views her consistently as someone in the agonies of unfulfilled love, a prolonged scream of frustrated yearning that Chekhov would probably not have recognised.'[76]

One of the major problems for today's directors of Chekhov is that, for many people, Stanislavski's interpretations are often taken to be 'authentic' Chekhov. Yet time and again the playwright complained of this kind of gloomy interpretation. In 1902, he wrote to Alexander Tikhonov:

> You say you wept over my plays. You are not the only one. But I did not write them for this. It was Stanislavsky who made them so tearful. I intended something quite different.[77]

Reviewers and directors alike produce variations on the gloomy Chekhov inspired by Stanislavski's sombre vision of his plays. Milton Shulman of the *Standard*, reviewing Philip Prowse's 1984 production of *The Seagull*, confidently asserts that: '*The Seagull* by Chekhov is a play about people who have resigned themselves to unhappiness but still cling precariously to hope.'[78] The production attempted, according to Shulman, to convey an 'atmosphere of compassionate futility', and no mention is made of any positive vision of reality that might be present in the play or the production. There has been a tradition on the British stage in particular to play Chekhov in this lugubrious manner. St John Irvine's review of Filmer's 1929 production of *The Seagull* at the Arts Theatre Club in London evocatively captures the mood of that production:

> Wave after wave of gloom rolled off the stage ... When someone said, 'There must be many fish in the lake!', he spoke as if he was certain that anyone who ate a fish would immediately come out in a rash or contract ptomaine poisoning.[79]

Patrick Miles quotes the reaction of the expatriate Russian director, Komisarjevsky, to mid-1920s British productions which aped Stanislavski's approach. After seeing *The Seagull*, he wrote that he had 'rarely laughed so heartily ... when the nonsense to which this simple play had been reduced by a *meaningful*, monotonous and dreary production was accepted by the audience as a *highbrow* affair'.[80]

Not everyone in Britain in the early part of the century was taken in by the misinterpretation of Chekhov's plays as dramas of pessimism. Frank Swinnerton, for example, wrote in a review in *Nation* in 1920 that to present Chekhov as a 'solemn' playwright was inaccurate:

> This is really to falsify the spirit of Chekhov, who was an artist and a humorist ... Until this fact is grasped, and Chekhov is played with some lightness and naturalness of deportment, we shall always lose the true quality of his dramatic work.[81]

Charles Sturridge's 1985 London production of *The Seagull* provides a clear illustration of the difficulties involved in finding the appropriate balance between the comic and tragic elements of the play. In the opening scene of the play, Sturridge directed Phoebe Nicholls in the role of Masha in an appropriately comic manner by having her play her famous first line in a parodically melodramatic fashion that clearly indicated to the audience that her 'tragic' behaviour was decidedly excessive. Michael Billington, reviewing this production, praises Sturridge's attempt to emphasise the comic potential of the script and describes how the actor achieved this effect: 'When Phoebe Nicholls' Masha says she is in mourning, she flings herself tempestuously on a chaise-longue and then spreads her arms wide adding "for my life": it gets a laugh.'[82]

In the same production, the director added a piece of business at the end of the play that was also highly melodramatic. However, unlike his earlier use of this overtly theatrical form, which had been in sympathy with Chekhov's own gently parodic use of it, Sturridge created a moment of pure melodrama which was in no sense ironical. The kind of cheap theatricality employed in this piece of business epitomises the sort of melodramatic 'event' that Chekhov was desperately trying to avoid in his dramas of 'indirect' action and the sort of theatrical overkill that reminds one of Stanislavski at his worst. Francis King described his negative response to what occurred. 'When brutally violating Chekhov's subtly mordant close to the play, [Masha] sprays the stage with vomit at the news of Konstantin's suicide, the director once again displays his imperfect sympathy with his author.'[83] As Milton Shulman pointed out, 'the usual impact' of the explicitly non-theatrical ending specified by Chekhov in his stage directions 'is devastating'. Sturridge's *coup-de-theatre*, in the form of Masha's vomiting, is paradoxically less effective in that it strains for the kind of theatricality that is alien to Chekhov's drama. As Shulman rightly states: 'Not only does this action make nonsense of the doctor's intention to prevent Arcadina hearing about her son's death, but it negates and spoils the play's understated climax by introducing an element of physical vulgarity that affronts Chekhov's fastidious and cultivated style.'[84]

Directors who are tempted to introduce obviously theatrical business into their *mise-en-scène* might do well to remember that Chekhov's stated aim was to write plays that would *not* conform to the theatrical demands of melodrama and the well-made play but be true to life. It is the ordinary quality of what happens in a Chekhov play that needs to be remembered by directors. Important events do occur but they should not be foregrounded if the director wishes to realise Chekhov's play.

In *The Seagull* several characters are playing lotto at the time of Konstantin's [Treplev's] suicide and thus this potentially theatrical event is barely noticed by those on-stage. This was precisely the effect that Chekhov had tried, unsuccessfully, to achieve in his earlier plays. He had at last managed to 'write a play in which people come and go, eat, talk about the weather, and play cards … and at the same time their happiness is made or their lives are being ruined'.[85] Chekhov realised how innovative his play was and that it was 'contrary to all the rules of dramatic art' in that 'I began it *forte* and ended it *pianissimo*'.[86] It is to Sturridge's credit that, when he came to revive his production, he restored Chekhov's own understated ending to the play.

One of the more important directorial decisions that needs to be made when directing *The Seagull* is how to interpret the key role of Treplev himself. He is a complex and ambiguous character. Any director who examines the playtext closely will find evidence that Treplev should not be interpreted as being either a misunderstood genius or an untalented nincompoop. He shares some of the playwright's own ideals, yet also has some of the failings that Chekhov saw in the intellectuals of his day. The status accorded Treplev's playlet in any overall production is of pivotal significance. It has been variously interpreted as a work of genius and as a piece of decadent nonsense. Hanna Scolnicov argues that the unnamed playlet should be called *The Seagull*. She claims that: 'The evaluation of the inset *Seagull* is crucial, for at stake is our understanding of Chekhov's own artistic aims and achievements.'[87]

Treplev is clearly someone who believes that new forms of dramatic art are required. Like Chekhov, he rejects the thesis dramas of his day but, unlike the writer of *The Seagull*, Treplev also seems to reject the kind of realistic drama in which he is in fact appearing as a character:

> TREPLEV. ... the theatre's in a rut nowadays, if you ask me — it's so one-sided. The curtain goes up and you see a room with three walls. It's evening, so the lights are on. And in the room you have those geniuses, those high priests of art, to show you how to eat, drink, love, walk about and wear their jackets. Out of mediocre scenes and lines they try to drag a moral, some commonplace that doesn't tax the brain and might come in useful about the house.[88]

Chekhov is no more to be identified with Treplev than he should be identified with Trigorin, the other writer in the play, simply because that character happens to share some of Chekhov's own writing habits. Treplev's play is clearly modelled on the sort of experimental dramas being written at the time by 'decadent' or 'symbolist' writers, the terms being used as synonyms in Chekhov's day. We know that Chekhov had an ambivalent attitude towards the Symbolists. He was certainly excited by the Belgian symbolist dramatist, Maurice Maeterlinck. While he was still working on *The Seagull*, Chekhov wrote to Suvorin recommending that some of this Belgian's work be performed in Russia: 'Why don't you try staging Maeterlinck at your theater? If I were a director of your theater, in two years I would make a Decadent Theater of it — or try to.'[89] Chekhov may even have been influenced by Maeterlinck's innovative staging of *The Blind* in which, as he told Suvorin, there was 'a magnificent scenic effect ... with the sea and a lighthouse in the distance'.[90] Treplev's play is provided with a similarly magnificent scenic effect in the form of a 'real' backdrop of a lake with a 'real' moon reflected in it.[91]

Despite an obvious attraction to certain aspects of symbolism, particularly the movement's commitment to finding new forms to express inner subjective reality, Chekhov would have found the nihilistic and anti-scientific aspects of the movement totally unacceptable. As Laurence Senelick points out:

> [Chekhov's] attitude toward the Russian decadents was satirical when it was not downright hostile. He is reputed to have said, 'they're swindlers, not decadents! They try to palm off rotten goods — religion, mysticism and all kinds of devilishness ... They've concocted it all to delude the public. Don't you believe them!'[92]

Chekhov's ambivalence towards the symbolist movement is reflected in *The Seagull* and can be profitably reflected in production. Even though the psychological reasons for Treplev's choosing to write a symbolist drama are clearly connected with his desire to struggle against the power that his mother has over him, the integrity of Treplev's aims need not be questioned. His efforts to achieve an identity, both artistic and personal, that was independent of Irina would surely have been seen in a favourable light by Chekhov whose own desire 'to be a free artist and nothing more'[93] is well known. Treplev's desire for personal freedom is mirrored in Chekhov's description of himself as someone who eventually managed to squeeze 'the slave out of himself, drop by drop' and who woke up one morning and felt that the blood in his veins was 'no longer that of a slave but that of a real human being'.[94] For Chekhov, both personal and artistic emancipation were desirable and inseparable, and it is part of Treplev's tragedy that, unlike Nina, he cannot achieve either. Rejecting the idea that talent and freshness is all that a writer needs, Chekhov wrote:

> Talent and freshness can ruin a great deal — that's near the truth. Outside of a plenitude of material and talent, something of no lesser importance is needed. Maturity is needed for one thing; secondly, a *sense of personal freedom* is indispensable. Yet only of late this sense began to burn within me.[95]

Near the end of the play Treplev comes to the realisation that he has failed to achieve artistic independence. Looking at his own writings he says: 'I've talked so much about new techniques, but now I feel I'm gradually getting in the old rut.' He even loses faith in the belief that 'new forms' are necessary — a belief that had sustained him up until this point: 'Yes, I'm more and more convinced that old or new techniques are neither here nor there.'[96] Having lost any sense of artistic purpose, he is confronted by Nina who, while she may not be an exceptionally talented actress, has nevertheless found her 'vocation' and is 'not afraid of life'. His response to her shows just how much he lacks any developed sense of artistic freedom and identity:

> TREPLEV. [*Sadly.*] You've found your road and you know where you're going, while I drift about in a maze of dreams and images, not knowing who needs my stuff or why. I've no faith and I don't know what my vocation is.[97]

Chekhov superbly suggests Treplev's lack of maturity, personal freedom and independence in this character's very last line. Nina has just embraced Treplev impulsively and run out through the garden. Left on his own, his last pathetic words suggest that, even at this stage in his life, he is unable to cut the umbilical cord that binds him to his mother: '[*After a pause.*] It'll be a pity if anyone sees her in the garden and tells Mother. It might upset her.'[98] Treplev demonstrates the fact that he now sees himself as a failure both as a human being and as an artist, by slowly tearing up all of his manuscripts and then leaving the stage to shoot himself.

From a directorial standpoint, Chekhov's depiction of Treplev seems to suggest that this character's aims concerning the need for new forms of dramatic art should be presented positively. What he aspires to is admirable, but, unfortunately, he is not the genius that Stanislavski thought him to be, and his dramatic achievement does not match his aspirations.

By presenting Treplev as a serious artist who fails to achieve his ideals, a director can avoid the inappropriate extremes of interpretation that are sometimes indulged in. Too often, Treplev is presented as either a fool or a genius when, in fact, Chekhov's text suggests the potential for a much richer complexity of characterisation. The one-dimensional interpretations of this character are often the result of directors failing to achieve the necessary balance between the tragic and comic elements. As Arthur Ganz puts it: 'the admirers of the comic Chekhov … are likely to find in Treplev … a hysterical, attitudinizing would-be Hamlet, whereas the advocates of the sensitive, melancholy playwright will see a frustrated artist driven to suicide'.[99] Vera Gottlieb makes a similar but more general point when she claims that 'the very essence of a Chekhov play lies in its balance'. She quotes Irving Wardle in support of her argument that British productions rarely achieve that balance. Wardle asserted that British Chekhov fails because directors there 'cannot hold a balance between sympathetic involvement and comic detachment'.[100]

One recent London production of *The Seagull* directed by John Caird appears to have continued the British tradition of one-sided interpretations of Chekhov. Michael Billington's review in *The Guardian* outlines the disastrous results that follow from approaching this play in such an unsubtle way. Having argued that the 'visual fussiness and overelaboration' of the *mise-en-scène* 'works against the spirit of the play', Billington outlines his major criticism of Caird's direction:

> But the production itself also tends to italicise emotional, as well as visual, effects. We all know that Chekhov described the play as a comedy. But it seems to me nonsense to treat Konstantin's [Treplev's] play as if it were a load of symbolist tosh with Nina rushing round the stage like a jet-propelled angel. It diminishes Konstantin, it undercuts Dorn's faith in his talent and it obliterates the point that K's theme — the division between matter and spirit — recurs throughout *The Seagull*. The art of directing Chekhov is to give us his polyphonic richness rather than to editorialise or to give undue stress to the tragic or comic element.[101]

Anthony Clark's 1990 production of the play for the Birmingham Repertory Company was flawed in a similar fashion. Paul Taylor, the reviewer for *The Independent*, described the way in which the director trivialised Treplev's play by having a group of peasants 'provide absurdly irrelevant sound effects' during the performance, and the on-stage audience perform 'antics' liable to raise a few cheap laughs from the audience in the auditorium:

> Disrupting the cohesiveness and solemnity of the occasion, an untimely plague of midges reduces this group [the on-stage audience] to a set of fractious individuals scratching and smacking their flesh and producing what sounds like a subversive mockery of applause.[102]

The Royal Shakespeare Company's production of *The Seagull* used the Michael Frayn translation that Anthony Clark had chosen earlier the same year. Terry Hands, however, directed the play in a much more 'polyphonic' manner. Paul Taylor, who had not disliked Clark's production, nevertheless recognised how superior Hands' interpretation was, particularly when it came to the presentation of Treplev's play:

> The treatment of that inset playlet is a good example of the shrewdness and sensitivity of Hands' approach. By having Arcadina and the onstage audience chomp Turkish Delight or swat at an invisible plague of flies, directors often minister to a sense that Konstantin's high-flown symbolist drama is merely ridiculous and deserves its humiliating public failure. Minimising such distractions and focusing attention on the make-shift stage, this production lets you feel the sad vulnerability as well as the risibility of his botched search for a new artistic form ... (For), if the play is talentless, what this version of its production makes sure you register is the beauty of the aspiration behind it.[103]

Treplev's play, as Billington noted, does indeed concern itself with themes that are important to Chekhov's play as a whole. This is one of the major reasons why directors who overlay this scene with gratuitous comic business run the risk of achieving the same results as the Shakespearean clowns who, as Hamlet says, are willing to 'set on some quantity of barren spectators to laugh too; though, in the mean time, some necessary question of the play be then to be considered'.[104]

The struggle between spirit and matter is a 'necessary question' not just of Treplev's play but of *The Seagull* as whole. Nina's character, the World Spirit, describes a world that has reached a state of entropy, which *Webster's Dictionary* defines as 'the degradation of the matter and energy in the universe to an ultimate state of inert uniformity'. This depressing condition depicted in Treplev's play is actually a grotesque parodic version of the state of inert uniformity that epitomises the lives of the characters in Chekhov's play. Their world is one that seems purposeless. They are lumps of matter without any spiritual dimension that would give their lives meaning. They have no faith. Sorin is the supreme example of entropic man. At the end of his life, having worked in what, on the face of it, might seem to be a meaningful occupation, he denies its significance, and searches pathetically for meaning in trivial hedonistic pursuits. He says to Dorn:

> SORIN. [*Laughs.*] It's all right for you to talk, you've enjoyed yourself. But what about me? Twenty-eight years I've worked for the Department of Justice, but I haven't lived yet, haven't experienced anything — that's what it comes to. So I want a bit of fun, it stands to reason. You've always had your own way and you don't care, which is why you're so given to idle chatter. But I want a bit of life, so I drink sherry at dinner and smoke cigars and so on. That's all there is to it.[105]

Sorin lives what Sartre would have called an 'inauthentic' life because he refuses to take any responsibility for his actions, or rather, for his inaction. He is reduced to an entropic state in which he becomes physically immobilised and spends much of his time asleep. Sorin has made his life 'absurd' by adopting a 'nothing to be done' attitude to life that involves the belief that his present condition is the result of fate rather than his own inaction. He has never enjoyed living in the country yet he continually returns there:

> SORIN. ... Isn't it typical? I've never done what I liked in the country. At one time I'd take a month off and come down here for a break and so on, but there'd be so much fuss and bother when you got here — you felt like pushing off the moment you arrived. [*Laughs.*] I was always glad to get away. Anyway, now I'm retired I've nowhere else to go, that's what it comes to. I have to live here, like it or not.[106]

Sorin is only an extreme case of what Chekhov shows to be the normal condition of living for most of the characters in *The Seagull*. They fritter their lives away, are constantly bored, and are ultimately aware of their failure to live fulfilling lives. Dorn, the materialist who rejects the idea of any transcendent spiritual purpose to life, realises that life's meaning is totally created by human beings who act purposefully in accordance with their ideals. His response to Sorin's 'bad faith' may, at first, seem rather blunt, but it is very much in tune with Chekhov's own cool objective appraisal of the nature of life. Furthermore, Dorn's insistence that Sorin face life parallels Chekhov's project of making audiences aware of their own inauthentic and wasted lives.

Without making any overt judgements, Chekhov was implying that the behaviour of people such as Sorin, who live their lives dreaming about what they would like to have done rather than actually doing anything to achieve their desires, was both comical and avoidable. Just as Masha wished to elevate the sadness she feels at not being loved by Treplev into a romantic melodrama, so Sorin wishes to dignify his failure by having it transformed into a sentimental novel of self-justification. Chekhov's Dr Dorn is quick to attack such escapist self-dramatising:

SORIN. I'd like to give Constantine a plot for a novel. It ought to be called *The Man who Wanted — L'homme qui a voulu*. In youth I wanted to become a writer — I didn't. I wanted to speak well — I spoke atrociously. [*Mocks himself.*] 'And all that sort, er, of thing, er, don't yer know.' I'd be doing a summing up sometimes, and find myself jawing on and on till I broke out in a sweat. I wanted to marry — I didn't. I wanted to live in town all the time — and here I am ending my days in the country and so on.
DORN. You wanted to become a senior civil servant — and did.
SORIN. [*Laughs.*] That's one thing I wasn't keen on, it just happened.
DORN. To talk about being fed up with life at the age of sixty-two — that's a bit cheap, wouldn't you say?
SORIN. Don't keep on about it, can't you see I want a bit of life?
DORN. That's just silly. All life must end, it's in the nature of things.
SORIN. You're spoilt, that's why you talk like this. You've always had what you wanted, so life doesn't matter to you, you just don't bother. But even you'll be afraid of dying.
DORN. Fear of death's an animal thing, you must get over it. It only makes sense to fear death if you believe in immortality and are scared because you've sinned. But you aren't a Christian for a start, and then — what sins have you committed? You've worked for the Department of Justice for twenty-five years, that's all.
SORIN. [*Laughs.*] Twenty-eight.[107]

It is important for directors not to over-sentimentalise Sorin, or to play Dorn as a totally unfeeling doctor. Too often in productions Sorin's self-pitying comments are played with little sense of the comic irony that is needed to undercut them. Instead of Dorn being an objective *raisonneur* gently laughing at a character who is bemoaning the inevitable fact that he is getting old and wishes that he could have his time over again, the doctor is often played as someone who has become so cynical and hard-hearted that he refuses to treat a patient who is 'seriously ill' with anything else but placebos like Valerian drops, soda or quinine.[108]

Treplev's playlet depicts in symbolist fashion what he sees as the current state of the world and, while that world is a depressingly bleak place where 'all life, all life, all life has completed its melancholy cycle and died', it is not beyond redemption. Chekhov's vision of reality included a belief in the idea of gradual progress that would happen not just through natural selection, but through human intervention, and Treplev's play also incorporates this 'epic vision'. Treplev expresses both his dislike of life as it currently is and his faith in a better long-term future for humanity, in a symbolist form that is quite unlike the form of realism being developed by Chekhov, but the belief that a sense of purpose, symbolised by the World Spirit, is necessary to bring about improvements in the lot of humanity was central to Chekhov's evolutionary vision. The fact that this progress would take a long time concerned Chekhov deeply. In the 1902 letter to Tikhonov, in which he expressed his certainty that people would 'create another and better life for themselves' once they realised how 'bad and dreary' their lives were, he added: 'I will not live to see it, but I know it will be quite different, quite unlike our present life'.[109] Treplev is likewise aware of the gradual nature of change. Nina, playing the role of the World Spirit, is given the following speech:

> NINA. ... Like a prisoner flung into a deep, empty well, I know not where I am or what awaits me. All is hidden from me except that in the cruel, unrelenting struggle with the Devil, the principle of Material Force, I am destined to triumph. Then shall Spirit and Matter unite in wondrous harmony, then shall the reign of Cosmic Will commence. But that will only come about after a long, long succession of millennia, when Moon, bright Sirius and Earth shall gradually have turned to dust. Until then there shall be horror upon horror.[110]

Rather than present Treplev's play as either a work of genius or 'tosh', a director needs to present this symbolist drama in a manner that reflects Chekhov's ambivalent attitude towards this character and his art. It is not Treplev's vision of reality that is defective, but the form in which he expresses it. The weakness of Treplev's play is that it is too removed from real life. Chekhov's art involved presenting 'life as it is' as realistically as was possible. This 'life' was a depiction of 'life as it should not be'. Without sacrificing artistic objectivity by introducing any judgemental 'thesis' and without abandoning the conventions of stage realism, Chekhov attempted to imply an idea of 'life as it should be'.

Treplev's approach to writing is criticised in *The Seagull* by other characters. We can discount the criticisms made by Irina, who, because she perceives her son's play as a personal attack on the type of drama she performs in, is biased in her dismissal of it as 'experimental rubbish'. Several other characters have no reason to be prejudiced against Treplev's dramatic efforts. Dr Dorn, for instance, liked the play and was especially impressed by its content: 'You took your plot from the realm of abstract ideas, and quite right too, because a work of art simply must express some great idea.' However the form in which Treplev expressed his vision did not impress the doctor as much. In particular, he is disturbed by the vagueness of this symbolist play and proceeds to give Treplev what turns out to be a prophetic warning:

> DORN. And then a work of art must express a clear, precise idea. You must know why you write, or else — if you take this picturesque path without knowing where you're going you'll lose your way and your gifts will destroy you.[111]

As we have seen, Treplev loses faith in himself and his art and, because he has no purpose or aim, kills himself.

Nina supplies the other telling criticism of Treplev's art when she complains to him that: 'Your play's hard to act, there are no living people in it.'[112] Trigorin appears to have no reason to attack Treplev's work and comments on what he believes to be the reason for the younger writer's limited success. His comment supports Nina's earlier judgement:

> TRIGORIN. Things aren't going too well, he still can't find his real level. There's something vaguely odd about his stuff, and some of it seems rather wild. None of his characters is ever really alive.[113]

Treplev's reaction to Nina's criticism is significant in that it indicates to anyone familiar with Chekhov's own artistic credo just how different his symbolist aesthetic is from his creator's realism. Knowing that Chekhov would certainly not have agreed with Treplev's artistic views is useful in helping a director or actor decide how sympathetically or otherwise to portray this character. Attacking the conventions of realism, Treplev scornfully exclaims: 'Living people! We should show life neither as it is nor as it ought to be, but as we see it in our dreams.'[114] This statement is the complete antithesis of Chekhov's own views about drama. Not long after he had written *The Seagull*, he criticised the Norwegian dramatist Bjoernson for writing a play that had 'no action, no living characters and no dramatic interest'.[115]

Like the other self-dramatising characters in this play, Treplev cannot come to terms with reality and consequently makes of his own life a symbolist drama in which he dreams that he is the doomed suffering tragic hero.[116] At the end of the play, Treplev expresses his unhappiness in the overblown language he had used in his symbolist playlet. In that early drama, 'the principle of Material Force' had destroyed life on Earth with the result that:

> NINA. ... It is cold, cold, cold. Empty, empty, empty. Terrible, terrible, terrible. [*Pause.*] The bodies of living creatures have turned to dust, and eternal matter has converted them into stones, water, clouds ... I am lonely ... Like a prisoner flung into a deep empty well, I know not where I am or what awaits me.[117]

In Act Four, Treplev describes his own depressed and lifeless state as follows:

> TREPLEV. I'm lonely, I haven't the warmth of anyone's devotion. I feel cold, as in a vault, and all I write is so dry, stale, dismal. Stay here Nina, I beg you, or let me go with you.[118]

The lack of maturity that is evident in Treplev's appeal with its excessive histrionic self-pity suggests that Chekhov did not wish Treplev to be interpreted as a 'hero'. Characters like Masha, Sorin and Treplev all suffer genuine pain, and Chekhov's depiction of them suggests that he wishes his audiences to pity them, but the response of all three characters to their suffering is excessive. Their vain attempts to assume a tragic stature and their adoption of a fatalistic attitude to life make them ludicrous as well as pathetic. As Laurence Senelick rightly points out: 'Abnegation of responsibility on grounds of human impotence was not sympathetic to Chekhov's way of thinking.'[119]

It is precisely because Nina is able to take responsibility for her own life by facing reality, rather than running away from it, that she, like the World Spirit she once impersonated, is 'destined to triumph'. She overcomes her earlier romantic fantasies about life and the theatre and no longer needs the comforting support of dreams and symbols — reality is sufficient. Nina's mature adjustment to reality is represented by her refusal to see herself any longer as a seagull. The seagull acquires various layers of symbolic significance in Chekhov's play, and, as Senelick has pointed out, both Treplev and Trigorin use the seagull to symbolically 'position' Nina in the role of victim:

> When, in Act IV, she repudiates the soubriquet, 'I'm a seagull. No, not that', she rejects not only Treplyov's martyr-bird, but Trigorin's fictitious happy-free-and-then-ruined creature. Nina, having found her calling, is not ruined but survives, if only in an anti-romantic, workaday world.[120]

In a scene in Act Two, Treplev associated himself with the dead seagull. He threatens to kill himself unless Nina returns his love. Nina's response to this immature piece of emotional blackmail is to reject his heavy-handed symbolism, and this should prepare an audience for her later refusal to be identified with this lifeless object:

> [TREPLEV *lays the seagull at her feet.*]
> NINA. What does that signify?
> TREPLEV. I meanly killed that seagull this morning. I lay it at your feet.
> NINA. What's wrong with you? [*Picks up the seagull and looks at it.*]
> TREPLEV. [*After a pause.*] I shall soon kill myself in the same way.
> NINA. You've changed so much.
> TREPLEV. Yes, but who changed first? You did. You're so different to me now, you look at me coldly and you find me in the way.
> NINA. You're touchy lately and you always talk so mysteriously, in symbols or something. This seagull's a symbol too, I suppose, but it makes no sense to me, sorry.[121]

As Peter Holland points out, it is a sign of Nina's essential sanity that she can finally reject this symbolic identification with the seagull. Characteristically, it is Treplev who 'would rather talk in symbols than face up to the reality of his life, a childish egocentricity that culminates in his suicide'.[122]

It is appropriate that the audience ultimately associates the seagull with Treplev rather than with Nina. The inert physical presence of the bird, when it is first brought on stage and later when it appears in stuffed form are suitably overblown symbols for the decadent writer who first attempts suicide and then succeeds in killing himself. Chekhov, whose own mastery of symbolic realism was becoming increasingly subtle, was able to use this crude symbolism in much the same way that he used melodrama — for the purpose of parody. John Gielgud, who played the role of Treplev in Esme Filmer's 1925 production, failed to detect Chekhov's parodic deflation of the young symbolist, believing him to be 'a very romantic character, a sort of miniature Hamlet'. Despite this sentimentalised approach to the role, even Gielgud could not override Chekhov's comic intentions, as, much to the actor's chagrin and dismay, audiences refused to take the symbolic seagull seriously:

> I resented the laughter of the audience when I came on in the second act holding the dead seagull, but on a very small stage it did look rather like a stuffed Christmas goose, however carefully I arranged its wings and legs beforehand.[123]

Chekhov's potentially tragic characters are depicted with a degree of ironic detachment that critics like Vera Gottlieb compare to Brecht's distancing techniques.[124] Certainly Chekhov created a perceptible gap between the tragic inner lives of his characters and their comic public behaviour and, if this gap is made perceptible in production, then that 'anaesthesia of the heart', that Bergson thought was necessary in comedy in order to allow an audience to laugh at what would otherwise be perceived as a painful situation, can be achieved. Stanislavski's production used very little 'anaesthesia' and produced a tragic, bleeding heart version of *The Seagull*. Esme Filmer tried, less successfully, to do the same, but the comic potential of the symbolically portentous seagull could not be suppressed.

In more recent productions of the play, particularly in Britain, directors have attempted to foreground the comic aspects of the drama, but at the cost of the tragic elements. So much 'anaesthesia' is administered that the heart is stopped altogether. Charles Osborne's review of Mike Alfreds' production of *The Seagull* in 1991 describes such a directorial approach:

> Coarsening Chekhov, however, appears to have been the principal intention of this staging. Chekhov called his play a comedy, but it is directed (by the perpetrator of this 'new version') as extremely crude farce. It's all very well to break away from the English sentimental Chekhov of a generation ago, but in this instance the baby of elegant comedy has been thrown out with the bath-water of autumnal melancholy.[125]

The manner in which directors have recently interpreted the scene in which Irina Arkadina temporarily manages to stop her lover, Trigorin, from leaving her and running off with Nina illustrates the dangers involved in overstressing the comic aspect of the scene. In addition, these productions reveal the hermeneutic problems that inevitably face directors who produce plays from an earlier period. The significance of the playwright's work that would have been clear to the play's original audiences may now be misinterpreted or become unreadable to a modern audience.[126]

In a speech that is deeply insulting to the aging Irina Arkadina, Trigorin asks her to set him free so that he can indulge in the fulfilment of his dream of experiencing what he calls 'young love'. He romantically envisions an 'enchanting and magical love that sweeps you off your feet into a make-believe world' and, claiming that 'this love has come at last', asks Irina 'Why should I run away from it?' Irina appears to be in a hopelessly vulnerable position when she responds to his appeal. Chekhov's stage direction says that she is 'trembling' when she replies: 'No, no, no. You can't talk to me like that, I'm only an ordinary woman. Don't torture me, Boris. I'm terrified.' However, within a page of dialogue, Chekhov has this quite extraordinary woman win back control of her man, even if only for the time being. Chekhov shows us Irina using all of her theatrical skills to dominate Trigorin. She turns the situation into a melodramatic 'scene' and plays her role with all of the skill and all of the theatrical quackery of a Sarah Bernhardt.[127] The 'scene' commences when Irina transforms herself from trembling defensiveness into angry attack:

> TRIGORIN. ... But now, you see, this love has come at last, it calls me on. Why should I run away from it?
> IRINA. [Arkadina] [*Angrily.*] You must be mad.
> TRIGORIN. Perhaps I am.
> IRINA. You're all conspiring to torment me today. [*Cries.*]
> TRIGORIN. [*Clutches his head.*] She doesn't understand, she won't understand.
> IRINA. Am I really so old and ugly that you don't mind talking to me about other women? [*Embraces and kisses him.*] Oh, you're mad. My marvellous, splendid man. You're the last page in my life. [*Kneels down.*] My delight, my pride, my joy! [*Embraces his knees.*] If you leave me for one hour I shan't survive, I shall go mad, my wonderful, splendid one. My master.[128]

Despite Trigorin's embarrassment at this public display of Irina's passion for him, he is unable to stop her using every technique in her power to keep him. She insists that he is a 'reckless boy' who needs to be protected from doing 'something crazy'. She asserts her ownership of him: 'you're mine, all of you'. Finally, she praises his artistic skills to the skies, and then, using all of her own artistry, she destroys his resolve to leave her and restores her control over him:

> IRINA. [Arkadina] ... Too much hero-worship, you think? Think I'm flattering you? Then look in my eyes, come on. Do I look like a liar? There, you see, I'm the only one who appreciates you, I'm the only one who tells you the truth, my wonderful darling. You will come, won't you? You won't desert me, will you?

> TRIGORIN. I've no will of my own, never have had. I'm a flabby, spineless creature that always does what it's told — surely that's not what women like. Take me then, carry me off, but don't ever let me move one step from your side.
> IRINA. [*To herself.*] Now he's mine. [*Off-handedly and casually.*] Actually, you can stay on if you want. I'll leave on my own and you can come later, in a week's time. What's the hurry after all?
> TRIGORIN. No, we may as well go together.
> IRINA. As you like. We'll go together if you say so.[129]

In this scene, Chekhov has reverted to the method of 'direct action' that was the standard practice of dramatists of the time who wrote well-made plays and romantic melodramas. This overtly theatrical scene is however given realistic justification by Chekhov, because it is Irina Arkadina, a specialist actress in these theatrical genres, who 'performs' the scene. Despite the fact that Irina is not spoofing the conventions of melodramatic acting but using them in a serious manner to win back Trigorin, the very fact that such a 'performance' is placed by Chekhov in a larger drama of 'indirect action' encourages an audience to notice how stylistically different this scene is from much of the rest of the play. In such a theatrically low-key context, Irina's melodramatic behaviour cannot help appearing excessive and even ludicrous, and consequently she cannot help appearing to be acting. The gap between her real terror at losing Trigorin and the absurdly theatrical methods she employs to keep him, if presented in performance, is likely to create the appropriate balance between the tragic and the comic aspects of her character.

The difficulty for the actor performing this scene is precisely that of playing both the sympathetic and the laughable aspects of the character. In Charles Sturridge's production of *The Seagull*, the scene was reduced to the level of physical farce. Victoria Radin vividly described the comic business that Irina [Vanessa Redgrave] employed to win back Trigorin [Jonathan Pryce]. She 'grabs [him] by the knees, throws him to the ground and crawls between his out-spread legs while fondling his bottom and declaring him to be a great writer'.[130] The major problem of taking a farcical approach to this scene, and to Chekhov in general, is that the tragi-comic balance is inevitably lost. Michael Billington's review of Vanessa Redgrave's performance highlights the fact that, by playing this role in a farcical manner, the 'anaesthesia of the heart' became total and it was difficult to feel in any way sympathetic toward Irina Arkadina. Sturridge's production:

> ... comes equipped with a performance by Vanessa Redgrave as Arkadina that often borders on the grotesque and that suggests a profound misunderstanding of the nature of Chekhov's genius ... I don't deny that Ms Redgrave is fascinating to watch (not least in the scene where she uses every erotic trick in the book to keep hold of Trigorin). But in editorialising about Arcadina, she misses any

sense of her residual humanity: this is a woman who (according to the text) once took medicine to a wounded washerwoman and bathed her children in a tub. You'd never guess that from Ms Redgrave's focus on Arkadina's egotistic triviality.[131]

This farcically one-sided and judgemental approach to the role of Irina appears to have been part of the director's interpretation, rather than an invention of Redgrave's.[132] Sturridge's production had originally had Samantha Eggar playing Irina, but, as Francis King noted in his review, the requisite tragi-comic balance was lacking, with the result that Irina became 'funny' but was in no way 'moving':

> What is otherwise amiss with this production is crystallised in Samantha Eggar's performance as Arkadina. Certainly, the character is selfish, silly and trivial. But the finest exponents of the role — Joan Plowright, Peggy Ashcroft and above all Isabel Jeans — found in her, as Chekhov himself surely did, both humanity and pathos.[133]

Vera Gottlieb has forcibly argued that Sturridge's production utilised the techniques of English farce in this scene in particular, and consequently 'vulgarized both the character and the play at that moment'.[134] Francis King is surely not claiming too much when he asserts, in his review of the revival of this Sturridge production, that 'the sight of Arkadina and Trigorin grappling amorously with each other on the floor is surely alien to this most subtle of playwrights'.[135]

However, while there is general critical awareness that Chekhov's plays are not simply farces, current British directors, who exhibit a laudable determination to avoid the earlier tragic 'gloom and doom' approach, still seem to find it difficult to produce these plays without introducing crassly inappropriate comic stage-business. John Caird, in his production of *The Seagull*, with Judy Dench as Irina, had his actors play the scene in which Irina tries to stop Trigorin from leaving her in a manner that even outdoes Sturridge in its use of overtly farcical and grossly inappropriate business. Sturridge's Irina 'rugby-tackles Pryce [Trigorin] to the floor, pins him down and massages his haunches as he springs more or less free, thus demonstrating her sexual power over him'.[136] In Caird's production, the hapless Trigorin is not even allowed to wrestle free from Irina's sexual advances:

> In Arkadina's third-act scene of abasement, he is flattened while Dench, in a display of ridiculous vulgarity, changes the usual knee-clutching business to knee-trembling sexual interference. She kisses his feet, gropes his privates and works her way up to an orgasmic embrace. She gets to her feet, lights a cigar and, while the writer instinctively reaches for his notebook, casually throws

down, 'Do stay if you want to'. It is a highly charged comic moment, but unjustifiably coarse.[137]

Many modern directors of *The Seagull* seem to believe that their audiences will be unable to grasp the significance of Arkadina's playing this scene as authentic melodrama, and so, they cut the specific business specified by Chekhov and replace it with easily understood farcical business. In fact, even though a modern audience may not have direct experience of the kind of melodramas that actors like Sarah Bernhardt or Arkadina played in, the heightened language and gestures used by Irina in this scene are easily readable as being excessive. The clear contrast between this heightened behaviour and the ordinary everyday mode of address used by the characters, including Irina, elsewhere in the play, makes it possible for the scene to be played for both its pathos and humour. Certainly, if Jeremy Kingston's reaction is reliable, then Susan Fleetwood's performance as Irina in Terry Hands' 1991 revival of his earlier production achieved precisely that double perspective on the character that is so vital if an audience is to be induced to both laugh at and be sympathetic towards her. Irina turns from her son:

> ... whose self-respect she has shattered to weave her spell upon Trigorin, whipping her tears into fury, enveloping the poor fellow in a she-bear's hug and gobbling him up. Half-way through this outburst of furious sobbing a change in tone comes into her voice, faint but definite. She is expressing the panic of a woman whose lover may be leaving her, but the artist in her, the actress, is feeling its way forward again. Like Roger Allam's mellifluous Trigorin noting down little phrases for his stories, she is noticing the sound of her rage. Its timbre may be helpful when next she plays in *La Dame aux Camellias*.[138]

*The Seagull* is in some ways a transitional drama that shows Chekhov in the process of abandoning outdated theatrical conventions or using them in a new way. The fact that Chekhov had not yet totally emancipated himself from the use of the conventions of the well-made play led one critic to describe *The Seagull* as 'the last of Chekhov's *piece-à-thèse*'.[139] It is certainly true that the author does propound the thesis that people need endurance in order to find fulfilment in both art and life. While the play certainly uses much of the machinery of romantic melodrama and the well-made play, Chekhov had already begun to use these conventions parodically. By the time he came to write his next play, *Uncle Vanya*, many of the overtly theatrical clichés present in *The Seagull* had gone. The playwright's epic vision is not stated, but rather implied in the action — an action that mirrors the drama of ordinary daily life in a much more realistic manner than had been achieved in *The Seagull*.

# ENDNOTES

[1] Chekhov, A., quoted in Nilsson, N. A. 'Intonation and Rhythm in Cechov's Plays', in Eekman, T., ed., *Anton Cechov 1860–1960: Some Essays*, E. J. Brill, Leiden, 1960, p. 173.

[2] Heim, M., 'Chekhov and the Moscow Art Theatre', in Barricelli, J-P., ed., *Chekhov's Great Plays: A Critical Anthology*, New York University Press, New York, 1981, p. 139.

[3] Styan, J. L., *Chekhov in Performance*, Cambridge University Press, Cambridge, 1971, p. 9.

[4] Seymour, A., 'Summer Seagull, Winter Love', *The London Magazine*, May 1964, p. 63.

[5] John Barber, in his review of Charles Sturridge's 1985 production of *The Seagull*, noted that Samantha Eggar's way of playing this aside was funny, but 'the amusement comes a little too pat, so that the pitifulness often gets lost. Samantha Eggar, ... as the fading actress, actually faces the stalls, conspiratorially, to win a laugh on 'Now he's mine!' when Trigorin at last yields.' (Barber, J., *Daily Telegraph*, 29 April 1985.)

[6] Frayn, M., in Chekhov, A., *The Seagull*, Allen & Unwin, London, 1989, p. xviii. Some directors avoid the problem of trying to justify the soliloquies realistically by not attempting to achieve verisimilitude at all. John Caird's 1994 production employs the kind of symbolist approach to the play's production that is in line with Meyerhold's ideas about how Chekhov should be interpreted. Robert Hewison reports how the 'symbol, fantasies and incestuous desires' evident in the play 'appear to justify Caird's treatment of the text as more of a dream-play than we have become used to. It helps to make sense of the breaks Chekhov made with the otherwise naturalistic conventions of the script by giving several characters brief soliloquies delivered directly to the audience.' (Hewison, R., *Sunday Times*, 17 July 1994.)

[7] Alan Seymour excuses Chekhov's use of earlier dramatic forms on the grounds that he was still learning his trade. 'If *The Seagull* seems to bristle with tricks left over from the nineteenth-century melodrama (the relentless 'planting' of Konstantin's eventual suicide, for example) these can be allowed, for this was the first play of Chekhov's mature period, the first play of this new kind.' Seymour then astutely points out that, because Chekhov had not as yet fully developed his new form of realistic drama, he created difficulties for future directors searching for the appropriate style in which to play this drama. 'Any of the plays sets great problems to their director and in this hybrid the problems are magnified.' (Seymour, A., op. cit., pp. 63–4.)

[8] Chekhov, A., Letter to A. S. Suvorin, 18 October 1896, in Friedland, L. S., *Letters on the Short Story, the Drama, and Other Literary Topics by Anton Chekhov*, Dover Publications, New York, 1966, p. 147.

[9] Heim, M., op. cit., p. 134.

[10] Heim, M., loc. cit.

[11] Avilova, L., *Chekhov in My Life: A Love Story*, Methuen, London, 1989, pp. 88–9.

[12] Ibid., pp. 92–3.

[13] Slonim, M., *Russian Theater from the Empire to the Soviets*, Methuen, London, 1963, p. 121.

[14] Gillès, D., *Chekhov: Observer without Illusion*, Funk & Wagnalls, New York, 1968, pp. 221–2.

[15] Nemirovich-Danchenko, V., Letter to A. Chekhov, 21 August 1898, in Benedetti, J., ed., *The Moscow Art Theatre Letters*, Routledge, New York, 1991, p. 31.

[16] Karlinsky, S., *Anton Chekhov's Life and Thought*, University of California Press, Berkeley, 1975, p. 282.

[17] Kommissarzhevskaya, V., Letter to A. Chekhov, 21 October 1896, in Karlinsky, S., op. cit., p. 283.

[18] Chekhov, A., Letter to M. P. Chekhov, 18 October 1896, in Hellman, L., *The Selected Letters of Chekhov*, Hamish Hamilton, London, 1955, pp. 193–4.

[19] Chekhov, A., Letter to A. S. Suvorin, 22 October 1896, in Hellman, L., op. cit., pp. 194–5.

[20] Chekhov, A., Letter to M. P. Chekhov, 15 October 1896, in Friedland, L. S., loc. cit.

[21] Chekhov, A., Letter to A. Koni, 11 November 1896, in Hellman, L., op. cit., p. 197.

[22] Chekhov, A., Letter to E. Shavrova, 1 November 1896, in Hellman, L., op. cit., pp. 195–6.

[23] Chekhov, A., quoted in Balukhaty, S. D., ed., *The Seagull Produced by Stanislavsky*, Dennis Dobson, London, 1952, p. 22.

[24] Chekhov, A., quoted in Hollosi, C., 'Chekhov's Reaction to Two Interpretations of Nina', *Theatre Survey*, Vol. 24, Nos 1 & 2, 1983, p. 118.

[25] Hollosi, C., loc. cit.

²⁶ Ibid., p. 125. Hollosi is correct to point out that there can be no single definitive interpretation of *The Seagull* or of any role in the play, but it does not follow from this that all interpretations are equally valid. She is perfectly accurate when she states that: 'Almost all of the major characters in Chekhov's plays are ambiguous; their interpretation poses no small task for directors and actors. The figure of Nina Zarechnaya in *The Seagull*, in particular, has been construed in many ways. She has been seen as a soaring seagull; a tumbled, tousled bird; a talentless country girl; an emerging artist of promise; a high-reaching neurotic wreck; a future actress of Arkadina's vein; and so on.' (Hollosi, C., op. cit., p. 117.) What I wish to contest in Hollosi's argument is her belief that all of these interpretations are in some way equally valid.

²⁷ Ibid.

²⁸ Stanislavski, C., *My Life in Art*, Eyre Methuen, London, 1980, p. 321.

²⁹ Ibid., p. 322.

³⁰ Meyerhold, V., in Braun, E., ed., *Meyerhold on Theatre*, Eyre Methuen, London, 1969, p. 30.

³¹ Chekhov, A., quoted in Stanislavski, C., op. cit., p. 356.

³² Chekhov, A., Letter to M. Gorky, 9 May 1899, in Karlinsky, S., op. cit., p. 357.

³³ Stanislavski, C., op. cit., p. 357.

³⁴ Ibid., p. 358.

³⁵ Braun, E., *The Director and the Stage*, Methuen, London, 1982, p. 65.

³⁶ Ibid., p. 63.

³⁷ Nemirovich-Danchenko realised later that such a division of artistic labour was unworkable. The idea that 'in the artistic region we would have equal rights' and that 'he had the last word in the region of *form* and I in the region of *content*' was, as an artistic solution to the problems of direction, 'by no means a wise one' because, as he soon discovered, 'form could not be torn from content'. This point of artistic demarcation Nemirovich-Danchenko ruefully remarked, 'was to become the most explosive in our mutual relations'. (Nemirovich-Danchenko, V., *My Life in the Russian Theatre*, Geoffrey Bles, London, 1968, p. 107.) As Benedetti has noted: 'For Nemirovich, work on *The Seagull* represented the ideal. Stanislavski was bewildered by the play. Nemirovich spent two days going through the text, analysing and explaining. The *concept* therefore was his; Stanislavski's staging was an embodiment of that concept. That was how Nemirovich conceived their working relationship: himself, content; Stanislavski, form. It is significant that in all his correspondence with Chekhov, Nemirovich refers to himself as the director.' (Benedetti, J., op. cit., p. 14.) Stanislavski was eventually to insist on combining the functions of interpretation and staging when directing and this combination has now become the normal role for directors today.

³⁸ Magarshack, D., *Stanislavsky: A Life*, Faber & Faber, London, 1986, p. 181.

³⁹ Gillès, D., op. cit., pp. 228–9.

⁴⁰ Magarshack, D., op. cit., p. 184.

⁴¹ Chekhov, A., *The Seagull*, in Hingley, R., *The Oxford Chekhov*, Vol. 2, Oxford University Press, London, 1967, p. 280.

⁴² Nemirovich-Danchenko, V., quoted in Balukhaty, S. D., op. cit., p. 63.

⁴³ Nemirovich-Danchenko, V., Letter to A. Chekhov, 18–21 December 1898, in Benedetti, J., op. cit., p. 44.

⁴⁴ Chekhov, A., Letter to N. M. Yezhov, 21 November 1898, quoted in Hollosi, C., op. cit., p. 122.

⁴⁵ Yezhov, N. M., Letter to A. Chekhov, n.d., quoted in Hollosi, C., loc. cit.

⁴⁶ Knipper, O., quoted in Balukhaty, S. D., op. cit., p. 81.

⁴⁷ Stanislavski, C., op. cit., p. 354.

⁴⁸ Ibid., p. 355.

⁴⁹ Ibid.

⁵⁰ Ibid. The supposedly 'giftless' Nina, in Stanislavski's production, can magically acquire the necessary talent to become 'a true actress' in order that the director can create a *coup-de-théâtre* in which the sentimental tear-jerking potential of the scene is milked to its limit.

⁵¹ Ibid.

⁵² Hollosi, C., op. cit., p. 123.

⁵³ Ibid., p. 119.

⁵⁴ Chekhov, A., *The Seagull*, p. 245.

55 Chitau-Karmina, M., quoted in Hollosi, C., loc. cit.
56 Ibid.
57 Ibid., p. 120.
58 Ibid., p. 124.
59 Ibid., p. 122.
60 Nemirovich-Danchenko, V., op. cit., p. 121.
61 Pinter, H., 'Writing for the Theatre', in *Pinter Plays*, Vol. 1, Methuen, London, 1976, p. 11.
62 Williams, R., *Drama in Performance*, Penguin, Harmondsworth, 1972, pp. 130–1.
63 Chekhov, A., Letter to A. S. Suvorin, 21 October 1895, in Hellman, L., op. cit., p. 189.
64 Ibid.
65 Brooks, C. and Heilman, R. B., *Understanding Drama*, Holt, Rinehart & Winston, New York, 1966, p. 492.
66 Chekhov, A., *The Seagull*, in Hingley, R., *The Oxford Chekhov*, Vol. 2, p. 233.
67 Steiner, G., *The Death of Tragedy*, Faber & Faber, London, 1961, p. 161.
68 Chekhov, A., *The Seagull*, p. 233.
69 Ibid., p. 247.
70 An early version of the play explicitly stated at the end of Act One that Dr Dorn was Masha's father. In the final version of the play, references to 'my child' appear to have a more innocent avuncular meaning. Some directors in their productions do suggest the possibility that Dorn could be Masha's father.
71 Ibid., pp. 269–70.
72 Stanislavski, C., in Balukhaty, S. D., op. cit., p. 139.
73 Ibid.
74 Holland, P., 'The Director and the Playwright: Control Over the Means of Production', *New Theatre Quarterly*, Vol. 3, No. 11, August 1987, p. 213.
75 Stanislavski, C., in Balukhaty, S. D., op. cit., p. 253.
76 Holland, P., op. cit., p. 214.
77 Chekhov, A., quoted in Melchinger, S., op. cit., p. 62. In the textual notes appended to Jean-Claude Van Itallie's 1974 translation of *The Seagull*, Paul Schmidt correctly identifies Chekhov's negative attitude towards interpretations that made his characters into cry-babies:
> The stage direction *almost crying (skvoz slyozy)* is one that Chekhov uses over and over in his plays; it occurs four times in this one. The Russian phrase literally means 'through tears', but on no account does it mean that Chekhov wants the actor or actress in question to cry, or even necessarily to come near it. So many of them did, especially under Stanislavski's over-wrought direction, that Chekhov had to write to Stanislavski's partner at the Moscow Art Theater, Nemirovich-Danchenko, on October 23, 1903: 'I often use the phrase "almost crying" in my stage directions, but that indicates only a character's mood, not actual tears.'

(Schmidt, P., 'Textual Notes', in Chekhov, A., *The Seagull, A New Version*, Van Itallie, J-C., trans., Harper & Row, New York, 1977, p. 93.)
78 Shulman, M., *Standard*, 27 April 1984.
79 Irvine, St J., *Observer*, 29 September 1929, quoted in Miles, P., *Chekhov on the British Stage*, Sam & Sam, England, 1987, p. 21. The temptation to parody such gloomy productions has proved irresistible and, as Laurence Senelick has noted, when he examined Burenin's 1917 parody of Chekhov, 'the parodist is confusing the play with the production', in this case Stanislavski's Moscow Art Theatre productions. In Burenin's parody entitled 'Cherry Jam on a Treacle Base. A white drama with mood. And not a single act', Chekhov is seen as the writer of proto-absurdist plays full of hopelessness and despair:
> Yes, on the whole life is, so to speak, a hole. What are human beings born for? To fall into the hole. Life has no meaning. Here I sit in an old, sort of baronial, aristocratic house, though in fact it's remarkably bourgeois. I sit and smear the table with treacly jam made from Vladimir cherries. There in the orchard, the actors and actresses, made up as birds, are chirping and cuckooing. There, beside the table, the property flies are flying on the strings which Messrs Nemirovich-Danchenko and Stanislavsky are tugging with remarkable effort. The gramophone reproduces the buzzing of flies. What is all this for? Why is all this? For, so to speak, 'mood' and the play's success, because without actors and actresses' chirping and cuckooing, without

flies' buzzing, it would flop … But in a thousand, in a million years new people will be born. And they too will smear treacly cherry jam on the table as I am now doing. But they, these people of a far-off day, will probably be more intelligent and will not create and present pseudo-realistic plays with mood, in which there is no meaning and in which over the course of four acts characters, for no reason at all, carry on dialogues like those in language primers for French and German … (Burenin, V. P., quoted in Senelick, L., 'Stuffed Seagulls: Parody and the Reception of Chekhov's Plays', *Poetics Today*, Vol. 8, No. 2, 1987, p. 290.)

[80] Miles P., op. cit., p. 13.

[81] Swinnerton, F., *Nation*, 17 July 1920, quoted in Miles, P., op. cit., p. 9.

[82] Billington, M., *Guardian*, 29 April 1985.

[83] King, F., *Sunday Telegraph*, 5 May 1985.

[84] Shulman, M., *Standard*, 29 April 1985.

[85] Ibid., pp. 74–5.

[86] Chekhov, A., Letter to A. S. Suvorin, 21 November 1895, in Friedland, L. S., op. cit., p. 146.

[87] Scolnicov, H., 'Chekhov's Reading of *Hamlet*', in Scolnicov, H. and Holland, P., eds, *Reading Plays: Interpretation and Reception*, Cambridge University Press, Cambridge, 1991, p. 201.

[88] Chekhov, A., *The Seagull*, p. 236.

[89] Chekhov, A., Letter to A. S. Suvorin, 2 November 1895, quoted in Van Itallie, J-C., op. cit., p. 90.

[90] Chekhov, A., Letter to A. S. Suvorin, 12 July 1897, quoted in Friedland, L. S., op. cit., p. 265.

[91] The lake and the moon are of course no more real than are the other staging and lighting effects used in *The Seagull*, but just as Hamlet attempts to convince an audience that he is a real person with an actual 'motive and cue for passion' as opposed to the player who only acts his passion, so in Chekhov's play we are asked to see the setting for Treplev's play not as a 'theatrical set', but as something that is as 'real' as the setting of *The Seagull* as a whole. Since that setting is itself a 'theatrical set', the paradox involved in the attempt to create any 'illusion of reality' is foregrounded.

[92] Senelick, L., 'Chekhov's Drama, Maeterlinck, and the Russian Symbolists', in Barricelli, J-P., ed., *Chekhov's Great Plays: A Critical Anthology*, New York University Press, New York, 1981, pp. 161–2.

[93] Chekhov, A., Letter to A. N. Pleshcheyev, 4 October 1888, in Yarmolinsky, A., *Letters of Anton Chekhov*, The Viking Press, New York, 1973, p. 81.

[94] Chekhov, A., Letter to A. S. Suvorin, 7 January 1889, in Yarmolinsky, A., op. cit., p. 107.

[95] Ibid.

[96] Chekhov, A., *The Seagull*, p. 277.

[97] Ibid., p. 280.

[98] Ibid., p. 281.

[99] Ganz, A., *Realms of the Self: Variations on a Theme in Modern Drama*, New York University Press, New York, 1980, p. 38.

[100] Gottlieb, V., 'Chekhov in Limbo: British Productions of the Plays of Chekhov', in Scolnicov H. and Holland, P., eds, *The Play Out of Context: Transferring Plays from Culture to Culture*, Cambridge University Press, Cambridge, 1989, p. 163.

[101] Billington, M., *Guardian*, 9 July 1994.

[102] Taylor, P., *Independent*, 23 February 1990. It should be noted that Mr Taylor found the comic business surrounding the performance of Treplev's play 'witty', regardless of its inappropriateness.

[103] Taylor, P., *Independent*, 8 November 1990.

[104] Shakespeare, W., *Hamlet*, Act 3, Scene 2.

[105] Chekhov, A., *The Seagull*, p. 250.

[106] Ibid., p. 234.

[107] Chekhov, A., *The Seagull*, p. 271.

[108] David Magarshack quotes from a letter to Suvorin in which Chekhov gave some medical advice to the 58-year-old publisher who had been suffering from giddy spells. The prescription was much the same as that offered by Dr Dorn to Sorin in *The Seagull*, and this suggests that, far from being heartless, Dorn is providing what was considered at the time to be the best treatment for this medical condition. (See Magarshack, D., *The Real Chekhov*, Allen and Unwin, London, 1972, pp. 42–3, footnote 1.)

[109] Chekhov, A., Letter to A. Tikhonov, 1902, quoted in Magarshack, D., *Chekhov the Dramatist*, p. 14.

[110] Chekhov, A., *The Seagull*, p. 241.
[111] Ibid., p. 246.
[112] Ibid., p. 238. Nina's taste may not be very sophisticated and she appears to like the sort of romantic melodramas that Treplev's mother acts in. Some of her criticisms of Treplev's new form of drama might apply equally well to Chekhov's new dramatic form. She complains that 'There's not much action, it's just a lot of speeches. I think a play needs a love interest'. Nevertheless, Nina's comment that Treplev's play did not depict 'living people' would have been regarded as a major fault by Chekhov, who was himself so committed to using the conventions of realism.
[113] Ibid., p. 276.
[114] Ibid., p. 238.
[115] Chekhov, A., Letter to A. S. Suvorin, 20 June 1896, quoted in Magarshack, D., *Chekhov the Dramatist*, p. 20.
[116] Many of the themes that were important in Russian symbolist literature are utilised by Chekhov in his depiction of Treplev. P. Gurev, in a book on Russian symbolist poetry, outlines some of these recurring motifs. Chekhov's use of these themes testifies to both his knowledge of this literary movement and his subtle debunking of the more pretentious aspects of it. 'The theme of solitude is the fundamental motif of symbolist poetry. In all of the experiences of the symbolist poets, we encounter, either directly or in reflected form, the fact of their estrangement not only from the life of groups, but also from the life of another individual, even their beloved. Solitude is by turns extolled as the delight and happiness of life — it alone remains to the man not wishing to mingle with the crowd — and cursed: he strains to break out of it, seeks salvation among people, in love for a woman, but in vain. He remains alone and alienated from all ... All the forces of his soul recede deep into the individual; his surroundings interest him less and less, and he separates himself from life, as it were, with a translucent screen through which everything seems to him less real, phantomlike. The real world loses something in palpability and weight, and reality comes to resemble a dream; but, in exchange, the images engendered by the soul acquire the brilliance and force of actuality.' (Gurev, P., 'Summing Up Russian Symbolist Poetry', in Rabinowitz, S., ed., *The Noise of Change: Russian Literature and the Critics (1891–1917)*, Ardis, Ann Arbor, 1986, pp. 106–10.)
[117] Chekhov, A., *The Seagull*, p. 241.
[118] Ibid., p. 279.
[119] Senelick, L., 'Chekhov's Drama, Maeterlinck, and the Russian Symbolists', in Barricelli, J-P., op. cit., p. 164.
[120] Senelick, L., 'Chekhov and the Irresistible Symbol: A Response to Peter Holland', in Redmond, J., *Drama and Symbolism: Themes in Drama 4*, Cambridge University Press, Cambridge, 1982, p. 246.
[121] Chekhov, A., *The Seagull*, p. 253.
[122] Holland, P., 'Chekhov and the Resistant Symbol', in Redmond, J., op. cit., p. 235.
[123] Gielgud, J., *Early Stages*, The Falcon Press, London, 1948, p. 84.
[124] See Gottlieb, V., *Chekhov and the Vaudeville*, Cambridge University Press, Cambridge, 1982, pp. 126 and 128.
[125] Osborne, C., *Daily Telegraph*, 25 April 1991.
[126] These problems of interpretation are made more difficult in the case of a writer such as Chekhov because, not only are audiences increasingly removed from the time in which the plays were written, they are also culturally removed because these works are Russian, not English, in origin. For a discussion of these particular problems of directorial interpretation, see Scolnicov, H. and Holland, P., op. cit.
[127] Chekhov saw Bernhardt perform and wrote: 'We are far from worshipping Sarah Bernhardt as a talent.' In her portrayal of Adrienne Lecouvreur Chekhov admitted 'There were brief passages in her acting which moved us almost to tears', but he added that 'the tears failed to well up only because all the enchantment is smothered in artifice. Were it not for that scurvy artifice, that premeditated tricksiness, that over-emphasis, honest to goodness, we would have burst into tears, and the theatre would have rocked with applause'. (Chekhov, A., 'More about Sarah Bernhardt', December 1881, in Senelick, L., *Russian Dramatic Theory from Pushkin to the Symbolists*, University of Texas Press, Austin, 1981, p. 87.)
[128] Chekhov, A., *The Seagull*, p. 265.
[129] Ibid., pp. 265–6.
[130] Radin, V., *New Statesman*, 9 August 1985.

[131] Billington, M., *Guardian*, 5 August 1985.

[132] Trigorin is another character who is often played judgementally and not from his own point of view. We know that Chekhov disliked the fact that Stanislavski played this character as a dandy. In Anthony Clark's 1990 production, Chekhov's weak-willed writer was made into a rather nasty seducer: 'Expatiating on the hollowness of his fame, Guinness [Trigorin] lets you see, in the faintly calculating look in his eyes, how the novelist is using this soul-bearing [sic] exercise as a way of besotting the girl [Nina] further.' (Taylor, P., *Independent*, 23 February 1990.)

[133] King, F., *Sunday Telegraph*, 5 May 1985.

[134] Gottlieb, V., 'Chekhov in Limbo: British Productions of the Plays of Chekhov', in Scolnicov, H. and Holland, P., op. cit., p. 166.

[135] King, F., *Sunday Telegraph*, 11 August 1985.

[136] Coveney, M., *Financial Times*, 5 August 1985.

[137] Coveney, M., *Observer*, 10 July 1994.

[138] Kingston, J., *The Times*, 12 July 1991.

[139] Karlinsky, S., op. cit., p. 281.

# Chapter 5. *Uncle Vanya*: 'A Glimmer of Light Shining in the Distance'

> *Futility and fatality, the unromantic fatality of everyday events, the overwhelming weight of boredom and banality are its central themes.* (Marc Slonim)[1]
>
> *The spine of the play: to make life better, find a way to be happy.* (Harold Clurman)[2]

*Uncle Vanya*, which received its Moscow premiere in October 1899, appears to be in many ways a more conventional play than *The Seagull*. One reviewer of the Moscow Art Theatre 1924 touring production commented that '*Uncle Vanya* is a play not far removed in construction from the old time melodrama thrillers of the American stage'.[3]

Despite the play's apparent simplicity, it has proved to be just as open to radically opposing interpretations as any of Chekhov's dramas. Both in Russia and the West, the gloom and doom version of *Uncle Vanya* has tended to predominate with both critics and directors. Fiona Scott-Norman, a Melbourne critic reviewing Gale Edwards' 1991 production, baldly states, '*Vanya* is about the futility of life'. She argues that, even though the play may not have had this pessimistic meaning at the time it was written, now, 'in our modern, Godless, society, that is the only interpretation, because we cannot share the hope of Sonya that we will find peace when we die'.[4] Certainly Oleg Yefremov's Moscow Art Theatre production that toured to London in 1989 carried on the Stanislavskian tradition of presenting Chekhov's dramas as if they were tragedies. This bleak view of Chekhov almost inevitably leads to critics and reviewers inappropriately associating his cautiously optimistic vision of reality with the 'nothing to be done' school of Absurdism. So, Milton Shulman begins his review of Yefremov's production as follows:

> Chekhov's *Uncle Vanya* has never been a barrel of laughs but the Slavic gloom into which it is plunged by the Moscow Art Theatre's production at the Lyttelton is not merely dramatic but philosophical. Everything from the vast set wreathed in mist and gardens steeped in dead brown leaves to the movements of the actors carrying their burdens of despair like heavy knapsacks, proclaims a mood almost as glum as a light comedy conceived by Samuel Beckett.[5]

In the light of such depressing interpretations, it may appear surprising that a critic of the standing of David Magarshack should sum up his analysis of the play by confidently asserting that the 'principal theme of *Uncle Vanya*, therefore, is not frustration, but courage and hope'.[6]

The fact that *Uncle Vanya*, in common with many of Chekhov's other dramas, has been interpreted in a variety of ways led the *Melbourne Times* critic, Chris

Boyd to make the ludicrous suggestion that the play might not mean anything at all:

> *Uncle Vanya* is surely Chekhov's most beguiling and baffling play. Though its portentous themes peal through the 20th century, one must first ask, is Chekhov really attempting to *say* anything? The play is, after all, open to countless readings.[7]

Since any director will inevitably 'impose an interpretation' on a play such as *Uncle Vanya* and make it 'say' something, it is surely wiser that such interpretative decisions be guided by informed critical argument, rather than simply suggesting that the play should mean whatever the director wishes it to mean.

Chekhov originally offered *Uncle Vanya*, which had played successfully for two years in the provinces, to the Moscow Maly Theatre, one of the oldest state theatres, rather than to the Moscow Art Theatre. However, every play produced in state theatres had first to be passed by the official Theatrical and Literary Committee. When this august body decided that the play could not be presented until certain changes had been made, Chekhov withdrew his offer from the Maly and offered it to the Moscow Art Theatre instead. For all of his reservations about Stanislavski's production of *The Seagull*, Chekhov seems to have appreciated the fact that this new, private theatre company which would perform his play without alterations was likely to be more attuned to the nature of his innovative dramaturgy than the more traditional government-controlled theatre company. He was not disappointed, for although the first night of the Moscow Art Theatre production of *Uncle Vanya* did not elicit as rapturous a response as that accorded the first night of their production of *The Seagull*, nevertheless the play became an enormous success. A month after it opened, Chekhov wrote enthusiastically to A. L. Vishnevsky, the actor who played the role of Uncle Vanya, about how grateful he was to have discovered the Moscow Art Theatre:

> ... I thank heaven that after having sailed the sea of life, I have finally landed on so wonderful an island as the Art Theater. When I have children, I will force them to pray to God eternally for all of you.[8]

The relatively small amount of correspondence and contemporary commentary concerning the Moscow Art Theatre production of *Uncle Vanya* that has survived is particularly revealing in respect of the increasing tensions that were beginning to develop between the two founders of the Art Theatre. Nemirovich-Danchenko clearly felt that he had a deeper understanding of Chekhov's play than Stanislavski, and he was not frightened to express this view in his correspondence with both the playwright and the director. An examination of this artistic quarrel, combined with Chekhov's own recorded comments about this production, supply directors of today with valuable hints about how the playwright and the two theatrical directors of the Moscow Art Theatre thought *Uncle Vanya* should be interpreted. The fact that artistic consensus was reached may go some way to explain why this production was such a success. Three days before the play opened, Meyerhold wrote to thank Chekhov for having given him some useful advice on how to approach the role of Johannes in Hauptmann's *Lonely People*. In the course of this letter, he described his impressions of how Stanislavski and Nemirovich-Danchenko were conducting the rehearsals of *Uncle Vanya*:

> The play is extremely well put together. What I note most of all in the production as a whole is the sense of restraint from beginning to end. For the first time the two directors complement each other perfectly; one, a director and actor, has great imagination, although inclined to go too far in the actual staging; the other, a director and dramatist, defends the interests of the author. And he seems quite evidently to have the upper hand. The frame does not hide the picture. Not only are the basic ideas carefully preserved by not burying them in a heap of useless details, they are rather skilfully brought out.[9]

Meyerhold clearly suggests that Stanislavski normally lacked 'restraint' but that, in this case, his tendency to invent all sorts of extraneous business, which buried the central ideas of a play, had been kept in check by Nemirovich-Danchenko. Meyerhold knew that Chekhov would be sympathetic to such criticism of Stanislavski, as the playwright had only recently written a letter to him in which he had warned the actor that he would have to resist the director's tendency to go for exaggerated effects that were theatrical rather than lifelike.[10]

In his memoirs, *My Life in the Russian Theatre*, Nemirovich-Danchenko recalled Stanislavski's love of both melodramatic excess and naturalistic exaggeration in the preparation of his *mise-en-scène*.[11] Stanislavski's obsession with what Meyerhold called the 'heap of useless details', which had been a feature of his earlier work, affected the early rehearsals of *Uncle Vanya*. Benedetti notes that 'Stanislavski found his way into the character of Astrov with difficulty', and this 'insecurity in the early stages of rehearsal' manifested itself in a tendency for him to become 'overactive'. Astrov was given all sorts of irrelevant 'business' by the actor:

> Thus he wandered round the house and garden, noting everything, examining the plants, picking the heads off dead flowers. Above all he swatted mosquitoes ... The production plan contains instructions to everyone to swat them and even, as an added protection, to put handkerchiefs over their faces.[12]

In his memoirs, Nemirovich-Danchenko could not resist quoting Chekhov's humorous criticism of this weakness in Stanislavski's approach to the role:

> Like every innovator he [Stanislavski] fell into extremes, but as every detail went through my direction I was in a position to cast aside anything that seemed superfluous or questionable.
>
> Within a year, in *Uncle Vanya*, he would cover up the head against mosquitoes, would stress the chirp of the cricket behind the stove; for these effects theatrical criticism would go to great lengths to abuse the Art Theatre. Even Chekhov, half jesting, half in earnest, would say: 'In my next play I'll make the stipulation: "The action takes place in a land which has neither mosquitoes nor crickets nor any other insects which hinder conversation between human beings."'[13]

At the time of the first Moscow Art Theatre production of *Uncle Vanya*, Nemirovich-Danchenko was much more upset by Stanislavski's work on the play than the entry in his memoirs indicates. In a long letter written on the day the play opened, he complained to Stanislavski about the way the production had developed. He felt that, due to the restricted rehearsal times, he had not been able to communicate to the director certain major reservations that he had about some of his directorial decisions. Nemirovich-Danchenko laments:

> … we have so little time for discussion that one cannot negotiate fully and logically. And we both are aware that it is awkward to disagree during rehearsals. It is embarrassing in front of the actors, don't you think?[14]

Claiming to be attempting to satisfy the needs of 'the interesting and better part of the public' rather than merely the reviewers, Nemirovich-Danchenko, apart from insisting that Stanislavski know Astrov's lines better, asked him to make certain changes to the production. One of these 'concessions' that he felt 'obliged' to ask for concerned the theatrical business that Stanislavski had devised for himself:

> 1) in your role as Astrov I don't want a handkerchief on your head to keep off mosquitoes, it's a detail I simply cannot take. And I can tell you for certain that Chekhov won't like it; I know his tastes and creative nature extremely well. I can tell you for certain that this particular detail doesn't introduce anything new. I'll wager that it will merely be numbered among those 'excesses' which just irritate and bring no advantage either to the theatre or to the work you are doing … Finally, even from the point of view of real life it is far-fetched. In short I cannot find any appreciable argument for it, not one serious argument of any kind whatsoever. And precisely because there is no argument for it I cannot see why you won't give it up when I ask you.[15]

At first, Stanislavski refused to give up these bits of business, clinging to them as if they were some sort of security blanket. So, as Benedetti notes, 'the handkerchief and the mosquitoes remained. Only gradually, as rehearsals progressed and confidence grew, did the welter of detail disappear.'[16] The artistic 'restraint' that Meyerhold had noticed developing during rehearsals in the production as a whole was gradually incorporated by Stanislavski into his own performance as Dr Astrov and, to his surprise, this resulted in a characterisation that was universally admired. He is reported to have said to Olga Knipper in astonishment: 'I do nothing and the public loves it.'[17]

The useful lesson that can be learnt from Stanislavski's experience in playing the role of Astrov is that much of the art of acting Chekhov lies in the ability of the actor to play his or her role with an almost classical simplicity. Chekhov's advice to the actors rehearsing in Karpov's St Petersburg production of *The Seagull* remains as useful for today's actors and directors as it was in 1896. 'Above all,' Karpov reports Chekhov saying, 'avoid theatricality. Try to be as simple as possible. Remember that they are all ordinary people.'[18] Stanislavski came to see the value of such an understated approach to characterisation.[19]

As a director, Stanislavski never overcame his habit of burying the central ideas of Chekhov's plays in 'a heap of useless details'. It was Meyerhold who pinpointed the potential for Chekhov's plays to be treated in this manner. As the Russian critic S. Balukhaty noted:

> In Meyerhold's opinion the use of images which are impressionistically scattered onto a canvas makes up the basic characteristic of Chekhov's dramatic style; it provides the director with material suitable for filling out the characters into bright, defined figures (types). Hence, the characteristic enthusiasm of directors for details which distract from the picture as a whole.[20]

One of the clearest examples of the kind of problems that arise from such excessive 'filling out' of a character can be seen when one examines the performance given by Antony Sher as Astrov in Sean Mathias' 1992 production of *Uncle Vanya*. Anyone who has seen Sher's performances as the homicidal Richard in *Richard III*, or as the arch hypocrite Tartuffe in Molière's play of the same name, will realise that this actor has a highly theatrical and often idiosyncratic approach to his roles. Christopher Edwards, in his review of Mathias' production, thought that Sher's performance as Astrov was 'vital', but makes the damning comment that 'Sher will never be a true ensemble actor, I imagine'.[21] Other reviewers echo this criticism. Malcolm Rutherford of the *Financial Times* pointed out that Sher 'must be one of the hardest actors to discipline to a team performance, particularly when he is not the captain'.[22]

Nothing is more fatal in playing Chekhov than if an actor draws attention to himself as a star performer rather than as a member of an ensemble, but this was precisely what Sher appears to have done. Kenneth Hurren in the *Mail on Sunday* talked about 'a couple of "actorish" performances' which marred what was otherwise felt to be a fine production. Sher's performance Hurren described as 'amusingly full of tricks from some actors' handbook'.[23] Many reviewers noted the self-centred nature of Sher's performance. Even Christopher Edwards, who liked his interpretation of Astrov, pointed out that Sher 'cannot help but grab attention and he goes about it with his usual thoroughness here'.[24] The most revealing review of Mathias' production and Antony Sher's performance was that written by Charles Spencer for the *Daily Telegraph*. Spencer's analysis of why this *Uncle Vanya* 'misses greatness', despite having the services of 'an exceptionally distinguished cast', suggests that this production fell into the trap of being overtly theatrical rather than attempting to be natural and lifelike:

> In Sean Mathias's staging you are too often aware that you are watching unusually gifted actors *acting*. The best Chekhov productions create the illusion that you are watching not a carefully constructed play but the untidy sprawl of life itself. Here there's a self-consciousness, a determination to be fresh and original at all costs. Mathias appears to have little time for the art which conceals art.[25]

Chekhov's commitment to the use of the conventions of realism meant that, unlike Mathias, he was attempting to create art in a form that by definition tried to hide its artifice. Sher, consciously or not, adopted the piece of 'business' with the handkerchief which Stanislavski had so loved and which Nemirovich-Danchenko had so despised. Spencer, like Nemirovich-Danchenko before him, points to the inappropriateness of such theatrical trickery:

> I must confess that I have a particular problem with Antony Sher, greatly admired by many, who plays Astrov. Mr Sher is famous for his hyperactive flamboyance and he is unable to repress it even in Chekhov. The Doctor makes his first entrance drenched in sweat and panting for breath before going through an elaborate ritual of wetting a handkerchief and placing it absurdly on his head. Of course all of this is meant to show that Astrov has just ridden a long way and that it's very hot, but what you actually think is here's old Antony Sher indulging in another elaborate piece of business. How long, you wonder, will it be before he's lying prone on the floor? Answer: about two minutes, and he has plenty of other tricks up his sleeve as the evening wears on.[26]

Sher's performance as Astrov epitomises the kind of histrionic excess that Chekhov constantly railed against. The playwright's love of brevity and understatement is constantly attested to in the advice he gave to other writers during the whole of his career. So, in a letter written just prior to the Moscow Art Theatre production of *Uncle Vanya*, we find Chekhov explaining what he found 'lacking' in Maxim Gorky's writing:

> I'll begin by saying that in my opinion you lack restraint. You are like a spectator in a theater who expresses his enthusiasm so unreservedly that he prevents himself and others from listening.[27]

A few weeks later Chekhov elaborated on this criticism. Having praised Gorky's talent, he added:

> The only weak point is the lack of restraint, the lack of grace. When a man expends the fewest possible movements on a given act, that is grace. In your movements one is aware of superfluity.[28]

It is precisely this 'lack of grace' that characterised Antony Sher's performance. By doing too much he made the play's central action more difficult to read.

Gregory Mosher's television version of *Uncle Vanya* did not simply fail to follow Chekhov's advice about the play, but instead appeared to be perversely trying to incorporate as many of the elements that the author had specifically objected to in Stanislavski's production. This Anglo-American venture, produced by the BBC in association with WNET New York in 1990, involved a stylistically uneasy combination of British and American actors. The verisimilitude that Chekhov's drama demands was destroyed by having Serebryakov played by the Scottish actor, Ian Bannen, while his daughter, Sonya, was played by the American actress Rebecca Pidgeon. Having heard Dr Astrov, the man she loves, state that the only thing that still thrills him is 'beauty', Sonya laments:

> SONYA. [*Alone.*] Oh, how dreadful not to be beautiful. It's dreadful. And I know I'm not beautiful, I know, I know, I know. Coming out of church last Sunday I heard some people talking about me and one woman said, 'She's such a nice, kind girl. What a pity she's so plain.' So plain.[29]

The problem in this production is that dramatic credibility is further strained by the fact that, no matter how hard she tries to deny the fact, Ms Pidgeon is a remarkably beautiful woman. The result is that she appears to be remarkably lacking in perception about her own appearance and Dr Astrov seems to be simply blind. Mary Elizabeth Mastrantonio is appropriately beautiful in the role of Helen, Serebryakov's young wife, but her strong American accent again has the effect of drawing attention to the incongruity of mixing actor nationalities in a production otherwise attempting to achieve complete realism.

Mosher's directorial perversity however is even more evident in his rejection, conscious or otherwise, of Chekhov's advice on how he wished certain sections of the play to be performed in order to avoid misinterpretation. Olga Knipper, who was playing the role of Helen in the Moscow Art Theatre production, had had difficulty in arriving at a satisfactory interpretation of the role, with the result that her performance on the opening night was unsatisfactory.[30] She wrote to Chekhov about her difficulties in accepting some of Stanislavski's ideas on how to play certain scenes. Knipper wrote that she was:

> ... rather put out by a comment of Stanislavski's on Astrov's last scene with Helen [Yeliena]. He wants Astrov to address Helen as an ardent lover seizing

on his passion as a drowning man clutches at a straw. In my opinion if that were the case Helen would follow him and wouldn't have the courage to answer, 'You really are absurd'. On the contrary, he speaks to her in the most cynical way, even somehow making fun of his own cynicism. Am I right or not?[31]

Chekhov's response was clear. As far as he was concerned, Stanislavski's interpretation, as presented by Knipper, was totally incorrect. To play Astrov as an ardent lover, Chekhov claimed, was 'Wrong, quite wrong'. The playwright then provided an extremely lucid explanation of why such an approach was incorrect:

> Astrov is attracted to Helen [Yeliena], she captivates him with her beauty, but in the last act he already knows there's nothing doing. He knows Helen's going away for good so far as he's concerned and in this scene he speaks to her in the same tone as when he talks about the heat in Africa. And he kisses her quite casually because he has nothing better to do. If Astrov makes a great to-do about this scene the entire mood of Act Four, which is quiet and apathetic, will be ruined.[32]

This potentially useful advice was ignored in Mosher's production. Ian Holm, a deeply gloomy Astrov, played this scene with the same passionate intensity advocated by Stanislavski, while Mary Elizabeth Mastrantonio's Helen wept tears of anguish at her inability to find the courage to have an affair with the tortured doctor.

Ronald Hingley claims that Chekhov 'found Stanislavski's interpretation over-flamboyant'.[33] One can only speculate on what the playwright would have made of Mosher's directorial embellishments to *Uncle Vanya*. One of the most glaring examples of this American director's distortion of Chekhov's meaning occurred at the climactic moment in Act Three when Vanya makes his inept attempt to shoot Serebryakov. At this point in the play Marina is comforting Sonya while, off-stage, Vanya and the Professor appear to be continuing their earlier on-stage quarrel. Chekhov's text runs as follows:

> MARINA. ... Don't grieve, my poor darling. [*Looking at the centre door, angrily.*] Dear me, the feathers are flying. A plague on those geese!
> [*A shot off stage.* HELEN [Yeliena] *is heard to scream.* SONYA *shudders.*]
> MARINA. Oh, a curse upon you!
> SEREBRYAKOV. [*Runs in, staggering and terrified.*] Stop him, stop him! He's gone mad!
> [HELEN *and* VOYNITSKY [Vanya] *are seen struggling in the doorway.*]
> HELEN. [Yeliena] [*Trying to take the revolver from him.*] Give it to me. Give it to me, I tell you!
> VOYNITSKY. [Vanya] Let me go. Let go of me. [*Frees himself, runs in and looks around for* SEREBRYAKOV.] Where is he? Ah, there he is. [*Fires at him.*] Bang!

[*Pause.*] Missed him, did I? Missed him again, eh? [*Angrily.*] Oh, hell, hell! Hell and damnation! [*Bangs the revolver on the floor and sinks exhausted in a chair.*
SEREBRYAKOV *looks stunned.*
[HELEN *leans against the wall almost fainting.*] HELEN. Get me away from here. Take me away, I don't care if you kill me, but I can't stay here. I can't.
VOYNITSKY. [*Desperately.*] Oh, what am I doing? What am I doing?
SONYA. [*Quietly.*] Nanny darling! Nanny!

CURTAIN.[34]

At this point in the play, we have an almost perfect example of Chekhov's tragi-comic technique. This highly melodramatic scene, replete with two pistol shots, may initially suggest to an audience that Vanya has committed suicide off-stage, like Treplev in *The Seagull*. Chekhov then increases the theatrical excitement by introducing the theatrical twist of having the possibility of suicide removed and replacing it by the even more dramatic situation of a potential murder occurring on-stage. Having developed the melodramatic possibilities of the scene to their utmost, Chekhov then proceeds, through the use of comic bathos, to transform it into something that, if it were not also potentially tragic, would be akin to farce. Effective tragic action turns into empty comic gesture.

In Mosher's production, the off- and on-stage shots are present, as in Chekhov's script, but the director adds an extra piece of stage business that is entirely at variance with the tragi-comic tone of the play. After David Warner as Vanya says 'Bang!', he is given a line which he delivers in a quietly menacing fashion. That line — 'All right. All right. One more time.' He then slowly approaches Serebryakov, who stands stock-still, fearlessly staring Vanya in the eyes, points the revolver under the professor's chin and then pulls the trigger. A click rather than an explosion is heard, and Vanya then '*sinks exhausted into a chair*'. Mosher's interpolation is certainly highly theatrical and is part of a tradition of melodramatic overstatement that accorded with Stanislavski's taste for excess, but it is the complete antithesis of the Chekhov's artistic attempt to 'show life and men as they are, and not as they would look if you put them on stilts'.[35]

Chekhov's advice to the actress playing the role of Sonya provides further evidence of his deep desire to avoid externalised melodramatic performance. In her *Reminiscences*, the actor I. S. Butova recounts Chekhov's comments:

> Anton Pavlovich once saw a performance of *Uncle Vanya*. In the third act Sonya went down on her knees on the line 'Father, you must be merciful!', and kissed his hands. 'You mustn't do that, that isn't what drama is', said Anton Chekhov. 'The whole meaning or drama of a person lies internally, not in outer manifestations. There was drama in Sonya's life prior to this moment, and there

will be subsequently, but this is just an occurrence, a continuation of the pistol shot. And the pistol shot is not a drama either, but an occurrence.'[36]

Almost all of the directorial flourishes introduced by Mosher in his production of *Uncle Vanya* helped to transform the play into an extremely portentous and bleak tragedy. Chekhov's ironic humour, which is found, for example, in Vanya's ludicrous attempt to shoot the professor, was almost totally submerged in the gloomy fatalism that predominated in this version of the play. What was missing in this production was a sense of the dualistic vision of reality, inherent in Chekhov's works, that manifests itself in the form of synthetic tragi-comedy. In all of Chekhov's plays, and in *Uncle Vanya* in particular, the vision of reality is expressed in terms of both a short view and a long view. The short view is essentially pessimistic and is expressed in a tragic form, while the long view is essentially optimistic and is associated with the comic aspect of the play. Dr Astrov and Sonya are the two characters in the play who embody the combined short and long views of life. Arriving at an appropriate interpretation of these roles can be the key for a director seeking to find that delicate balance between hope and despair at the heart of Chekhovian tragi-comedy. It is, of course, up to any given director to find the specific *mise-en-scène* that, at the particular time of his or her production, will realise that interpretation for an audience.

While Dr Astrov is not a portrayal of Chekhov himself, the playwright invested this character with many of his own beliefs. In particular, Chekhov's dualistic vision of reality is reflected in Astrov's alternation between moods of hope and despair. Just as the terminally sick Dr Chekhov knew that, from his individual short-term view, there was little he could do to improve humanity's lot during his brief lifetime, so Dr Astrov, in his darker moods, is depressed by the fact that his own puny efforts seem pointless and will even fail to be noticed. At the beginning of the play the overworked doctor is in just such a depressed mood. He has just lost a patient and this reminds him of the limitations of his profession and his own inability to significantly improve the lot of the peasants. Astrov, in this mood, loses the scientific objectivity that is vital for survival in the profession of medicine where the inevitability of death is a given. He recounts how his personal emotions became involved when his patient died. This leads him to voice his current feeling that perhaps his work, and life in general, are futile:

> ASTROV. ... They brought someone in from the railway, a switchman. I got him on the table to operate, and damned if he didn't have to die on me under chloroform. Then just at the worst possible moment my feelings did come to life and I felt as guilty as if I'd murdered the man. I sat down and closed my eyes like this. And I thought of the men and women who will be alive a hundred or a couple of hundred years after we've gone, those we're preparing the way

for. Will they have a good word to say for us? You know, Nanny, they won't even remember us.

MARINA. Men may forget, but God will remember.

ASTROV. Thank you for saying that. You put it well.[37]

Astrov's long-term epic vision of a better life, evidenced by his reference to the future generations for whom he and others are working, is at this point eclipsed by his short-term sense of futility. What we witness here is a momentary loss of faith on Astrov's part. We later find out that, unlike Marina and Sonya, Astrov has no belief in God to sustain him. In Act Two, after having drunk too much vodka, he embarks on a late-night talk with Sonya in which he describes this lack of faith and sense of hopelessness by using a metaphorical image:

> ASTROV. ... You know, sometimes when you walk in a wood on a dark night there's a glimmer of light shining in the distance, isn't there? Then you don't notice how tired you are or how dark it is or how the thorns and twigs hit you in the face. As you well know, I work harder than anyone else round here, the most awful things are always happening to me and there are times when the whole business really gets me down. But for me there's no light shining in the distance.[38]

Despite Astrov's awareness that from his personal individual viewpoint there is no hope, he nevertheless continues to behave in a manner that takes into account future generations. Like Chekhov, he continues to practise medicine and also, like the playwright, he plants trees in order to halt the environmental degradation that would adversely affect the living conditions of those yet unborn. Though Dr Astrov does not appear to believe in any afterlife, he retains his faith in the idea of creating a better future for humanity. When Astrov describes the ways in which the Russian forests 'are crashing down before the axe',[39] he does not ascribe this ecological disaster to fate. According to Astrov, it is human beings who are responsible because they have chosen to behave in this irresponsible manner:

> ASTROV. ... Man has been endowed with reason, with the power to create, so that he can add to what he's been given. But up to now he hasn't been a creator, only a destroyer. Forests keep disappearing, rivers dry up, wild life's become extinct, the climate's ruined and the land grows poorer and uglier each day.[40]

The fact that Astrov says that man has been a destroyer 'up to now', implies that in the future he could be a creator. If the degradation had come about because it was in the nature of things to degenerate, then Chekhov would indeed have presented a world view in which there was 'nothing to be done'. However, Astrov's argument suggests that the disasters that occur to the environment are the result of 'no-one doing anything'. It is 'all because man's so lazy'[41] that he 'destroys everything with no thought for the morrow'.[42] Astrov has little faith in the present but it is because he does have faith in the 'morrow' that he plants his trees:

> ASTROV. ... You don't take any of this seriously, and — and perhaps I really have got a bee in my bonnet. But when I walk past our village woodlands which I've saved from the axe or hear the rustle of my own saplings, planted with my own hands, I feel that I too have some slight control over the climate and that if man is happy a thousand years from now I'll have done a bit towards it myself. When I plant a young birch and later see it covered with green and swaying in the breeze my heart fills with pride ...[43]

While Helen may be indolent and incapable of involving herself in any useful occupation, she is intelligent enough to see her own lack of worth when compared to Astrov. She admits to Sonya that she is 'just a tiresome character and not a very important one',[44] but she recognises, like Sonya, that part of what makes the doctor attractive is his belief in the possibility of creating a better future:

> HELEN. [Yeliena] ... he has courage, flair, tremendous vision. When he plants a tree he's already working out what the result will be in a thousand years' time, already glimpsing man's future happiness. People like that are rare and should be cherished.[45]

Astrov's vision is not one that includes personal happiness. The vodka he drinks may temporarily anaesthetise the pain of enduring the grinding nature of his work, but what sustains him is faith in the future. The passion he shows for his research into and documentation of the environmental degradation of his district is made abundantly clear in the long speeches that Chekhov gives him in Act Three, when he explains his research to Helen. It is only when he realises that she is not really interested in environmental issues and has something else on her mind that he stops his heartfelt description of his work. There is absolutely no sense of irony in these speeches, but rather a tone of serious commitment:

> ASTROV. ... The general picture is one of gradual and unmistakable decline, and it obviously needs only another ten or fifteen years to become complete. You'll tell me it's the influence of civilization, that the old life obviously had to make way for the new. All right, I see what you mean. If roads and railways had been built in place of the ravaged woodlands, if we had factories, workshops and schools, the peasants would have become healthier, better off and more intelligent. But you see, nothing of the sort has happened.[46]

It is only when Astrov realises the real purpose of Helen's private consultation that the bantering ironic tone appears. He wags his finger at her and calls her 'a little box of tricks', 'little vampire', and a 'beautiful furry little weasel'.[47] Attracted as he is to Helen's beauty, he evinces no real passion for her. Indeed, when the time comes for him to say goodbye, he realistically appraises the situation by pointing out to Helen that their would-be affair was really only a comic interlude which for a brief time took the place of his real passion:

> ASTROV. ... No sooner do you and you husband turn up in this place than people here who are getting on with their work, all busy creating something, have to drop everything and do nothing all summer but attend to you and your husband's gout. You two have infected us all with your idleness. I've been under your spell and I've done nothing for a whole month while all the time people have been falling ill and the villagers have been grazing their cattle in my newly planted woods ... And I'm quite sure of this. If you'd stayed on here we'd have had a full-scale disaster on our hands. It would have been the end of me and you wouldn't have come out of it too well either. All right then, off with you. The show is over.[48]

When directors overemphasise the 'love' between Astrov and the professor's wife they push the play towards the type of clichéd boulevard dramas that Chekhov was trying to avoid. Chekhov depicts Astrov in an anti-romantic fashion, not as some thwarted passionate lover but as a realist who sees life without illusions and endures. It is Uncle Vanya, or Uncle Johnny as he should be in English, who attempts to be the passionate lover, and Chekhov depicts his attempts at seduction in a comic fashion.

Nothing could be more ludicrous than Vanya's perfect comic entrance bearing autumn roses for Helen and finding her in the arms of Astrov. It is Vanya who, having wasted his own life, blames the professor for his own lack of vision and then makes the comically ludicrous claim, which even he realises is silly, that, but for the professor, he would have been a man of genius:

> VOYNITSKY. [Vanya] My life's ruined. I'm gifted, intelligent, courageous. If I'd had a normal life I might have been a Schopenhauer or a Dostoyevsky. But I'm talking nonsense, I'm going mad. Mother dear, I'm desperate. Mother!
> MRS. VOYNITSKY. [*Sternly*.] Do as Alexander says.[49]

Vanya's pain is real, but his reaction to what is in effect a mid-life crisis is ludicrously inappropriate. Here he acts with a lack of maturity and emotional independence similar to Treplev in *The Seagull*, but in this case it is even more grotesque as Vanya is middle-aged and still behaves like a child in his mother's presence. It is Astrov who is forced to make Vanya face the harsh reality of his life when the unhappy self-pitying man asks the doctor to help him either to create a new life or help him out of this one. Astrov gives advice to Vanya similar to that which Dr Dorn had given to Sorin in *The Seagull* when that character bemoaned his unlived life. He refuses to bolster Vanya's illusions:

> VOYNITSKY. [Vanya] ... What am I to do? What am I to do?
> ASTROV. Nothing.

> VOYNITSKY. Give me some medicine or something. Oh my God I'm forty-seven. Suppose I live to be sixty, that means I still have thirteen years to go. It's too long. How am I to get through those thirteen years? What am I to do? How do I fill the time? Oh can you think — ? [*Feverishly clutches* ASTROV's *arm.*] Can you think what it would be like to live one's life in a new way? Oh, to wake up some fine, clear morning feeling as if you'd started living all over again, as if the past was all forgotten, gone like a puff of smoke. [*Weeps.*] To begin a new life — Tell me, how should I begin? Where do I start?
> ASTROV. [*Annoyed.*] Oh, get away with you. New life indeed. Our situation's hopeless, yours and mine.
> VOYNITSKY. Is it?
> ASTROV. I'm perfectly certain of it.
> VOYNITSKY. Please give me something. [*Pointing to his heart.*] I've a burning feeling here.
> ASTROV. [*Shouts angrily.*] Oh, shut up! [*More gently.*] Those who live a century or two after us and despise us for leading lives so stupid and tasteless, perhaps they'll find a way to be happy, but as for us — There's only one hope for you and me, that when we're resting in our graves we may have visions. Even pleasant ones perhaps. [*Sighs.*][50]

While he holds out no hope for any salvation in his own lifetime or in any afterlife, Astrov is able to endure because of his faith in future generations. Astrov is one of those characters in Chekhov's plays and short stories who embody what Morris Freedman has called 'Chekhov's morality of work'. The importance of interpreting this character in terms both of his short-term pessimism and his long-term optimism cannot be overstressed as it is only when both are realised on stage that Chekhov's tragi-comic vision can be experienced by an audience. Freedman is accurate when he points to the centrality of Astrov in the action of *Uncle Vanya*:

> It seems to me especially meaningful that the most energetic, the most vital, the most balanced, the most intelligent, and, all in all, the most attractive person in the play carries the point that work as it has meaning after death is the only good and meaningful work that we can ultimately do.[51]

Sonya shares Astrov's faith in the efficacy of work but, unlike him, she is consoled by her belief in God and an afterlife. It is this faith that allows her to endure her individual pain at not being loved by Dr Astrov. The inconsolable Vanya, having lost his faith in the usefulness of work, comes to the realisation that he has wasted his life. While Chekhov may not have believed in God, there is little doubt that he could appreciate the sustaining power of such a belief for those who could have faith. Both Astrov's faith in ecology and Sonya's faith in God could be interpreted as a rather blatant thesis, advocating the need for faith, were it not for Chekhov's ironic undercutting of their most committed utterances.

Astrov's examination of the maps that show the ecological damage occurring in Russia and his fervent resolution to do something to reverse this process is undercut by the fact that Helen [Yeliena] is far more interested in him as an attractive man than as a visionary man of ideas. The scene witnessed by the audience is not one in which an environmental thesis is driven home. Instead, the scene is one of comic 'crossed wires' in which the committed Astrov is so engrossed in advancing his thesis that he is comically unaware that Helen [Yeliena] is not listening to his ideas.

In a similar fashion, Sonya's long speech of faith at the end of the play is undercut by the fact that she is preaching to the unconverted. Vanya appears to have little faith in the existence of Sonya's God and, even though he has now resumed working, he no longer has faith in the value of work. Sonya's lyrical last speeches are played against a background of Vanya's quiet sobbing. There is no need for the actor to convey any tone of irony in Astrov's speeches about his faith in ecological management. Helen's amused response to his 'lecture' provides the scene as a whole with that tone. Similarly the actress playing Sonya can let the character's faith in the afterlife shine out in all its sustaining commitment at the end of the play. The sharp juxtaposition of Sonya's hope with Vanya's despair undercuts the power of her polemics while it enriches the tragi-comic complexity of the play's conclusion:

> SONYA. Well, it can't be helped. Life must go on. [*Pause.*] And our life will go on, Uncle Vanya. We shall live through a long succession of days and endless evenings. We shall bear patiently the trials fate has in store for us. We shall work for others — now and in our old age — never knowing any peace. And when our time comes we shall die without complaining. In the world beyond the grave we shall say that we wept and suffered, that our lot was harsh and bitter, and God will have pity on us ... And we shall find peace. We shall, Uncle, I believe it with all my heart and soul ... Poor, poor Uncle Vanya, you're crying. [*Through tears.*] There's been no happiness in your life, but wait, Uncle Vanya, wait. We shall find peace. [*Embraces him.*] We shall find peace.[52]

Regardless of whether audience members share Sonya's faith in the compensating rewards of the afterlife, it does seem to be important that the actor playing the role should show that Sonya believes what she says. Imposing an ironic undercutting of this last speech of Sonya's makes the play into an unremittingly bleak experience that is alien to the tragi-comic experience that occurs when Chekhov's vision of reality is fully realised. For this reason, the kind of interpretation of the role of Sonya given by Frances de la Tour in Christopher Fettes' critically acclaimed 1982 production is appropriate and did not warrant Francis King's final criticism. Having praised this actor for bringing 'her incomparable gift for pathos to the role of the plain, yearning Sonya' and saying that she was able in her performance to 'wring the heart', King comments:

> My only criticism of her performance is that, when she delivers that last pitiable speech in which she tries to comfort Vanya with a promise of final rest, she does so as though Sonya really believes what she is saying. I am sure that she does not.[53]

I can find no supporting evidence, either external or internal, for King's assertion that Sonya doesn't believe what she says. Again Freedman seems to me to be nearer the truth when he says that, in the world of *Uncle Vanya*, 'perhaps the only meaning in life is to be found in looking for meaning in life'.[54] While no specific faith is valorised by Chekhov in *Uncle Vanya,* the necessity of having something to believe in is advocated by the playwright. To deny this leads to the sort of misinterpretation made by Eric Bentley in his well-known article on the play. Bentley refuses to see Astrov's position as in any way positive or normative and proceeds to give a character analysis that, if it were to be followed in a production of the play, would result in an essentially absurdist version of the action. In Bentley's view, Astrov is like all of the characters in the play — a daydreamer who talks but does nothing:

> Astrov is not to be congratulated on his beautiful dreams; he is to be pitied. His hope that mankind will someday do something good operates as an excuse for doing nothing now. It is an expression of his own futility, and Astrov knows it. Even in the early version he was not really a Wood Demon. That was only the ironical nickname of a crank. In the later version even the nickname has gone, and Astrov is even more of a crank. When Yelena [Helen] arrives he leaves his forests to rot. Clearly they were no real fulfillment of his nature but an old-maidish hobby like Persian cats.[55]

Dr Astrov may appear to be a crank to those characters who do nothing to improve life, but to those, such as Sonya, who work, he appears to be almost heroic. It is hardly surprising that in Act One, when confronted by Sonya's adulation and the other characters' scepticism at his attempts to do something to save Russia's forests, he should cover his embarrassment by calling himself a 'crank'. Astrov's real attitude is revealed in his long late-night discussion with Sonya, when, having drunk a lot of vodka, he pours out his feelings to her. He admits that he may appear odd to others, but that is only because these others think 'shallow little thoughts' and 'not one of them can see farther than the end of his own nose'.[56] It is quite clear from his behaviour and the tone of this speech that Astrov is frustrated by the small-mindedness of those around him who, because of their irresponsible lack of effective action, make him seem the odd one out. No one else seems to be doing anything:

> ASTROV. ... They come crawling up to you, look at you sideways on and then complain. 'Oh, he's a psychopath' or 'He talks a lot of hot air'. And when they don't know how to label me they say, 'He's an odd fellow, odd.' I like forests.

So that's odd. I don't eat meat, so that's odd too. They don't have straightforward, decent, free relationships any more either with nature or with other people. That's gone entirely. [*Is about to have a drink.*][57]

If one grants the fact that Astrov and, to a certain degree, Sonya are normative characters in *Uncle Vanya* who embody Chekhov's morality of useful work, then it becomes difficult to justify absurdist critical interpretations of the play, such as that put forward by Eric Bentley, or bleak productions, such as that of Gregory Mosher. In most productions of the play that I have seen, Marina's simple expression of faith that, even though future generations may not remember the work people like the doctor have done to improve people's lives, 'God will remember' was followed by a bitter response from the doctor. Astrov's line, 'Thank you for saying that. You put it very well',[58] was delivered in an extremely patronising manner, with heavy irony, implying that this silly old woman was clearly talking nonsense. If we accept that Chekhov presents faith, whether in future generations or in the afterlife, as infinitely preferable to the inertia and despair that results from having no faith in anything, then it is quite possible that Astrov's reply to Marina, the one person he admits having 'a soft spot for',[59] might more appropriately be delivered without irony. It then becomes the expression of genuine gratitude at being reminded that it is more productive to have faith in the long view rather than succumb to the despair that results from concentrating only on the short view of life.

It is clear that Chekhov, the scientifically trained materialist, did not believe in God. But he equally felt that humans needed to believe in something in order to avoid the despair and inertia that results from an acceptance of the absurdity of life. In March 1892, in a letter to a friend, he wrote: 'I have no religion now'.[60] Chekhov expresses here a similar perception to that voiced by Astrov in *Uncle Vanya* when that doctor was at his most depressed: 'there's no light shining in the distance'.[61] Chekhov, however, even in his darkest moments, did not entirely accept this bleak perception. He felt that some kind of disease was afflicting him.

Chekhov's own double perception of short-term hopelessness and long-term faith was, as we have seen, reflected in the seemingly contradictory beliefs of Dr Astrov, whose concern for the future seems to be combined with a personal fatalism. A brief entry in his *Notebooks* captures perfectly Chekhov's own contradictions where the question of faith was concerned. It reads: 'He was a rationalist, but he had to confess that he liked the ringing of church bells.'[62] To claim categorically that God either exists or doesn't exist was seen as simplistic by the playwright. Chekhov's views on the whole question of faith were complex. In his diary he once wrote:

> Between 'There is a God' and 'There is no God' lies a great expanse which the sincere sage traverses with much difficulty. The Russian knows only one of

these two extremes, for the middle ground between them does not interest them. Hence, he usually knows nothing or very little.[63]

Chekhov's *Notebooks* are littered with comments concerning the need to have a purpose in life. It is not difficult to see how Astrov's aim to improve the environment for future generations would be seen as admirable by the person who wrote: 'We judge human activities by their goal; that activity is great of which the goal is great.'[64] It is also clear that the expressions of faith made by such characters as Marina and Sonya were unlikely to have been seen as the naive mumblings of a pair of misguided believers by the person who wrote:

> Faith is a spiritual faculty; animals have not got it; savages and uncivilized people have merely fear and doubt. Only highly developed natures can have faith.[65]

Three years before he died we find Chekhov still concerned with advocating the need to have some kind of faith. So, having given details of the advanced stage of his illness, he warns his friend, Victor Mirolubov, against becoming a follower of a philosophical society created by Vasili Rosanov, but suggests that he still hold on to his beliefs, even if only in his 'own decency': 'One should believe in God; if one doesn't have faith, though, its place should not be taken by sound and fury but by seeking and more seeking, seeking alone, face to face with one's conscience.'[66]

Organised religion, like organised political parties and movements, was inimical to Chekhov but, as I argued earlier, this does not imply that he had no use for faith in a general humanist sense.

If directors of *Uncle Vanya* were to take account of Chekhov's own beliefs, they might see more clearly how inappropriate it is to interpret Astrov as a bitter failure crushed by the boredom and inertia that surrounds him, and they would not trivialise the vision of reality expressed by characters like Sonya and Marina. A balance between hope and despair needs to be realised on stage in any production that hopes to adequately present Chekhov's play.

Gary Saul Morson has written one of the more useful recent articles on Chekhov in general, and on *Uncle Vanya* in particular, in which he provides valuable insights that are of great use to directors. In the first place, he reminds us of some of Chekhov's concerns that permeate both the form and content of his plays:

> It might be said that the fundamental theme of Chekhov's plays is theatricality itself, our tendency to live our lives 'dramatically'. 'True life' does not generally conform to stage plots, except when people try to endow their lives with a spurious meaningfulness by imitating literary characters and scenes ... That is what Chekhov's major characters typically do. His plays center on histrionic

people who imitate theatrical performances and model themselves on other melodramatic genres.[67]

As we saw in the previous chapter on *The Seagull*, characters such as Masha, Sorin, Treplev and Irina constantly overdramatise their situations. They vainly and ludicrously try to give their prosaic lives the kind of significance that characters in romantic melodramas have. It was precisely Voynitsky's tendency to fantasise his own pathetic life that led to Astrov and Sonya attempting to make him face the reality of his life. Typical of Uncle Vanya's fantasised dramatic scenarios is the one in which he imagines what his life might have been if he, instead of the professor, had married Helen. In one of those undisguised soliloquies that function rather awkwardly in this essentially realistic drama, Voynitsky plays the role of a young lover in his imagined drama:

> VOYNITSKY. [Vanya] [*Alone.*] She's gone. [*Pause.*] To think that ten years ago I used to meet her at my sister's when she was only seventeen and I was thirty-seven. Why didn't I fall in love then and ask her to marry me? It would have been the most natural thing in the world. And she'd be my wife now. Yes. And tonight the storm would have woken us both. She'd be scared of the thunder and I'd hold her in my arms and whisper, 'Don't be afraid. I'm here.'[68]

Chekhov's parodic use of romantic melodrama undermines any heroic potential in Vanya's reverie. The audience should see a forty-seven-year-old man behaving in an entirely inappropriate manner — like an adolescent dramatising his sexual fantasies. The choice of who to cast in the role of Vanya is important, since it is vital that the character does not assume heroic dimensions. It is essential that the appropriate physical events be created on stage in order to trigger the desired physic events in the audience. Michael Redgrave's playing of Vanya in Stuart Burge's 1963 television production of Laurence Olivier's Chichester Festival production gave the character a deeply tragic quality partly because the actor's nobility was transferred to the character. The casting of the less heroic Wallace Shawn in Louis Malle's 1994 film, *Vanya on Forty-Second Street*, by contrast was a key factor in highlighting the comically ordinary nature of 'Uncle Johnny'. For Chekhov's tragi-comic characterisation to be achieved on stage, it is vital that an audience sees the gap between Vanya's claim that he could have been a Schopenhauer and his actual ordinariness. As Morson observes:

> In most plays, people behave 'dramatically' in a world where such behaviour is appropriate. The audience, which lives in the undramatic world we all know, participates vicariously in the more interesting and exciting world of the stage ... In *Uncle Vanya*, by contrast, the world in which the characters live resembles everyday life, but the characters nevertheless go on behaving 'dramatically'. Consequently, actions that would be tragic or heroic in other plays here acquire tonalities of comedy or even farce.[69]

In *Uncle Vanya*, Chekhov creates situations that are potentially tragic for the play's nominal protagonist. Despite this, Vanya's attempts to have himself seen as a person of tragic stature are constantly undercut by Chekhov. Vanya's ludicrous attempts to seduce Helen [Yeliena] and kill her husband make him comically pathetic rather than tragically heroic. His claim that Serebryakov stopped him from being a Schopenhauer or a Dostoevsky is a further example of his comic tendency to overplay his part. Vanya can attack Serebryakov for acting the role of an important scholar who pretends to know all about art, but he seems largely unaware of his own role-playing. Again, Morson makes an astute observation about the difficulties that face the actor playing one of those characters who overdramatise their lives:

> One reason the play has proved so difficult to stage in the right tonality — as critics and directors have constantly noted — is that the actors must overact and call attention to their theatrical status *but without ceasing to play real people who truly suffer*. They must not over-overact. Their performance must allude to but not shatter the dramatic frame.[70]

By actively subverting the theatricality of melodrama, Chekhov produces a kind of drama in which there are no clear-cut heroes or villains. Harvey Pitcher is surely correct when he says that, though some Chekhovian characters are more sympathetic than others, it is dangerous to take sides in their presentation. No character should be judged by the director and actor to be 'good' or 'bad'. As Pitcher says:

> To regard the Professor, for example, as an 'evil exploiter' and Vanya as a 'virtuous victim' misses the whole point of Vanya's portrayal, which is to show the plight of a man who really has no one but himself to blame for the mess that he has made of his life.[71]

Vera Gottlieb has pointed out that, in many recent British productions, the decision to interpret Chekhov's plays without due regard to their 'sad comicality' has resulted in grave distortions of their meaning:

> Thus the interpretation of the plays as tragedies simply ignores both the content *and* the form; while those productions which have recently played up the comedy have also failed to fuse form and content exactly because the comedy has not been seen as emanating from the philosophy and ideas of the plays — comic styles have been explored, but not the serious function of the comedy.[72]

The delicate balance between the comic and the tragic is difficult, but not impossible to achieve. In a 1990 production of *Uncle Vanya* directed by Paul Unwin, the role of Vanya was performed by Timothy West in a manner that led Christopher Edwards, the theatre critic of the *Spectator*, to describe the performance as 'the most convincing performance of the part I have seen'. What

Edwards saw was a performance in which the 'sad comicality', alluded to by Gottlieb, was clearly achieved:

> … Vanya's spluttering rages and the truculent moodiness that lie behind them expose the 47-year-old as a dour, immature adolescent. It is Vanya's tragedy to be ridiculous. The famous moment where he fires at the Professor and misses, twice, sums Vanya's life up. Farcically, he has missed all of his opportunities. But this is precisely what makes the play so affecting. When he bursts into tears of frustration West is both ridiculous and heart-rending at the same time.[73]

If the critic for the *Guardian*, David Foot, is to be believed, however, the same production failed to create the requisite tragi-comic balance for the production as a whole, mainly as a result of the bleak manner in which Patrick Malahide interpreted the role of Astrov. Foot had no problem with this interpretation, since he wrongly assumed that the vision of reality embodied in Chekhov's play is completely tragic. 'Paul Unwin, the director, is faithful enough to the pessimistic spirit of the play', Foot claims and, consistent with this one-sided view, proceeds to praise the actor's interpretation of the doctor's role:

> Patrick Malahide's Astrov, wearisome, embittered, idealism painfully thwarted, is portrayed with unrelenting despair. Here is both the most complicated and interesting character on view.[74]

If Unwin tipped the balance of his production towards the tragic, then the Renaissance Theatre Company production, jointly directed by Peter Egan and Kenneth Branagh, overbalanced the play towards the comic. The company advertised their production on the poster as 'The Bouncing Chekhov', which, as Allison Pearson noted, made it appear that 'Anton Pavlovich, the master of sleight of mind and heart, needed the *Carry On* treatment'. Pearson described the effect of this particular approach:

> Half the cast act as though they are in a Chekhov play: their vivid inner lives surface in details which suggest they have made the long mental journey to the Serebryakov estate. The rest have apparently taken an Awayday to Ayckbourngrad. It is a missed opportunity with a great play that is all about wasted chances.[75]

Pearson's last comment highlights the fact that the particular tonality chosen by a given director does not simply affect the style of production, it largely determines the meaning of the play. Vera Gottlieb goes even further when she points out that such directorial decisions have a political dimension to them. She argues that Chekhov uses comedy for philosophical and political purposes. Comedy is used as a kind of 'alienation effect' that works against the creation of any 'cathartic experience' and highlights both the choices that the characters have made and the fact that they could have made different choices. The distancing effect of comedy allows spectators to see the situation more clearly than if they are encouraged to have the kind of uncritical empathetic response that pure tragedy tends to promote.

Chekhov seems to have been acutely aware of the function of comic distancing well before Brecht popularised the idea. He explained to Suvorin what a writer had to do to awaken the reading public's awareness: 'One must shock it, rather, and then it will think more.'[76] It was by using the 'shock' of comic incongruity in *Uncle Vanya* that Chekhov was able to make his audiences see how many of the characters had wasted their lives. Chekhov's purpose in doing this was to raise the consciousness of the audience to a level that might make them question the ways in which they are leading their own lives. Morson suggests that the self-dramatising characters who refuse to face reality in *Uncle Vanya* act as reminders to audience members of their own escapist tendencies:

> ... the audience contemplates real people — people like themselves — who live citational lives, that is, lives shaped by literary role-playing, lives consisting not so much of actions as of allusions. We are asked to consider the extent to which our own lives are, like the title of the play, citational.[77]

Morson's argument suggests that Chekhov's plays are part of that time-honoured tradition that employs comedy as a form of social corrective. This certainly seems to be consistent with Chekhov's comment in his *Notebooks* that: 'Man will only become better when you make him see what he is like.'[78]

As with Morson, Gottlieb's analysis is significant because it restores the emphasis on the function and purpose of Chekhov's plays at a time when far too many productions of his plays are simply exercises in the creation of mood:

> ... the debate about tragedy and comedy goes deeper than questions of content and form, and becomes a philosophical and political debate. To put it crudely: the tragic view of human impotence in the face of seemingly inevitable forces, implies an *acceptance* of the world order as it manifests itself and works out its design in the characters on stage. The assumption of human impotence, the acceptance of 'that which is', the belief in ungovernable external forces, and the insistence on 'absolutes', all become part of a retrograde world view. This philosophy, I would suggest, was complete anathema to Chekhov, whose concern as a scientist and as a writer was with the exposure of contradictions, and not an annulment or denial of contradictions. His aim was to expose, and not to tranquilize, what Coleridge called 'the lethargy of custom'.[79]

*Uncle Vanya* is a play about lost opportunities that embodies an implied criticism of the behaviour that produces such wasted lives. It only makes sense to criticise or blame people or characters if they are seen to have the freedom of action that makes them responsible for their behaviour. The characters in this play are not the helpless playthings of fate. Chekhov's criticism of his characters is not however expressed polemically — in his dramatic universe there are no villains to be vilified or heroes to be the subject of adulation. The devastation of the environment that is recorded in *Uncle Vanya* has come about not because humans are venal, but because, as Astrov says, 'they're backward and ignorant'[80] and 'man's so lazy'.[81] Because the playwright believed that ignorance can be cured by education, and laziness by work, Chekhov's vision of reality always expresses long-term hope. An understanding of Chekhov's vision of reality will inevitably lead directors to create the physical events on stage that will cause the audience to experience the appropriate psychic events. Consequently, it is vital that this optimistic element be present in productions of this play. *Uncle Vanya*, as Allison Pearson points out, depicts a 'recognition' situation in which, 'the characters have measured out their lives in linseed-oil bills and snowy days around the samovar, only to be agonisingly awakened to the might-have-beens and the should-have-beens by the arrival of outsiders.'[82]

The past life *has* been wasted and the present life, 'life as it is', *is* awful; but the future, 'life as it should be', *may* well be better if humans can learn from their mistakes. In the short term, there is nothing for the characters to do but endure. This does not mean that they should sit around and mope but, rather, do as Astrov and Sonya and even Uncle Vanya do in their different ways: work. Chekhov believed that 'the power and salvation of a people lie in its intelligentsia, in the intelligentsia who think honestly, feel, and can work'.[83] This idea was to be of central importance in his next play, *Three Sisters*.

## ENDNOTES

[1] Slonim, M., *Russian Theater from the Empire to the Soviets*, Methuen, London, 1963, p. 128.

[2] Clurman, H., 'Director's Notes for *Uncle Vanya*', in *On Directing*, Collier Macmillan, New York, 1974, p. 261.

[3] Anon., *World*, 29 January 1924.

[4] Scott-Norman, F., *In Press*, 3 July 1991.

[5] Shulman, M., *Evening Standard*, 15 September 1989.

[6] Magarshack, D., *Chekhov the Dramatist*, Eyre Methuen, London, 1980, p. 225. Richard Gilman, in an article in which he took the Broadway theatre reviewers to task for what he felt was their inept criticism of Mike Nicols' 1973 production, made a similar point to Magarshack when he said that none of these critics 'said the important non-clichéd thing about *Uncle Vanya*: that like the other three last great plays of Chekhov it is not about failure but about *stamina*'. (Gilman, R., 'Broadway Critics Meet *Uncle Vanya*', *Theatre Quarterly*, Vol. 4, No. 13, February–April 1974, p. 68.)

[7] Boyd, C., *Melbourne Times*, 10 July 1991.

[8] Chekhov, A., Letter to A. L. Vishnevsky, 3 November 1889, in Yarmolinsky, A., *Letters of Anton Chekhov*, The Viking Press, New York, 1973, p. 355. Nemirovich-Danchenko records several other favourable comments made by Chekhov about the time that *Uncle Vanya* was produced: 'Anton Pavlovitch's feeling for the Art Theatre grew steadily. I remember the dates when there were letters from him containing such expressions: 'I am ready to be a door-keeper in your theatre'; or 'I envy the rat which lives under the walls of your theatre'; or, in answer to a disturbed letter of mine ... 'A trembling note is audible in your words. Oh, don't give up! The Art Theatre is the best page of that book which will one day be written about the contemporary Russian theatre. This theatre is your pride; it is the only theatre that I love, though I haven't been in it even once.' (Nemirovich-Danchenko, V., *My Life in the Russian Theatre*, Geoffrey Bles, London, 1968, pp. 195–6.)

⁹ Meyerhold, V., Letter to A. Chekhov, 23 October 1899, in Benedetti, J., *The Moscow Art Theatre Letters*, Routledge, New York, 1991, pp. 58–9.

¹⁰ A reading of Chekhov's letter to Meyerhold written in early October 1889 (see Benedetti, J., op. cit., pp. 56–7) must surely explode the myth, largely created by Stanislavski in his *My Life in Art*, that Chekhov was incapable of giving actors any useful advice. Stanislavski would have his readers believe that Chekhov, when asked to talk to actors about his plays, 'would grow confused, and in order to find a way out of this strange situation and get rid of us, he would take advantage of his usual statement: "Listen, I wrote it down, it is all there."' (Stanislavski, C., *My Life in Art*, Eyre Methuen, London, 1980, p. 361.) In fact, Meyerhold, who was acknowledged to be one of the Moscow Art Theatre's most talented actors, actively sought Chekhov's advice. 'Dear and respected Anton Pavlovich, ... I have been given the role of Johannes in Hauptmann's *Lonely People*. Would you help me to study this role? Write and tell me what you expect from someone playing the role of Johannes? How do you see Johannes?' (Meyerhold, V., Letter to A. Chekhov, 29 September 1889, in Benedetti, J., op. cit., p. 55.) Meyerhold's reaction to Chekhov's detailed advice shows that he found the playwright's comments on role interpretation to be lucid, perceptive and useful to the actor. 'I clasp your hand warmly and thank you for having pointed out what you thought was typical of Johannes. Only someone like you could be content to sketch in the general characteristics yet with such mastery that the character emerges with complete clarity ... Moreover everything you indicated ... immediately suggests a host of details which are in tonal harmony with the basic tonality of the portrait of an intellectual who is lonely, elegant, healthy and at the same time sad.' (Meyerhold, V., Letter to A. Chekhov, 23 October 1899, in Benedetti, J., op. cit., p. 58.)

¹¹ Nemirovich-Danchenko's description of Stanislavski's *mise-en-scène* for *Tsar Fyodor* provides ample evidence that this director adored melodramatic excess. Employing 'movements, costumes and properties, by no means always historically accurate', Stanislavski set about creating his grandiose spectacle: 'If the original hats were high, he must make them excessively high; if the sleeves were long, he must make them so long as to necessitate their being continually tucked in; if the door in the manor was small, he had to reproduce a door so small as to force the actors to bend low in order to pass through. He had read somewhere that the boyers, in appearing before the Tsar, bowed thrice to the ground. Well, in our rehearsals the boyers got down on their knees, touched the floor with their foreheads, rose and went down again — not less than twenty times ... And from this bright piling up of colours, images, outcries, we had to turn about-face to the sad everyday realities of Chekhov.' (Nemirovich-Danchenko, V., op. cit., pp. 153–4.) Stanislavski found this 'about-face' much harder to achieve than his partner.

¹² Benedetti, J., *Stanislavski: A Biography*, Methuen, London, 1988, p. 93.

¹³ Nemirovich-Danchenko, V., op. cit., p. 163.

¹⁴ Nemirovich-Danchenko, V., Letter to C. Stanislavski, 26 October 1889, in Benedetti, J., *The Moscow Art Theatre Letters*, p. 59.

¹⁵ Ibid., p. 60.

¹⁶ Benedetti, J., *Stanislavski: A Biography*, p. 94.

¹⁷ Stanislavski, C., quoted in Benedetti, J., op. cit., p. 97. The actor Leonid Leonidov has left a graphic description of how effective Stanislavski's histrionically low-key performance was: 'I have seen many good performances and many great actors, but never have I experienced anything like it before. I realised what it was: here one believed everything; here was no trace of theatricality; it almost seemed that there were no actors on the stage and no previously contrived *mise-en-scènes*. Everything was so simple, just as in real life, but beneath this simplicity one became aware of the seething cauldron of human passions.' (Leonidov, L., quoted in Magarshack, D., *Stanislavsky: A Life*, Faber and Faber, London, 1986, p. 192.)

¹⁸ Chekhov, A., quoted in Magarshack, D., *Chekhov the Dramatist*, p. 184.

¹⁹ At this time, Stanislavski was in the process of discovering through practice the key elements of what would later become his system of acting. His much admired playing of Astrov had been preceded by an equally truthful characterisation of Lovborg in Ibsen's *Hedda Gabbler*. This performance, according to Benedetti, marked a critical moment in Stanislavski's development as an actor. 'It is difficult to locate precise turning points in an actor's career but it is worth noting that this performance follows immediately on the encounter with Chekhov and the demands his plays made on the actor's inner life. In subsequent seasons Stanislavski gave performances in which the psychological is emphasized rather than external appearance and technique.' (Benedetti, J., op. cit., p. 87.)

²⁰ Balukhaty, S., quoted in Bitsilli, P., *Chekov's Art: A Stylistic Analysis*, Ann Arbor, 1983, p. 116.

²¹ Edwards, C., *Spectator*, 7 March 1992.

22 Rutherford, M., *Financial Times*, 27 February 1992.
23 Hurren, K., *Mail on Sunday*, 1 March 1992.
24 Edwards, C., loc. cit.
25 Spencer, C., *Daily Telegraph*, 27 February 1992.
26 Ibid.
27 Chekhov, A., Letter to M. Gorky, 3 December 1898, in Yarmolinsky, A., op. cit., p. 320.
28 Chekhov, A., Letter to M. Gorky, 3 January 1899, in Yarmolinsky, A., op. cit., p. 323.
29 Chekhov, A., *Uncle Vanya*, in Hingley, R., *The Oxford Chekhov*, Vol. 3, Oxford University Press, London, 1964, p. 40.
30 Knipper resisted Stanislavski's direction in this production and the result was that, on opening night, she acted poorly. Nemirovich-Danchenko reported to Chekhov that 'Knipper caused us great annoyance. At the dress rehearsal people said she was fascinating, enchanting, etc. Today she got flustered and overplayed the whole part from beginning to end.' (Nemirovich-Danchenko, V., Letter to A. Chekhov, 27 October 1889, in Benedetti, J., *The Moscow Art Theatre Letters*, p. 63.) Knipper knew that she had performed badly and in a letter to Chekhov, having said 'I played so appallingly — why?', she attempted to give an explanation for her failure. 'The problem to my mind is this: they wanted me to forget my own conception of Elena because the director found it boring but I had not been able to carry the idea right through. They imposed a different conception on me on the grounds that it was essential for the play. I held out for a long time and was still opposed to it at the end ... On the first night I was infernally nervous and simply panicked ... If I had been able to play the way I wanted, probably the first night would not have worried me so ... It's awful to think of the future, of the work ahead, if I have to resist the director's yoke again.' (Knipper, O., Letter to A. Chekhov, 27–29 October 1889, in Benedetti, J., op. cit., p. 65.)
31 Knipper, O., Letter to A. Chekhov, 26 September 1889, quoted in Hingley, R., op. cit., p. 301. The role of Astrov was one of Stanislavski's most successful portrayals. Nemirovich-Danchenko wrote to Chekhov: 'We present Astrov as a materialist in the best sense of the term, incapable of loving, relating to women with elegant cynicism. There is sensitivity but no passion there. And all this in that half-joking form women find so attractive.' (Nemirovich-Danchenko, V., quoted in Benedetti, J., *Stanislavski: A Biography*, p. 96.) Olivier's justly famous interpretation of Astrov in his 1963 production of the play followed closely the kind of approach outlined by Nemirovich-Danchenko.
32 Chekhov, A., Letter to O. Knipper, 30 September 1889, quoted in Hingley, R., op. cit., pp. 301–2.
33 Ibid., p. 301.
34 Chekhov, A., *Uncle Vanya*, pp. 56–7.
35 Chekhov, A., quoted in Fen, E., ed., *Chekhov Plays*, Penguin, Harmondsworth, 1954, p. 19.
36 Butova, I. S., *Reminiscences*, quoted in Worrall, N., *File on Chekhov*, Methuen, London, 1986, p. 48. Hingley has pointed out that the incident referred to in Butova's work 'actually precedes the shot and does not follow it as Chekhov is made to suggest'. (Hingley, R., op. cit., p. 302.)
37 Chekhov, A., *Uncle Vanya*, p. 20.
38 Ibid., pp. 38–9.
39 Ibid., p. 27.
40 Ibid., p. 28.
41 Ibid., p. 27.
42 Ibid., p. 48.
43 Ibid., p. 28.
44 Ibid., p. 42.
45 Ibid.
46 Ibid., p. 48.
47 Ibid., pp. 49–50.
48 Ibid., p. 63.
49 Ibid., p. 55.
50 Ibid., pp. 60–1.
51 Freedman, M., 'Chekhov's Morality of Work', *Modern Drama*, Vol. 5, No. 1, 1962, p. 88.
52 Chekhov, A., *Uncle Vanya*, p. 67.

[53] King, F., *Sunday Telegraph*, quoted in *London Theatre Record* for 15 July–15 August 1982.
[54] Freedman, M., op. cit., p. 89.
[55] Bentley, E., 'Chekhov as Playwright', *Kenyon Review*, Vol. 11, No. 2, Spring 1949, pp. 233–4.
[56] Chekhov, A., *Uncle Vanya*, p. 39.
[57] Ibid.
[58] Ibid., p. 20.
[59] Ibid., p. 39.
[60] Chekhov, A., Letter to I. L. Leontyev-Shcheglov, 9 March 1892, in Yarmolinsky, A., op. cit., p. 202.
[61] Chekhov, A., *Uncle Vanya*, p. 39.
[62] Koteliansky, S. S. and Woolf, L., eds, *The Notebooks of Anton Tchekhov*, The Hogarth Press, London, 1967, p. 61.
[63] Chekhov, A., quoted in Simmons, E. J., *Chekhov : A Biography*, Jonathan Cape, London, 1963, p. 588.
[64] Koteliansky, S. S. and Woolf, L., op. cit., p. 6.
[65] Ibid., p. 26. Given such positive views towards people with an ability to believe in something greater than themselves, it should not be so surprising to discover that, as Simon Karlinsky puts it: 'Chekhov's own favourite among the hundreds of stories he wrote was *The Student*, a very brief story that, in moving and utterly simple terms, states the case for the importance of religious traditions and religious experience for the continuation of civilization.' (Karlinsky, S., 'The Gentle Subversive', Introduction to Karlinsky, S. and Heim, M. H., *Anton Chekhov's Life and Thought*, University of California Press, Berkeley, 1975, p. 13.)
[66] Chekhov, A., Letter to V. Mirolubov, 17 December 1901, in Hellman, L., *The Selected Letters of Anton Chekhov*, Hamish Hamilton, London, 1955, p. 296.
[67] Morson, G. S., 'Prosaic Chekhov: Metadrama, the Intelligentsia, and *Uncle Vanya*', *Tri-Quarterly*, No. 80, Winter 1990–91, p. 134.
[68] Chekhov, A., *Uncle Vanya*, p. 35. Chekhov gives Helen a similar type of undisguised soliloquy in Act Three when she meditates out loud about her feelings for Astrov. Despite having increasingly mastered the conventions of realism in *Uncle Vanya*, Chekhov had not yet found a way of entirely avoiding the use of pre-realistic stage conventions.
[69] Morson, G. S., op. cit., p. 135.
[70] Ibid., p. 136. It was precisely because of Anthony Sher's tendency to 'over-overact' in Sean Mathias' 1992 production that his performance as Astrov was marred.
[71] Pitcher, H., *The Chekhov Play*, Chatto & Windus, London, 1973, p. 7.
[72] Gottlieb, V., 'The Politics of British Chekhov', in Miles, P., ed., *Chekhov on the British Stage*, Cambridge University Press, Cambridge, 1993, p. 153.
[73] Edwards, C., *Spectator*, 17 November 1990.
[74] Foot, D., *Guardian*, 10 November 1990.
[75] Pearson, A., *Independent on Sunday*, 18 August 1991.
[76] Chekhov, A., Letter to A. S. Suvorin, 17 December 1891, in Friedland, L. S., *Chekhov: Letters on the Short Story, the Drama, and Other Literary Topics*, Dover Publications, New York, 1966, p. 102.
[77] Morson, G. S., loc. cit.
[78] Koteliansky, S. S. and Woolf, L., op. cit., p. 15.
[79] Gottlieb, V., loc. cit.
[80] Chekhov, A., *Uncle Vanya*, p. 48.
[81] Ibid., p. 27.
[82] Pearson, A., loc. cit.
[83] Koteliansky, S. S. and Woolf, L., loc. cit.

# Chapter 6. *Three Sisters*: 'Oh if we could only know!'

*In his plays he [Chekhov] expresses the view that it would take at least two to three hundred years, or perhaps even a thousand years, to bring about a cardinal change in human nature, and in the* Three Sisters *he makes the idealist Vershinin his mouthpiece on the future of mankind.* (David Magarshack)[1]

*And really the whole structure of the play is designed to undercut Vershinin. He insists that life is always becoming 'steadily easier and brighter'. But more than three years go by in the course of the play, and nothing changes – not at any rate for the better – nothing even begins to change.* (Michael Frayn)[2]

*Three Sisters*, more than any of Chekhov's plays, has been read as a deeply pessimistic, almost nihilistic play, by many critics, both in Russia and in the West. Beverly Hahn described it as 'a profoundly sad play', before adding, 'Lionel Trilling calls it one of the saddest works in all literature'.[3] Many productions have likewise been extremely bleak affairs. Chekhov's so-called 'pessimism' led one reviewer of Theodore Komisarjevsky's 1926 London production to describe the playwright as 'the dramatist of disillusionment, of frustrated hopes, and of human failure'.[4] In 1984, Simon Karlinsky optimistically claimed: 'In the West, the durable cliché of the morose, despondent Chekhov has lately been caving in under the onslaught of informed critical writing and of the productions of the plays that do not reduce them to gloom and twilight.'[5] Karlinsky's observations have turned out to be a case of wishful thinking because, two decades later, many critics and directors continue to regard Chekhov as a pessimistic Absurdist before his time. Richard Gilman, in a much praised book on Chekhov's plays, having given his chapter on *Three Sisters* the mock-Beckettian subtitle 'I Can't Go On, I'll Go', proceeds to explicitly link Chekhov with that Absurdist dramatist. We are told that Beckett's *Waiting for Godot* has such profound affinities with *Three Sisters*'.[6] After claiming that what Chekhov dramatises is not an *action* but a *condition,* Gilman outlines his Absurdist 'nothing to be done' reading of the play:

> That *Three Sisters* doesn't seem to be taking us anywhere is, once again, a matter of Chekhov's having written it so that we see time's effects not as rational or even irrational consequences, not as consequences at all but as an accumulation, like the sand that more and more covers Winnie in Beckett's *Happy Days*, where time is rendered in a visual metaphor. Eventful immobility, or movement around a still center, or a circle, or a series of flat planes rather than a more or less straight line — any of these images will help free us from an inherited,

chronologically and narratively anchored way of looking at *Three Sisters*, a perspective disastrous to understanding.[7]

Like many critics who analyse *Three Sisters*, Gilman correctly indicates the importance of 'time' in this play, but his assumption that Chekhov's use of time is similar to the way Beckett uses the concept is unwarranted and, to use his own expression, 'disastrous to understanding'. The kind of stasis that is presented in *Happy Days* and that is given verbal form by Pozzo in *Waiting for Godot* has little to do with Chekhov. When Pozzo cries out: 'Have you not done tormenting me with your accursed time! It's abominable! When! When! … one day we were born, one day we shall die, the same day, the same second, is that not enough for you?',[8] he is indeed presenting a non-chronological picture of time. In Beckett's Absurdist world there is, as Estragon says, 'Nothing to be done'.

Chekhov's world, by contrast, is deeply embedded in chronological time. His audiences are shown characters who are quite literally 'wasting their time'. As I argued earlier, Chekhov's play does not depict a world in which there is nothing to be done, but one in which 'no one is doing anything'. Through their own inertia and passivity, the characters in *Three Sisters* make their lives absurd. They may abdicate their responsibility for action and even see themselves as 'Beckettian' fated characters, but this is not what the overall action of Chekhov's play depicts. Chekhov employs the idea of time passing as a warning and, in this, is closer to Andrew Marvell's concept of time than Beckett's. Marvell was acutely aware of how short a time human beings have on earth and so wished to avoid wasting it:

> But at my back I alwaies hear
> Time's wingéd Charriot hurrying near:
> And yonder all before us lye
> Desarts of vast Eternity.[9]

Chekhov, like Marvell, is implicitly reminding his audience not to waste their lives in the way that the characters on-stage waste theirs. Far from being static, time in Chekhov's plays runs away so fast that characters are bewildered at its speed. Andrew, at the end of the play, begins his vivid description of the wasted lives of the Prozorovs and those like them with an anguished version of the 'ubi sunt' theme: 'Where is my past life, oh what has become of it …?'[10]

Critics such as Gilman and, as we shall see, such directors as Mike Alfreds privilege the nihilistic characters such as Dr Chebutykin who espouse an Absurdist view of life.[11] Chebutykin's point of view, however, is not identical to the playwright's view expressed in the action of the play.[12] As Howard Moss has noted:

> The doctor may comfort himself with bogus philosophy and claim nothing matters but the others tend to confirm not his thesis but its perverse corollary.

By the indecisiveness of their actions, by their inability to deal head-on with what is central to their lives, they make, in the end, what matters futile.[13]

The kind of Absurdist interpretation advocated by critics like Gilman continues in more recent productions of *Three Sisters*. In 1986, two years after Karlinsky had heralded the demise of the 'gloom and twilight' school of Chekhov, Mike Alfreds directed the play in a manner that led Michael Billington to describe this painfully drawn-out production as 'the most unrelievedly tragic *Three Sisters* I have seen for some time'.[14] Alfreds discussed his interpretation of the play with David Allen who quotes the director as saying:

> Chekhov calls *Three Sisters* a drama. It is certainly not a comedy, although it is full of bitter ironies and has comic moments. It is a dramatic play that is aspiring towards tragedy (although it does not quite fit the classic definition of tragedy — none of the characters has true tragic stature) ... The play discloses a world in which people are lost ... The active theme of the play is how people cope with failure, either by constructing fantasies of a future happiness, or withdrawing into cynicism, or by trying to pretend that all is well ... There needs to be in performance too, an emotional danger, and a sense of a desolate emotional landscape.[15]

Here is Gilman's Beckettian Chekhov realised with a vengeance! As Sheila Fox commented after seeing Alfreds' production: 'This is bullet-in-the-back-of-the-neck Chekhov. Three and a half hours of full-throttle futility and hopelessness.'[16]

With some exceptions, notable for their rarity, there have been few productions in the West that have presented *Three Sisters* as a truly optimistic drama. Even Magarshack, who pioneered the attack on the pessimistic school of Chekhov interpretation, could find little evidence to support the more extreme Soviet readings which see in his work a powerful prediction of the bright future that was to result from the Communist Revolution of 1917. As Magarshack points out, Chekhov 'was never impressed by the facile optimism of the revolutionaries who believed that by sweeping away the old order they would establish peace and harmony on earth'.[17]

Karlinsky may have been rather too hopeful in his claims about the 'caving in' of the 'gloom and twilight' school of Chekhov interpretation. He was more accurate about the ways in which, 'In the Soviet Union, the equally short-sighted image of the politically correct proto-bolshevik Chekhov, bequeathed by the Ermilovs of the 1930s and 40s'[18] was giving way to more balanced views of his work. It is rare today for characters such as Trofimov in *The Cherry Orchard* or Vershinin in *Three Sisters* to be performed as though they were the heroic mouthpieces of Chekhov's supposedly radical revolutionary ideals. The pessimistic 'Absurdist' Chekhov is certainly more in evidence today than the optimistic 'Soviet' version, but neither of these polarised readings of his plays does them justice. The complexity of Chekhov's vision of reality is lost when the plays are interpreted in a monopathic manner. Many reductionist readings result, at least partially, from a simplistic reading of the playwright's 'political' stance. As Vera Gottlieb claims: 'The ideas voiced in all of Chekhov's work, whether literary or dramatic, are certainly not those of a reactionary, nor indeed of a revolutionary, but of a progressive or humanist.'[19]

Mike Alfreds' 'reactionary' interpretation of *Three Sisters* delivered the clear message to the audience that hopelessness was the core feature of the human condition and that, as one reviewer put it, 'Chekhov is really writing about the illusion of happiness, the absurdity of our quest for it'.[20] It was just such an extremely pessimistic reading that led Michael Billington to conclude his review of this production with the heartfelt cry: 'What I hunger for is more of the peculiar Chekhovian balance between hope for the race and deep personal despair.'[21]

Given Stanislavski's propensity to interpret Chekhov's plays as tragedies, one might have supposed that he would be the director accorded the dubious honour of having initiated the long line of gloomy productions of *Three Sisters*. Perhaps surprisingly, Stanislavski's production eventually turned out to be one which presented a balance between 'hope' and 'despair'. As Nick Worrall has noted, 'Chekhov himself was well pleased with the production which, when he saw it in September 1901, he said was staged better than the play was written'.[22] Worrall points out that Stanislavski's 'production of *Three Sisters* can be described as an ideological fusion of opposites — form and content, positive and negative, optimism and pessimism, meaning and non-meaning, and even, "East" and "West"'.[23] The Soviet critic, N. M. Stroyeva quotes evidence from Stanislavski's production score that suggests an unusual sensitivity on the director's part towards the more positive aspects of Chekhov's vision of reality. Stanislavski stated that those working on the production should do nothing that would cause them 'to miss our main quarry, which is to present the author's final and optimistic summing up, which compensates for the many sad parts of the play'.[24] So Stroyeva argues that:

> The surmounting of the sorrow at the end of this play is the most important task of all for a director. He sees the 'affirmative thought of the author' as Chekhov's characters, even in times of deepest personal grief, find the strength to raise themselves to the level of dreams about the future happiness of humanity. Stanislavski directed that Olga's final words be spoken 'as buoyantly as possible'.[25]

Stanislavski did not arrive at his balanced interpretation of *Three Sisters* immediately. It seems likely that he once again relied on Nemirovich-Danchenko to clarify for him the meaning of the play. Certainly, as Worrall points out, Nemirovich-Danchenko 'had a greater enthusiasm, initially, for the work of Chekhov than did Stanislavsky'.[26] Furthermore, apart from having a greater artistic affinity with Chekhov than did Stanislavski, Nemirovich-Danchenko was also closer to the playwright in matters of ideology. The 'progressive or humanist' Chekhov had a concern for social issues that was shared by the co-founder of the Moscow Art Theatre. As Senelick points out: 'The Art Theatre was liberal but far from radical; its social conscience resided mainly in Nemirovich, for Stanislavsky was essentially apolitical'.[27]

Nemirovich-Danchenko's contribution to the production of *Three Sisters* was attested to by A. L. Vishnevsky, the actor cast as Kulygin, in a letter to Chekhov,[28] but his efforts were not publicly acknowledged. Worrall comments: 'Despite the significant part played by Nemirovich-Danchenko in rehearsals, especially during January, the only directors' names to appear on the production poster were those of K. S. Stanislavsky and V. V. Luzhsky'.[29] Nemirovich-Danchenko had less of a problem than Stanislavski in acknowledging the artistic contribution made by his co-director in the initial production. In *My Life in the Russian Theatre* he wrote: '*The Three Sisters* has remained the best production of the Art Theatre, not only because of the superb ensemble, but also because of the fine *mise-en-scène* by Stanislavsky'.[30]

In 1940, two years after Stanislavski's death, the eighty-three-year-old Nemirovich-Danchenko undertook his own production of *Three Sisters*. His reading of the play was certainly a more optimistic one than Stanislavski's. Laurence Senelick outlines some of the differences between the two Moscow Art Theatre directors' views of the play's action:

> In 1901, Leonid Andreev had declared the play's theme-song to be 'To want to live, excruciatingly, agonisingly, painfully to want to live!' But Stanislavsky had notated this tune so as to be sung, 'It's impossible to live'. Nemirovich, in line with Stakhanovite optimism, chose to sing two different tunes: longing for a better life (not a plangent, whiny longing to escape life, but something active though devoid of the element of struggle), and deep faith in the future, in Tusenbach's storm about to break over the land and sweep away deceit, money-grubbing and antipathy to work. The characters were seen not as futile and trivial, but as fine minds in magnificent and handsome bodies. They were to be interpreted in a style of 'virile strength'.[31]

Nemirovich-Danchenko's reading of *Three Sisters*, which he outlined in his autobiography, aptly illustrates the ways in which it is so easy to lose the precarious balance between 'hope' and 'despair' that is so important an element of Chekhov's vision of reality. Writing in 1938, only two years before his relatively optimistic production of the play, but referring to the original 1901 production in which he had collaborated with Stanislavski,

Nemirovich-Danchenko describes what he took to be the vision expressed in the play:

> The events of the play crept along even as life itself during this epoch, in a tired sort of way, without any visible logic. Human beings acted under the influence of chance happenings; they did nothing to build their own lives. Here is the substance of his first act: a birthday party, the spring, gaiety, birds singing, bright sunshine. And of the second act: triviality gradually takes into its hands the power over the sensitive, nobly inclined human beings. Of the third act: a conflagration in the neighbourhood, the entire street is aflame; the power of triviality grows intenser, human beings somehow flounder in their experiences. The fourth act: autumn, the collapse of all hopes, the triumph of triviality. Human beings are as chess pawns in the hands of invisible players. The absurd and the pathetic, the noble and the worthless, the intelligent and the stupid, are all interwoven ...[32]

Statements such as, 'Human beings acted under the influence of chance happenings', and, 'Human beings are as chess pawns in the hands of invisible players', can easily be interpreted as existential statements about the hopelessness of the human condition. This is the 'Absurdist' Chekhov, who supposedly depicts a world in which there is 'Nothing to be done'. This is precisely how the right-wing reactionary critic of Suvorin's *New Times,* Viktor Burenin, interpreted the 1901 production. Chekhov, he claimed, 'is the minstrel of hopelessness'.[33] But, as Vera Gottlieb has convincingly argued, 'Chekhov is *not* Beckett'.[34]

A closer look at Nemirovich-Danchenko's analysis of *Three Sisters* reveals a more balanced and less pessimistic reading than appears at first sight. When he writes, 'they did nothing to build their own lives', he implies that it was possible for these characters to have created better lives for themselves, but that, by their inaction, they abdicated their responsibility to do so. Chekhov's characters in *Three Sisters* and, indeed, in all of his four major plays, behave in a ridiculously unreasonable way in the face of the social situation in which they find themselves. They behave foolishly and, to a large extent, create their 'silly trivial lives' themselves. The American woman who, having seen a production of *Three Sisters* in 1942, observed that she 'could not see much sense in three adults spending four acts in *not* going to Moscow when all the time they had the price of a railroad ticket'[35] was perhaps more perceptive than is generally acknowledged. There *is* something ludicrously 'incongruous' about the Prozorov sisters not doing anything. Again Gottlieb perceptively notes that Chekhov's characters carry 'some measure of responsibility for their own lives, and it is partly this which in Russian terms makes the plays *comedies*'.[36] The characters make their lives pointless by their refusal to act.

Gottlieb has argued elsewhere that our conventional view of farce and comedy where 'situation or circumstance dictate character and action — and render characters impotent' — a view which has much in common with 'Absurdist' work – is contrasted in Russia by what is 'virtually an oppositional reading' in which comic and farcical 'action and circumstance arise largely *from* character: there is potential for change, albeit often unrealised on stage'.[37] Because they do nothing effective to alter their situation, Chekhov's characters become, at least potentially, the objects of comedy's critical laughter. Chekhov's comedy accords with the Classic and Neo-Classic 'social corrective' theories of comedy and depends on the belief that humans are corrigible. Again, Gottlieb is surely correct when she points out that: 'The *leitmotif* of play after play is *'tak zhit nelzya'* — one cannot and must not live like that'.[38] Chekhov uses farce and comedy to achieve a similar aim to that espoused by Molière, who claimed that 'the purpose of comedy is to correct the vices of men'.[39] Gottlieb is again perceptive when she claims that Chekhov 'uses farce, as he does melodrama, to expose the farcical'.[40]

As we shall see, Stanislavski did not find it easy to see the comedy in Chekhov and, according to Senelick, the 'brightness' of the first production of *Three Sisters* 'was dimmed by the "lachrymosity" which Chekhov complained Stanislavsky had added to his work and which intensified over time'.[41]

*Three Sisters* was the first of Chekhov's plays to be written specifically for the Moscow Art Theatre and the playwright attended the first reading of his initial draft to the company on 29 October 1900. The reading was followed by a discussion which, according to Stanislavski, angered Chekhov: 'After the reading of the play, some of us, talking of our impressions of the play, called it a drama, and others even a tragedy, without noticing that these definitions amazed Chekhov.'[42] The playwright walked out of the meeting and, when Stanislavski called on him at his hotel, he found Chekhov still furious:

> I do not remember ever seeing him so angry again … But the real reason (for Chekhov's anger) was that he had written a happy comedy and all of us had considered the play a tragedy and even wept over it. Evidently Chekhov thought that the play had been misunderstood and that it was already a failure.[43]

Simon Karlinsky has argued that the above account given by Stanislavski is a piece of revisionism, written decades after the event, that bears little relation to the facts. He claims that Stanislavski's 'interpretation of the play is flatly contradicted by Chekhov's own letters at the time he was writing *Three Sisters* and by all the other contemporary documentation we have, in which *Three Sisters* is invariably referred to as a drama'.[44]

Chekhov wrote to Olga Knipper expressing his doubts about Stanislavski's ability to respond sensitively enough to his new play. 'Let it lie on the table a bit … Four important female parts, four young women of the upper class; I cannot leave that to Stanislavsky — with all due respect for his gifts and understanding. I must have at least a peek at the rehearsals.'[45] Edward Braun has argued that Chekhov feared that Stanislavski might caricature the military characters in the play: 'Reluctant to surrender all control to Stanislavsky, Chekhov nominated in his absence a certain Colonel Petrov to act as military consultant on the production.'[46] According to Harvey Pitcher, 'Chekhov had made up his mind in advance that the play was bound to be a failure'. The playwright had reached this conclusion as a result of being 'alarmed by reports of how Stanislavsky was interpreting *Three Sisters*'.[47]

Whatever the truth of Stanislavski's version of what happened at the first reading of *Three Sisters* and Nemirovich-Danchenko's claim that Chekhov 'several times repeated "I've written a vaudeville piece!"',[48] Chekhov set about rewriting the play. When it was completed he did not call it "a Comedy", which had been his genre description of *The Seagull* and was to be his description of *The Cherry Orchard*, nor did he choose a rather vaguer description similar to "Scenes from Country Life" that he had used to characterise *Uncle Vanya*. Instead, whether ironically or not, he chose to call *Three Sisters* "a Drama". Nemirovich-Danchenko's failure to 'understand why he called his play [a vaudeville]',[49] and the response of the Moscow Art Theatre personnel after the first reading may have made Chekhov decide on this generic classification. He wrote to Vera Kommissarzhevskaya that the play 'has turned out to be boring ... its mood, I am told, is gloomier than gloom'.[50]

Stanislavski tended to assume that it was Chekhov, and not himself, who had misinterpreted the plays. In 1907, he confidently asserted:

> As a matter of fact he never was able to criticise his own plays and he always listened to the opinions of others with interest and astonishment. The opinion that astonished him most of all — to the day of his death he could not accept it — was that his *Three Sisters* (and later *The Cherry Orchard*) was a serious drama of Russian life. He was sincerely convinced that it was a gay comedy, almost a farce.[51]

Stanislavski appears to have lacked a clear idea about what kind of play he was directing. In 1909, he wrote to Baron Drizen and, as Laurence Senelick states, 'confusedly tried to explain'[52] his approach to the play:

> We understood one thing: the play needed sadness and affliction. We attain this sadness by means of laughter, since three quarters of the play rests on laughter. For the audience, however, there was no laughter, the play emanated an appalling sorrow.[53]

Stanislavski's confusion about the precise type of play he was dealing with may have arisen as a result of his growing awareness that neither Chekhov's extreme view of the play as a comedy/farce, nor his own equally one-sided view of the play as a tragedy/serious drama, adequately described the nature of *Three Sisters*.

In his 1901 production of the play, Stanislavski worked against his natural bent by attempting to incorporate the more optimistic and comic aspects of the play. With the benefit of hindsight, he writes in his memoir, *My Life in Art*:

> The men of Chekhov do not bathe, as we did at that time, in their own sorrow. Just the opposite; they, like Chekhov himself, seek life, joy, laughter, courage. The men and women of Chekhov want to live and not to die. They are active and surge to overcome the hard and unbearable impasses into which life has plunged them.[54]

Achieving an appropriate balance between 'hope' and 'despair' and between the 'absurd' and the 'pathetic' in any production of *Three Sisters* depends to a large extent on how a director interprets particular characters. What Joseph Wood Krutch once said about interpreting Tennessee Williams' *A Streetcar Named Desire* applies with equal validity to *Three Sisters*: 'Everything depends on, as the phrase goes, which side the author is on'.[55] Much of Chekhov's play concerns itself with deliberations about 'the meaning of life'. Indeed, as Daniel Gillès correctly observes:

> The meaning of life ... It is this question, continually stated or implied but never resolved, on which the whole play is founded. Around this central theme Chekhov built his drama like a musical composition, a series of questions in many voices that cross, harmonise, contradict one another, soar, or sink in despair.[56]

Since it is Tuzenbach and Vershinin who carry on much of the explicit discussion about the meaning of life in this play, the way they are interpreted is crucial. The degree of sympathy or antipathy the audience feels towards particular characters is largely determined by the director's interpretation. A director of *Three Sisters* who instructs the actor playing Vershinin to present the character as though he were merely a garrulous windbag mouthing empty platitudes will inevitably lead an audience to discount the import of this character's speeches. Since Vershinin expresses the view that life, though difficult, does have meaning and will gradually improve through human effort, any interpretation that makes him a fool effectively negates his ideas. The voice of 'hope' is in this way effectively silenced and 'despair' at the meaningless of life becomes the predominant vision of reality expressed.

In Mike Alfreds' 1986 production of *Three Sisters*, we find a clear example of how the director's decision to devalue Vershinin led to a bleak reading. One must assume that Alfreds believed that the author was *not* on Vershinin's side, since he gave his audience little room to find anything of value in Vershinin's ideas. David Nathan's review of the production mentioned 'John Price's Vershinin whose own pretensions to philosophical depth have never seemed so shallow',[57] while Michael Coveney observed that 'John Price makes of Vershinin's philosophising an acknowledged bore factor'.[58] Here was 'the windbag as local saint'.[59] In Alfreds' production Vershinin was not simply presented as being intellectually shallow but was also an emotional cripple. Eric Shorter wryly commented: 'Is John Price's Vershinin capable of deep feeling? Probably not.'[60] With such a demolition job carried out by Alfreds on the major voice of optimism and hope in the play, it is hardly surprising that most reviewers shared the opinion expressed by Helen Rose that 'this twitchy nervous production, suffused with doom from the outset, offers an unrelievedly pessimistic view of human hope'.[61]

Seemingly, it is difficult for critics and directors to avoid polarised readings of Chekhov's characters. Vershinin in *Three Sisters* is presented either as 'a marrowless colonel whose integrity is questionable from the start',[62] a person whose 'only conversational topic' is his 'philosophy which he trots out at any opportunity', and which is made up of 'trivial ideas',[63] or as an 'idealist', Chekhov's 'mouthpiece on the future of mankind'.[64] *Three Sisters*, possibly more than any other Chekhov play, has been subject to polarised readings both by critics and directors. When the gloom and doom 'Absurdist' reading is rejected, it is often replaced by a reading of unalloyed optimism, but this is just as limiting and reductionist a view as the pessimistic one. An advocate of the 'Absurdist' Chekhov, Richard Gilman, finds little difficulty in characterising the optimistic Soviet reading of the play as 'pernicious nonsense'. Presumably assuming that he — unlike those pesky Bolshies! — writes from an ideologically free position, Gilman attacks this 'misreading by Chekhov's countrymen and women': 'Where ideology enters, Soviet (to stick to the now outdated word) criticism of Chekhov has been especially guilty of distortion in regard to the subject of the future in his plays, wishing to turn him into a prophet of the age that followed his, the bolshevik millennium'.[65]

The problem with Gilman's argument is that it only attacks straw men such as the Soviet critic Vladimir Yermilov who simplistically describe Chekhov's characters as happy martyrs, willing 'to postpone love and happiness to the future, for those who come after them',[66] but fails to see that his own view of a Beckettian Chekhov is as simplistic a piece of 'pernicious nonsense' as that peddled by Yermilov.

Michael Frayn is one of several writers who, despite alluding to evidence that would suggest the inadequacy of any one-sided view of the play and its characters, nevertheless plumps for a reading that invalidates any of Vershinin's 'philosophy' and places Chekhov in the 'nothing to be done' school. Frayn correctly highlights the importance of the particular moment in history when *Three Sisters* first appeared:

> The play was written, it is true, at the beginning of a new and hopeful century, when belief in progress was high, and when the pressures upon the archaic

despotism of imperial Russia were plainly becoming irresistible. Many people shared with Vershinin and Tusenbach the vision of a future in which everything would in one way or another be totally changed. Some influential commentators have argued that Chekhov was one of them ... But he made it abundantly clear in his letters ... that the characters in his plays express their own views, not his.[67]

The fact that characters such as Vershinin 'express their own views' does not mean that Chekhov did not share many of that character's beliefs. That Chekhov is *not* Vershinin any more than he is the nihilistic Chebutykin, does not mean that he is absent from his work.[68] The relationship between the beliefs of the author and those of his characters is an ambiguous and complex one. To begin with, Chekhov rejected the overly simplified characterisation that was common in melodrama. In his early play *Ivanov,* he had attacked the simplistic value system of Lvov, who classified people as 'either saints or blackguards.'[69] Chekhov's characterisation of Vershinin is essentially non-judgemental. He is neither a villain nor a hero. In certain ways he is portrayed unsympathetically and yet he expresses ideas for which the author felt great sympathy. Vershinin may indeed be a weak man, a philanderer, someone who does not live up to his ideals, and someone who *is* a windbag, but this does not invalidate what he says. Chekhov's strategy is to present a gap between the admirable things that his characters say about what must be done to make life better and the disastrous failure on their part to actually do anything to bring this better world into being. There is nothing wrong with Vershinin's dream for a better future, any more than there was anything wrong with Martin Luther King's 'dream' of a non-racist society in the United States, although, unlike the civil rights campaigner, Vershinin fails to turn his talk into action.

*Three Sisters* begins on a note of hope and optimism that is even reflected in the weather: '*Outside the sun is shining cheerfully*'.[70] Both Olga and Irina are, quite literally, full of the joys of spring. Almost immediately, however, their vision of happiness, symbolised by their desire to return to an idealised 'Moscow', is immediately undercut by the negative comments of Chebutykin and Tuzenbach who are having a quite separate conversation in the neighbouring room:

> OLGA. ... Heavens, how marvellous! When I woke up this morning and saw the great blaze of light and knew that spring had come — I felt so happy and excited, I felt I just had to go back to Moscow.
> CHEBUTYKIN. [*To* SOLYONY *and* TUZENBACH.] Not a chance in hell.
> TUZENBACH. Absolute nonsense of course.[71]

Chekhov thus prepares his audience for the disillusionment of at least two of the Prozorov sisters. Masha, the unhappily married third sister, is barely included in her sisters' dream of a better future, but their brother Andrew is part of the 'Moscow' myth that is deflated by the next room commentators:

> OLGA. Yes, to Moscow! As soon as we can.
> [CHEBUTYKIN and TUZENBACH *laugh*.]
> IRINA. Andrew's probably going to be a professor and he won't live here anyway. There's nothing stopping us except poor Masha here.
> OLGA. Masha can come and spend the whole summer in Moscow every year.
> [MASHA *softly whistles a tune*.]
> IRINA. I only pray it will work out all right.[72]

The dreams of the Prozorovs are empty precisely because they are not backed up by actions. Merely praying for something to happen does not produce results in Chekhov's world.

In *Three Sisters*, Chekhov again takes up the theme of wasted lives. Andrew [Andrey], instead of becoming a professor, as he had hoped, has become a county councillor working for the man who is his wife's lover. He comes to see that he has failed to realise his potential:

> ANDREW. [Andrey] Where is my past life, oh what has become of it — when I was young, happy and intelligent, when I had such glorious thoughts and visions, and my present and future seemed so bright and promising? Why is it we've hardly started living before we all become dull, drab, boring, lazy, complacent, useless and miserable?[73]

Unlike Sorin and Vanya, whose bad faith leads them to blame others for their plight, Andrew, while not taking responsibility for his failure, at least does not blame others for his inaction. Masha is one character who acknowledges herself as the cause of her failure, but she can only cope with this admission by denying its importance in words that echo the leitmotif of Chebutykin. Immediately after '*the muffled sound of a distant shot*' that signals Tuzenbach's death, the distressed Masha cries out: 'I've made a mess of my life. I don't want anything now. I'll be all right in a moment – It doesn't matter.'[74] It is the alcoholic and depressive Dr Chebutykin who most fully acknowledges his own responsibility for failure. Chekhov even cut the line, 'I've done nothing all my life and I've never had time to do anything all my life',[75] probably because this might have suggested that the doctor was shuffling off his responsibility for his inaction. In the final version of this speech of Chebutykin in Act I, the self-hating doctor bitterly blames himself for his failure and almost complete withdrawal from involvement in life. He offers no excuses:

> CHEBUTYKIN. [*Laughs*.] You know, I've never done a thing and that's a fact. Since I left the university I haven't lifted a finger, I've never even read a book. I've read nothing but newspapers.[76]

Chekhov's lifelong interest in community welfare and education suggests that his attitude, the attitude he wished his audiences to have, towards the kind of wilful ignorance and lethargy epitomised by Chebutykin, was a negative one. Dr Astrov in *Uncle Vanya* has much in common with Dr Chebutykin, but their respective modes of behaviour in the face of life's hardships differ markedly. Like Dr Chebutykin, Dr Astrov has had to put up with a hard life and has suffered the anguish of losing patients during operations. Like Chebutykin, Astrov cannot find consolation in the idea of any transcendental significance to life. He honestly admits, 'there are times when the whole business really gets me down. But for me there is no light shining in the distance. I don't expect anything for myself any more and I don't care for other people either.'[77] Unlike Chebutykin, however, Astrov involves himself in life. As he rightly claims: 'I work harder than anyone else around here.'[78] He has made a continuing intensive study of the environmental degradation affecting the neighbourhood and is doing something to improve the present situation. The positive attitude that Chekhov has toward this active character is in sharp contrast to the negative attitude he has toward Chebutykin, whose response, even to the senseless killing of Tuzenbach which he did nothing to stop, is to lapse into lethargy and mouth his nihilistic catch phrase:

> CHEBUTYKIN. [*Sits down on a bench at the back of the stage.*] I'm worn out. [*Takes a newspaper out of his pocket.*] They may as well have a cry. [*Sings softly.*] Tararaboomdeay, let's have a tune today. Anyway, what does it all matter?[79]

Chekhov has no need to say explicitly that Chebutykin's behaviour is irresponsible and untenable. All he has to do is depict Chebutykin as he is and leave the audience to evaluate his behaviour.

Chekhov's desire to avoid any explicit judgement of his characters is often forgotten by directors. This is especially the case when dealing with the character of Natasha. Perhaps taking their cue from a comment in one of Chekhov's letters to Stanislavski, in which he asked that Natasha cross the stage 'à la Lady Macbeth, with a candle',[80] critics and directors turn Natasha into a melodramatic villain. Even Magarshack, who points out that Chekhov 'warned the actor playing Solyony not to make him "too coarse", that is to say, not to make him into a melodramatic villain',[81] characterises Natasha in just such a 'coarse' manner. He calls her behaviour 'vindictive' and describes her as 'a ruthless predator'.[82] Later on in his analysis, he refers to 'Natasha's truly devilish behaviour'.[83] Demonising of Natasha is taken to its ultimate extreme in Brustein's melodramatic interpretation of *Three Sisters*. Since he believes that 'the conflict between culture and vulgarity provides the major theme',[84] Brustein describes Chekhov's characters in black-and-white terms. The three sisters become synonymous with 'culture' and Natasha with 'vulgarity'. He reads Chekhov's characterisation as though he were analysing Strindberg's *Ghost Sonata*:

> Women, to be sure, often play a destructive role in Chekhov's plays ... Natasha ... is unique in the blackness of her motives. She might be a member of the Hummel family of vampires: sucking up people's nourishment, breaking foundations, speculating in houses. She is a malignant growth in a benevolent organism and her final triumph, no matter how Chekhov tries to disguise it, is the triumph of pure evil.[85]

What is lost by such a judgemental interpretation of Natasha is any sense of Chekhov's implied criticism of the ineffectual passive behaviour of the Prozorovs. One director, Jonathan Miller, was aware that the traditional reading of Natasha's character as some sort of satanic force was not supported by Chekhov's text:

> The worst thing one can say about her is that she knows exactly what she wants. She simply embodies the general banality of the sisters' environment, without conscious vindictiveness or any recognition of what she is doing. Once she has a stake in the big house, the sisters simply become an irrelevance in her life and, however wounding her treatment of them, her mind is on other things at the time.[86]

Harvey Pitcher notes that, while Natasha may be 'an odious character ... there is such an impatient desire to find someone to blame in *Three Sisters*, such a gleeful rush to castigate Natasha for her most obvious failings, that comment on her has often been very superficial'.[87]

In order to restore the 'objectivity' of Chekhov's characterisation of Natasha, directors need to do something akin to what Peter Brook did for the characters of Goneril and Regan in his production of *King Lear*. Brook refused to present Cordelia as a Cinderella figure who is destroyed by her two ugly sisters. Instead, Brook took the Chekhovian approach of objectivity and refrained from judging Goneril and Regan, allowing them to be played in a morally neutral fashion from their own point of view.

With the notable exception of Miller's production, Natasha has rarely been played in English-speaking countries in a non-judgemental way. Because she is seen as 'common' and the three sisters as 'cultured', directors have tended to present the play from an upper-middle class elitist standpoint, and middle-class audiences have been only too happy to identify with the dispossessed sisters and hate the *arriviste* Natasha. The snobbery inherent in this standard interpretation is well brought out by Marina Majdalany in an article in which, while attempting to 'maintain objectivity' and resisting 'the temptation to redress the balance by tilting it in Natasha's favour', she tries to give her 'a fair appraisal':

> While all commentators of Chekhov's play dwell at length upon the aesthetic longings of the three sisters and tenderly evoke their sensitivity bruised by frustration, no comparable sympathy is extended to Natasha, their brother's young wife. She is indeed vain, selfish and even ruthless, as she has been

categorised; but what all these attributions have crowded out is the fact that, first and foremost, she is a disoriented *petite bourgeoise*, socially insecure and lonely in an alien and hostile environment.[88]

The hostility addressed towards Natasha by the three sisters takes the form of a kind of 'effortless superiority' that is akin to the patronising behaviour practised in England by the 'gentry' towards the 'great unwashed'. Olga and Masha deride Natasha's lack of dress sense; they laugh at her attempts to speak one of the foreign languages that they have been fortunate enough to have learnt, but have largely forgotten; they patronisingly explain that her inappropriate behaviour is the result of not having been brought up in the way that they have.

Once we step back from the judgemental position in relation to the characters in *Three Sisters*, we find much of the behaviour of the 'malignant growth' at least understandable, and much of the behaviour of the 'benevolent organism' reprehensible. How fair is it that critics and directors alike harshly censure Natasha's affair with the successful Protopopov while 'not a word condemns Masha's passion for Vershinin'?[89] Masha betrays a husband who, for all his limitations, works hard and loves her, while Natasha betrays a weak lazy gambler who can say of her: 'there's something degrading about her too, as if she is some kind of blind, groping, scruffy little animal. She's not a human being anyway.'[90] Why is it that Masha's behaviour is seen as less reprehensible than Natasha's? Natasha's dismissal of the Prozorovs' old servant of thirty years, Anfisa, on the 'economic rationalist' grounds that 'she can't work any more'[91] is certainly cruel. However, the public humiliation that Masha inflicts on her cuckolded husband when, in reply to his saying to her, 'You're really a marvellous creature. I'm happy, happy, oh so happy', she sharply retorts, 'I'm bored, bored, oh so bored',[92] is hardly less vicious. As Majdalany justly observes: 'For all Masha's extolled sensitivity, the callousness she displays towards the long suffering Kulygin is breathtaking, even by modern standards.'[93]

*Three Sisters* is not simply about a clash between 'culture' and 'vulgarity', but a confrontation between contrasting groups of people, one of which is 'passive' and the other 'active' in the face of life's problems. Just as in *The Cherry Orchard* Chekhov was to juxtapose Lopakhin's active entrepreneurial approach to the problem of saving the estate with the ineffectual passivity of Gayev and Mrs Ranevsky, so in this play similar opposing groups are contrasted. Harvey Pitcher points out the significance of this juxtaposition:

> In the characters of Natasha and the unseen, but not unimportant Protopopov, Chekhov was introducing representatives of a new and rising middle class; and it is impossible not to contrast what these two achieve in the play with what the Prozorovs fail to achieve.[94]

Majdalany likewise has noted how Chekhov incorporated the social background of his time into both *Three Sisters* and *The Cherry Orchard*: 'It is well known that Chekhov observed the social change that was taking place in Russia, of which the dominant feature was the emergence of the new commercial middle class, and dramatised it through Natasha and later, in *The Cherry Orchard*, through Lopakhin.'[95]

The general theme of wasted potentiality is given specific application in Chekhov's depiction of the failure of the intelligentsia and the gentry to adjust to the changing social circumstances. As Pitcher puts it:

> The sheltered lives of families like the Prozorovs, who were conscious of their social and cultural superiority, and whose house had until recently been full of orderlies ready to carry out their slightest wish, may tend to sap all personal initiative and to produce a charming but ineffectual breed. *Three Sisters* shows clearly how the upper classes could no longer rely on this position of unchallenged superiority, and how their authority might rapidly pass to more vigorous elements from classes below. Andrew has to take orders from Protopopov, just as Natasha assumes the position of authority in the sisters' household.[96]

Natasha's vulgarity triumphs largely because she actively pursues her aims for herself and her children, while the Prozorov family fail to do anything to stop her. The result is that they are progressively driven out of their house. It is important that the significance of Natasha's development from the shy, awkward outsider of Act I into the confident householder of Act IV should not be lost on an audience. If Natasha's rapacious behaviour is meant to be viewed negatively, so also is the effete inactivity of the Prozorovs. As Majdalany acutely observes:

> In observing this evolution, the audience should recognise that Natasha's 'sins of commission' are balanced by the Prozorovs' 'sins of omission'. The asperities of her selfishness collide with the granite of their egotism: she is vulgar and strives to become genteel; they are refined and never even attempt to groom her understanding or her manners. She grasps, they withdraw; she pushes, they recoil.[97]

The playwright presented his audience with provincial Russian society as he saw it. As Ronald Hingley notes, 'Chekhov's works abound in denunciations of provincial Russian towns'.[98] Provincial towns, including his birthplace, Taganrog, seemed alike in their sterility. In 1887, at Easter, Chekhov described his hometown in a manner that suggests both his awareness of the potentiality of the place and his disgust at the way that potentiality has not been realised:

> Sixty thousand inhabitants busy themselves exclusively with eating, drinking, procreating, and they have no other interests, none at all. Wherever you go

there are Easter cakes, eggs, local wine, infants, but no newspapers, no books ... The site of the city is in every respect magnificent, the climate glorious, the fruits of the earth abound, but the people are devilishly apathetic. They are all musical, endowed with fantasy and wit, highstrung, sensitive, but all this is wasted.[99]

This cultural desert is very little different from the one agonisingly described by Andrew in the last act of *Three Sisters*. Life as it is lived in the Prozorovs' hometown — 'a provincial town, — it might be Perm'[100] — has become totally trivial. Andrew's own failure to realise his potential is part of a social malaise that has infected the whole society:

> ANDREW. [Andrey] ... We've never produced a single scholar, or artist or anyone with a touch of originality ... All these people do is eat, drink and sleep till they drop down dead. Then new ones are born to carry on the eating, drinking and sleeping ... the children are crushed by vulgarity, lose any spark of inspiration they might have had, and — like their fathers and mothers before them — turn into a lot of miserable corpses, each exactly like his neighbour.[101]

The Prozorov sisters, their brother Andrew, Tuzenbach, Vershinin, Chebutykin, in fact most of the characters in the play apart from Natasha and the servants, are highly educated, yet all of these members of the intelligentsia manage to waste their lives in precisely the way that Andrew describes in his long 'disguised soliloquy' near the end of the play:

> ANDREW. [Andrey] ... And to save themselves getting bored to tears and put a bit of spice in their lives, they go in for all this sickening gossip, vodka, gambling, litigation. Wives deceive their husbands and husbands tell lies and pretend they're deaf and blind to what's going on ...[102]

The intelligentsia may well be wasting their lives, but Chekhov nevertheless does not give up faith in progress. Science and the work of inconspicuous individuals will, Chekhov asserts, eventually bring about an improvement in humanity's lot. The fact that the vision of a more hopeful future is carried by fallible characters such as Vershinin is further evidence of how great a gap there is between 'life as it is' and 'life as it should be'.

Stanislavski's dealings with Chekhov led him to recognise the playwright's cautiously optimistic vision of reality:

> Anton Pavlovich was very offended when he was called a pessimist ... Anton Pavlovich was the most optimistic believer in the future I ever met. He would sketch with animation and faith a beautiful picture of the future life of Russia. As for the present, he related to it honestly and was not afraid of the truth.[103]

Chekhov's 'optimism', however, did not involve a belief in the transformation of Russian society through revolution, as the Soviet critics and directors tried to suggest. Rather, as a follower of Darwin's theories, Chekhov saw change as a gradual evolutionary process. Chekhov depicts what he sees and what he sees does not reflect the kind of vision that Soviet artists admire in which active heroes change the world. Part of the suffering that these characters endure lies in their consciousness of the gulf that has opened between their words and their actions, between their dreams and the reality they live. Vershinin, for example, is perfectly well aware that his behaviour, especially with regard to his affair with Masha, has not been admirable. Alone with Olga just before his departure he asks her forgiveness:

> VERSHININ. Ah well, thank you for everything. And if there's been anything at all amiss, please forgive me. I've talked much too much. Please forgive that too. Don't think too badly of me.[104]

The fallibility of Chekhov's characters is of central importance in the total action of the play. It is only by making perceptible the gap between what characters say and what they do that the playwright can lead members of his audience to recognise their own failure to bring about social improvement in Russia. The critique of Vershinin's behaviour made by Pitcher is essentially valid. He states: 'Vershinin's fine words and noble aspirations have never been matched by any comparable achievements in his personal life; and this combination of noble sentiments with practical ineffectuality seems to epitomise the well-meaning Russian liberal of the late nineteenth century.'[105]

What Pitcher says about Vershinin applies with equal validity to most of the characters in *Three Sisters*, particularly to the Prozorov family. This failure to match word with deed was intended to strike a chord of recognition in the audience. There is, for example, nothing inherently stupid or wrong with Irina's lyrically expressed ideal that 'Man should work and toil by the sweat of his brow, whoever he is — that's the whole purpose and meaning of his life, his happiness and his joy.'[106] Chekhov would almost certainly have felt great sympathy with Irina's sentiment, if not her manner of expression. However, what he presents to his audience is not some mouthpiece for himself, but a silly young woman who, as her sister Olga says, 'wakes at seven and lies in bed at least till nine, just thinking'.[107] The comic incongruity that results from the perception of the gap between Irina's words and her deeds is highlighted when Chekhov provides Olga with the stage instruction: '*Laughs*'. It is Irina's behaviour, not her ideas, that is laughable.

In similar fashion there is something comical about the aristocratic Tuzenbach, who, on his own admission, has 'never done a hand's turn'[108] all his life, agreeing with Irina about the supreme value of work. However, even if we find it incredible that Tuzenbach would ever have made a success of working in a brickworks, we should not discount his arguments in favour of work. Although the Soviet critics failed to see that there was a gap between the content of

Tuzenbach's 'visionary' speech and his own behaviour, they were nevertheless correct not to discount that content. Tuzenbach's stirring words, written in 1900, must have seemed a remarkable example of Chekhovian prescience to those who lived in the exciting period immediately after the Russian revolution of 1917. It is not surprising that Tuzenbach's fallibility should have gone unnoticed when the triumphant Bolsheviks read or heard his rousing speech:

> TUZENBACH. ... The time has come, an avalanche is moving down on us and a great storm's brewing that'll do us all a power of good. It's practically on top of us already and soon it's going to blast out of our society all the laziness, complacency, contempt for work, rottenness and boredom. I'm going to work and in twenty-five or thirty-years' time everyone will work. Everyone.[109]

Often in a Chekhov play, a character, however blind to their own failings, will highlight the mistakes of others with perfect lucidity and may, sometimes unknowingly, destroy the illusions of another character. We saw earlier how Olga's and Irina's dream of getting to Moscow was undercut by the apparently unrelated comments of Chebutykin and Tuzenbach. Vershinin continues this explosion of the sisters' 'Moscow myth' by presenting what he sees as its reality. Moscow conjures up thoughts for him that are depressing, even suicidal. In contrast, he sees the place where the sisters live in a positive light:

> VERSHININ. ... You have a good healthy climate, what I call a real Russian climate. There are the woods and the river, and you've silver birches too. Charming modest birches, they're my favourite tree. This is a good place to live.[110]

Vershinin's comments serve to highlight the fact that there is very little that is wrong with the physical environment in which the Prozorovs live. What makes the place intolerable is the way the inhabitants live their lives. Instead of making use of the talents and educational privileges they have been given, the Prozorovs have started to go to seed since the death of their father. Andrew talks of their father having 'inflicted education on us', and confesses, 'since he died I've started putting on weight and in one year I've filled out like this, just as if my body had shaken off some kind of burden'.[111] In the course of the play, Chekhov makes it quite clear to his audience that what this member of the intelligentsia has cast off is the burden of responsibility. Having been born into an educationally privileged level of society, Andrew wastes his many talents and, instead of fulfilling his achievable dream to become a university professor, turns into a compulsive gambler who whines about his failure. He sells his and his sisters' share of their inheritance to pay his gambling debts, yet, significantly, even though his sisters know what he is doing, they do nothing to stop him.

Masha, infected by the same malaise of idleness and negativity as her brother, also denies the value of her education. 'Knowing three languages is a useless luxury in this town,' she asserts, then adds, 'We know much too much.'[112] It is this denial of the value of education and, in particular, its power to effect improvement in the quality of life, however minimal, that draws from Vershinin the first of several 'philosophical' speeches. The audience's reading of the content of these speeches depends on whether this army officer is taken seriously. There is considerable evidence to suggest that Chekhov had a high estimation of the cultural standing of such officers. Following the 1874 army reforms of General D. A. Milyutin, the Russian army became associated with education. According to Hingley, 'The army became a place where peasants first learnt to read and write ... Chekhov was sympathetically disposed towards the Russian Army'.[113] Stanislavski quotes Chekhov as saying that he didn't want the soldiers in *Three Sisters* to be presented as caricatured 'heel-clickers':

> 'There's none of that,' he argued rather heatedly, 'military personnel have changed, they have become more cultured, many of them have even begun to realize that in peacetime they should bring culture with them into remote backwaters.'[114]

The association of education and culture with the military is pointed out by Masha in the play when she compares civilians with the military:

> MASHA. ... Other places may be different, but in this town the most decent, the most civilized and cultivated people are the military ... But civilians in general are often so rude, disagreeable and bad-mannered.[115]

Despite his tendency to be long-winded, there is no reason to doubt the probable truth of Vershinin's claim that the Prozorov sisters can make a contribution to the improvement of society. Vershinin's speech has a variety of effects on his listeners. Andrew slips away *'unobserved'* — he appears to be a lost cause — but it is this speech that brings Masha to life for the first time in the play and marks the beginning of her attraction toward Vershinin. While Vershinin is clearly not Chekhov's alter ego, many of the sentiments that he expresses are similar to those we know Chekhov believed in. In performance, it becomes necessary not to present Vershinin as someone who talks nonsense, but as someone who is attractive because of his commitment to positive ideas. When played in the committed way I have suggested, it is hard to imagine how an audience would not see some validity in Vershinin's 'aria':

> VERSHININ. Oh, what a thing to say! [*Laughs.*] You know much too much. I don't think there exists, or even could exist, a town so dull and dreary that it had no place for intelligent, educated men and women. Let's suppose that among the hundred thousand inhabitants of this town — oh, I know it's a backward, rough sort of place — there's no one else like you three. Well, you obviously can't hope to prevail against the forces of ignorance around you. As you go on living you'll have to give way bit by bit to these hundred thousand people and

be swallowed up in the crowd. You'll go under, but that doesn't mean you'll sink without trace — you will have some effect. Perhaps when you're gone there will be six people like you, then twelve and so on, and in the end your kind will be in the majority. In two or three hundred years life on this earth will be beautiful beyond our dreams, it will be marvellous. Man needs a lift like that, and if he hasn't yet got it he must feel he's going to get it, he must look forward to it, dream about it, prepare for it. That means he must have more vision and more knowledge than his father or grandfather ever had. [*Laughs.*] And here are you complaining you know much too much.

MASHA. [*Takes off her hat.*] I'm staying to lunch.[116]

Hingley argues that changes Chekhov made to the script 'serve to emphasize his [Vershinin's] lack of interest in what anyone else has to say'.[117] Chekhov had rewritten Vershinin's response to Tuzenbach's claim that to create a better future 'we must get ready for it and work for it'. Originally Chekhov had Vershinin reply: 'That may well be so.' His revision was: 'Yes, yes of course.' Hingley claims that this revision is a 'casual' remark. However, even the revised line — 'Yes, yes of course' — need not be said 'casually' or in a dismissive way. Any good actor could deliver that line 'enthusiastically' and thus portray Vershinin as deeply interested in Tuzenbach's observations. Such readings are dependent on directorial decisions. It is perfectly possible to interpret Vershinin's quick changing of the subject after Tuzenbach joins in the conversation as a realisation on his part that his 'aria' is socially inappropriate. He has only a little earlier said to Andrew, 'I'm afraid your sisters must be rather bored with me already'.[118] Having made such a long and serious speech, it is quite in character for Vershinin to become aware that he has been talking too much. He realises that, while this is a topic that he feels passionately about, it is hardly the time or the place to embark on a philosophical debate with Tuzenbach. Thus, when Tuzenbach joins in the conversation by arguing that we must work now to bring about a better future, Vershinin agrees, but proceeds to change the subject, so as not to bore the ladies. He resorts to small talk about 'what a lot of flowers' there are in this 'splendid house'. This equally playable interpretation of Chekhov's text avoids presenting Vershinin as the self-centred egotist that Hingley depicts.

Despite his belief that people should work, Tuzenbach denies the efficacy of any human effort to improve life. It is in response to his pessimistic view that, even in two or three hundred years 'life itself won't change',[119] that Vershinin puts forward what is essentially an expression of his own faith in progress. The discussion between the two military men is a variant on the nature/nurture debate that is still an issue today. Vershinin's argument is remarkably similar to Chekhov's own belief in the possibility of gradual progress that can be brought about through the nurturing efforts of humans working to improve what has been provided by nature. Like Dr Astrov in *Uncle Vanya*, Vershinin sees little chance of immediate rewards for human effort, but passionately believes in the long-term benefits:

> VERSHININ. ... My hair's going grey now and I'm growing old, but the trouble is I know so precious little. Still, when it comes to the things that really matter, there I do know my stuff pretty well, I think. And I only wish I could make you see that happiness — well, we haven't got it, we've no right to it, in fact it isn't meant for us at all. Our business is to work and go on working, and our distant descendants will have any happiness that's going. [*Pause.*] I won't have it, but my children's children may.[120]

Tuzenbach presents the argument in favour of a fixed idea of nature. His views, while not as nihilistic as those expressed by Dr Chebutykin, are nevertheless close to the 'nothing to be done' school of thinking, since he believes that nature programs all behaviour including that of humans.

> TUZENBACH. ... Forget your two or three hundred years, because even in a million years life will still be the same as ever. It doesn't change, it always goes on the same and follows its own laws. And those laws are none of our business. Or at least you'll never understand them.[121]

To illustrate his views, Tuzenbach compares human behaviour to that of the migratory habits of cranes who 'still keep flying without ever knowing why they do it or where they're going'.[122] This view of nature and life as being without purpose was one that Chekhov denied. As someone with a belief in scientific progress, Chekhov could not help regarding such fatalistic views as life-denying.

Certainly, while Chekhov does not explicitly judge Tuzenbach, he provides the newly invigorated Masha with a powerful speech which undermines Tuzenbach's idea that life is programmed and purposeless:

> MASHA. But what's the point of it all?
> TUZENBACH. The point? Look, it's snowing out there. What's the point of that? [*Pause.*]
> MASHA. I feel that man should have a faith or be trying to find one, otherwise his life just doesn't make sense. Think of living without knowing why cranes fly, why children are born or why there are stars in the sky. Either you know what you're living for, or else the whole thing's a waste of time and means less than nothing.[123]

Even though Masha is deeply unhappy at having to say farewell to Vershinin, she expresses her faith in the idea of life having a purpose. Tuzenbach had asserted that humans, like the cranes, live 'without knowing why they do it or where they're going'. Originally Masha's speech finished by rejecting the inevitability of this state of ignorance:

> MASHA. Oh, listen to the band. They're all leaving us, and one has gone right away and will never, never come back, and we shall be left alone to begin our lives again. {We must go on living, we must. I shall go on living, my dears, one must live. [*Looks upwards.*] There are migrating birds up there, they fly past every spring and autumn, they've been doing it for thousands of years and they don't know why. But they fly on and they'll go on flying for ages and ages, for many thousand years, until in the end God reveals his mysteries to them.}[124]

Chekhov cut the lines {…} at the request of Olga Knipper, who was playing Masha. She had written to him and asked: 'Does it matter if I make a cut in my last speech? If I find it difficult to say?'[125] Chekhov had also been asked by Nemirovich-Danchenko to make cuts in the final speeches of the play: 'About the 4th act. It needs cutting. I've just sent you a telegram but, to give a few details, three long speeches for the three sisters is not a good idea. It's both out of key and untheatrical. A cut for Masha, a big cut for Irina. Only Olga can offer some consolation. Yes?'[126] Whether or not these cuts were desirable is open to question. Certainly, Chekhov agreed to make them, but we should still note the importance that he gave, even in the final version, to the expression of hope by all three sisters. In Chekhov's final version it is Olga who most fully expresses both the anguish the Prozorovs feel in the face of 'life as it is' and the hope that all three sisters have that one day they will come to understand the purpose of life. Olga's speech reiterates Vershinin's vision of life in which the present generation must prepare the way for a better life for those yet unborn:

> OLGA. … Oh, my God! In time we shall pass on forever and be forgotten. Our faces will be forgotten and our voices and how many of us there were. But our sufferings will bring happiness to those who come after us, peace and joy will reign on earth and there will be kind words and kind thoughts for us and our times.[127]

Chekhov concludes the play by juxtaposing the nihilistic Chebutykin's 'Nothing matters' with Olga's repeated wish that 'we might find out what our lives and sufferings are for'. She does not doubt that things do matter, that life does have a purpose, but she longs for that purpose to be revealed: 'If we could only know, oh if we could only know!'[128]

Like Vershinin, the three sisters believe in the possibility of a better future and all of them have some inkling of how they might make some contribution to help realise this future. Irina believes that the purpose of life 'will be known one day … but till then life must go on, we must work and work and think of nothing else'.[129] The three sisters all assert the value of that quintessentially Chekhovian virtue of endurance and this is combined, as it was by Nina in *The*

*Seagull* and Sonya in *Uncle Vanya*, with a faith in the future. It is left to Vershinin in his parting speech to elucidate the means by which this better future can be achieved. If played sympathetically, Vershinin's final philosophical 'aria', without resorting to judgemental preaching, can suggest to an audience ways in which they can do something to improve the condition of their own lives:

> VERSHININ. ... Life isn't a bed of roses. A lot of us think it's a hopeless dead end. Still you must admit things are getting brighter and better all the time, and it does look as if we'll see a real break in the clouds before very long ... Oh, if that could only happen soon. [*Pause.*] If we could only combine education with hard work, you know, and hard work with education.[130]

It was to be in *The Cherry Orchard* that Chekhov would show his audience, even more explicitly than in *Three Sisters*, the failure of an educated class who don't know how to work. In that last play, we find in the character of Lopakhin a more sympathetic representative than Natasha of that class which, while knowing how to work, lacks education.

It should be clear that fallible creatures like Vershinin need not be presented as knights in shining armour in order for their ideas to be given some validity. It should also be clear that this validity is necessary if Chekhov's vision of reality is to be realised on stage. The ideas of Vershinin and Tuzenbach as well as those of the nihilistic Chebutykin and Solyony need to be balanced against each other. The 'philosophers' in *Three Sisters*, despite their personal inadequacies, must be seen as 'serious' people in order for their ideas to have any value for an audience. To privilege the more nihilistic characters, as so often happens in productions today, is to distort the Chekhovian vision.

It is not surprising that there are certain moments in history when the Chekhovian preferred reading that I am advocating seems more pertinent than at other times. One can see why, after many years of Stalinist oppression, the hopeful vision of reality expressed by Vershinin would sound rather hollow to an audience grown cynical after having experienced the failure of the Bolshevik dreams. One important Russian production, that I believe attempted to realise the kind of balance between hope and despair that I have suggested is at the heart of the Chekhovian vision, was that directed by Georgii Tovstonogov in 1965. The historical moment gave this director the opportunity to present Chekhov's *Three Sisters* in a way that neither distorted the playwright's vision nor presented a world view that seemed too removed from the audience's own experience.

Tovstonogov's production occurred towards the end of the 'Thaw', a brief period of liberalisation in Russia after years of Stalinist oppression. At the time, it became possible again to express Chekhov's sense of hope in a possible better future without resorting to the blind optimism of the more extreme Soviet productions. Equally, because the 'Thaw' was a time of hope, the bleak 'Absurdist' approach to the play did not seem to be appropriate. Comparing his interpretation with that made by Nemirovich-Danchenko in his 1940 production, Tovstonogov pointed out the ways in which his approach was different. He argued that Nemirovich-Danchenko's production suggested 'that the blame for a ruined life lay beyond the limits of human personality. Fine and noble people were victimised by the times and the social order.'[131] This depiction of Chekhov's characters as sensitive victims unable to do anything to control their fates seemed questionable to Tovstonogov:

> Is it only environment that prevents people from living fully, intelligently, and beautifully? It is important to assert that it is not something or someone from outside that destroys, but that the Chekhovian characters themselves — intelligent, subtle, suffering people — destroy one another by their own passivity and irresolution.[132]

Instead of assessing whether Tovstonogov's reading of the play accurately produces the action implied by Chekhov's playtext, Senelick uncharacteristically resorts to stereotyping the director as a Soviet stooge. He asserts:

> A modern Soviet conscience had to attribute much of the fault to the characters themselves and their weak wills. Their indifference and cruelty had to be faced up to, not justified.[133]

It not true that Tovstonogov 'had to' attribute the fault to the characters. Rather, he recognised that Chekhov's play contains an implied criticism of the behaviour of his characters which was intended to induce spectators to look critically at their own 'silly trivial lives'. Tovstonogov was able to see the action of Chekhov's play clearly partly because he was not drawn into a 'saints or blackguards' approach to the playwright's work. He saw the problems that result from such polarised readings. If the 'gloom and twilight' version of Chekhov has become the default reading of *Three Sisters* in the Western world, then the 'welcome bright world' version became the default reading in Soviet Russia. Tovstonogov wished to avoid both extremes in his own production:

> In opposition to the notion of Chekhov as pessimist, another extreme attitude arose: interpreters began to look for traits of the fighting revolutionary in Chekhov's heroes. His protagonists were credited with a strong will and much energy, with courage and optimism. Historical and psychological truth was sacrificed to this conception.[134]

Tovstonogov's belief that, in *Three Sisters*, Chekhov 'not only sympathises with his heroes and loves them, but also judges them in anger'[135] is, I would argue, essentially accurate. Chekhov's 'judgements', however, always remain implicit rather than explicit. Chekhov rarely loses his 'objectivity', even in depicting a character such as Natasha. He allows the audience to make their own judgement of her behaviour. Tovstonogov's balanced approach resulted in a production that, while different from Nemirovich-Danchenko's 1940 version, did not contradict it. His 1965 production may not have been 'permeated with faith in a better future' as he claimed Nemirovich-Danchenko's 1940 production had been, but, by directing his production 'against "the slave in man", as Chekhov put it, against the amazing ability of the intelligentsia to find justification for its inertia and indifference',[136] Tovstonogov did not exclude the possibility of creating a 'better future'.

*Three Sisters* is possibly the most difficult Chekhov play to classify in terms of its genre. Chekhov called it 'A Drama in Four Acts' and this at least suggests that he was aware that it was darker in tone than his other plays. He admitted as much in a letter to Vera Kommissarzhevskaya:

> *Three Sisters* is finished... The play has turned out dull, protracted and awkward; I say — awkward, because, for instance, it has four heroines and a mood, as they say, gloomier than gloom itself ... My play is complex like a novel and its mood, people say, is murderous.[137]

It has, as Gordon McVay has noted, 'inspired a bewildering variety of interpretations': '*Three Sisters* has been viewed both as a tragedy and as a comedy, as a poignant testimony to the eternal yearning for love, happiness, beauty and meaning, or as a devastating indictment of the folly of inert gentility and vacuous day-dreaming.'[138]

Certainly, the play continues the exploration of life as a constant struggle between hope and despair that had been so movingly dramatised in *Uncle Vanya*. It is easy to see why the tragic theme of loss and waste can easily overwhelm the theme of faith in a better future and lead directors to interpret the play as a lament. It remains important however to constantly attempt to present a balance between the darker and brighter elements of the play. McVay is one critic who is aware of the dual nature of *Three Sisters*. While asserting that the play is 'a profoundly serious piece in the questions it raises', he notes the fact that 'hardly any theme or character in the play remains untouched by laughter'.[139] McVay's analysis of *Three Sisters* is one that any director might well keep in mind when directing this play. He accurately describes the balance that needs to be struck in performance between presenting the bleak reality that Chekhov describes with cool objectivity and communicating the underlying aim of suggesting possibilities for changing that reality for the better:

> In *Three Sisters*, the burden of sorrow and non-achievement is balanced, and even perhaps transcended, by the yearning for happiness and fulfilment. The portrayal of life as it is engenders a longing for life as it should be.[140]

Chekhov's objectivity and his overall aim should co-exist in any production. In his final play, *The Cherry Orchard*, Chekhov perfected the synthesis between these two elements of his dramaturgy.

## ENDNOTES

[1] Magarshack, D., *The Real Chekhov*, George Allen and Unwin, London, 1972, p. 126.

[2] Frayn, M., *Chekhov Plays*, Methuen, London, 1988, p. lix.

[3] Hahn, B., *Chekhov: A Study of the Major Stories and Plays*, Cambridge University Press, Cambridge, 1979, pp. 284–5.

[4] A. E. W. in *Star*, 17 February 1926, quoted in Emeljanow, V., ed., *Chekhov: The Critical Heritage*, Routledge and Kegan Paul, London, 1981, p. 300.

[5] Karlinsky, S., 'Russian Anti-Chekhovians', *Russian Literature*, Vol. 15, 1984, p. 183.

[6] Gilman, R., *Chekhov's Plays: An Opening into Eternity*, Yale University Press, New Haven, 1995, p. 148.

[7] Ibid., p. 159.

[8] Beckett, S., *Waiting for Godot*, Faber and Faber, London, 1965, p. 89.

[9] Davison, D., ed., *Andrew Marvell: Selected Poetry and Prose*, Harrap and Company, London, 1952, p. 84.

[10] Chekhov, A., *Three Sisters*, in Hingley, R., *The Oxford Chekhov*, Vol. 3, Oxford University Press, London, 1964, p. 133.

[11] Not all of Chekhov's depictions of medical men are sympathetic, and we should be aware that sympathetically drawn characters like Dr Dorn or Dr Astrov are no more to be identified with Dr Chekhov than is Dr Chebutykin. Chekhov follows the advice given to his elder brother Alexander that the dramatist should never identify with his characters. 'Who wants to know about my life and yours, my thoughts and your thoughts? Give people people – don't give them yourself ...' [Chekhov, A., Letter to A. Chekhov, 8 May 1889, in McVay, G., *Chekhov's 'Three Sisters'*, Bristol Classical Press, 1995, p. ix.]

[12] In a similar way, the 'Absurdist' view expressed by Macbeth in which he depicts life as being 'full of sound and fury, signifying nothing' is not the view expressed by Shakespeare in the play as a whole.

[13] Moss, H., 'Three Sisters', *The Hudson Review*, Vol. 30, No. 4, 1977, p. 531.

[14] Billington, M., *Guardian*, 3 April 1986.

[15] Alfreds, M., quoted in Allen, D., 'Exploring the Limitless Depths: Mike Alfreds Directs Chekhov', *New Theatre Quarterly*, Vol. 2, No. 8, November 1986, p. 332.

[16] Fox, S., *City Limits*, 3 April 1986.

[17] Magarshack, D., loc. cit.

[18] Karlinsky, S., loc. cit.

[19] Gottlieb, V., 'The Politics of British Chekhov', in Miles, P., ed., *Chekhov on the British Stage*, Cambridge University Press, Cambridge, 1993, p. 148.

[20] Coveney, M., *Financial Times*, 2 April 1986.

[21] Billington, M., loc. cit.

[22] Worrall, N., 'Stanislavsky's Production of *Three Sisters*', in Russell, R. and Barratt, A., eds, *Russian Theatre in the Age of Modernism*, Macmillan, London, 1990, p. 27.

[23] Worrall, N., op. cit., p. 2.

[24] Stanislavski, C., quoted in Stroyeva, N. M., 'The *Three Sisters* at the MAT', *Tulane Drama Review*, Vol. 9, No. 1, 1964, p. 52.

[25] Stroyeva, N. M., op. cit., p. 51.

[26] Worrall, N., op. cit., p. 11.

[27] Senelick, L., *The Chekhov Theatre*, Cambridge University Press, Cambridge, 1997, p. 64.

[28] See Worrall, N., op. cit., p. 5.

[29] Ibid., p. 9.

[30] Nemirovich-Danchenko, V., *My Life in the Russian Theatre*, Geoffrey Bles, London, 1968, p. 210.

[31] Senelick, L., op. cit., p. 189.

32 Nemirovich-Danchenko, V., op. cit., p. 207.
33 Burenin, V., quoted in Senelick, L., op. cit., p. 65.
34 Gottlieb, V., 'Chekhov in Limbo: British Productions of the Plays of Chekhov', in Scolnicov, H. and Holland, P., eds, *The Play Out of Context: Transferring Plays from Culture to Culture*, Cambridge University Press, Cambridge, 1989, p. 171.
35 Corrigan, R., 'The Plays of Chekhov', in Corrigan, R. and Rosenberg, J. L., eds, *The Context and Craft of Drama*, Chandler Publishing Company, Scranton, 1964, p.139.
36 Gottlieb, V., loc. cit.
37 Gottlieb, V., 'Why this Farce?', *New Theatre Quarterly*, Vol. 7, No. 27, August 1991, p. 224. The essential difference between the oppositional philosophies of farce and comedy according to Gottlieb 'is that whereas "absurdism" demonstrates that "life" is absurd, and much French and English farce places its emphasis on situation, Chekhov's emphasis is on the absurdity of his characters'. (p. 226.)
38 Gottlieb, V., 'The Politics of British Chekhov', p. 148.
39 Molière, *Defence of Tartuffe*, 1669, quoted in Brownstein, O. L. and Daubert, D. M., eds, *Analytical Sourcebook of Concepts in Dramatic Theory*, Greenwood Press, Westport, 1981, p. 93.
40 Gottlieb, V., 'Why this Farce?', p. 225.
41 Senelick, L., op. cit., p. 66.
42 Stanislavski, C., *My Life in Art*, Eyre Methuen, London, 1980, p. 371.
43 Ibid.
44 Karlinsky, S. and Heim, M. H., *Anton Chekhov's Life and Thought*, University of California Press, Berkeley, 1975, p. 393.
45 Chekhov, A., Letter to O. L. Knipper, 15 September 1900, quoted in Valency, M., *The Breaking String*, Oxford University Press, Oxford, 1966, p. 208.
46 Braun, E., *The Director and the Stage*, Methuen, London, 1982, p. 67.
47 Pitcher, H., *Chekhov's Leading Lady*, John Murray, London, 1979, p. 83.
48 Nemirovich-Danchenko, V., op. cit., p. 209.
49 Ibid.
50 Chekhov, A., Letter to V. Kommissarzhevskaya, 13 November 1900, in Yarmolinsky, A., *Letters of Anton Chekhov*, The Viking Press, New York, 1973, p. 383.
51 Stanislavski, C., 'Memories of Chekhov', in Hapgood, E. R., ed., *Stanislavski's Legacy*, Max Reinhardt, London, 1958, p. 98.
52 Senelick, L., op. cit., p. 59.
53 Stanislavski, C., Letter to Baron Drizen, 3 November 1909, quoted in Senelick, L., op. cit., pp. 59–60.
54 Stanislavski, C., *My Life in Art*, pp. 373–4.
55 Krutch, J. W., *'Modernism' in Modern Drama*, Cornell University Press, New York, 1953, p. 128.
56 Gillès, D., *Chekhov: Observer without Illusion*, Funk & Wagnalls, New York, 1968, p. 319.
57 Nathan, D., *Jewish Chronicle*, 11 April 1986.
58 Coveney, M., loc. cit.
59 Ratcliffe, M., *Observer*, 6 April 1986.
60 Shorter, E., *Daily Telegraph*, 3 April 1986.
61 Rose, H., *Time Out*, 9 April 1986.
62 Styan, J. L., *Chekhov in Performance*, Cambridge University Press, Cambridge, 1971, p. 151.
63 Melchinger, S., *Anton Chekhov*, Frederick Ungar, New York, 1972, p. 140.
64 Magarshack, D., loc. cit.
65 Gilman, R., op. cit., p. 176.
66 Yermilov, V., quoted in Gilman, R., loc. cit.
67 Frayn, M., op. cit., p. lviii.
68 Maurice Valency makes the interesting observation that Chekhov, far from being 'absent' from his plays and 'detached' from his characters, is 'present' and 'engaged' with them. He states: 'In *The Three Sisters*, Vershinin evidently speaks for Chekhov, and his views are clear. But Chebutykin also speaks for Chekhov, and his views are equally clear ... The indeterminate area between faith and scepticism

measures the extent of Chekhov's spiritual discomfort. Vershinin speaks for his faith; Chebutykin, for his doubt.' (Valency, M., op. cit., p. 243.)

[69] Chekhov, A., Letter to A. S. Suvorin, 30 December 1888, in Karlinsky, S., op. cit., p. 79.
[70] Chekhov, A., *Three Sisters*, p. 73.
[71] Ibid.
[72] Ibid., p. 74.
[73] Chekhov, A., *Three Sisters*, p. 133.
[74] Ibid., p. 136.
[75] Ibid., p. 312.
[76] Ibid., p. 77.
[77] Chekhov, A., *Uncle Vanya*, pp. 38–9.
[78] Ibid., p. 38.
[79] Chekhov, A., *Three Sisters*, p. 138.
[80] Chekhov, A., Letter to C. Stanislavski, 2 January 1901, in Karlinsky, S., op. cit., p. 391. Chekhov in this letter was not so much emphasising Natasha's evil qualities as trying to stop Stanislavski from introducing a piece of inappropriate 'business' for Natasha. As Stroyeva notes: 'Originally, as Stanislavsky had written Chekhov, the plan was to have "Natasha go through the house at night, putting out lights and looking for burglars under the furniture"'. (Stroyeva, N. M., op. cit., p. 48.) Chekhov tactfully steered Stanislavski away from this rather crude send-up of Natasha by suggesting a more subtle theatricality. 'It seems to me, though, that it would be better to have her walk across the stage in a straight line without a glance at anyone or anything à la Lady Macbeth, with a candle — that way it would be much briefer and more frightening.' (Karlinsky, S., loc. cit.)
[81] Magarshack, D., op. cit., p. 138.
[82] Ibid.
[83] Ibid., p. 181.
[84] Brustein, R., *The Theatre of Revolt*, Little, Brown and Company, Boston, 1964, p. 160.
[85] Ibid., pp. 157–8.
[86] Miller, J., quoted in Allen, D., 'Jonathan Miller Directs Chekhov', *New Theatre Quarterly*, Vol. 5, No. 17, February 1989, pp. 56–7.
[87] Pitcher, H., *The Chekhov Play*, Chatto and Windus, London, 1973, p. 127.
[88] Majdalany, M., 'Natasha Ivanovna, the Lonely *Bourgeoise*', *Modern Drama*, Vol. 26, 1983, p. 305.
[89] Ibid., p. 307.
[90] Chekhov, A., *Three Sisters*, p. 130.
[91] Ibid., p. 112.
[92] Ibid., p. 118.
[93] Majdalany, M., loc. cit.
[94] Pitcher, H., op. cit., p. 123.
[95] Majdalany, M., op. cit., p. 308.
[96] Pitcher, H., op. cit., p. 124.
[97] Majdalany, M., op. cit., p. 306.
[98] Hingley, R., *Russian Writers and Society 1825–1904*, Weidenfeld and Nicolson, London, 1967, p. 170.
[99] Chekhov, A., Letter to N. A. Leykin, 7 April 1887, in Yarmolinsky, A., op. cit., p. 46.
[100] Chekhov, A., Letter to M. Gorky, 16 October 1900, in Friedland, L. S., *Letters on the Short Story the Drama and Other Literary Topics by Anton Chekhov*, Dover Publications, New York, 1966, p. 156.
[101] Chekhov, A., *Three Sisters*, p. 133.
[102] Ibid.
[103] Stanislavski, C., 'A. P. Chekhov at the Arts Theater', in Turkov, A., ed., *Anton Chekhov and His Times*, University of Arkansas Press, Fayetteville, 1995, p. 116.
[104] Chekhov, A., *Three Sisters*, p. 135.
[105] Pitcher, H., op. cit., p. 126.
[106] Chekhov, A., *Three Sisters*, p. 75.

[107] Ibid., p. 76.
[108] Ibid.
[109] Ibid.
[110] Ibid., p. 81.
[111] Ibid., p. 84.
[112] Ibid.
[113] Hingley, R., op. cit., pp. 208–9.
[114] Stanislavski, C., op. cit., p. 111.
[115] Chekhov, A, *Three Sisters*, p. 95.
[116] Ibid., p. 84.
[117] Ibid., p. 311.
[118] Ibid., p. 83.
[119] Ibid., p. 98.
[120] Ibid., p. 99.
[121] Ibid.
[122] Ibid.
[123] Ibid., p. 100.
[124] Ibid., p. 138 and {p. 311}.
[125] Knipper, O., Letter to A. Chekhov, quoted in Hingley, R., *The Oxford Chekhov*, Vol. 3, p. 311.
[126] Nemirovich-Danchenko, V., Letter to A. Chekhov, 22 January 1901, in Benedetti, J., ed., *The Moscow Art Theatre Letters*, New York, 1991, p. 99.
[127] Chekhov, A., *Three Sisters*, p. 139.
[128] Ibid.
[129] Ibid.
[130] Ibid., p. 135.
[131] Tovstonogov, G., 'Chekhov's *Three Sisters* at the Gorky Theatre', *Tulane Drama Review*, Vol. 13, No. 2, 1968, p. 149.
[132] Ibid.
[133] Senelick, L., op. cit., p. 204.
[134] Tovstonogov, G., op. cit., p. 148.
[135] Ibid., p. 149.
[136] Ibid., p. 153.
[137] Chekhov, A., Letter to V. F. Kommissarzhevskaya, 13 November 1900, in McVay, G., op. cit., p. xvi.
[138] McVay, G., op. cit., p. v.
[139] Ibid., p. 67.
[140] Ibid., p. 19.

# Chapter 7. *The Cherry Orchard*: Complete Synthesis of Vision and Form

*Today, as never before, Chekhov productions argue with one another, and each one of them provokes discussion. This is because everyone has his own Chekhov. This is true of producers [directors] and actors, and also of audiences and critics. They do not always see eye to eye ... But let us pause and ask ourselves: why are there such divergent interpretations, and are they, in general, justified? Perhaps there does exist a standard 'reading of Chekhov' for all time, a model that can be violated only at one's peril? Does this diversity of interpretation have something to do with producer's [director's] license, or is it prompted by the inherent features of Chekhov's plays with their polyphony and counterpoint, so that different people hear different voices?* (Marianna Stroyeva)[1]

*Chekhov, to sum up, transcended the superficiality that often adheres to optimistic literature and at the same time escaped the morbidity that besets pessimistic profundity; and he kept a characteristic balance in other important respects ... [It is by] remembering especially the plain yet somehow elusive fact that there was ever sympathy in his comedy and some degree of comedy in his sympathy, that we may hope to bring his plays authentically to the stage.* (John Gassner)[2]

A month after Chekhov had written to the actress Mariya Petrovna Lilina informing her that his new play, *The Cherry Orchard*, 'has turned out not a drama, but a comedy, in places even a farce',[3] her husband Stanislavski wrote to the playwright and informed him that the play 'is not a comedy, nor a farce as you have written, this is a tragedy, whatever escape towards a better life you open up in the last act'.[4] So began the interpretative controversy that has continued to this day. Unfortunately, the quarrel about which genre more aptly describes *The Cherry Orchard* has generated more heat than light. Generations of directors and critics have placed themselves in warring factions that mirror the original polarised positions set up by Chekhov and Stanislavski. As Gilman rightly points out:

> ... from the beginning of its life on stage and in the critical and popular minds the play has swung between interpretative polarities: naturalism and poetry, social lament and social prophesy, more controversially comedy and something very close to a tragic mood ... What we might call 'the comic versus the melancholic' became a debate at the start.[5]

In the West, the belief that Chekhov was a deeply pessimistic writer developed as a result of critics and directors in Europe and America slavishly following the Moscow Art Theatre interpretations made famous by Stanislavski and

Nemirovich-Danchenko. Writing in 1966, Nicholas Moravcevich argued that the West developed 'a full-fledged cult of Chekhovian gloom', which was not challenged till after World War II. As a result, 'a whole generation of theatre-goers spent their lives believing that the Chekhovian play calls for a refined sensibility, melancholy disposition, red eyes, and a handkerchief'.[6] Like Gilman, Moravcevich saw interpretative approaches to Chekhov in terms of polarities. From the time when the Moscow Art Theatre produced *The Seagull*:

> ... the critical controversy over the rightful interpretation of Chekhovian plays, like a great pendulum, completed two full turns. Its initial swing towards the *larmoyante*, mournful, and somnolent gained momentum through the productions of Stanislavski and Nemirovich-Danchenko, whose popular success easily obliterated the author's occasional feeble protests that the Moscow Art Theatre directors and ensemble very frequently saw in his works dimensions and themes he had no intention of revealing.[7]

According to Kenneth Tynan, British versions of Chekhov in the immediate post Second World War years were even more *larmoyante* [tearful] than those created by the Moscow Art Theatre. Indeed, when the Russian company brought their production of *The Cherry Orchard* to London in 1958, Tynan used their interpretative approach as the norm by which to judge the failings of English Chekhov. In particular Tynan attacked the way that productions in Britain tended to turn the Russian play into a distinctively upper-class English affair:

> The great thing about the Moscow Art Theatre's production of *The Cherry Orchard* is that it blows the cobwebs off the play. And who put them there? Why we ourselves. We have remade Chekhov's last play in our image ... Our *Cherry Orchard* is a pathetic symphony, to be played in a mood of elegy. We invest it with a nostalgia for the past which, though it runs right through our culture, is alien to Chekhov's. His people are country gentry: we turn them into decadent aristocrats. Next, we romanticise them. Their silliness becomes pitiable grotesquerie; and at this point our hearts warm to them. They are not Russians at all: they belong to the great line of English eccentrics ... Having foisted on Chekhov a collection of patrician mental cases, we then congratulate him on having achieved honorary English citizenship. Meanwhile the calm, genial sanity of the play has flown out the window.[8]

Trevor Griffiths, whose controversial 'new English version' of *The Cherry Orchard* was directed by Richard Eyre in 1977, attests to the resilience of the 'pathetic symphony' approach to the play that Tynan had pilloried in the late nineteen-fifties. Griffiths felt alienated from the kind of Chekhov that 'especially from the early sixties on ... had come to seem, in his content as much as his form, inalienably bound up with the fine regretful weeping of the privileged fallen on hard times'.[9] As a Marxist, Griffiths was less worried about questions of genre than about political questions. What he objected to in previous English translations and productions was that they created a 'reactionary' rather than a 'progressive' Chekhov. This Griffiths attributed to the fact that: 'For half a century now, in England as elsewhere, Chekhov has been the almost exclusive property of theatrical class sectaries for whom the plays have been plangent and sorrowing evocations of an "ordered" past no longer with "us", its passing greatly to be mourned.'[10]

Griffiths' political interpretation of *The Cherry Orchard* was an attempt to reactivate the element of social criticism that he felt was implied in Chekhov's play and was a reaction against those productions that transformed the play into a sentimental elegy. Griffiths' version of the play, by not allowing audiences to feel enough for the characters whose world was passing away, lost some of the essential Chekhovian balance between the happiness associated with future hopes and the sadness associated with the loss of the past. Nevertheless, his version of *The Cherry Orchard* was salutary because it restored the element of hope and the possibility of social improvement that had been totally lacking in earlier English productions.

David Magarshack's reaction against the kind of tearful productions that Griffiths hated was to attack them for being too gloomy. He has argued strongly that Chekhov's plays should be interpreted as comedies. Unfortunately his sensible advice has, on occasion, been taken too far. Moravcevich claims that as a result of following Magarshack's approach, 'everything serious and sombre that the author ever expressed in his plays was deliberately minimised and tucked beneath the alleged optimism and skittish boisterousness of the Chekhovian comic muse.'[11]

The positive effect of Magarshack's emphasis on the comedic elements in Chekhov has undoubtedly been that productions that follow his approach tend to include some humour and even optimism. It is now rarer to find directors presenting totally lugubrious interpretations of a play such as *The Cherry Orchard*. However, there have been certain directors who have pushed Magarshack's corrective idea to an extreme. We find some productions of Chekhov's play that reduce it to farce.

In 1977, Andrei Serban directed the play in New York. Within an impressionistic setting, the production, while not avoiding the play's class politics, emphasised its farcical elements. There were scenes of almost slapstick physicality. Senelick commented: 'understatement was less common than athleticism: Dunyasha performed a striptease and at one point tackled Yasha like a football player.'[12] The overall effect, according to Senelick, was that, 'The visual images were often striking, but the meaning was often perverse, and the result unmoving'.[13] The cause of this failure to move the audience almost certainly lay in the overemphasis on comedy which, as Bergson noted, requires from spectators an 'anaesthesia of the heart'. Rocco Landesman is probably correct when he asserts: 'Serban takes Chekhov's statement that *The Cherry Orchard* is a comedy too literally'. Arguing that Serban has turned Chekhov's *comédie humaine* into the *Comédie Française*, Landesman points out how both the staging and the interpretation are overstated. The production presented yet another polarised reading of the play that made it ludicrous rather than comic:

> ... literalness is the problem with every aspect of this production. To show that the characters are all children, Serban has them play with toys; to present the threat of a new, strange world, Serban puts in a physical stranger in the background. When Gayev speaks of 'glorious nature' the backdrop of smokestacks gets brighter. But worst of all is Serban's Trofimov, whose vision of the coming brave new world is literalized in a Soviet army overcoat with red lapels. He and Anya, it seems, go off together to start a new and better society.[14]

Possibly one of the most extreme examples of the tendency to privilege the comical, or even farcical, aspects of *The Cherry Orchard* at the expense of the more sombre elements is provided by Joel Gershmann's 1986 postmodern production. In what the director called 'a comic *Cherry Orchard* for the 80s', Gershmann almost totally destroyed the nexus between the playwright's play and this ninety-minute production of it. Senelick's description gives us some idea of just how far the director was willing to go in order to raise a laugh:

> Spilling out of this cornucopia of Reagan-era pop culture was a Gaev obsessed by television rather than billiards, Anya and Varya played by men in drag, and Yasha and Firs their female counterparts. In the finale, Ranevskaya and her brother departed for the future carrying a giant American Express card, as Lopakhin entered with a buzzing chainsaw. The anarchic exuberance of iconoclasm provoked a good deal of laughter ...[15]

Magarshack's corrective to the gloom and doom interpretations of Chekhov may have been salutary, but when the comic aspects of Chekhov's plays are overemphasised, as they were in Gershmann's production, an equally unbalanced reading results. Examining this production, Ronald Leblanc attempted to answer the question: 'Does Gershmann's farcical production of *The Cherry Orchard* "liberate" Chekhov or does it instead "destroy" him?'[16] His answer is that the production does both:

> By emphasising the play's humorous elements, Gershmann's version certainly liberates the comic Chekhov from the Stanislavskian captivity of naturalism and psychological realism that long imprisoned his play. But in combining rock music, drug use, and sexual promiscuity with a highly emotional style of acting, the American director at the same time so modernised and vulgarised Chekhov that he rendered him virtually unrecognisable.[17]

Leblanc seems to me to have incorrectly analysed Gershmann's production. The comedy created by all of the business the director introduced did not so much 'liberate the comic Chekhov', as liberate the comic Gershmann. Furthermore, Leblanc incorrectly assumes that 'the comic Chekhov' cannot be liberated if one employs the 'psychological realism' that Stanislavski advocated. Just because Stanislavski's own use of 'psychological realism' was in the service of an overly lugubrious interpretation of Chekhov's play does not mean that it cannot be used in such a way as to allow for the comic aspects of the play to be realised on stage.

The problem with polarised approaches to Chekhov, be they the tragic approach popularised by Stanislavski or the comic approach encouraged by critics like Magarshack, is that they both lose the vital sense of balance between apparently conflicting polarities. In terms of characterisation, for instance, we need a both/and rather than an either/or approach. I have argued that Vershinin in *Three Sisters* should not be played as simply either 'an empty windbag' or 'a heroic visionary', but as a flawed human being with a worthwhile vision of the future. Similarly, in *The Cherry Orchard*, it is vital that the character Trofimov should not be played as either 'the heroic visionary Bolshevik' or as 'an emotionally immature student', but as a combination of both. Michael Frayn is one of the few writers to see that Chekhov presents characters like Trofimov from a dual perspective. Noting that in some English productions Trofimov had been played as a totally 'inadequate and immature personality', Frayn writes:

> Chekhov plainly takes Trofimov seriously as a man who holds sane and genuine convictions for which he is prepared to suffer. But then to go to the opposite extreme, as was done in Trevor Griffiths' adaptation of the play and to turn him into a 'positive hero' in the Socialist Realist sense, is also an absurdity.[18]

The both/and approach to characterisation needs to be applied not just to individual characters but to the entire cast. This is part of what Raymond Williams is driving at when he argues that:

> ... the contradictory character, of the group and its feeling, has to be conveyed in the tone: a kind of nobility, and a kind of farce, have to co-exist. (This is not, by the way, a cue for the usual question: are we supposed to laugh or cry at such people and such situations? That is a servile question: we have to decide our response for ourselves. The point is, always, that the characters and situations can be seen, are written to be seen, in both ways; to decide on one part of the response or the other is to miss what is being said.)[19]

An audience is more likely to experience that complex response to his plays which, for want of a better term, we call 'Chekhovian', if this fusion of opposites is effected in performance. A number of critics and directors are aware of the need for this fusion to be made apparent to audiences. Herbert Müller, for example, notes:

> In his humanity [Chekhov] was ... more keenly aware at once of the ludicrous and the tragic aspects of man's folly and futility. Humor runs all through his serious drama. It is only slightly more pronounced in *The Cherry Orchard*, which he labelled a comedy, and which might be called the quintessence of tragicomedy.[20]

Styan, perhaps more clearly than any other critic, sums up Chekhov's extraordinary achievement in *The Cherry Orchard*. He points out the difficulty that Chekhov faced in trying to achieve his desired sense of balanced ambiguity and the many ways in which, as we have seen, such a balance is easily lost in polarised interpretations of the play. Styan writes:

> In *The Cherry Orchard*, Chekhov consummated his life's work with a poetic comedy of exquisite balance, but so treads the tightrope that his audience has a hard time keeping its wits. This ultimate exercise in Chekhovian comedy is a lesson in funambulism. If, like recent Soviet audiences watching the work of the Moscow Art Theatre, they want rousing polemics from Trofimov, they can hear them. If, like most Western audiences, they want to mourn for Mme Ranevsky and her fate, they can be partly accommodated. It is possible to see Lyuba and Gayev as shallow people who deserve to lose their orchard, or as victims of social and economic forces beyond their control. It is possible to find Anya and Trofimov far-sighted enough to want to leave the dying orchard, or terribly ignorant of what they are forsaking. But if production allows either the heroics of prophesy or the melodrama of dispossession to dominate, then all of Chekhov's care for balance is set at nought and the fabric of the play is torn apart.[21]

Chekhov's characters function on both objective and subjective levels. On the subjective level of the subtext, life may indeed appear tragic, since characters in Chekhov's later plays are sadly aware that they have wasted their lives. On the objective level of the text, however, these same characters often behave in a silly trivial manner that is essentially comic. The audience's perception of the inter-relationship between these two levels of reality creates Chekhovian synthetic tragi-comedy. Chekhov's tragi-comedy is synthetic because the tragic and comic dimensions of a character's behaviour are perceived at the same time. Vanya's entry with a bunch of flowers for Helen in Act III of *Uncle Vanya* is both tragic *and* comic. In a Shakespearean tragi-comedy, by contrast, there is a tendency to alternate serious and comic scenes.

Again, Chekhov's tragi-comedy is synthetic in the way that it deals with characters. In Chekhov, there is no clear separation into high and low characters as occurs in a play such as *A Midsummer Night's Dream*. Instead, each character combines traits that are both noble and ludicrous. As Karl Guthke comments:

> ... this device of internal character dichotomy realises its tragi-comic effect by exploring the two sides of the *dramatis persona* in such a way that they not only offset each other, but impart their aesthetic quality (comic and tragic respectively) to each other. Thus a ludicrously disproportioned physiognomy may make an isolated noble mind all the more tragic in its suffering while the contrast with the highly valuable human substances will make the shortcomings of the outward appearance all the more comical ...[22]

One can readily see how, when dealing with a play such as *The Cherry Orchard* in which the land-owning gentry are dispossessed of their estates, a director like Stanislavski, with his wealthy merchant background, should quite naturally sympathise with those 'dispossessed' characters. It is equally clear how a playwright such as Chekhov, the grandson of a serf, whose ideal was personal freedom and who had 'squeezed the slave out of himself, drop by drop'[23] should have a much more ironic attitude to the demise of a highly privileged class.

Peter Holland's sociological analysis provides a partial explanation of Stanislavski's interpretation of the play. Holland, who sees Stanislavski 'imposing the values of his own class on Chekhov's play' argues that Chekhov's science-based 'gently liberalizing progressivism' was appropriated by Stanislavski, 'whose every instinct throughout his life was as reactionary as his theatre work was supposedly revolutionary and radical in its method'.[24]

Robert Corrigan's attack on Stanislavski's misinterpretation of *The Cherry Orchard* is not couched in socio-political terms, but in terms of what he sees as the director's privileging of the actor over the playwright:

> Because Stanislavski, in the final analysis, failed to distinguish between art and nature, because he was more concerned with creating *natural truthfulness* of character rather than expressing with *artistic rightness* the role of a character who served a specific function in the playwright's formulation of a statement about life in theatrical terms, it was inevitable that Stanislavski would be a failure as an actor and director of Chekhov's plays.[25]

Like Holland, Corrigan's analysis is only a partial explanation of Stanislavski's misreading of Chekhov's play, and both critics are too extreme in their criticisms of the director. Stanislavski was not a totally insensitive man. What he saw in Chekhov's play was indeed there. There *is* a tragic element in his dramas and this element is to be located in the subtext that constitutes the inner life of his characters. It is perhaps one of the greatest achievements of the co-founders of the Moscow Art Theatre that they developed an acting system that allowed actors to play not just the externalised text, but also the hidden subtext. The use of this system was the essential means required for the full realisation of Chekhov's plays. As Alexandr Skaftymov rightly observed:

> K. S. Stanislavski and V. I. Nemirovich-Danchenko detected the most significant principle of the dramatic development in Chekhov's plays, the so-called 'undercurrent'. Behind the surface of quotidian episodes and details they revealed the presence of a ceaseless inner intimate-lyrical current ...[26]

Stanislavski was involved in an attempt to develop a naturalistic system of acting based on theories of human behaviour that were currently being propounded by psychologists such as Ribot and Pavlov. He was deeply interested in the hidden subjective reasons and causes for overt objective behaviour. Quite naturally, he was sensitive to this new inner reality, which in Chekhov tends to be tragic. Stanislavski's weakness, I believe, stems from the *overemphasis* he placed on this tragic subtext, which led him to encourage his actors to allow these darker elements to almost totally suppress the comic elements of the text.

A similar overemphasis on the subtext is to be found in Harvey Pitcher's critical analysis of Chekhov's plays. Pitcher recounts how Chekhov had been dissatisfied at the overly theatrical manner in which the actress played Sonya in the Moscow Arts Theatre production of *Uncle Vanya*: '[She] had at one point in Act III thrown herself at her father's feet and started to kiss his hand.' Pitcher proceeds to quote Chekhov's reaction, but his comment following Chekhov's statement reveals that Pitcher has only partially seen what the playwright was driving at:

> 'That's quite wrong,' he [Chekhov] commented, 'after all, it isn't a drama. The whole meaning, the whole drama of a person's life are contained within, not in outward manifestations ... A shot, after all, is not a drama, but an incident.' This is a helpful indication of Chekhov's general approach to playwriting, and suggests that his presentation of the characters' inner lives might be regarded as the central feature of Chekhov's plays.[27]

'The ostensible action of *The Cherry Orchard* is very simple.'[28] What the audience sees is the presentation of a story in which a group of impoverished owners of an estate have gathered together in the vain hope that they can save the property. They reject a practical plan that, while saving them financially, would involve cutting down the orchard and demolishing the old house. As the owners of the orchard do nothing to save the estate, the orchard is sold to a rich man of peasant stock. The former owners and their children leave, expressing their various hopes about their future life.

The general structure of the play is built around a pattern that Chekhov used in all of his plays after *Ivanov*. It consists of an arrival, a sojourn, and a departure. 'The principal action of *The Cherry Orchard* is not dramatised.'[29] Behind the humdrum life of the text, however, is an extremely complex story which, as Valency says:

> ... is told in snatches first by Anya, then by Lyubov Andreyevna herself. Nobody dwells on it. It is known to all the characters, and they have no desire to hear it again from anyone. It is an exposition without the slightest urgency.[30]

There are, in fact, several stories which are not dramatised but which are alluded to. Mrs Ranevsky's love affair and her attempted suicide would have made the perfect subject for a Scribean melodrama. Every character has their own individual story which, though not dramatised, is mentioned indirectly in the play, and awareness of their stories helps to make the behaviour of each character comprehensible to an audience. For instance, a director must make an audience aware that the reason that 'the eternal student', Trofimov, has not yet finished his degree and has been thrown out of the university is not because of laziness but because of his political activities.[31]

A detailed analysis of the opening scene of the play reveals just how systematic Chekhov is in his depiction of the two lives of his characters. It also reveals the clues that he has provided for actors to assist them in portraying this duality of character. *The Cherry Orchard* opens in the nursery of the main house. It is near dawn and Lopakhin is in an obvious state of excitement and expectation:

> LOPAKHIN. The train's arrived, thank God. What time is it?[32]

Lopakhin's excitement is objectively shown to the audience, but the reason for it remains a hidden part of his subjective life. We immediately learn that Lopakhin had intended to meet the train on which Mrs Ranevsky and the rest of her entourage were expected to arrive, but that he had fallen asleep. The gap between Lopakhin's subjective intention to meet the train and the objective fact of his failure to do so is thus established by Chekhov, who then gives Lopakhin the play's first 'disguised soliloquy'. Although he is ostensibly talking to the maid Dunyasha, Lopakhin is essentially musing out loud to himself, especially since the maid is so preoccupied with her own inner life that she fails to listen to him. The first 'disguised soliloquy' provides for the audience the dramatically necessary exposition. More importantly, it establishes the existence of Lopakhin's inner life, his subtext, by allowing his normally hidden private hopes and beliefs to rise briefly to the visible surface of the text's dialogue. As Magarshack says:

> ... their inner life bursts through the outer shell of their everyday appearance and overflows into a torrent of words. It is this spontaneous and almost palpable transmutation into speech of hidden thoughts and deeply buried emotions that is perhaps the most subtle expression of dramatic action in a Chekhov play.[33]

In the opening 'disguised soliloquy' of *The Cherry Orchard*, Chekhov was careful to provide a realistic motivation for Lopakhin's speech by making it seem like the natural response to his already illustrated state of excitement. Lopakhin reveals part of the reason why he has risen before dawn to meet Liuba Ranevsky. He tells how, as a child, he had been a peasant on the Ranevsky estate. Liuba had shown sympathy towards him when his father had beaten him. Lopakhin, though he has now risen to be a rich and powerful man, has never ceased to be grateful to Liuba for her kindness:

> LOPAKHIN. ... 'Don't cry, little peasant,' she said. 'You'll soon be right as rain.' [*Pause.*] Little peasant. It's true my father was a peasant, but here I am in my white waistcoat and brown boots, barging in like a bull in a china shop. The only thing is, I am rich. I have plenty of money, but when you really get down to it I'm just another country bumpkin. [*Turns the pages of his book.*] I was reading this book and couldn't make sense of it. Fell asleep over it. [*Pause.*][34]

This momentary closing of the gap between the two levels of reality, in which the subtext bubbles up into the text, provides the spectators with the information necessary for them to see another gap that will be of central importance later in the play. Objectively Lopakhin is a rich man, subjectively he is still a peasant.[35] The disjunction between his two lives is realised theatrically by creating an obvious gap between Lopakhin's elegant clothes and his gauche and clumsy movements. Lopakhin is aware of the gap between what he feels himself to be and what he is and has attempted to bridge the gap. The ignorant peasant attempts to educate himself, but fails. He can't understand the book he is reading. The gap between his aims and his achievement is emphasised by the fact that he not only fails to understand what he is reading but, having fallen asleep, also fails to meet the train.

Lopakhin now proceeds to upbraid the maid, Dunyasha:

> LOPAKHIN. You're too sensitive altogether, my girl. You dress like a lady and do your hair like one too. We can't have that. Remember your place.[36]

Lopakhin's observation is objectively correct and, as we find out later when Dunyasha reveals a little of her own inner life, she does have vague hopes of climbing socially. Her manner of dressing, her affected ladylike behaviour, epitomised by her 'fainting', her white lady's hands and her constant powdering of her nose are noticeably at variance with her actual social position. The absurdity of Dunyasha's pretensions operates as a parody of Lopakhin's situation. His style of dressing doesn't correspond with his behaviour. It is precisely his problem that he is not sure of his 'place' — peasant or rich man. Consequently, there is an ironic disparity between what Lopakhin says to Dunyasha and what he himself does. This disparity between what characters say and what they actually do helps to communicate Chekhov's dramatic world in which the characters' actions fail to live up to their aims.

## The Cherry Orchard: Complete Synthesis of Vision and Form

The most extreme example of the kind of dislocation between the subjective and objective lives of the characters is provided by Yepikhodov, the accident-prone clerk, who enters immediately after Lopakhin's admonition of Dunyasha:

*Yepikhodov comes in carrying a bunch of flowers. He wears a jacket and brightly polished high boots which make a loud squeak. Once inside the room he drops the flowers.*[37]

Yepikhodov seems, on the surface, to be a clown-like figure. His boots squeak, he drops the flowers, he breaks a billiard cue, he bumps into furniture, he finds blackbeetles in his kvass, he wakes up with an enormous spider on his chest and, to top it all, he talks in an extremely pretentious and silly manner. This walking disaster, who in some translations is given the nickname of 'Two and twenty misfortunes', cannot help appearing ludicrous to both the other characters and to an audience. Viewed from the outside, on the objective level, he is, as Magarshack describes him, 'a conceited half-wit who imagines himself a highly educated person because he possesses the bovine patience to wade through "learned" books he has not the brain to understand'.[38]

But Yepikhodov, with his pretensions to learning and his absurd manner of speaking, is not simply the one-dimensional character who appears in the text. That is merely his objective manifestation; how he appears to others. His subjective inner life is far from farcical. He is, in fact, so unhappy with himself and his maladroitness that he seriously contemplates committing suicide, and it is for this reason that he carries a gun.

The manifestations of the gap between Yepikhodov's inner and outer lives are essentially physical. His subjective self is almost totally cut off from the objective world. The yawning gap between his inner and outer selves, shown by his inability to express what he inwardly feels except through his ludicrous manner of speech and behaviour, is further underlined by what Bergson would call his comic 'inelasticity'.[39] Yepikhodov's inner self is unable to control his outer self or the world of physical objects which overpowers him. Indeed, it almost appears that the physical world is actively plotting against him. The result is that Yepikhodov's sensitive action of bringing flowers, possibly for Mrs Ranevsky, but more probably for Dunyasha, whom he loves, is undercut when he drops the flowers.

Yepikhodov's pain is hidden from other characters partly because he tries to hide it. Just as Lopakhin, in the famous non-proposal scene with Varya in Act IV, will talk about the weather to hide what he is really feeling, so Yepikhodov, apart from allowing himself a sigh that wells up from the subtext of his inner life, covers his own anguish by discussing trivialities:

> YEPIKHODOV. There are three degrees of frost this morning and the cherry trees are in full bloom. I can't say that I think much of our climate. [*Sighs.*] That I can't. It isn't exactly co-operative, our climate isn't. Then if you'll permit a further observation, Mr Lopakhin, I bought these boots the day before yesterday and, as I make so bold to assure you, they squeak like something out of this world. What could I put on them?[40]

Lopakhin, whose own inner life is occupied with his own concerns about greeting Mrs Ranevsky and telling her his plan to save the estate, pays little attention to Yepikhodov's worries. His cursory dismissal of Yepikhodov leads the clerk to reveal a tiny part of his anguished inner life. In what is in effect a miniature 'disguised soliloquy', Yepikhodov momentarily closes the gap between his inner and outer lives by bringing his own subtext into the text:

> LOPAKHIN. Leave me alone. I'm tired of you.
> YEPIKHODOV. Everyday something awful happens to me. Not that I complain. I'm used to it. Even raise a smile.[41]

Even though Lopakhin may not register the significance of Yepikhodov's remark an audience should be made aware of its significance. From this point in the play, whenever Yepikhodov smiles at the 'disasters' that occur to him, the audience should see the ludicrous behaviour that is manifested in the text and also be aware of the suffering that is being endured in the hidden subtextual inner life behind this maladroit character's smile. As Yepikhodov exits, he bumps into a chair and presumably grins as he departs.

The vain and rather stupid Dunyasha, who doesn't understand anything that Yepikhodov says to her, has only one interest in the clerk and that is that 'he's crazy about me'.[42] We learn that the besotted Yepikhodov has already proposed to her. As we see in Act II, Dunyasha's slight interest in Yepikhodov vanishes the moment that the odious social climbing servant Yasha arrives. At this early point of the play, Dunyasha has no other love interest. She says to Lopakhin, 'I do sort of like him'[43] and continues to provide important information for the audience concerning Yepikhodov. In an early example of what Magarshack called the 'messenger' element, Dunyasha informs her uninterested stage companion:

> He's a most unfortunate man, everyday something goes wrong. That's why he gets teased here. They call him 'Simple Simon'.[44]

At this point in the play, the audience has been given all the necessary information to be able to read Yepikhodov as a tragi-comic character. Without knowledge of both his subjective and objective lives, how he sees himself and how others see him, an audience would not be able to read the extraordinary scene that occurs at the beginning of Act II, which I will analyse later.

## The Cherry Orchard: Complete Synthesis of Vision and Form

Just before the arrival of Mrs Ranevsky [Liuba], the old servant, Firs, crosses the stage muttering unintelligibly. In his characterisation of Firs, Chekhov creates an extreme example of the disjunction between a character's subjective and objective lives. Firs is a man who exists almost entirely in his subjective inner world. Cut off from the world because of his deafness, he is quite literally living in the past: '*He wears old-fashioned servant's livery and a top hat.*'[45] He treats the middle-aged Gayev as though he were still a child. He lives his life as though the emancipation of the serfs had never happened. He is physically cut off not just from the subjective lives of the other characters, which is the normal situation for most of Chekhov's characters, but also cut off from their objective lives, since most of their behaviour is expressed in speech that he can't hear.

After Firs' brief traversal of the stage in Act I, Mrs Ranevsky and Gayev enter. At this point, Chekhov employs the technique of the 'tactless comment' to illustrate how unaware Liuba Ranevsky is of the inner lives of others:

> MRS. RANEVSKY. [Liuba] The nursery! My lovely room! I slept here when I was a little girl. [*Weeps.*] And now I feel like a little girl again. [*Kisses her brother and* VARYA, *and then her brother again.*] Varya hasn't changed a bit, she still looks like a nun. And I recognised Dunyasha. [*Kisses* DUNYASHA.]
> GAYEV. The train was two hours late. Pretty good, eh? What price that for efficiency?[46]

Liuba is so bound up with her subjective world that she is unaware of the subjective lives of others. Consequently, she makes two 'tactless' remarks. Her remark about Varya looking like a nun might not at first be read as tactless by an audience as it has not as yet learnt anything about the adopted daughter's inner life. It is only later that we find out that Varya is single but in love with Lopakhin, who has not yet declared his own love for her. We soon learn that Varya, possibly out of frustration at Lopakhin's failure to declare his love, has contemplated becoming a nun. To make the audience aware that Varya is not pleased with Liuba's comment, the actress playing Varya need only show signs of embarrassment at the tactless remark.

Liuba's second 'tactless comment' is immediately perceivable to an audience. She says that she has recognised Dunyasha, and by implication this suggests that she has failed to recognise Lopakhin. Having been made aware of Lopakhin's inner life in his 'disguised soliloquy', the audience is aware of how much this 'peasant', as he subjectively sees himself, desires to be recognised by Liuba, the woman he so admires and loves, and for whom he has thought out a plan to save the estate. The audience has just heard Lopakhin's last line before he goes out to welcome Liuba: 'I wonder if she'll know me, we haven't seen each other for five years'.[47] An audience must therefore be well aware of the deep disappointment Lopakhin feels subjectively at not being recognised while the maid was remembered. The actor playing Lopakhin should re-enter the stage in a manner that shows his disappointment.

Gayev's remark about the lack of efficiency of the railways is another example of creating a perceivable disparity between what a character says and what he does. Gayev is aware of others' inefficiency but is totally unaware that he is one of the most inept and inefficient persons in the play.

The opening section of the play that I have just analysed is only three pages in its printed form yet, through Chekhov's application of such dramatic devices as the 'disguised soliloquy' and the 'messenger element', the audience is supplied with enough information to construct a coherent subtext for each of the characters. Providing that directors guide their actors to create their subtextual life, then an audience will be able to perceive the systematically established gap that appears between the objectively presented text and the implied subtext. By the use of the 'disguised soliloquy' and the 'messenger element', Chekhov was able to satisfy the demands of realism and yet overcome its limitations by communicating more than is said in the dialogue. He was able to present the humdrum surface of life, while at the same time presenting fully rounded characters, each of whom, like real human beings, has already lived through past experiences which have affected the way each acts, thinks and feels at the time when the audience sees them.

It is because an audience has been provided with access to the inner life of a character such as Lopakhin that the otherwise bizarre scene in which he intrudes on Varya and Anya in Act I becomes intelligible. The two sisters have been talking about the family's shortage of money and the desperate need that they have to pay off the interest on the mortgage on the estate:

> ANYA. ... Have you paid the interest?
> VARYA. What a hope.
> ANYA. My God, how dreadful.
> VARYA. This estate is up for sale in August.
> ANYA. Oh my God!
> LOPAKHIN. [*Peeping round the corner and mooing like a cow.*] Moo-oo-oo. [*Disappears.*][48]

Lopakhin's intrusion is impossible for an actor to justify or for an audience to interpret unless it is grounded in reality. Lopakhin has probably overheard the sisters' fatalistic conversation and, given that he believes that he has a plan that will save the estate, he jokingly pokes fun at the pessimism expressed by the two young women. With some sort of realistic justification, such as the one I have suggested, the bizarre animal noise becomes playable and intelligible.

Possibly one of the most subtle uses that Chekhov makes of the disjunction he has created between the two lives of his characters in *The Cherry Orchard*

## The Cherry Orchard: Complete Synthesis of Vision and Form

relates to the 'love' relationship between Lopakhin and Varya which culminates in the 'non-proposal' scene towards the end of Act IV. Before analysing this justly famous scene it is important to examine precisely how Chekhov provides his audience with all the information necessary to read it.

The first mention of a possible marriage between Varya and Lopakhin is given in the scene between Anya and Varya that takes place immediately after Lopakhin's bizarre 'mooing' episode. The sisters quite naturally begin to talk about him:

> ANYA. ... Has he proposed, Varya? [VARYA *shakes her head.*] But he does love you. Why can't you get it all settled? What are you both waiting for?
> VARYA. I don't think anything will come of it. He's so busy he can't be bothered with me, he doesn't even notice me. Wretched man, I'm fed up with the sight of him. Everyone's talking about our wedding and congratulating us, when there's nothing in it at all actually and the whole thing's so vague. [*In a different tone of voice.*] You've got a brooch that looks like a bee or something.
> ANYA. [*Sadly.*] Yes mother bought it.[49]

The audience is now apprised of the fact that there is general consensus among the other characters that Lopakhin and Varya will marry each other. What is also of interest is that Anya believes that Lopakhin does love Varya. Clearly, with everyone expecting this marriage and yet with Lopakhin, for some reason or other, not proposing, Varya is placed in a situation that is painful for her. Not surprisingly, she changes the subject and Anya picks up the hint and goes on to change the subject herself.

One of the clichéd ways of solving problems in nineteenth-century well-made plays was to marry off the indigent hero or heroine to a wealthy partner. In this case the *scène-à-faire* would be the proposal scene which would bring about the reversal in the fortune of the hero or heroine, and this would then lead to the happy ending. Chekhov keeps teasing his audience with this possible wish-fulfilment ending. The very real possibility that Varya will prove to be the saviour of the estate as a result of marrying Lopakhin is avoided by her. Instead, her 'plan' involves a dream in which Anya achieves that desired end:

> VARYA. [*Standing near the door.*] You know darling, while I'm doing my jobs round the house I spend the whole day dreaming. I imagine marrying you off to a rich man. That would set my mind at rest and I'd go off to a convent, then on to Kiev and Moscow, wandering from one holy place to another. I'd just wander on and on. What bliss![50]

The spectators have just heard that Varya has been vainly waiting for a proposal from Lopakhin. More significantly, they have *not* heard her suggest that she would refuse him if he finally did propose to her. Consequently, they are able to read Varya's description of the prospect of being a nun as 'bliss' as a cover for her true feelings. Being a nun is certainly not Varya's first choice of occupation. Even in the abortive proposal scene near the end of the play — a scene which acts as a parody of all such clichéd scenes in the drama of the time — Varya places herself in a situation where she hopes that Lopakhin will finally get round to asking for her hand.

The Varya–Lopakhin marriage is again alluded to at the end of Act I. Lopakhin has outstayed his welcome and, just before he exits, tries once too often to get Gayev and Liuba to think about his unpalatable plan to save the estate:

> LOPAKHIN. ... [*To* MRS. RANEVSKY.] Think it over about those cottages, let me know if you decide to go ahead and I'll get you a loan of fifty thousand or so. Give it some serious thought.
> VARYA. [*Angrily.*] Oh do for heaven's sake *go*.
> LOPAKHIN. All right I'm going. [*Goes.*]
> GAYEV. Ill-bred lout. Oh I beg your pardon, Varya's going to marry him. He's Varya's 'young man'.
> VARYA. Don't overdo it, Uncle.
> MRS. RANEVSKY. But I should be only too pleased, Varya. He's such a nice man.[51]

Gayev is always tactlessly talking out of place. Later in Act I, he describes his sister as 'a loose woman'[52] in earshot of Liuba's daughter, Anya. Here, he tactlessly makes insulting comments about Lopakhin in front of his possible future wife. As usual, the rest of his family try to get him to keep quiet. Importantly, the audience learns that Liuba Ranevsky, if not Gayev, approves of the match between Varya and Lopakhin. As we shall see, Liuba's approval is extremely important to Lopakhin.

The third major discussion of the Varya–Lopakhin marriage takes place in the middle of Act II. Liuba has just accused Lopakhin and his ilk of leading 'drab lives' and of talking a lot of 'rubbish'. He agrees with her but, after a pause, launches into a speech that recapitulates his first 'disguised soliloquy' in Act I, in which he informed us that subjectively, despite his wealth, he still feels himself to be a peasant:

> LOPAKHIN. Quite right. To be honest, the life we lead is preposterous. [*Pause.*] My father was a peasant, an idiot who understood nothing, taught me nothing, and just beat me when he was drunk, with a stick too. As a matter of fact I'm just as big a numbskull and idiot myself. I never learned anything and my handwriting's awful. A pig could write as well as I do, I'm ashamed to let anyone see it.
> MRS. RANEVSKY. You ought to get married my friend.
> LOPAKHIN. Yes, that's true enough.
> MRS. RANEVSKY. Why not marry Varya? She's a very nice girl.

## The Cherry Orchard: Complete Synthesis of Vision and Form

> LOPAKHIN. True.
> MRS. RANEVSKY. She's a nice simple creature. She works all day long, and the great thing is she loves you. And you've been fond of her for some time too.
> LOPAKHIN. All right, I've nothing against it. She is a very nice girl. [*Pause.*][53]

One 'messenger', Anya, has told Varya that Lopakhin loves her. Now another 'messenger', Liuba, has told Lopakhin that Varya loves him and reminds him that he seems 'fond' of her. Lopakhin works from morn till night and Varya is likewise a worker. While neither party seems to be wildly in love with the other in any romantic sense, the match is nevertheless extremely suitable. Varya has not voiced any abhorrence at the idea and Lopakhin has nothing against it. The ground for their proposal scene would seem to have been prepared. Certainly, Liuba thinks that the preparations are complete since, later in Act II, after she has been flustered by the begging Passer-By and has given him a gold coin that the family can ill afford to lose, she covers her own embarrassment at the incident by borrowing more money from Lopakhin, and then tactlessly announcing the Varya–Lopakhin engagement in front of the stunned couple. Their ensuing embarrassment again fails to result in any overt proposal:

> VARYA. ... Oh mother, we've no food in the house for the servants and you gave him all that money.
> MRS. RANEVSKY. What's to be done with me? I'm so silly. I'll give you all I have when we get home. Yermolay, lend me some more money.
> LOPAKHIN. At your service.
> MRS. RANEVSKY. Come on, everybody, it's time to go in. Varya, we've just fixed you up with a husband. Congratulations.
> VARYA. [*Through tears.*] Don't make jokes about it, Mother.
> LOPAKHIN. Amelia, get thee to a nunnery.[54]

Varya, who is often likened to a nun, is placed in an extremely awkward position by her mother's remark. She sees her mother 'sponge' yet more money from Lopakhin. For her to happily go along with Liuba's announcement could only make it appear that she is also after Lopakhin's money. Lopakhin, who had shown his anger at the Passer-By for frightening Varya, is clearly out of his depth in the face of Varya's distress at her mother's tactless announcement about their marriage. In his embarrassment, he could hardly have chosen a less felicitous quotation than the garbled line from *Hamlet* about a 'nunnery'.

The next reference to the Varya–Lopakhin marriage occurs at the beginning of Act III where Trofimov, who objects to Varya keeping such a close watch on Anya and himself and who claims to be 'above love', pokes fun at the poor young woman who reacts with anger:

> TROFIMOV. [*Teasing her.*] Mrs Lopakhin! Mrs. Lopakhin!
> VARYA. [*Angrily.*] Seedy-looking gent![55]

The antagonism between the two continues later in the Act and leads to a revealing interchange between Liuba and Varya that explains much to an audience about why Varya finds her situation in relation to her possible engagement to Lopakhin so difficult to deal with. It provides information that will be vital for helping an audience to read the Act IV non-proposal scene:

> TROFIMOV. [*Teasing* VARYA.] Mrs. Lopakhin!
> VARYA. [*Angrily.*] Hark at the eternal student. He's already been sent down from the university twice.
> MRS. RANEVSKY. Why are you so cross Varya? If he teases you about Lopakhin, what of it? If you want to marry Lopakhin, do — he's a nice attractive man. And if you don't want to, don't. Nobody's forcing you darling.
> VARYA. I'm perfectly serious about this, Mother, I must tell you quite plainly. He is a nice man and I do like him.
> MRS. RANEVSKY. Well, marry him then. What are you waiting for? That's what I can't see.
> VARYA. I can't very well propose to him myself, can I? Everyone's been talking to me about him for the last two years. Everyone goes on and on about it, but he either says nothing or just makes jokes. And I see his point. He's making money, he has a business to look after and he hasn't time for me. If I had just a bit of money — even a hundred roubles would do — I'd drop everything and go away. I'd go to a convent.
> TROFIMOV. What bliss![56]

Trofimov's cruelly ironic response, which echoes Varya's earlier comment about entering a convent, is nevertheless appropriate, since the audience now hears from her own mouth how seriously she wishes to marry Lopakhin, rather than become a nun. After crying, Varya leaves the stage to reprimand Yepikhodov who has now broken a billiard cue. The antagonism between Varya and Yepikhodov and the remarkable difference between them in terms of their respective efficiency will also prove important when the audience comes to interpret the non-proposal scene. It is this antagonism that leads to a brief moment of real interaction between Varya and Lopakhin in Act III. It is one of the few moments in the play when they are on-stage alone together. Having had an argument with Yepikhodov, Varya loses her temper and, thinking that he is coming back into the room, she lashes out with a stick as Lopakhin, rather than the clerk, enters. He has just returned from the auction at which he bought the cherry orchard:

> VARYA. ... Oh, so you're coming back, are you? ... Then take that. [*Lashes out just as* LOPAKHIN *comes in.*]
> LOPAKHIN. Thank you very much.
> VARYA. [*Angrily and derisively.*] I'm extremely sorry.
> LOPAKHIN. Not at all. Thank you for such a warm welcome.

## The Cherry Orchard: Complete Synthesis of Vision and Form

> VARYA. Oh don't mention it. [*Moving away, then looks round and asks gently.*] I didn't hurt you did I?
> LOPAKHIN. No, it's all right. I'm going to have a whacking bruise though.[57]

The defensive cover of joking is briefly dropped when Varya's tone becomes 'gentle', and an audience might well hope that this might at last be the scene where they can talk to each other and perhaps even become engaged. However, Chekhov thwarts the audience's expectations once again by bringing on Pishchik to interrupt the would-be lovers.

When Lopakhin announces to everyone that he has bought the cherry orchard, Mrs Ranevsky is '*overwhelmed*' and nearly faints. Varya's response appears to involve the total rejection of Lopakhin, for she '*takes the keys from her belt, throws them on the floor in the middle of the drawing room and goes out*'.[58] Certainly, Lopakhin seems to think that Varya's behaviour marks the end of their relationship. Towards the end of his speech in which he recounts what happened at the auction and muses amazedly at his good fortune, he refers to Varya's melodramatic exit:

> LOPAKHIN. ... [*Picks up the keys, smiling fondly.*] She threw away the keys to show she's not in charge here now. [*Jingles the keys.*] Oh well, never mind.[59]

Following this apparent rejection by the aristocratically brought up Varya, Lopakhin almost aggressively adopts the pose of the crass new owner as he orders the band to play. He tells those present that they can 'just watch Yermolay Lopakhin get his axe into the cherry orchard, watch the trees come crashing down'.[60] Almost immediately, the more sensitive side of this man who cares for the Ranevsky family, and especially for Liuba, manifests itself when he tries to comfort the woman he so admires and loves:

> LOPAKHIN. [*Reproachfully.*] But why, oh why, didn't you listen to me before? My poor friend, you can't put the clock back now. [*With tears.*] Oh, if all this could be over quickly, if our miserable, mixed-up lives could somehow hurry up and change.[61]

Pishchik, however, tells Lopakhin to 'leave her alone' and takes Liuba into another room. This second rejection by the members of the class that he has tried to help leads Lopakhin to revert to the coarse peasant self that the gentry imply is his true nature. He becomes the vulgar 'ill-bred lout' that Gayev had said that he was and that he secretly feared was true. There is both sadness and bitterness mixed in with the rich peasant's joy at owning the estate. Chekhov alerts us to this by supplying the actor with the stage instruction '*ironically*':

> LOPAKHIN. Hey, what's up? You in the band, let's have you playing properly. Let's have everything the way *I* want it. [*Ironically.*] Here comes the new squire,

the owner of the cherry orchard! [*Accidentally jogs a small table, nearly knocking over the candelabra.*] I can pay for everything.[62]

It seems as if Lopakhin's bitterness is partly a result of his own failure to succeed in his original plan to save the cherry orchard for the Ranevsky family and is surely, in part, due to the loss of any hopes he might have had of marrying Varya. His coarse behaviour is a response to their rejection of him. As a character who has failed to squeeze the last drop of 'slave' out of himself, he hardly seems to have expected anything better. However, Lopakhin is to get one more chance in Act IV to propose marriage to Varya.

With about five minutes to spare before the Ranevsky family have to leave the estate, Mrs Ranevsky speaks to Lopakhin about her two remaining worries. Her first worry concerns Firs, but she is assured, wrongly as it turns out, that Firs has been sent to hospital. Liuba now tries for the last time to get Lopakhin to propose to Varya. Her first move is to try and make him take pity on her. When he fails to respond in the '*Pause*', Liuba is forced to be more direct with him:

> MRS. RANEVSKY. My other worry's Varya. She's used to getting up early and working, and now she has nothing to do she's like a fish out of water. She's grown thin and pale and she's always crying, poor thing. [*Pause.*] As you know very well, Yermolay, I had hoped — to see her married to you, and it did look as if that was how things were shaping.[63]

Having begun her last-ditch attempt to get Lopakhin to propose to Varya, Liuba does everything she can to enable the couple to be alone together. Presumably she gives instructions to Anya to prepare Varya for the big event and begins to clear the room of other people. Liuba's speech and actions continue as follows:

> [*Whispers to ANYA, who nods to CHARLOTTE. They both go out.*] She loves you, you're fond of her, and I haven't the faintest idea why you seem to avoid each other. It makes no sense to me.
> LOPAKHIN. It makes no sense to me either, to be quite honest. It's a curious business, isn't it? If it's not too late I don't mind going ahead even now. Let's get it over and done with. I don't feel I'll ever propose to her without you here.[64]

The audience must feel at this point that, at last, they are going to get the long awaited proposal scene that will, at the last minute, solve everyone's problems. Lopakhin will get his bride, Varya will get her man and the family will now have access to money through Varya's marriage so that all the characters can live happily ever after. But this is Chekhov, not Scribe or Sardou. The hint that all may not go well in the forthcoming proposal scene is given by Lopakhin when he says that, without Liuba being present, he doesn't think he will be able

## The Cherry Orchard: Complete Synthesis of Vision and Form

to propose. The new owner of the cherry orchard still sees himself as a peasant and Varya as one of the gentry. He thus feels that it is inappropriate for him to step above his class to ask her to marry him. Early in the play, Lopakhin had said to Dunyasha: 'Remember your place'. Now, unlike Dunyasha or the other servant, Yasha, Lopakhin finds it almost impossible see his new 'place' in the changing social order. He needs Liuba, the woman whom he has admired, respected and even loved since childhood, to *actively* support him in his proposal.

The scene continues with rising excitement on the part of both Liuba and Lopakhin and the only other remaining person, Yasha, is ordered out of the room. The one sour note that is sounded occurs when it is discovered that the valet has drunk the champagne that could have been used to celebrate the engagement:

> MRS. RANEVSKY. [Liuba] That's a very good idea. Why, it won't take more than a minute. I'll call her at once.
> LOPAKHIN. There's even champagne laid on. [*Looks at the glasses.*] They're empty, someone must have drunk it. [*Yasha coughs.*] That's what I call really knocking it back.
> MRS. RANEVSKY. [*Excitedly.*] I'm so glad. We'll go out. Yasha, *allez!* I'll call her. [*Through the door.*] Varya, leave what you're doing and come here a moment. Come on! [*Goes out with* YASHA.][65]

Liuba, having unsuccessfully attempted to call Varya into the room, makes the fatal mistake of leaving the room to get her. This leaves Lopakhin on his own without the support that he needs in order to have the nerve to ask Varya to marry him. The audience sees the nervous Lopakhin waiting for Varya and Liuba to return. The audience, like Lopakhin, hears the off-stage encouragement of Varya to go into the room to be proposed to:

> LOPAKHIN. [*With a glance at his watch.*] Yes. [*Pause.*]
> [*Suppressed laughter and whispering are heard from behind the door. After some time* VARYA *comes in.*][66]

Finally, Varya appears, but she is without Liuba, and the non-proposal scene takes place. Both parties know why they are in the room alone. Both of them wish to get engaged, yet both are incapable of asking the other. Lopakhin needs the assistance of Liuba or at least the help of Varya herself. Varya feels that she cannot ask Lopakhin to marry her. She is, after all, the financially dependent one. Her gentrified upbringing and her perception of her gender role, as we discovered earlier, precludes her from popping the question, or even overtly encouraging Lopakhin to do so. She must be courted. As Magarshack accurately notes:

> Face to face with Varya he [Lopakhin] is so conscious of her social superiority that he cannot bring himself to propose to her, while Varya … is quite incapable

Interpreting Chekhov

of disregarding the conventions which demand that the lady has to wait for the gentleman to propose to her.[67]

In this play that is centrally concerned with the idea of change, Chekhov depicts Varya and Lopakhin as two people whose objective outer lives have changed radically. He has risen and she has fallen, economically and socially. However, because Chekhov recognises that change is painful, he shows that Varya and Lopakhin are unchanged in their subjective selves. The 'tragic' serious subtext underlies the 'comic' triviality of the text.[68] Chekhov has provided the means to access the text and subtext and perceive the disjunction between the two. Providing that the director encourages the actors to play the two elements, an audience should experience the full complexity of the Varya/Lopakhin relationship.

The 'non-proposal' scene that follows Varya and Lopakhin being left alone on stage, incorporates behaviour that is similar to that required in the acting exercise called 'passing the ball'. This exercise involves the actors passing back and forth to each other the responsibility for progressing the scene. The audience should clearly sense the movement of responsibility. This scene is like a tennis match in terms of 'passing the ball':

VARYA. [*Spends a long time examining the luggage.*] That's funny, I can't find it anywhere.
(Subtext: 'Well we are alone. I'm waiting for you to make your proposal.' Passes ball.)

LOPAKHIN. What are you looking for?
(Subtext: 'Oh no, please. You start.' Passes ball.)

VARYA. I packed it myself and I still can't remember. [*Pause.*]
(Subtext: 'No, you are the one who has to ask.' [*Pause.*] 'Well, go on. Say it.' Passes ball.)

LOPAKHIN. Where are you going now, Varya?
(Subtext: 'Where will you go if you don't stay here with me?' Passes ball.)

VARYA. Me? To the Ragulins'. I've arranged to look after their place, a sort of housekeeper's job.
(Subtext: 'Well, unless I stay here and continue to run this estate, I will be forced into the demeaning position of being a lowly housekeeper for the Ragulins. It's up to you.' Passes ball.)

LOPAKHIN. That's in Yashnevo, isn't it? It must be fifty odd miles from here. [*Pause.*] So life has ended in this house.
(Subtext: 'Yashnevo? Surely you don't want to be that far away from here, and from me? [*Pause.*] Well from your lack of response, I assume that you don't care. You realise that life in this house is over unless you stay here?' Passes ball.)

## The Cherry Orchard: Complete Synthesis of Vision and Form

VARYA. [*Examining the luggage.*] Oh, where can it be? Or could I have put it in the trunk? Yes, life has gone out of this house. And it will never come back.
(Subtext: 'I can't stay here forever. Are you going to say anything? Yes life in this house is over unless you choose to let it continue by doing something like living here with me.' Passes ball.)

LOPAKHIN. Well, I'm off to Kharkov. By the next train. I have plenty to do there. And I'm leaving Yepikhodov in charge here, I've taken him on.
(Subtext: 'Please hurry up and make some effort to show me whether you want to marry me or not. There's not much time. Since you don't seem to want to stay, I've had to replace you. I've chosen Yepikhodov. How do you feel about that?' Passes ball.)

The choice of Yepikhodov, the most inept, accident-prone person in the play, certainly seems a strange choice of character to replace the highly efficient Varya. What Lopakhin seems to be trying to do here is to goad Varya into objecting to Yepikhodov's appointment. He knows how much she dislikes 'Simple Simon'. All he needs is to get Varya to respond by saying something like, 'How on earth can you think of employing that fool?', and he will be able to respond with something like, 'Well who else is there who can do the job properly?' This in turn is likely elicit the response, 'I can'. Once Lopakhin can engineer some such overt response from Varya to the effect that she wishes to stay, the possibility of his proposing to her becomes much more likely. What actually happens in Chekhov's non-proposal scene is that Varya is too proud to object overtly to Lopakhin's choice of Yepikhodov as manager for the estate:

VARYA. Oh, have you?
(Subtext: 'Surely not? Oh well. If that's what you really want, it's up to you.' Passes ball.)

This seems to me to be the moment when an audience should be made to feel that Varya's inner life expressed in the subtext is going to bubble up into the text and so establish the sort of contact between her and Lopakhin that will lead to the desired proposal. Lopakhin's ploy nearly succeeds but Varya's proud self-control triumphs over her desires. Seeing that there is no response from Varya, even after he has attempted to goad her to speak, Lopakhin gives up any hope of marrying Varya. He resorts to talking about the weather until he is rescued from this embarrassing scene by being called elsewhere:

LOPAKHIN. This time last year we already had snow, remember? But now it's calm and sunny. It's a bit cold though. Three degrees of frost, I should say.
(Subtext: 'I see, she doesn't want me. I've got to get away from here somehow. I've no idea what to say to her now. I feel a complete fool standing here.')

VARYA. I haven't looked. [*Pause.*] Besides, our thermometer's broken. [*Pause.*]

(Subtext: 'I see, he doesn't want me. [*Pause.*] I feel totally wretched and don't know what to do or say.')

The painful scene is brought to an end by an external means:

[*A voice at the outer door:* 'Mr. Lopakhin!']
LOPAKHIN. [*As if he had long been expecting this summons.*] I'm just coming. [*Goes out quickly.*]
(Subtext: 'Thank God! I can go.')
[VARYA *sits on the floor with her head in a bundle of clothes, quietly sobbing. The door opens and* MRS. RANEVSKY *comes in cautiously.*]
MRS. RANEVSKY. Well? [*Pause.*] We'd better go.[69]

Varya allows her anguish to surface from her inner life only *after* Lopakhin has left and Liuba enters only when it is too late to help the couple to achieve what they both desire. The gap between aim and achievement could hardly be more poignantly expressed. The wonder is that Chekhov was able to find the way to allow an audience to experience the characters' dual lives through the interaction of the grotesque comic text and the pathetic tragic subtext. Neither Varya nor Lopakhin can express objectively their subjective feelings because it is impossible for them to escape from their subjective view and enter the objective world where they could communicate with each other.

'Life as it should be' is implied by Chekhov throughout the play. Though little is actually achieved by the characters, there is a prevailing sense of the possibility of a better future. This optimistic vision is carried mainly by the younger generation, particularly Anya and Trofimov. Audiences may experience the sadness associated with the fate of Gayev and Mrs Ranevsky but this is balanced by a sense of hope for the future. If the characters cannot themselves achieve a better future, the audience can. Trofimov may be laughed at for his comic rigidity, especially his absurd priggishness about 'love'. Chekhov uses the conventions of nineteenth-century melodrama to poke fun at the student who claims to be 'above love'. In Act III, his extreme reaction to Liuba's statement, 'Fancy being your age and not having a mistress!', is as absurdly histrionic as Arcadina's ham-acting in *The Seagull*. Chekhov gives Trofimov a melodramatic exit, which is itself humorous, but then proceeds to move into the realm of farce by having him return to make a second exit, which is then followed by his falling down a flight of stairs. This really is a 'banana skin' farcical *lazzi*. Trofimov's ideas, however, like those of Vershinin in *Three Sisters*, should not be discounted by an audience. As Robert Corrigan has noted:

> Throughout his life Chekhov constantly made the statement that 'the truth about life is ironical' and since he was showing 'life as it is' almost all of his dramatic devices were ironic. The irony is best seen in the disparity between what his characters say and what they do. Thus we find in all of his plays

characters making brilliantly incisive remarks about themselves and other people, and yet they are said in such a way and are put in such an incongruous and ludicrous context that we do not stop to take them seriously when we hear them. The force of these statements is driven home cumulatively; we are suddenly aware as the play ends that in their actions the characters have done just the opposite to what in their dialogue they have expounded they should do.[70]

One of the clearest examples of this ironic technique in *The Cherry Orchard* occurs when Trofimov expounds on what is wrong in the Russia of his day. He has just criticised the human race for being 'crude, stupid and profoundly miserable' and claims that: 'It's time we stopped admiring ourselves. The only thing to do is work'.[71] This last statement is truly ironic in that Trofimov seems to do very little work. The irony deepens when the mature-aged student launches into what in Hingley's translation runs to twenty-four lines. This 'tirade' is in fact the longest speech of the play. This searing indictment of the laziness of the intelligentsia in Russia concludes with the deadly earnest and rather humourless Trofimov making one final attack on this group within society:

TROFIMOV. ... I loathe all these earnest faces. They scare me, and so do earnest conversations. Why can't we keep quiet for a change?
LOPAKHIN. I'm always up by five o'clock, you know. I work from morning till night ...[72]

The sight and sound of the earnest and prolix intellectual, Trofimov, railing against everything that he himself embodies is certainly comic and undercuts the character. Lopakhin is quick to point out how, in contrast to people like Trofimov, he actually does work. Even though Trofimov is undercut by the fact that he does not practise what he preaches, his arguments make good sense. Commenting on this speech, Raymond Williams concedes that Trofimov 'does practically no work', but astutely argues: 'This does not mean that he is wrong, or that what he says can be disregarded'.[73]

We should remember that this speech of Trofimov's was one that the censors insisted on cutting because the material was felt to be too inflammatory in its criticism of the intelligentsia's lack of action in assisting in the improvement of the appalling social conditions that Chekhov depicts as prevailing at the time. Once we concentrate less on the singer and more on the song, we can recognise the truth and importance of the content of Trofimov's speech:

TROFIMOV. ... Here in Russia very few people do work at present. The kind of Russian intellectuals I know ... aren't looking for anything. They don't do anything. They still don't know the meaning of hard work ... They talk of nothing but weighty issues and they discuss abstract problems, while all the time everyone knows the workers are abominably fed and sleep without proper bedding, thirty or forty to a room — with bedbugs everywhere, to say nothing of the stench, the damp, the moral degradation.[74]

Trofimov's 'tirade' expresses opinions about the intelligentsia that are remarkably similar to comments Chekhov made several years earlier. He wrote in a letter to I. I. Orlov about the failure of the intelligentsia to improve the quality of life in Russia:

> I have no faith in our intelligentsia, hypocritical, false, hysterical, ill-bred, lazy; I have no faith in them even when they suffer and complain, for their oppressors come from the same womb as they ... whatever comes to pass, science keeps advancing, social-consciousness increases ... And all this is being done ... despite the intelligentsia *en masse* ...[75]

Knowing that Chekhov had this mistrust of the intelligentsia, it is tempting for a director to see Trofimov as Chekhov's mouthpiece. According to Graham Greene, Tyrone Guthrie even had the eternal student 'interestingly made-up to look like Chekhov himself'.[76] The point is, however, that Trofimov is himself a member of the intelligentsia and is the object of Chekhov's irony. Like the good advice given by Polonius in *Hamlet*, Trofimov's good sense is not to be taken on its face value. While a reactionary production of *The Cherry Orchard* is likely to present Trofimov as a comically inadequate and pretentious student, the more radical productions, such as that of Trevor Griffiths, present the character as a serious Bolshevik visionary. In both cases, the dualistic nature of Chekhov's characterisation is obscured and the disjunctive gap between 'what is believed and what is lived' closed.[77] In contrast, Chekhov's Trofimov is both fool and seer.

Perhaps the most extreme example of Chekhov's depiction of the two lives that his characters lead is to be found at the opening of Act II. Chekhov was aware that this act was different from anything else he had written and was worried that it might not be 'theatrical' enough. He wrote to his wife, Olga Knipper:

> My play is moving, and I'm finishing copying Act Three today and starting Act Four. Act Three is the least boring, but the second act is as boring and as monotonous as a cobweb.[78]

It opens with a group of four characters employed by the Ranevsky family lounging around in the open air not long before sunset. The fates of Charlotte, Yasha, Dunyasha and Yepikhodov will all be determined by what happens to the cherry orchard. Anya's governess, Charlotte, is the most vulnerable of this quartet as her charge has now grown up,[79] and it is she who speaks first, in a 'disguised soliloquy'. We discover that she acquired her performing skills from her parents, who died when she was young, and that she had been adopted by a 'German lady'. She recounts how she feels herself to be alone and an outsider. At the moment when her speech becomes most poignant and moving Chekhov undercuts her by introducing a totally comic effect:

> CHARLOTTE. [*Meditatively.*] ... Well, I grew up and became a governess. But where I come from and who I am I've no idea. Who my parents were I don't know either, very likely they weren't even married. [*Takes a cucumber out of her pocket and starts eating it.*] I don't know anything. [*Pause.*] I'm longing for someone to talk to, but there isn't anyone. I'm alone in the world.[80]

Eating a cucumber at the most 'tragic' moment in her speech is a perfect example of what Bergson is talking about when he outlines as a general law of comedy that: 'Any incident is comic that calls our attention to the physical in a person when it is the moral side that is concerned'.[81]

As the context shows us, the 'someone' she is longing to talk to at this moment is Yepikhodov. The clerk, however, fails to register Charlotte's subtextual appeal because he is longing to talk to Dunyasha. He serenades his loved one. It is through the words of the song that he is able to express his subtextually felt love for the maid. She is not interested in his attentions at this moment, as she is more interested in making herself attractive to Yasha, whom she is longing to talk to. She brusquely dismisses the serenade. Meanwhile, Yasha is not really interested in Dunyasha's attentions, as he seems more interested in admiring himself. Each of the characters, except Yasha, hurts the one who is asking for contact, and each lays themselves open to being hurt by the one they wish to contact. Again, the interplay between the 'physical' and the 'moral' is emphasised by Chekhov. Where Charlotte had her cucumber, Yepikhodov has his guitar, Dunyasha has her hand-mirror and Yasha has his cigar:

> YEPIKHODOV. [*Playing the guitar and singing.*]
> 'I'm tired of the world and its bustle,
> I'm tired of my friends and my foes.'
> How nice to play the mandolin.
> DUNYASHA. That isn't a mandolin, it's a guitar. [*Looks at herself in a hand-mirror, and powders her face.*]
> YEPIKHODOV. To a man crazed with love it's a mandolin. [*Sings softly.*]
> 'If only my heart were delighted
> By the warmth of an ardour requited.'
> [YASHA *joins in.*]
> CHARLOTTE. The awful way these people sing — ugh! Like a lot of hyenas.[82]

As part of his attempt to impress Dunyasha, Yepikhodov pulls out a revolver that he says he thinks of using to end his woes. Eventually, Yepikhodov's total rejection of her leads Charlotte to leave, but not before, with heavy irony, she ridicules the clerk's amorous pretensions:

> DUNYASHA. [*To* YASHA.] You're ever so lucky to have been abroad, though.
> YASHA. Yes, of course. My sentiments precisely. [*Yawns, then lights a cigar.*]
> YEPIKHODOV. It stands to reason. Abroad everything's pretty comprehensive like. Has been for ages.
> YASHA. Oh, definitely.
> YEPIKHODOV. I'm a cultured sort of person and read all kinds of remarkable books, but I just can't get a line on what it is I'm really after. Shall I go on living or shall I shoot myself, I mean? But anyway, I always carry a revolver. Here it is. [*Shows them his revolver.*]
> CHARLOTTE. Well, that's that. I'm off. [*Slings the gun over her shoulder.*] Yepikhodov, you're a very clever man and a most alarming one. Women must be quite crazy about you. Brrr! [*Moves off.*] These clever men are all so stupid, I've no one to talk to. I'm lonely, oh so lonely. I'm on my own in the world, and — and who I am and what I'm for is a mystery. [*Goes out slowly.*][83]

Chekhov had juxtaposed the existential and tragic with the trivial and comic in *The Seagull* when he had Treplev shoot himself while his mother and friends were playing Lotto. In *The Cherry Orchard,* the tragic/comic juxtaposition was created without Chekhov feeling the necessity to employ any overtly theatrical device such as suicide. Chekhov's aim had always been to write a truly realistic play in which characters involve themselves with life's trivialities, while 'all the time their happiness is being established or their lives are broken up'.[84] As we saw earlier, Lopakhin and Varya quite literally 'talk of the weather'[85] while just such a personal disaster is happening to them. In the case of Yepikhodov, Chekhov finally achieved his aim. He knew that 'in real life, people do not shoot themselves, or hang themselves, or make confessions of love every minute'.[86] Chekhov's Yepikhodov is a potential suicide rather than an actual one.[87] Now, in *The Cherry Orchard,* through making it possible for an audience to read the two lives of his characters, Chekhov was able to be 'dramatically effective' without resorting to the theatrics of melodrama.

As soon as Charlotte leaves, the maladroit Yepikhodov continues his attempt to make himself 'interesting'. In his verbose manner, he relates the disasters that are always happening to him. He then pauses in the hope that Dunyasha will make some comment. She doesn't respond, and so he continues his would-be courtship of the girl with what must be one of the most inappropriate and, consequently, pathetically funny small-talk lines that one could make to someone as feather-brained as Dunyasha. His attempt to move her interest away from Yasha is the following:

> YEPIKHODOV. ... [*Pause.*] Have you ever read Buckle's *History of Civilisation*?[88]

Not surprisingly, the poor girl makes no response and so, after another pause, Yepikhodov screws up his courage and asks her directly to speak to him alone.

## The Cherry Orchard: Complete Synthesis of Vision and Form

The seemingly trivial scene, like that in which Irina Arcardin plays Lotto in *The Seagull*, takes place while momentous events are occurring, unbeknown to most of the characters on stage. A chance remark by Dunyasha averts a potential tragedy:

> YEPIKHODOV. ... [*Pause.*] Might I trouble you for the favour of a few words, Miss Dunyasha?
> DUNYASHA. All right, carry on.
> YEPIKHODOV. I would prefer it to be in private. [*Sighs.*]
> DUNYASHA. [*Embarrassed.*] Very well then, only first go and get me my cape. You'll find it in the cupboard or somewhere. It's rather damp out here.
> YEPIKHODOV. Oh certainly, I'm sure. At your service. Now I know what to do with my revolver. [*Takes the guitar and goes out strumming it.*]
> YASHA. Simple Simon! The man's a fool, between you and me. [*Yawns.*]
> DUNYASHA. Heavens, I hope he doesn't go and shoot himself. [*Pause.*][89]

An audience needs to be made aware that, had Dunyasha simply told Yepikhodov to leave her alone, the clerk would indeed have known what to do with his gun. He would, like Treplev, have shot himself. Instead, Dunyasha, while trying to get rid of him, asks her admirer to do her a little favour, and the happy clerk puts his gun away and picks up his guitar. Dunyasha, for one fleeting moment, contemplates the possibility of Yepikhodov committing suicide but, after a pause, she forgets the clerk and concentrates all of her attention on making herself agreeable to Yasha.

Throughout the play, trivial events mask significant happenings. For example, whenever anything occurs that Gayev finds hard to deal with, he either pops a sweet into his mouth or practises imaginary billiard shots. In Act III, a dance takes place while off-stage the estate is being sold. At the end of the play, a misunderstanding leads to the sick Firs being left behind to die in a locked house.

It is in Act II that Lopakhin makes the most concerted attempt to get Liuba Ranevsky to face the reality of her financial situation and abandon such fantasy plans as saving the estate by getting enough money from an aunt, or by marrying Anya to a rich man. Instead, he proposes the financially responsible, but emotionally unacceptable, idea of replacing the orchard and the old house with summer cottages that could be let profitably.

In a well-made play, Act II would set into motion activities that would either succeed or fail in the final act of the play. In *The Cherry Orchard,* however, the only viable plan to save the orchard is quashed. The reason again results from the inability of characters to change as society changes. Just as Varya and Lopakhin do not become engaged because they cannot adjust their subjective views of themselves and others to the changed circumstances in which they are now placed, so Gayev and Liuba still think and behave like rich landed gentry rather than bankrupts. Their response to Lopakhin's economically sensible plan is to avoid the question of economics altogether and to concentrate on outmoded concepts of tradition and class. Facing the fact that the cherry orchard does not produce a saleable crop every year, Gayev had responded in Act I with the economically useless statement that 'This orchard is even mentioned in the Encyclopedia'.[90] Now, in Act II, when time to do something about their plight is really running out, both Gayev and Liuba respond to Lopakhin's irrefutable argument that the estate will be lost unless they follow his plan with statements that show that they have simply refused to adjust to their changed situation:

> MRS. RANEVSKY.[Liuba] Cottages, summer visitors. Forgive me, but all that's so frightfully vulgar.
> GAYEV. I entirely agree.
> LOPAKHIN. I'm going to burst into tears or scream or faint. This is too much. I've had about all I can stand![91]

What the audience knows from this is that the estate will inevitably be lost and that no activities to save it will take place. One of Chekhov's innovations in this last play was to place the *anagnorisis* or recognition scene in Act II rather than, as was the usual dramatic method, near the end of the play. The whole of Act II is a series of recognitions that there is 'nothing to be done' about saving the cherry orchard because 'no one is doing anything' to save it. Liuba's complete disregard for her dire financial situation is captured perfectly by the fact that, though she knows that Varya is scrimping and scraping in order to pay for food to feed the servants, she goes around 'squandering money'. She spills what little money she has left on the ground and later gives a gold coin to the Passer-By. Each of the characters who comes up with their ideas on how to save the orchard is undercut by another character, usually someone who is important to the character with the idea. So when Gayev talks of 'a general who might let us have a loan', Liuba destroys that illusion with the remark: 'He's only talking nonsense. There is no such general'.[92]

Each character's vision of a better world is undermined by someone else. Trofimov's visionary future where, 'Mankind marches on, going from strength to strength'[93] once people learn to work, is undercut by Lopakhin, who points out that he already does 'work from morning till night'. His own vision of Russia is in turn undercut by Liuba:

> LOPAKHIN. ... When I can't sleep I sometimes think — the Lord gave us these huge forests, these boundless plains, these vast horizons, and we who live among them ought to be real giants.
> MRS. RANEVSKY.[Liuba] You're calling for giants. That's all very well in fairy-tales, but elsewhere they might be rather alarming.[94]

At this point in the Act, the recognition scene occurs. What everyone sees is that the orchard will be lost. In terms of the conventions of realism operating in this play, Gayev's observation that 'The sun has set, my friends', simply refers to the time of day. In addition, however, Chekhov informs his audience that, symbolically, the sun has set on the gentrified world of Gayev and Liuba. Chekhov uses Yepikhodov as a device to trigger the other characters' individual recognition scenes. All are aware that, like Yepikhodov, their inner subjective reality does not match up with the objective reality of their social situation. Each of the onstage characters project onto Yepikhodov their own sense of anguish at being unable to bridge the gap between their two lives:

[YEPIKHODOV *crosses the back of the stage playing his guitar.*]
MRS. RANEVSKY. [*Pensively.*] There goes Yepikhodov.
ANYA. [*Pensively.*] There goes Yepikhodov.
GAYEV. The sun has set, my friends.
TROFIMOV. Yes.
GAYEV. [*In a quiet voice, as if giving a recitation.*] Nature, glorious Nature, glowing with everlasting radiance, so beautiful, so cold — you, whom men call mother, in whom the living and the dead are joined together, you who give life and take it away —
VARYA. [*Imploring him.*] Uncle dear!
ANYA. Uncle, you're off again.
TROFIMOV. You'd far better pot the red in the middle.
GAYEV. I am silent. Silent.
[*Everyone sits deep in thought. It is very quiet. All that can be heard is* FIRS' *low muttering. Suddenly a distant sound is heard. It seems to come from the sky and is the sound of a breaking string. It dies away sadly.*][95]

The sun has indeed set on all of the characters' hopes and illusions. The sunshine of the opening of Act II has been replaced by darkness.

In a 'disguised soliloquy', which superficially appears to be a trivial piece of rhetoric, Gayev recognises the truth that Nature is 'cold' or, as Frayn translates it, 'indifferent'. There is no divine plan underpinning 'glorious Nature'. Left to Nature alone, the impecunious characters may be saved, as Pishchik is by pure luck, or ruined as are Gayev and Liuba. There is no plan in Nature's interaction with man. This clearly means that humans must actively do something to control their lives. Gayev's 'vision', though absurdly expressed, is not a stupid one, and it is too painful for the other characters to face. Consequently they silence him. It is in that silence that we hear the sound of the breaking string.

This discordant note reflects the disharmony felt by the characters. Chekhov, who loved to observe that 'You must never put a loaded rifle on the stage if no one is going to fire it',[96] has used Yepikhodov as his 'loaded rifle' in this scene. The clerk's traversal of the stage appears, at first, to merely be a piece of incidental realism. However, Yepikhodov serves a much deeper purpose here. On the realistic level, the sound is, as I have noted earlier, that of poor Yepikhodov's guitar string breaking. The accident-prone 'Simple Simon' has once again been unable to control the objective world. If Yepikhodov is Chekhov's 'loaded rifle', then the breaking string is the playwright firing it.[97]

All of the characters provide a different explanation for the sound and project onto it their own particular concerns. For the practical Lopakhin it is the sound of a cable breaking in one of the mines; for Gayev it is one of Nature's creatures, a heron (a large wading bird); for the eternal student it is a wise old owl. All agree that the sound is unpleasant. This sound crystallises the moment of recognition that the estate is lost. In a quite brilliant piece of dramatic writing, Chekhov reintroduces this same sound towards the end of the play. In doing so, he ensures that the moment of sad recognition, associated by the audience with the breaking string heard in Act II, is recalled. This is more likely to be effective if the director heeds Chekhov's advice to Stanislavski and keeps superfluous sound effects out of the production.

The second appearance of this sound is linked with another sound that makes concrete the general sense of impending loss associated with the breaking string.[98] The sound is, of course, that of the axes striking into the cherry trees. The abandoned Firs in the play's final disguised soliloquy rambles on about how life has somehow passed him by. His comments, and the sounds that end the play, sum up Chekhov's depiction of a social group who have, through their inability to adjust to change, wasted their lives. The audience sees that the way of life of the older generation of Gayev and Liuba is now over, but the hope remains that the younger generation of Anya and Trofimov will not repeat the cycle of wasted potential:

> FIRS. ... [*Mutters something which cannot be understood.*] Life's slipped by as if I'd never lived at all. [*Lies down.*] I'll lie down a bit. You've got no strength left, got nothing left, nothing at all. You're just a — nincompoop. [*Lies motionless.*] [*A distant sound is heard. It seems to come from the sky and is the sound of a breaking string. It dies away sadly. Silence follows, broken only by the thud of an axe striking a tree far away in the orchard.*]
>
> CURTAIN.[99]

*The Cherry Orchard* is not merely what Francis Fergusson called 'a theatre-poem of suffering and change',[100] for this suggests a too fatalistic and passive view. It fails to take into account the implied criticism of the characters who suffer the effects of change without doing anything to adjust to it. Nor will David Magarshack's interpretation of the play as being the depiction of 'the destruction of beauty by those who are utterly blind to it'[101] do as an adequate description of the play's action. In the first place, this interpretation lays the blame for the destruction of the cherry orchard on Lopakhin, whom Chekhov was at great pains to say was not some philistine peasant bent on the destruction of all that was beautiful. Lopakhin, a man with the hands of an artist, expresses this combined aesthetic and economic response to his poppies when offering to lend money to Trofimov. Both the cherry blossom and the poppies are 'beautiful', but only the latter has any economic value. The point is that when Lopakhin looks out at a field of poppies he sees *both* their beauty *and* their financial value:

> LOPAKHIN. I put nearly three thousand acres down to poppy in the spring and made a clear forty thousand roubles. And when my poppies were in flower, that was a sight to see.[102]

Magarshack's interpretation privileges Liuba and Gayev, the defenders of 'beauty' but Chekhov, while being equally aware of their good qualities, implicitly criticises them for their totally impractical approach to their financial problems.

Any balanced interpretation of Chekhov's last four plays needs to avoid taking an 'either/or' stance. In order to portray the duality of Chekhov's vision of reality, any sense of despair must be balanced by a sense of hope. Equally, any production that wishes to create the duality of the Chekhovian form must balance the tragic with the comic.

Chekhov's achievement of having written a play in which he did not have to use the overtly theatrical conventions of melodrama and the well-made play is truly remarkable. *The Cherry Orchard* is, on the surface, a play about real people living their everyday lives, yet this play, when properly performed, is far from being drab or ordinary. The interplay between their private yearnings and their public behaviour transforms these seemingly banal characters into truly extraordinary people and creates a drama that is full of emotional intensity.

## ENDNOTES

[1] Stroyeva, M., 'Everyone Has His Own Chekhov', *Soviet Literature*, No. 2, February 1980, p. 138.

[2] Gassner, J., 'The Duality of Chekhov', in Bristow, E. K., *Anton Chekhov's Plays*, W. W. Norton, New York, 1977, p. 410.

[3] Chekhov, A., Letter to M. P. Lilina, 15 September 1903, in Yarmolinsky, A., *Letters of Anton Chekhov*, The Viking Press, New York, 1973, p. 454.

[4] Stanislavski, C., Letter to A. Chekhov, in Benedetti, J., *The Moscow Art Theatre Letters*, Routledge, New York, 1991, p. 162.

[5] Gilman, R., *Chekhov's Plays: An Opening into Eternity*, Yale University Press, New Haven, 1995, p. 203.

[6] Moravcevich, N., 'The Dark Side of the Chekhovian Smile', *Drama Survey*, Vol. 5, No. 3, Winter 1996–7, p. 237.

[7] Ibid.

[8] Tynan, K., *Curtains*, Longmans, London, 1961, pp. 433–4.

[9] Griffiths, T., 'Introduction', in Chekhov, A., *The Cherry Orchard*, new English version by Griffiths, T., from Rapaport, H., trans., Pluto Press, London, 1981, p. v.

[10] Ibid.

[11] Moravcevich, N., op. cit., pp. 237–8.

[12] Senelick, L., *The Chekhov Theatre*, Cambridge University Press, Cambridge, 1997, p. 298.

[13] Ibid.

[14] Landesman, R., 'Comrade Serban in *The Cherry Orchard*', *Yale Theatre*, Vol. 8, Nos 2 & 3, Spring 1977, pp. 139–40.

[15] Senelick, L., op. cit., p. 336.

[16] Leblanc, R., 'Liberating Chekhov or Destroying Him? Joel Gershmann's Farcical Production of *The Cherry Orchard*', in Clayton, J. D., ed., *Chekhov Then and Now: The Reception of Chekhov in World Culture*, Peter Lang, New York, 1997, p. 59.

[17] Ibid., pp. 59–60.

[18] Frayn, M., 'Introduction', in Frayn, M., trans., *Chekhov Plays*, Methuen, London, 1988, p. lxvi.

[19] Williams, R., *Drama from Ibsen to Brecht*, Penguin, Harmondsworth, 1976, p. 117.

[20] Müller, H., *The Spirit of Tragedy*, Alfred A. Knopf, New York, 1956, p. 288.

[21] Styan, J. L., 'The Delicate Balance: Audience Ambivalence in the Comedy of Shakespeare and Chekhov', *Costerus*, Vol. 2, 1972, p. 181.

[22] Guthke, K. S., *Modern Tragi-Comedy*, Random House, New York, 1996, p. 84.

[23] Chekhov, A., Letter to A. S. Suvorin, 7 January 1889, in Yarmolinsky, A., op. cit., p. 107.

[24] Holland, P., 'The Director and the Playwright: Control over the Means of Production', *New Theatre Quarterly*, Vol. 3, No. 11, August 1987, p. 210.

[25] Corrigan, R., 'Stanislavski and the Playwright', in Corrigan, R., ed., *Theatre in the Twentieth Century*, Grove Press, New York, 1965, pp. 190–1.

[26] Skaftymov, A., quoted in Senderovich, S., '*The Cherry Orchard*: Cechov's Last Testament', *Russian Literature*, Vol. 35, 1994, p. 239.

[27] Pitcher, H., *The Chekhov Play: A New Interpretation*, Chatto and Windus, London, 1973, p. 4.

[28] Valency, M., *The Breaking String*, Oxford University Press, London, 1966, p. 268.

[29] Ibid.

[30] Ibid., p. 269.

[31] Michael Frayn notes that, in England, Trofimov has sometimes been portrayed 'as an inadequate and immature personality who is afraid to emerge from university and face the real world'. (Frayn, M., loc. cit.) Frayn argues that Trofimov is 'perpetually being thrown out of the university ... Exiled, of course, for his political activities ...' (Ibid.) Trofimov's 'story' is only glanced at obliquely in the play, but it must be subtextually implied in performance if Trofimov is not to be reduced to some silly pretentious failure whose opinions are not to be taken seriously.

[32] Chekhov, A., *The Cherry Orchard*, in Hingley, R., *The Oxford Chekhov*, Vol. 3, Oxford University Press, London, 1964, p. 145.

[33] Magarshack, D., *Chekhov the Dramatist*, Eyre Methuen, London, 1980, p. 169.

[34] Chekhov, A., *The Cherry Orchard*, p. 145.

[35] Lopakhin's problem is that he has changed his objective situation by becoming rich but, unlike his creator, has failed to 'squeeze the slave out of himself', and so remains, subjectively, a peasant.

[36] Chekhov, A., *The Cherry Orchard*, p. 146.

[37] Ibid.

[38] Magarshack, D., op. cit., p. 284.

[39] Bergson, H., 'Laughter', in Sypher, W., ed., *Comedy*, Doubleday Anchor, New York, 1956, p. 73.

[40] Chekhov, A., *The Cherry Orchard*, p.146.

[41] Ibid.

[42] Ibid.

[43] Ibid.

[44] Ibid., pp. 146–7.

[45] Ibid., p. 147.

[46] Ibid.

[47] Ibid.

[48] Ibid., p. 149.

49 Ibid., pp. 149–50.

50 Ibid., p. 150. Chekhov again teases his audience with the prospect of this clichéd solution to the family's financial problems when, later in Act I, Gayev echoes Varya's 'dream'. In a list of highly impractical ways that the estate might be saved, Gayev indulges in his fantasies: 'GAYEV. ... I have plenty of remedies, any amount of them, and that means that I haven't really got one. It would be a good thing if someone left us some money. It would be a good thing to marry Anya to a very rich man ...' (Ibid., p. 159.) Possibly the aristocratic Gayev cannot conceive of the very real possibility of their estate being saved through Varya marrying Lopakhin. In Gayev's eyes, Lopakhin is still an ignorant peasant. Being such a complete elitist, Gayev becomes ludicrous when he claims to have a close rapport with the peasants. 'GAYEV. ... I'm a man of the eighties ... I've suffered quite a lot for my convictions, I can tell you. Do you wonder the peasants like me so much? You have to know your peasant of course. You have to know how to ...' (Ibid., p. 161.)

51 Ibid., p. 156.

52 Ibid., p. 159.

53 Ibid., pp. 167–8.

54 Ibid., p. 172.

55 Ibid., p. 175.

56 Ibid., p. 178.

57 Ibid., pp. 184–5. In production it is quite common, and, I would argue, quite appropriate, for Lopakhin to cringe in terror when the stick bears down on him. This is, after all, the man who, though he has just bought the cherry orchard, subjectively is still a peasant who was commonly beaten by his father when he was young. It is a conditioned reflex that his behaviour reverts to that of his peasant youth, origin and experience.

58 Ibid., pp. 185–6.

59 Ibid., p. 186.

60 Ibid.

61 Ibid.

62 Ibid., p. 187.

63 Ibid., p. 194.

64 Ibid.

65 Ibid., p. 195.

66 Ibid.

67 Magarshack, D., op. cit., p. 278.

68 I am not suggesting that the subtext is as fixed as the text, but *something like* the subtext I suggest here is implied by Chekhov in his playtext. Different productions will, of course, highlight different aspects of the implied subtext.

69 Chekhov, A., *The Cherry Orchard*, pp. 197–8.

70 Corrigan, R., 'The Plays of Chekhov', in Corrigan, R. and Rosenberg, J. L., eds, *The Context and Craft of Drama*, Chandler Publishing Company, Scranton, 1964, p. 155.

71 Chekhov, A., *The Cherry Orchard*, p. 169.

72 Ibid., p. 170.

73 Williams, R., op. cit., p. 116.

74 Chekhov, A., *The Cherry Orchard*, p. 170. Chekhov's experiences as a doctor treating the peasants during epidemics and his research work on Sakhalin led him to have first-hand knowledge of suffering. For all that he in no way lives up to his ideals, Trofimov's description of the appalling conditions, the hardships endured by the peasants and the lack of concerted action by the intelligentsia has the ring of authenticity about it.

75 Chekhov, A., Letter to I. I. Orlov, 22 February 1899, in Friedland, L. S., *Letters on the Short Story, the Drama, and Other Literary Topics by Anton Chekhov*, Dover Publications, New York, 1966, pp. 286–7.

76 Greene, G., *Spectator*, 5 September 1941.

77 Williams, R., loc. cit. Chekhov's ambivalent attitude towards the Russian intelligentsia is captured well by Vladimir Nabokov. He writes: 'Chekhov's intellectual was a man who combined the deepest human decency of which man is capable with an almost ridiculous inability to put his ideals and principles into action; a man devoted to moral beauty, the welfare of his people, the welfare of the

universe, but unable in his private life to do any thing useful; frittering away his provincial existence in a haze of utopian dreams; knowing exactly what is good, what is worthwhile living for, but at the same time sinking lower and lower in the mud of a humdrum existence, unhappy in love, hopelessly inefficient in everything — a good man who cannot make good'. (Nabokov, V., *Lectures on Russian Literature*, Picador, London, 1981, p. 253.) Trofimov is a perfect example of such an 'intellectual'.

[78] Chekhov, A., Letter to O. L. Knipper, 9 October 1903, quoted in Hingley, R., *The Oxford Chekhov*, Vol. 3, p. 320.

[79] Charlotte covers her worries by constantly performing stage tricks. In Act IV, when the cherry orchard has been sold and her future is insecure, the anguish of her inner life bursts forth into the text breaking through her overtly comic behaviour:
   GAYEV. Charlotte's happy, she's singing.
   CHARLOTTE. [*Picking up a bundle which looks like a swaddled baby.*] Rock-a-bye baby. [*A baby's cry is heard.*] Hush, my darling, my dear little boy. [*The cry is heard again.*] You poor little thing! [*Throws the bundle down.*] And please will you find me another job? I can't go on like this. (Chekhov, A., *The Cherry Orchard*, p. 193.)

[80] Ibid., p. 162.

[81] Bergson, H., *Laughter: An Essay on the Meaning of the Comic*, Macmillan and Co., London, 1935, pp. 50–1.

[82] Chekhov, A., *The Cherry Orchard*, pp. 162–3.

[83] Ibid., p. 163.

[84] Chekhov, A., quoted in Lewis, A., *The Contemporary Theatre*, Crown Publishers, New York, 1971, p. 65.

[85] Ibid.

[86] Ibid.

[87] For Chekhov, the central problem of his dramaturgical approach was how to avoid the demand made by almost every critic 'that the hero and heroine be dramatically effective' (Chekhov, A., quoted in Lewis, A., loc. cit.), while at the same time avoiding theatrical clichés. Chekhov's elation at having avoided cheap theatrics is evident in the excited tone of the letter he wrote to his wife about the play in September 1903: 'However boring my play may be, I think there's something new about it. Incidentally, there's not a single pistol shot in the whole play'. (Chekhov, A., Letter to O. L. Knipper, quoted in Hingley, R., *The Oxford Chekhov*, Vol. 3, p. 320.)

[88] Chekhov, A., *The Cherry Orchard*, p. 163.

[89] Ibid., pp. 163–4.

[90] Ibid., p. 153.

[91] Ibid., p. 166.

[92] Ibid., pp. 168–9.

[93] Ibid., p. 170.

[94] Ibid., pp. 170–1.

[95] Ibid., p. 171.

[96] Chekhov, A., quoted in Magarshack, D., op. cit., p. 45.

[97] One can easily see why Chekhov objected to Stanislavski introducing extra sound effects. While they may have made the play seem more realistic, they were like having a whole series of unloaded rifles on stage. Every sound that Chekhov specifies has both a surface realistic reference and a deeper significance which, being 'loaded', adds meaning to the action of the play.

[98] The use of these two sound effects illustrates Chekhov's capacity to employ the two forms of symbolism outlined by Wimsatt that I noted in Chapter 2. The sound of the axe is both real [used to chop down the trees] and symbolic [an evocation of the end of an era]. The sound of the breaking string which, on its first use was both real [Yepikhodov's guitar string] and symbolic [an evocation of the end of an era] is here used only in its purely symbolic sense.

[99] Chekhov, A., *The Cherry Orchard*, p. 198. There is further evidence that Chekhov wished to suggest to his audience that the main characters had also 'let life slip by'. In an earlier draft of the ending of Act II, Chekhov had Charlotte help Firs look for the items that Liuba had dropped. While looking, she had commented: 'Mrs. Ranevsky's forever losing things. She's thrown away her life as well'. (Ibid., p. 324.)

[100] Fergusson, F., *The Idea of a Theater*, Doubleday Anchor, New York, 1953, p. 175.

[101] Magarshack, D., op. cit., p. 274.
[102] Chekhov, A., *The Cherry Orchard*, p. 190.

# Conclusion

*The Theatre is the world compressed, and with meaning.* (Jean-Paul Sartre)[1]

*Question: Can one interpret something one doesn't understand?* (Jean Vilar)[2]

Chekhov was fortunate to have had his plays performed by the actors of the Moscow Art Theatre. Whatever the agony he suffered seeing his plays presented in an uncongenial manner; whatever the limitations Stanislavski had as a director of his plays, Chekhov could not have found a group of actors more appropriately trained to perform his works. It was the system of acting devised by Stanislavski and taught to his students that made it possible for actors to explore the inner lives of their characters and to create the necessary subtext in performance. Without this acting system, there would have been no way for actors to communicate the conflict between their characters' public and private lives and thus present Chekhov's implied criticism of their failure to live up to their aspirations. Without actors capable of creating an inner life for their characters, audiences would have been able to perceive only the drab reality of 'life as it is' and would have been unaware of any implied vision of 'life as it should be'.

Today, most English actors and directors have a working knowledge of Stanislavski's acting system. However, the difference between English and Russian sensibilities creates a cultural divide that is difficult to bridge. English directors, for instance, seem to find it difficult to give due value to the positive ideas expressed by Chekhov's 'philosophers'. The difficulty stems from the fact that these characters tend to express their ideas in lengthy tirades. Such effusions are not easily accepted by English theatre practitioners and audiences brought up to value understatement or who feel that 'politics' or 'religion' are not proper subjects for polite conversation. What Gottlieb perceptively claims to be a peculiarly English phenomenon is, I would argue, equally evident in all English-speaking countries:

> The question of 'positive affirmations' is, perhaps a more contentious one: there is a peculiarly English embarrassment at people or characters who 'spout' positively about life or who talk idealistically or hopefully about the future ... hence, perhaps, the difficulty English actors, directors and audiences have with characters like Vershinin or Tuzenbach or Trofimov ... Debate, which sits uneasily on the English stage, is treated as something which emanates from Chekhov's charming idiosyncratic characters, not from the whole social fabric of the plays.[3]

Trevor Griffiths, who wrote a new English version of *The Cherry Orchard* in 1977, was acutely aware of this Anglo-Saxon fear of public expression of emotion which he felt was especially evident in the English language itself. In one interview he commented: 'There is something very contained about English, and when it does express deep emotion, it does so in simple rather than purple ways; in oblique and understated rather than rhetorical language.'[4]

Griffiths' solution to this cultural difference between Russian and English sensibilities was to anglicise the language of his version of *The Cherry Orchard*. It is worth noting that, whereas the critic, Kenneth Tynan, objected to the ways in which the English had transformed Chekhov's *The Cherry Orchard* into an English play that is 'in our image', Griffiths deliberately emphasised the fact that he had written an 'English' version. When interviewed about his version by David Allen in 1987, Griffiths commented:

> My translation is specifically called a new *English* version. To say that the play will be in the English language does imply — to me, at least — that it will be *anglicised* to a certain extent; that adjustments will be made to take account of the different history and a different national, cultural structure of feeling.[5]

Another contemporary English director, Mike Alfreds, takes an opposite approach to Griffith. Alfreds specifically avoids producing 'English' Chekhov. As David Allen has noted: 'In performing Chekhov, Alfreds argues that it is important to try to replace our Anglo-Saxon mode of emotional expression by a more extrovert, Slavic one.'[6]

Griffith is surely correct, however, to suggest that the overt emotionalism expressed in the long idealistic speeches of characters like Vershinin, Tuzenbach and Trofimov appears excessive to lovers of English reticence. It is perhaps because English directors feel embarrassed by this extrovert expression of feeling that they avoid asking their actors and audiences to take such characters seriously. In the English-speaking world, it is easier to present such passionate characters as eccentric 'gasbags' and to comically deflate their heartfelt faith in the future. The result is that, instead of embodying what Gottlieb calls the *leitmotif* of Chekhov's dramas, '*tak zhit nelzna* — one cannot and must not live like that', British, and English-speaking Chekhov in general, 'has enforced the idea that Chekhov's plays deal nostalgically with "the tragedy of dispossession"'.[7]

As we have seen, Chekhov's plays are not simply mood pieces stuffed full of interesting 'characters' fatalistically doomed to failure. His plays are social comedies which deal with issues that are of direct relevance to the lives of the audience. They provide a comic critique of the behaviour of his characters who have abdicated their responsibility to act according to their knowledge and ideals. Gottlieb is correct when she points out that the never-ending critical discussion of whether Chekhov's plays are tragedies or comedies 'goes deeper than questions of content and form, and becomes a philosophical and political debate'.[8] The decision to interpret Chekhov's plays as either tragedies or comedies has far-reaching ramifications. It is not simply the style of performance that is affected, but, more significantly, the meaning of the plays that is radically altered as a result of this decision:

> To put it perhaps crudely: the tragic view of human impotence in the face of seemingly inevitable forces implies an *acceptance* of the world order as it manifests itself and works out its design in the characters on stage. The assumption of human impotence, the acceptance of 'that which is', the belief in ungovernable external forces, and the insistence on 'absolutes', all become part of a retrograde world view. This philosophy, I would suggest, was complete anathema to Chekhov, whose concern as a scientist and as a writer was with the exposure of contradictions, and not an annulment or denial of contradictions. His aim was to expose, and not to tranquillise, what Coleridge called, 'the lethargy of custom'.[9]

Chekhov's aim has not always gone unnoticed, but critics like Gottlieb, Karlinsky and Magarshack, who emphasise the central role that such an aim plays in Chekhov's work, have always been in a minority. In addition, they have almost always written in reaction against the prevailing 'Absurdist' reading of the playwright. As early as 1927, we find one such critic expressing his dissatisfaction with critics of the 'nothing to be done' school of Chekhov:

> He wrote very often, not invariably, about the weak and unsuccessful ... When Chekhov presents such characters, he is not trying to rouse us into a state of false indignation against life and fate; he did not intend to put the blame for anything that is wrong with the world of men upon those vague and convenient scapegoats; he wanted us to put the blame where it belongs: on ourselves.[10]

I share the assumption expressed in a recent text on play directing that 'all plays, no matter how poor, have inherent meanings. Pinpointing them is often the problem'.[11] That problem has emerged particularly in those cases where directors have portrayed Chekhov as a proto-Absurdist and consequently have misinterpreted the meanings implied in his playtexts. The director's first function is to correctly interpret the meaning of a given playscript before embarking on the second function of finding the theatrical means to communicate that meaning to an audience. It is the first function of interpretation that I have focused on in this book.

It is an interesting fact of theatrical history that the two functions of the modern director were formerly carried out by separate people. As we have seen, Nemirovich-Danchenko saw his role in the production process as interpreter of the playtext, while Stanislavski undertook to find the theatrical means of realising that interpretation. Increasingly, Stanislavski took over both the interpretive and creative functions, and today most directors regard it as normal practice to carry out these dual functions. In some ways, this has placed an undue burden on directors. Not only are they expected to have a complete knowledge of the theatre arts, they are also expected to be experts in literary interpretation. That this is perhaps asking too much of most directors is, I believe, acknowledged by the fact that some of the more important and well-resourced companies employ dramaturgs to take on some of the functions formerly carried out by literary interpreters such as Nemirovich-Danchenko.

It is not the business of critics such as myself to legislate how a director should realise a playwright's play. What I believe a critic can do is help directors to arrive at an interpretation that lies within the 'parameters' and 'tolerances' of the playscript. Possibly the most useful preparation a potential director of a Chekhov play can make is to read Chekhov's other plays and short stories. The plays embody an exceptionally unified vision of reality and show a progressive mastery of form and consequently they are the perfect preface to help a director understand the nature of Chekhov's dramaturgy.

I have demonstrated how and why misinterpretations of Chekhov's plays have taken place in the past and continue in the present. This book will, of course, not stop such misinterpretations from continuing to occur. My hope is that prospective directors of Chekhov will be convinced by my argument and use their theatrical skills and creativity to mount productions that do not distort the playwright's vision of reality, and successfully communicate the richness of Chekhov's plays.

## ENDNOTES

[1] Sartre, J-P., Film of *The Condemned of Altona*, quoted in Hodge, F., *Play Directing: Analysis, Communication and Style*, Allyn and Bacon, Boston, 1994, p. 47.

[2] Vilar, J., 'Murder of the Director', in Corrigan, R., ed., *Theatre in the Twentieth Century*, Grove Press, New York, 1965, p. 146.

[3] Gottlieb, V., 'Chekhov in Limbo: British Productions of the Plays of Chekhov', in Scolnicov, H. and Holland, P., eds, *The Play Out of Context: Transferring Plays from Culture to Culture*, Cambridge University Press, Cambridge, 1989, pp. 166–7.

[4] Griffiths, T., quoted in Allen, D., '*The Cherry Orchard*: A New English Version by Trevor Griffiths', in Miles, P., ed., *Chekhov on the British Stage*, Cambridge University Press, Cambridge, 1993, p. 163.

[5] loc. cit.

[6] Allen, D., 'Exploring the Limitless Depths: Mike Alfreds Directs Chekhov', *New Theatre Quarterly*, Vol. 2, No. 8, November 1986, p. 321.

[7] Gottlieb, V., 'The Politics of British Chekhov', in Miles, P., op. cit., pp. 148–9.

[8] Ibid., p. 153.

[9] Ibid. Chekhov was quite aware of the importance of providing audiences and readers with a jolt in order to wake them from 'the lethargy of custom'. In a letter in which he suggested ways that Suvorin might increase the effect of his writing on his reading public, Chekhov stated: 'And why should you explain to the public? One must shock it, rather, and then it will think more'. (Chekhov, A., Letter to A. S. Suvorin, 17 December 1891, in Friedland, L. S., *Letters on the Short Story, the Drama, and Other Literary Topics by Anton Chekhov*, Dover Publications, New York, 1966, p. 102.)

[10] Robinson, M., 'M. Robinson Replies to the Notion that Chekhov's Characters "Are Forever Conquered by Life"', *Adelphi*, May 1927, in Emeljanow, V., ed., *Chekhov: The Critical Heritage*, Routledge and Kegan Paul, London, 1981, p. 319.

[11] Hodge, F., op. cit., p. 48.

# Select Bibliography

## Editions of Chekhov's plays and short stories consulted or cited

Bentley, E., ed. and trans., *The Brute and Other Farces by Anton Chekhov,* Grove Press, New York, 1958.

Bristow, E. K., trans. and ed., *Anton Chekhov's Plays*, W. W. Norton and Company, New York, 1977.

Chekhov, A. (unknown translator), *The Plays of Anton Chekhov,* J. J. Little and Ives Company, New York, 1935.

Chekhov, A. (unknown translator), *The Cherry Orchard,* Dover Publications, New York, 1991.

Dunnigan, A., *Chekhov: The Major Plays,* The New America Library, New York, 1964.

Fell, M. and West, J., trans., *Tchekoff: Six Famous Plays*, Gerald Duckworth and Co., London, 1949.

Fen, E., ed., *Chekhov Plays*, Penguin, Harmondsworth, 1954.

Frayn, M., trans., *Wild Honey,* Methuen, London, 1984.

Frayn, M., trans., *Chekhov Plays,* Methuen Drama, London, 1988.

Frayn, M., trans., *The Seagull*, Allen & Unwin, London, 1989.

Gems, P., *Uncle Vanya: A New Version,* Eyre Methuen, London, 1980.

Griffiths, T., ed., *The Cherry Orchard*, new English version, from Rapaport, H., trans., Pluto Press, London, 1981.

Guthrie, T. and Kipnis, L., trans., *The Cherry Orchard,* University of Minnesota Press, Minneapolis, 1965.

Hingley, R., *The Oxford Chekhov, Vol. 1, Short Plays,* Oxford University Press, London, 1968.

Hingley, R., *The Oxford Chekhov, Vol. 2, Platonov, Ivanov, The Seagull,* Oxford University Press, London, 1967.

Hingley, R., *The Oxford Chekhov, Vol. 3, Uncle Vanya, Three Sisters, The Cherry Orchard, The Wood Demon,* Oxford University Press, London, 1964.

Hingley, R., *The Oxford Chekhov, Vol. 4, Stories 1888–1889,* Oxford University Press, London, 1980.

Hingley, R., *The Oxford Chekhov, Vol. 5, Stories 1889–1891,* Oxford University Press, London, 1970.

Hingley, R., *The Oxford Chekhov, Vol. 6, Stories 1892–1893,* Oxford University Press, London, 1971.

Hingley, R., *The Oxford Chekhov, Vol. 7, Stories 1893–1895,* Oxford University Press, London, 1978.

Hingley, R., *The Oxford Chekhov, Vol. 8, Stories 1895–1897,* Oxford University Press, London, 1965.

Hingley, R., *The Oxford Chekhov, Vol. 9, Stories 1898–1904,* Oxford University Press, London, 1975.

Magarshack, D., trans., *Platonov,* Faber and Faber, London, 1964.

Magarshack, D., trans., *Chekhov: Four Plays,* Unwin Books, London, 1969.

Makaroff, D., trans., *Platonov,* Methuen, London, 1961.

Mamet, D., *Uncle Vanya* (an adaptation), Grove Press, New York, 1989.

Pavis-Zahradniková, E. and Pavis, P., *Anton Tchékhov: 'La Cerisaie',* Le Livre de Poche, Paris, n.d.

Ross, P. P., trans., *Anton Chekhov: Stories of Women,* Prometheus Books, New York, 1994.

Szogyi, A., *Ten Early Plays by Chekhov,* Bantam Books, New York, 1965.

Van Itallie, J-C., ed., *The Seagull: A New Version,* Harper & Row, New York, 1977.

Yarmolinsky, A., trans., *The Cherry Orchard,* The Avon Theatre Library, New York, 1965.

Young, S., trans., *Best Plays by Chekhov,* The Modern Library, New York, 1956.

**Chekhov correspondence cited**

Chekhov, A., Letter to V. Bibilin, 14 February 1886, quoted in Magarshack, D., *Chekhov the Dramatist,* Eyre Methuen, London, 1980, p. 151.

Chekhov, A., Letter to A. Chekhov between 10 and 12 October 1887, quoted in Hingley, R., *The Oxford Chekhov,* Vol. 2, pp. 284–5.

Chekhov, A., Letter to Alexander Chekhov, 23 October 1887, quoted in Valency, M., *The Breaking String,* Oxford University Press, London, 1966, p. 83.

Chekhov, A., Letter to Alexander Chekhov, 24 October 1887, quoted in Hingley, R., *The Oxford Chekhov,* Vol. 2, p. 285.

Chekhov, A., Letter to A. Chekhov, 20 November 1887, quoted in Hingley, R., *The Oxford Chekhov,* Vol. 2, p. 286.

Chekhov, A., Letter to A. Chekhov, 24 November 1887, quoted in Hingley, R., *The Oxford Chekhov,* Vol. 2, p. 287.

Chekhov, A., Letter to A. Chekhov, 8 May 1889, in McVay, G., *Chekhov's 'Three Sisters',* Bristol Classical Press, 1995, p. ix.

Chekhov, A., Letter to A. P. Chekhov, 10 May 1886 in Yarmolinsky, A., *Letters of Anton Chekhov*, The Viking Press, New York, 1973, p. 37.

Chekhov, A., Letter to A. P. Chekhov, 8 May 1889, in Yarmolinsky, A., op. cit., p. 117.

Chekhov, A., Letter to A. P. Chekhov, 11 April 1889, in Karlinsky, S. and Heim, M. H., *Anton Chekhov's Life and Thought*, University of California Press, Berkeley, 1975, p. 142.

Chekhov, A., Letter to M. P. Chekhov, 15 October 1896, in Friedland, L. S., *Letters on the Short Story, the Drama, and Other Literary Topics by Anton Chekhov*, Dover Publications, New York, 1966, p. 147.

Chekhov, A., Letter to M. P. Chekhov, 18 October 1896, in Hellman, L., *The Selected Letters of Chekhov*, Hamish Hamilton, London, 1955, pp. 193–4.

Chekhov, A., Letter to M. Chekhov, 3 December 1887, quoted in Hingley, R., *The Oxford Chekhov*, Vol. 2, p. 289.

Chekhov, A., Letter to E. N. Chirikov, 7 October 1903, in Friedland, L. S., op. cit., p. 202.

Chekhov, A., Letter to Davydov, 1 December 1887 in Hingley, R., *The Oxford Chekhov*, Vol. 2, p. 288.

Chekhov, A., Letter to S. P. Diaghilev, 30 December 1902, in Yarmolinsky, A., op. cit., p. 438.

Chekhov, A., Letter to S. P. Diaghilev, 12 July 1903, in Yarmolinsky, A., op. cit., p. 453.

Chekhov, A., Letter to F. A. Fyodorov-Yurkowsky, 8 January 1889, in Hingley, R., *The Oxford Chekhov*, Vol. 2, p. 296.

Chekhov, A., Letter to M. Gorky, 3 December 1898, in Yarmolinsky, A., op. cit., p. 320.

Chekhov, A., Letter to M. Gorky, 3 January 1899, in Yarmolinsky, A., op. cit., p. 323.

Chekhov, A., Letter to M. Gorky, 9 May 1899, in Karlinsky, S., op. cit., p. 357.

Chekhov, A., Letter to M. Gorky, 16 October 1900, in Friedland, L. S., op. cit., p. 156.

Chekhov, A., Letter to D. V. Grigorovich, 9 October 1888, in Yarmolinsky, A., op. cit., p. 84.

Chekhov, A., Letter to M. V. Kiseleva, 14 January 1887, in Yarmolinsky, A., op. cit., p. 41.

Chekhov, A., Letter to O. L. Knipper, 30 September 1889, quoted in Hingley, R., op. cit., pp. 301–2.

Chekhov, A., Letter to O. L. Knipper, 2 January 1900, quoted in Tulloch, J., *Chekhov: A Structuralist Study*, Macmillan Press, London, 1980, p. 107.

Chekhov, A., Letter to O. L. Knipper, 15 September 1900, quoted in Valency, M., op. cit., p. 208.

Chekhov, A., Letter to O. L. Knipper, 9 October 1903, quoted in Hingley, R., *The Oxford Chekhov*, Vol. 3, p. 320.

Chekhov, A., Letter to O. L. Knipper, 10 April 1904, in Yarmolinsky, A., op. cit., p. 466.

Chekhov, A., Letter to V. Kommissarzhevskaya, 13 November 1900, in Yarmolinsky, A., op. cit., p. 383.

Chekhov, A., Letter to V. Kommissarzhevskaya, 13 November 1900, in McVay, G., op. cit., p. xvi.

Chekhov, A., Letter to A. Koni, 11 November 1896, in Hellman, L., op. cit., p. 197.

Chekhov, A., Letter to Vukol Lavrov, 10 April 1890 in Karlinsky, S., op. cit., pp. 165–7.

Chekhov, A., Letter to I. L. Leontyev-Shcheglov, 7 November 1888, in Friedland, L. S., op. cit., p. 169.

Chekhov, A., Letter to I. L. Leontyev-Shcheglov, 31 December 1888, in Hingley, R., *The Oxford Chekhov*, Vol. 2, p. 295.

Chekhov, A., Letter to I. L. Leontyev-Shcheglov, 22 March 1890, in Karlinsky, S., op. cit., pp. 162–4.

Chekhov, A., Letter to I. L. Leontyev-Shcheglov, 9 March 1892, in Yarmolinsky, A., op. cit., p. 202.

Chekhov, A., Letter to I. L. Leontyev-Shcheglov, 24 October 1892 in Yarmolinsky, A., op. cit., p. 225.

Chekhov, A., Letter to I. L. Leontyev-Shcheglov, 20 January 1899, in Yarmolinsky, A., op. cit., p. 329.

Chekhov, A., Letter to N. A. Leykin, 7 April 1887 in Yarmolinsky, A., op. cit., p. 46.

Chekhov, A., Letter to N. A. Leykin, 4 November 1887, quoted in Hingley, R., *The Oxford Chekhov*, Vol. 2, p. 285.

Chekhov, A., Letter to N. A. Leykin, 15 November 1887 in Karlinsky, S., op. cit., pp. 70–1.

Chekhov, A., Letter to M. P. Lilina, 15 September 1903, in Yarmolinsky, A., op. cit., p. 454.

Chekhov, A., Letter to A. F. Marks, 1 October 1902, quoted in Hingley, R., *The Oxford Chekhov*, Vol. 1, p. 189.

Chekhov, A., Letter to O. P. Menshikov, 16 April 1897, in Yarmolinsky, A., op. cit., p. 286.

Chekhov, A., Letter to V. Meyerhold, early October 1889 in Benedetti, J., *The Moscow Art Theatre Letters,* Routledge, New York, 1991, pp. 56–7.

Chekhov, A., Letter to V. Meyerhold, October 1889, in Karlinsky, S., op. cit., p. 368.

Chekhov, A., Letter to V. Mirolubov, 17 December 1901, in Hellman, L., op. cit., p. 296.

Chekhov, A., Letter to L. S. Mizonova, 13 August 1893, in Yarmolinsky, A, op. cit., p. 237.

Chekhov, A., Letter to V. Nemirovich-Danchenko, 2 September 1903, in Friedland, L. S., op. cit., p. 201.

Chekhov, A., Letter to I. I. Orlov, 22 February 1899, in Friedland, L. S., op. cit., pp. 286–7.

Chekhov, A., Letter to A. N. Pleshcheyev, 4 October 1888, in Yarmolinsky, A., op. cit., p. 81.

Chekhov, A., Letter to A. N. Pleshcheyev, 9 October 1888, in Karlinsky, S., op. cit., p. 112.

Chekhov, A., Letter to A. N. Pleshcheyev, 13 November 1888, in Yarmolinsky, A., op. cit., p. 92.

Chekhov, A., Letter to A. N. Pleshcheyev, 2 January 1889, in Hingley, R., *The Oxford Chekhov*, Vol. 2, p. 295.

Chekhov, A., Letter to A. N. Pleshcheyev, 9 April 1889, in Josephson, M., ed., *The Personal Papers of Anton Chekhov*, Lear, New York, 1948, p. 150.

Chekhov, A., Letter to A. N. Pleshcheyev, 15 February 1890, in Yarmolinsky, A., op. cit., p. 125.

Chekhov, A., Letter to Yakov Polonsky, 22 February 1888, quoted in Magarshack, D., *Chekhov: A Life*, Westport, Greenwood Press, 1970, p. 144.

Chekhov, A., Letter to G. I. Rossolimo, 11 October 1889, in Yarmolinsky, A., op. cit., pp. 352–3.

Chekhov, A., Letter to C. Stanislavski, 2 January 1901, in Karlinsky, S., op. cit., p. 391.

Chekhov, A., Letter to Ye. M. Shavrova, 16 September 1891, in Friedland, L. S., op. cit., p. 17.

Chekhov, A., Letter to Ye. M. Shavrova, 28 February 1895, in Yarmolinsky, A., op. cit., pp. 256–7.

Chekhov, A., Letter to E. Shavrova, 1 November 1896, in Hellman, L., op. cit., pp. 195–6.

Chekhov, A., Letter to A. S. Suvorin, 30 May 1888, in Yarmolinsky, A., op. cit., p. 71.

Chekhov, A., Letter to A. S. Suvorin, 11 September 1888, in Karlinsky, S., op. cit., p. 107.

Chekhov, A., Letter to A. S. Suvorin between 4 and 6 October 1888, quoted in Hingley, R., *The Oxford Chekhov*, Vol. 2, p. 289.

Chekhov, A., Letter to A. S. Suvorin, 27 October 1888 in Yarmolinsky, A., op. cit., p. 88.

Chekhov, A., Letter to A. S. Suvorin, 27 October 1888, in Karlinsky, S., op. cit., p. 117.

Chekhov, A., Letter to A. S. Suvorin, 7 November 1888, in Yarmolinsky, A., op. cit., p. 91.

Chekhov, A., Letter to A. S. Suvorin, 11 November 1888, quoted in Magarshack, D., *Chekhov the Dramatist*, pp. 31–2.

Chekhov, A., Letter to A. S. Suvorin, 19 December 1888 quoted in Hingley, R., *The Oxford Chekhov*, Vol. 2, p. 290.

Chekhov, A., Letter to A. S. Suvorin, 30 December 1888, in Karlinsky, S., op. cit., p. 79.

Chekhov, A., Letter to A. S. Suvorin, 7 January 1889, in Karlinsky, S., op. cit., p. 84.

Chekhov, A., Letter to A. S. Suvorin, 7 January 1889, in Friedland, L. S., op. cit., p. 142.

Chekhov, A., Letter to A. S. Suvorin, 7 January 1889, in Yarmolinsky, A., op. cit., p. 107.

Chekhov, A., Letter to A. S. Suvorin, 6 February 1889, in Hingley, R., *The Oxford Chekhov*, Vol. 2, p. 297.

Chekhov, A., Letter to A. S. Suvorin, 14 February 1889, quoted in Magarshack, D., *Chekhov the Dramatist*, p. 23.

Chekhov, A., Letter to A. S. Suvorin, 11 March 1889 in Yarmolinsky, A., op. cit., p. 111.

Chekhov, A., Letter to A. S. Suvorin, 7 May 1889, in Karlinsky, S., op. cit., p. 143.

Chekhov, A., Letter to A. S. Suvorin, 15 May 1889, in Karlinsky, S., op. cit., pp. 143–4.

Chekhov, A., Letter to A. S. Suvorin, 28 October 1889, in Yarmolinsky, A., op. cit., p. 122.

Chekhov, A., Letter to A. S. Suvorin, 25 November 1889, in Friedland, L. S., op. cit., p. 193.

Chekhov, A., Letter to A. S. Suvorin, 9 March 1890, in Yarmolinsky, A., op. cit., p. 129.

Chekhov, A., Letter to A. S. Suvorin, 9 March 1890, in Karlinsky, S., op. cit., p. 159.

Chekhov, A., Letter to A. S. Suvorin, 1 April 1890, in Yarmolinsky, A., op. cit., p. 133.

Chekhov, A., Letter to A. S. Suvorin, 11 September 1890, in Karlinsky, S., op. cit., p. 171.

Chekhov, A., Letter to A. S. Suvorin, 9 December 1890, in Yarmolinsky, A., op. cit., p. 170.

Chekhov, A., Letter to A. S. Suvorin, 9 December 1890, in Karlinsky, S., op. cit., p. 174.

Chekhov, A., Letter to A. S. Suvorin, 17 December 1891, in Friedland, L. S., op. cit., p. 102.

Chekhov, A., Letter to A. S. Suvorin, 8 April 1892, in Karlinsky, S., op. cit., p. 221.

Chekhov, A., Letter to A. S. Suvorin, 28 May 1892, in Yarmolinsky, A., op. cit., p. 212.

Chekhov, A., Letter to A. S. Suvorin, 1 August 1892, in Yarmolinsky, A., op. cit., pp. 218–19.

Chekhov, A., Letter to A. S. Suvorin, 10 October 1892, in Yarmolinsky, A., op. cit., p. 223.

Chekhov, A., Letter to A. S. Suvorin, 18 October 1892, in Yarmolinsky, A., op. cit., p. 223.

Chekhov, A., Letter to A. S. Suvorin, 25 November 1892, in Yarmolinsky, A., op. cit., p. 227.

Chekhov, A., Letter to A. S. Suvorin, 25 November 1892, in Karlinsky, S., op. cit., p. 243.

Chekhov, A., Letter to A. S. Suvorin, 3 December 1892, in Yarmolinsky, A., op. cit., p. 227.

Chekhov, A., Letter to A. S. Suvorin, 2 January 1894, in Yarmolinsky, A., op. cit., p. 243.

Chekhov, A., Letter to A. S. Suvorin, 27 March 1894, in Karlinsky, S., op. cit., p. 261.

Chekhov, A., Letter to A. S. Suvorin, 21 October 1895, in Hellman, L., op. cit., p. 189.

Chekhov, A., Letter to A. S. Suvorin, 2 November 1895, quoted in Van Itallie, J-C., *The Seagull: A New Version*, Harper & Row, New York, 1977, p. 90.

Chekhov, A., Letter to A. S. Suvorin, 21 November 1895, in Friedland, L. S., op. cit., p. 146.

Chekhov, A., Letter to A. S. Suvorin, 20 June 1896, quoted in Magarshack, D., *Chekhov the Dramatist*, p. 20.

Chekhov, A., Letter to A. S. Suvorin, 18 October 1896, in Friedland, L. S., op. cit., p. 788.

Chekhov, A., Letter to A. S. Suvorin, 22 October 1896, in Hellman, L., op. cit., pp. 194–5.

Chekhov, A., Letter to A. S. Suvorin, 12 July 1897, quoted in Friedland, L. S., op. cit., p. 265.

Chekhov, A., Letter to A. S. Suvorin, 13 March 1898, in Yarmolinsky, A., op. cit., p. 308.

Chekhov, A., Letter to A. Tikhonov, 1902, quoted in Magarshack, D., *Chekhov the Dramatist*, p. 14.

Chekhov, A., Letter to A. L. Vishnevsky, 3 November 1889, in Yarmolinsky, A., op. cit., p. 355.

Chekhov, A., Letter to A. L. Vishnevsky, 7 November 1903, quoted in Moravcevich, N., 'Chekhov and Naturalism: From Affinity to Divergence', *Comparative Drama*, Vol. 4, No. 4, Winter 1970–71, p. 239.

Chekhov, A., Letter to N. M. Yezhov, 27 October 1887, quoted in Simmons, E. J., *Chekhov: A Biography*, Jonathan Cape, London, 1963, p. 163.

Chekhov, A., Letter to N. M. Yezhov, 21 November 1898, quoted in Hollosi, C., 'Chekhov's Reaction to Two Interpretations of Nina', *Theatre Survey*, Vol. 24, Nos 1 & 2, 1883, p. 122.

Danchenko, V., Letter to A. Chekhov, 27 October 1889, in Benedetti, J., op. cit., p. 63.

Knipper, O., Letter to A. Chekhov, 26 September 1889, quoted in Hingley, R., *The Oxford Chekhov*, Vol. 3, p. 301.

Knipper, O., Letter to A. Chekhov, 27–29 October 1889, in Benedetti, J., op. cit., p. 65.

Kommissarzhevskaya, V., Letter to A. Chekhov, 21 October 1896, in Karlinsky, S., op. cit., p. 283.

Meyerhold, V., Letter to A. Chekhov, 29 September 1889, in Benedetti, J., op. cit., p. 55.

Meyerhold, V., Letter to A. Chekhov, 23 October 1899, in Benedetti, J., op. cit., pp. 58–9.

Nemirovich-Danchenko, V., Letter to C. Stanislavski, 26 October 1889, in Benedetti, J., op. cit., p. 59.

Nemirovich-Danchenko, V., Letter to A. Chekhov, 21 August 1898, in Benedetti, J., op. cit., p. 31.

Nemirovich-Danchenko, V., Letter to A. Chekhov, 18–21 December 1898, in Benedetti, J., op. cit., p. 44.

Nemirovich-Danchenko, V., Letter to A. Chekhov, 22 January 1901, in Benedetti, J., op. cit., p. 99.

Stanislavski, C., Letter to Baron Drizen, 3 November 1909, quoted in Senelick, L., *The Chekhov Theatre*, Cambridge University Press, Cambridge, 1997, pp. 59–60.

Stanislavski, C., Letter to A. Chekhov, in Benedetti, J., op. cit., p. 162.

Yezhov, N. M., Letter to A. Chekhov, n.d., quoted in Hollosi, C., op. cit., p. 122.

**Books consulted or cited**

Abrams, M. H., *A Glossary of Literary Terms,* 3rd ed., Holt, Rinehart and Winston, New York, 1971.

Allen, D., *Performing Chekhov,* Routledge, London, 2000.

Avilova, L., *Chekhov in My Life,* Methuen Drama, London, 1989.

Balukhaty, S. D., ed., *The Seagull Produced by Stanislavsky*, Dennis Dobson, London, 1952.

Baring, M., *Landmarks in Russian Literature,* Methuen, London, 1960 (Chapter 7, 'The Plays of Anton Tcekhov', pp. 163–85).

Barnet, S., Berman, M. and Burto, W., *Types of Drama: Plays and Essays,* Little, Brown and Company, Boston, 1981.

Barricelli, J-P., ed., *Chekhov's Great Plays: A Critical Anthology,* New York University Press, New York, 1981.

Benedetti, J., *Stanislavski: A Biography*, Methuen, London, 1988.

Benedetti, J., *The Moscow Art Theatre Letters*, Routledge, New York, 1991.

Bentley, E., *The Playwright as Thinker*, Meridian Books, New York, 1960.

Bergson, H., *Laughter: An Essay on the Meaning of the Comic*, Macmillan and Co., London, 1935.

Bill, V. T., *Chekhov: The Silent Voice of Freedom*, Philosophical Library, New York, 1987.

Bitsilli, P. M., *Chekhov's Art: A Stylistic Analysis*, Ardis Publishers, Ann Arbor, 1983.

Bloom, H., *Anton Chekhov: Modern Critical Views*, Chelsea House Publishers, Philadelphia, 1999.

Brahms, C., *Reflections in a Lake: A Study of Chekhov's Four Greatest Plays*, Weidenfeld and Nicolson, London, 1976.

Braun, E., ed., *Meyerhold on Theatre*, Eyre Methuen, London, 1969.

Braun, E., *The Director and the Stage*, Methuen, London, 1983 (Chapter 5, 'Stanislavsky and Chekhov', pp. 59–76).

Brooks, C. and Heilman R. B., *Understanding Drama*, Holt, Rinehart and Winston, New York, 1966.

Brownstein, O. L. and Daubert, D. M., eds, *Analytical Sourcebook of Concepts in Dramatic Theory*, Greenwood Press, Westport, 1981.

Bruford, W. H., *Chekhov and his Russia: A Sociological Study*, Routledge and Kegan Paul, London, 1948.

Bruford, W. H., *Chekhov*, Bowes and Bowes, London, 1957.

Brustein, R., *The Theatre of Revolt*, Little, Brown and Company, Boston 1964 (Chapter 4, 'Anton Chekhov', pp. 135–79).

Butova, I. S., *Reminiscences*, quoted in Worrall, N., *File on Chekhov*, Methuen, London, 1986.

Callow, P., *Chekhov: The Hidden Ground*, Ivan R. Dee, Chicago, 1998.

Chekhov, A., *The Island: A Journey to Sakhalin*, Washington Square Press, New York, 1967.

Chudakov, A. P., *Chekhov's Poetics*, Ardis Publishers, Ann Arbor, 1983.

Clayton, J. D., *Chekhov Then and Now: The Reception of Chekhov in World Culture*, Peter Lang, New York, 1997.

Clyman, T. W., ed., *A Chekhov Companion*, Greenwood Press, Westport, 1985.

Constantine, P., trans., *The Undiscovered Chekhov: Thirty-Eight New Stories*, Seven Stories Press, New York, 1998.

Corrigan, R., *Theatre in the Twentieth Century,* Grove Press, New York, 1963.

Corrigan, R. W. and Rosenberg, J. L., *The Context and Craft of Drama,* Chandler Publishing Company, Scranton, 1964 (Corrigan, 'The Plays of Chekhov', pp. 139–67).

Debreczeny, P. and Eekman, T., eds, *Chekhov's Art of Writing,* Slavica Publishers, Columbus, 1977.

Delgado, M. M. and Heritage, P., eds, *In Contact with the Gods?: Directors Talk Theatre,* Manchester University Press, Manchester, 1996.

Donaldson, I., *Transformations in Modern European Drama,* Macmillan Press, London 1983.

Driver, T. F., *Romantic Quest and Modern Query: A History of the Modern Theater,* Delacorte Press, New York, 1970 (Chapter 10, 'Anton Chekhov', pp. 217–48).

Eekman, T., ed., *Anton Cechov 1860 – 1960: Some Essays,* E. J. Brill, Leiden, 1960.

Ehre, M., trans., *Chekhov for the Stage,* Northwestern University Press, Evanston, 1992 (translation of the four major plays).

Ehrenburg, I., *Chekhov, Stendhal and Other Essays,* Macgibbon and Kee, London, 1962 ('On Re-Reading Chekhov', pp. 10–77).

Ellis-Fermor, U., *The Frontiers of Drama,* Methuen, London, 1964.

Elsom, J., *Post-war British Theatre,* Routledge and Kegan Paul, London, 1979.

Emeljanow, V., *Chekhov: The Critical Heritage,* Routledge and Kegan Paul, London, 1981.

Esslin, M., *The Field of Drama,* Methuen, London, 1987.

Forsås-Scott, H., *Notes on 'The Cherry Orchard',* Longman York Press, Harlow, 1983.

Friedland, L. S., ed., *Anton Chekhov: Letters on the Short Story, the Drama, and Other Literary Topics,* Dover Publications, New York, 1966.

Furst, L. and Skrine, P., *Naturalism,* Methuen, London, 1971.

Ganz, A., *Realms of the Self: Variations on a Theme in Modern Drama,* New York University Press, New York, 1980.

Gaskell, R., *Drama and Reality: The European Theatre since Ibsen,* Routledge and Kegan Paul, London, 1972.

Gassner, J., *The Theatre in Our Times,* Crown Publishers, New York, 1963.

Gassner, J., *Directions in Modern Theatre and Drama,* Holt, Rinehart and Winston, New York, 1967.

Gerhardie, W., *Anton Chekhov: A Critical Study*, St. Martin's Press, New York, 1974.

Gielgud, J., *Early Stages*, The Falcon Press, London, 1948.

Gillès, D., *Chekhov: Observer without Illusion*, Funk & Wagnalls, New York, 1968.

Gilman, R., *Chekhov's Plays: An Opening into Eternity*, Yale University Press, New Haven, 1995.

Glicksberg, C. I., *Modern Literary Perspectivism*, Southern Methodist University Press, Dallas, 1970.

Gorky, M., *Reminiscences of Tolstoy, Chekhov and Andreev*, Hogarth Press, London, 1934.

Gorky, M., *Fragments from My Diary*, Penguin Books, Harmondsworth, 1940 (Chapter 19, 'Tchekoff', pp. 170–7).

Gottlieb, V., *Chekhov and the Vaudeville*, Cambridge University Press, Cambridge, 1982.

Gottlieb, V., *Chekhov in Performance in Russia and Soviet Russia*, Chadwyck–Healey, New Jersey, 1984.

Gottlieb, V. and Allain, P., eds, *The Cambridge Companion to Chekhov*, Cambridge University Press, Cambridge, 2000.

Grant, D., *Realism*, Methuen, London, 1970.

Gross, R., *Understanding Playscripts: Theory and Method*, Bowling Green University Press, Bowling Green, 1974.

Guthke, K. S., *Modern Tragi-Comedy*, Random House, New York, 1996.

Guthrie, T. and Kipnis, L., trans., *The Cherry Orchard*, University of Minnesota Press, Minneapolis, 1965.

Hahn, B., *Chekhov: A Study of the Major Stories and Plays*, Cambridge University Press, Cambridge, 1979.

Hellman, L., ed., *The Selected Letters of Anton Chekhov*, Hamish Hamilton, London, 1955.

Hingley, R., *Chekhov*, Unwin Books, London, 1966.

Hingley, R., *Russian Writers and Society*, Weidenfeld and Nicolson, London, 1967.

Hingley, R., *A New Life of Chekhov*, Oxford University Press, London 1976.

Hobgood, B. M., ed., *Master Teachers of Theatre: Observations on Teaching Theatre by Nine American Masters*, Southern Illinois University Press, Carbondale, 1988.

Hodge, F., *Play Directing: Analysis, Communication, and Style*, Allyn and Bacon, Boston, 1994.

Hornby, R., *Script into Performance: A Structuralist Approach*, Paragon House Publishers, New York, 1987.

Howard, J. E., *Shakespeare's Art of Orchestration*, University of Illinois Press, Urbana, 1984.

Jackson, R. L., ed., *Chekhov: A Collection of Critical Essays,* Prentice-Hall, New Jersey, 1967.

Jackson, R. L., ed., *Reading Chekhov's Text,* Northwestern University Press, Evanston, 1993.

Josephson, M., *The Personal Papers of Anton Chekhov,* Lear Publishers, New York, 1948.

Karlinsky, S., ed., *Anton Chekhov's Life and Thought: Selected Letters and Commentary,* University of California Press, Berkeley, 1975.

Kataev, V., *If Only We Could Know!: An Interpretation of Chekhov,* Ivan R. Dee, Chicago, 2002.

Katzer, J., ed., *1860–1960 A. P. Chekhov,* Foreign Languages Publishing House, Moscow, 1960.

Kirk, I., *Anton Chekhov,* Twayne Publishers, Boston, 1981.

Koteliansky, S. S. and Woolf, L., trans., *The Notebook of Anton Tchekhov*, The Hogarth Press, London, 1967.

Krutch, J. W., '*Modernism' in Modern Drama,* Russell and Russell, New York, 1962 (pp. 66–77).

Laffitte, S., *Chekhov,* Angus and Robertson, London, 1974.

Levin, I. and I., *Working on the Play and the Role: The Stanislavsky Method for Analysing the Characters in a Drama,* Ivan R. Dee, Chicago, 1992.

Lewis, A., *The Contemporary Theatre*, Crown Publishers, New York, 1971.

Magarshack, D., *Chekhov: A Life,* Greenwood Press, Westport, 1970.

Magarshack, D., *The Real Chekhov,* Allen and Unwin, London, 1972.

Magarshack, D., *Chekhov the Dramatist,* Eyre Methuen, London, 1980.

Magarshack, D., *Stanislavsky: A Life*, Faber and Faber, London, 1986.

Maugham, W. S., *Points of View,* Bantam Books, New York, 1961 (pp. 137–50).

McVay, G., *Chekhov's 'Three Sisters'*, Bristol Classical Press, London, 1995.

Meister, C. W., *Chekhov Bibliography,* McFarland and Company, Jefferson, 1985.

Melchinger, S., *Anton Chekhov,* Frederick Ungar, New York, 1972.

Miles, P., *Chekhov on the British Stage,* Cambridge University Press, Cambridge, 1993.

Miller, J., *Subsequent Performances,* Faber and Faber, London, 1986.

Mirsky, D. S., *A History of Russian Literature from its Beginnings to 1900,* Vintage Books, New York, 1961.

Müller, H., *The Spirit of Tragedy,* Alfred A. Knopf, New York, 1956.

Nabokov, V., *Lectures on Russian Literature,* Pan Books, London, 1983 (pp. 245–95).

Nemirovich-Danchenko, V., *My Life in the Russian Theatre,* Geoffrey Bles, London, 1968.

Nemirovsky, I., *A Life of Chekhov,* The Grey Walls Press, London, 1950.

Paris, B., ed., *Stella Adler on Ibsen, Strindberg and Chekhov,* Vintage Books, New York, 1999.

Peace, R., *Chekhov: A Study of the Four Major Plays,* Yale University Press, New Haven, 1983.

Pervukhina, N., *Anton Chekhov: The Sense and the Nonsense,* Legas, New York, 1993.

Pitcher, H., *The Chekhov Play: A New Interpretation,* Chatto and Windus, London 1973.

Pitcher, H., *Chekhov's Leading Lady,* John Murray, London, 1979.

Posell, E. Z., *Russian Authors,* Houghton Mifflin Company, Boston, 1970.

Priestley, J. B., *Anton Chekhov,* International Textbook Company, London, 1970.

Pritchett, V. S., *Chekhov: A Biography,* Penguin Books, London, 1988.

Prokofieva, R., trans., *Chekhov's 'Three Years'* , Foreign Languages Publishing House, Moscow, n.d.

Racin, J., *Tatyana Repina: Two Translated Texts by Alexei Suvorin and Anton Chekhov,* McFarland and Company, Jefferson, 1999.

Rapaport, I., *Acting: A Handbook of the Stanislavski Method*, Crown Publishers, New York, 1955.

Rayfield, D., *Chekhov: The Evolution of his Art,* Paul Elek, London, 1975.

Rayfield, D., *Chekhov's 'Uncle Vanya' and 'The Wood Demon',* Bristol Classical Press, London, 1995.

Rayfield, D., *Anton Chekhov: A Life,* Harper Collins, London, 1997.

Rayfield, D., *Understanding Chekhov,* University of Wisconsin Press, Madison, 1999.

Redmond, J., *Drama and Symbolism: Themes in Drama 4*, Cambridge University Press, Cambridge, 1982.

Salmon, E., ed., *Bernhardt and the Theatre of her Time*, Greenwood Press, Westport, 1984 (Senelick, L., Chapter 7, 'Chekhov's Response to Bernhardt', pp. 165–81).

Sanders, E., *Chekhov*, Black Sparrow Press, Santa Rosa, 1995.

Saunders, B., *Tchehov the Man*, Centaur Press, London, 1960.

Schuler, C. A., *Women in Russian Theatre*, Routledge, London, 1996.

Scolnicov, H. and Holland, P., eds, *The Play Out of Context: Transferring Plays from Culture to Culture*, Cambridge University Press, Cambridge, 1989.

Selden, R., *A Reader's Guide to Contemporary Literary Theory*, The Harvester Press, Brighton, 1985.

Senderovich, S. and Sendich, M., eds, *Anton Chekhov Rediscovered: A Collection of New Studies with a Comprehensive Bibliography*, Russian Language Journal, East Lansing, 1987.

Senelick, L., ed., *Russian Dramatic Theory from Pushkin to the Symbolists*, University of Texas Press, Austin, 1981.

Senelick, L., *Anton Chekhov*, Macmillan, 1985.

Senelick, L., *The Chekhov Theatre*, Cambridge University Press, Cambridge, 1997.

Shestov, L., *Chekhov and Other Essays*, University of Michigan Press, Ann Arbor, 1966.

Simmons, E. J., *Chekhov: A Biography*, Jonathan Cape, London, 1963.

Slonim, M., *Russian Theater from the Empire to the Soviets*, Methuen, London, 1963.

Smith, V. L., *Anton Chekhov and the Lady with the Dog*, Oxford University Press, London, 1973.

Stanislavski, C., *My Life in Art*, Eyre Methuen, London, 1980.

States, B. O., *Irony and Drama: A Poetics*, Cornell University Press, Ithaca, 1971.

Steiner, G., *The Death of Tragedy*, Faber & Faber, London, 1961.

Styan, J. L., *The Dark Comedy*, Cambridge University Press, Cambridge, 1968 (pp. 74–106).

Styan, J. L., *Chekhov in Performance*, Cambridge University Press, Cambridge, 1971.

Toumanova, N. A., *Anton Chekhov: The Voice of Twilight Russia*, Columbia University Press, New York, 1937.

Troyat, H., *Chekhov,* Macmillan Press, London, 1986.

Tulloch, J., *Chekhov: A Structuralist Study,* Macmillan Press, 1980.

Tulloch, J., *Shakespeare and Chekhov in Production and Reception,* University of Iowa Press, Iowa City, 2005.

Turkov, A., *Anton Chekhov and his Times,* University of Arkansas Press, Fayetteville, 1995.

Tynan, K., *Curtains,* Longmans, London, 1961.

Valency, M., *The Breaking String,* Oxford University Press, London, 1966.

Wellek, R. and N. D., eds, *Chekhov: New Perspectives,* Twentieth Century Views, Prentice-Hall Inc., New Jersey, 1984.

Williames, L. J., *Anton Chekhov the Iconoclast,* University of Scranton Press, Scranton, 1989.

Williams, R., *Drama from Ibsen to Eliot*, Penguin, Harmondsworth, 1953; 1964.

Williams, R., *Drama in Performance*, Penguin, Harmondsworth, 1968; 1972.

Winner, T., *Chekhov and his Prose,* Holt, Rinehart and Winston, New York, 1966.

Worrall, N., *File on Chekhov,* Methuen, London, 1986.

Yarmolinsky, A., ed., *Letters of Anton Chekhov,* The Viking Press, New York, 1973.

Yermilov, V., *A. P. Chekhov,* Foreign Languages Publishing House, Moscow, n.d.

Young, S., *The Theater,* Doran, New York, 1927.

## Articles, theses and reviews consulted or cited

Allen, D., 'Exploring the Limitless Depths: Mike Alfreds Directs Chekhov', *New Theatre Quarterly*, Vol. 2, No. 8, November 1986.

Allen, D., 'David Jones Directs Chekhov's *Ivanov*', *New Theatre Quarterly*, Vol. 4, No. 15, August 1988.

Allen, D., 'Jonathan Miller Directs Chekhov', *New Theatre Quarterly*, Vol. 5, No. 17, February 1989.

Allen, D., '*The Cherry Orchard*: A New English Version by Trevor Griffiths', in Miles, P., ed., *Chekhov on the British Stage*, Cambridge University Press, Cambridge, 1993.

Allen, D. and Ghelardi, M., 'Unfinished Pieces: From *Platonov* to *Piano*', *Modern Drama,* Vol. 42, No 4, 1999.

Anderson, G., 'The Music of *The Cherry Orchard:* Repetitions in the Russian Text', *Modern Drama*, Vol. 34, 1991.

Anon., Review of *Uncle Vanya, World,* 29 January 1924.

Aronson, A., 'The Scenography of Chekhov', in Bloom, H., *Anton Chekhov: Modern Critical Views,* Chelsea House Publishers, Philadelphia, 1999.

Ashton, B., Letter to *New Statesman,* 11 September 1970, quoted in Magarshack, D., *The Real Chekhov,* George Allen and Unwin, London, 1972.

Atkinson, B., Review of *The Cherry Orchard, New York Times,* 11 March 1928, quoted in Emeljanow, V., ed., *Chekhov: The Critical Heritage*, Routledge and Kegan Paul, London, 1981.

*Australian Theatre Record (The Cherry Orchard),* April 1987.

*Australian Theatre Record (The Cherry Orchard),* May 1987.

*Australian Theatre Record (Three Sisters),* November 1987.

*Australian Theatre Record (Three Sisters),* December 1987.

*Australian and New Zealand Theatre Record (The Cherry Orchard),* April 1989.

*Australian and New Zealand Theatre Record (Three Sisters),* August 1990.

*Australian and New Zealand Theatre Record (The Cherry Orchard),* May 1991.

*Australian and New Zealand Theatre Record (Uncle Vanya),* June 1991.

Azadovsky, K. and Vitale, S., 'Chekhov in Berlin and Badenweiler', *Soviet Literature,* Vol. 1, January 1980.

Babula, W., '*Three Sisters,* Time, and the Audience', *Modern Drama,* Vol. 18, 1975.

Balukhaty, S. D., '*The Cherry Orchard:* A Formalist Approach', in Jackson, R. L., ed., *Chekhov: A Collection of Critical Essays,* Prentice-Hall, New Jersey, 1967.

Barber, J., Review of *The Seagull, Daily Telegraph,* 29 April 1985.

Barricelli, J-P., 'Counterpoint of the Snapping String: Chekhov's *The Cherry Orchard', California Slavic Studies*, Vol. 10, 1997.

Barthes, R., 'The Death of the Author', in Rice, P. and Waugh, P., eds, *Modern Literary Theory*, Edward Arnold, London, 1990.

Beckerman, B., 'Dramatic Analysis and Literary Interpretation: *The Cherry Orchard* as Exemplum', *New Literary History,* Vol. 2, No. 3, Spring 1971.

Beckerman, B., 'The Artifice of "Reality" in Chekhov and Pinter', *Modern Drama,* Vol. 21, 1978.

Belgion, M., 'Verisimilitude in Tchekhov and Dostoievsky', *The Criterion,* Vol. 16, No. 62, October 1936.

Bentley, E., 'Chekhov as Playwright', *Kenyon Review*, Vol. 11, No. 2, Spring 1949.

Bentley, E., 'Craftsmanship in *Uncle Vanya*', in Wellek, R. and N. D., eds, *Chekhov: New Perspectives*, Twentieth Century Views, Prentice-Hall Inc., New Jersey, 1984.

Berdnikov, G., '*Ivanov*: An Analysis', in Jackson, R. L., ed., *Chekhov*, Prentice-Hall, New Jersey, 1967.

Berdnikov, G., 'Chekhov and Our Time', *Soviet Literature,* January 1980.

Bergson, H., 'Laughter', in Sypher, W., ed., *Comedy*, Doubleday Anchor, New York, 1956.

Billington, M., Review of *The Seagull, Guardian*, 29 April 1985.

Billington, M., Review of *The Seagull, Guardian*, 5 August 1985.

Billington, M., Review of *Three Sisters, Guardian*, 3 April 1986.

Billington, M., Review of *The Seagull, Guardian,* 9 July 1994.

Bloom, H., '"Simpler, More Truthful, More Himself": Chekhov', *Theater*, Vol. 24, No. 1, 1993.

Bloom, H., 'Introduction', in Bloom, H., *Anton Chekhov: Modern Critical Views*, Chelsea House Publishers, Philadelphia, 1999.

Borden, R. C., 'The Comic Chekhov on the Russian Stage, 1993–94', in Clayton, J. D., ed., *Chekhov Then and Now: The Reception of Chekhov in World Culture*, Peter Lang, New York, 1997.

Bordinat, P., 'Dramatic Structure in Cexov's *Uncle Vanja*', *Slavic and East European Journal,* Fall 1958.

Bordinat, P., 'Chekhov's Two Great American Directors', *The Midwest Quarterly*, Vol. 16, Nos 1–4, October 1974–July 1975.

Borny, G. J., 'The Subjective and Objective Levels of Reality in Chekhov's *Ivanov* and *The Cherry Orchard*: A Study in Dramatic Technique', unpublished honours thesis, University of New South Wales, 1969.

Borny, G. J., 'Appropriate Mis/Appropriations: Translating Racine's *Les Plaideurs'*, in *Dis/Orientations Conference Proceedings,* Australasian Drama Studies Association, Centre for Drama and Theatre Studies, Monash University, Melbourne, 1997.

du Bos, C., 'The Chekhovian Sense of Life', in Jackson, R. L., ed., *Chekhov: A Collection of Critical Essays*, Prentice-Hall, New Jersey, 1967.

Boyd, C., 'Chekhov's Most Beguiling and Baffling' (*Uncle Vanya*), *Melbourne Times,* 10 July 1991.

Brandon, J. R., 'Toward a Middle-View of Chekhov', *Educational Theatre Journal,* Vol. 13, December 1960.

Braun, E., 'From *Platonov* to *Piano'* and *'The Cherry Orchard',* in Gottlieb, V. and Allain, P., eds, *The Cambridge Companion to Chekhov,* Cambridge University Press, Cambridge, 2000.

Bristow, E. K., 'Circles, Triads, and Parity in *The Three Sisters',* in Barricelli, J-P., ed., *Chekhov's Great Plays: A Critical Anthology*, New York University Press, New York, 1981.

Brustein, R., 'Theatre Chronicle', *Hudson Review,* Vol. 12, 1959.

Burgess, M. A. S., 'The Nineteenth- and Early Twentieth-Century Theatre', in Auty, R. and Oblensky, D., *An Introduction to Russian Language and Literature,* Companion to Russian Studies Series, Vol. 2, Cambridge University Press, Cambridge, 1977.

Cameron, A., *'The Three Sisters'* (Gate Theatre, Dublin), *The Times,* 6 April 1990.

Carnicke, S. M., 'Stanislavsky's Production of *The Cherry Orchard* in the US', in Clayton, J. D., ed., *Chekhov Then and Now: The Reception of Chekhov in World Culture,* Peter Lang, New York, 1997.

Chances, E., 'Chekhov's *Seagull*: Etherial Creature or Stuffed Bird?', in Debreczeny, P. and Eekman, T., eds, *Chekhov's Art of Writing*, Slavica Publishers, Columbus, 1977.

Chizhevsky, D., 'Chekhov in the Development of Russian Literature', in Jackson, R. L., ed., *Chekhov: A Collection of Critical Essays*, Prentice-Hall, New Jersey, 1967.

Chudakov, A. P., 'The Poetics of Chekhov: The Sphere of Ideas', *New Literary History*, Vol. 9, Winter 1978.

Chudakov, A. P., 'Dr Chekhov: A Biographical Essay (29 January 1860–15 July 1904)', in Gottlieb, V. and Allain, P., eds, *The Cambridge Companion to Chekhov*, Cambridge University Press, Cambridge, 2000.

Chukovsky, K., 'Chekhov', in Katzer, J., ed., *1860 – 1960 A. P. Chekhov*, Foreign Languages Publishing House, Moscow, 1960.

Clayton, J. D., 'Cexov's *Djadja Vanja* and Traditional Comic Structure', *Russian Language Journal,* Vol. 40, Nos 136–7, 1986.

Clayton, J. D., 'Chekhov in Canada 1926–1980', in Clayton, J. D., ed., *Chekhov Then and Now: The Reception of Chekhov in World Culture,* Peter Lang, New York, 1997.

Clurman, H., 'Director's Notes for *Uncle Vanya'*, in *On Directing,* Collier Macmillan, New York, 1974.

Clyman, T. W., 'Chekhov: A Biography', in Clyman, T. W., ed., *A Chekhov Companion*, Greenwood Press, Westport, 1985.

Cole, D., 'Chekhov, *The Seagull*', in Bloom, H., *Anton Chekhov: Modern Critical Views*, Chelsea House Publishers, Philadelphia, 1999.

Conrad, J., 'Chekhov as Social Observer: *The Island of Sakhalin*', in Clyman, T. W., ed., *A Chekhov Companion*, Greenwood Press, Westport, 1985.

Corrigan, R., 'Some Aspects of Chekhov's Dramaturgy', *Educational Theatre Journal*, Vol. 7, May 1955.

Corrigan, R., 'The Plays of Chekhov', in Corrigan, R. and Rosenberg, J.L., eds, *The Context and Craft of Drama*, Chandler Publishing Company, Scranton, 1964.

Corrigan, R., 'Stanislavski and the Playwright', in Corrigan, R., ed., *Theatre in the Twentieth Century*, Grove Press, New York, 1965.

Coveney, M., Review of *The Seagull*, *Financial Times*, 5 August 1985.

Coveney, M., Review of *Three Sisters*, *Financial Times*, 2 April 1986.

Coveney, M., Review of *The Seagull*, *Observer*, 10 July 1994.

Cross, A. G., 'The Breaking Strings of Chekhov and Turgenev', *Slavonic and East European Review* (University of London), Vol. 47, 1969.

Croyden, M., 'People Just Eat Their Dinners: The Absurdity of Chekhov's Doktors', *Theatre Quarterly*, Vol. 11, 1968.

De Sherbinin, J. W., 'Chekhov and Christianity, in Clayton, J. D., ed., *Chekhov Then and Now: The Reception of Chekhov in World Culture,* Peter Lang, New York, 1997.

Durkin, A. R., 'Chekhov's Narrative Technique', in Clyman, T. W., ed., *A Chekhov Companion*, Greenwood Press, Westport, 1985.

Edwards, C., 'Balancing Acts' (*Three Sisters*), *The Spectator*, 11 August 1990.

Edwards, C., Review of *Uncle Vanya*, *Spectator*, 17 November 1990.

Edwards, C., Review of *Uncle Vanya*, *Spectator*, 7 March 1992.

Eekman, T., 'Cechov and the Europe of His Day', in Eekman, T., ed., *Anton Cechov 1860–1960: Some Essays*, E. J. Brill, Leiden, 1960.

Eekman, T., 'Chekhov as Correspondent', in Clyman, T. W., ed., *A Chekhov Companion*, Greenwood Press, Westport, 1985.

Eichenbaum, B., 'Chekhov at Large', in Jackson, R. L., ed., *Chekhov: A Collection of Critical Essays*, Prentice-Hall, New Jersey, 1967.

Esslin, M., 'Chekhov and the Modern Drama', in Clyman, T. W., ed., *A Chekhov Companion,* Greenwood Press, Westport, 1985.

Fergusson, F., '*The Cherry Orchard:* A Theater-Poem of the Suffering of Change', in Barricelli, J-P., ed., *Chekhov's Great Plays: A Critical Anthology*, New York University Press, New York, 1981.

Fischer-Lichte, E., 'Intercultural Aspects in Post-Modern Theatre: A Japanese Version of Chekhov's *Three Sisters*', in Scolnicov, H. and Holland, P., eds, *The Play Out of Context,* Cambridge University Press, Cambridge, 1989.

Fisher, R. T. Jr, 'Chekhov's Russia: A Historian's View', in Clyman, T. W., ed., *A Chekhov Companion*, Greenwood Press, Westport, 1985.

Flath, C. A., '*The Seagull:* The Stage Mother, the Missing Father, and the Origins of Art', *Modern Drama*, Vol. 42, No. 4, 1999.

Foot, D., Review of *Uncle Vanya, Guardian*, 10 November 1990.

Fox, S., Review of *Three Sisters, City Limits*, 3 April 1986.

Freedman, J., 'Center Stage: Chekhov in Russia 100 Years On', *Modern Drama*, Vol. 42, No. 4, 1999.

Freedman, M., 'Chekhov's Morality of Work', *Modern Drama*, Vol. 5, No. 1, 1962.

French, P., 'Chekhov on Film', in Bloom, H., *Anton Chekhov: Modern Critical Views,* Chelsea House Publishers, Philadelphia, 1999.

Gassner, J., 'Chekhov and the Sublimation of Realism', in *Masters of the Drama*, 3$^{rd}$ ed., Dover Publications, New York, 1954.

Gassner, J., 'The Duality of Chekhov', in Bristow, E. K., *Anton Chekhov's Plays*, W. W. Norton, New York, 1977.

Gauss, R., 'Lydia Borisovna Yavorskaya 1871–1921: A Biography', *Theatre Perspectives International,* October 1998.

Gerould, D., '*The Cherry Orchard* as Comedy', *Journal of General Education*, Vol. 11, January 1958.

Gerould, D., 'The Pitoëff's Chekhov', in Clayton, J. D., ed., *Chekhov Then and Now: The Reception of Chekhov in World Culture,* Peter Lang, New York, 1997.

Gilman, R., 'Broadway Critics Meet *Uncle Vanya*', *Theatre Quarterly*, Vol. 4, No. 13, February–April 1974.

Gilman, R., 'Chekhov', in *The Making of Modern Drama,* Da Capo Press, New York, 1987.

Gilman, R., '*Ivanov:* Prologue to a Revolution', *Theater,* Vol. 22, No. 2, 1991.

Goldberg, L., 'Chekhov's Comedy: *The Cherry Orchard*', *Scripta Hierosolymitana*, Vol. 19, 1967.

Golomb, H., 'Communicating Relationships in Chekhov's *Three Sisters*', in Senderovich, S. and Sendich, M., eds, *Anton Chekhov Rediscovered: A Collection of New Studies with a Comprehensive Bibliography*, Russian Language Journal, East Lansing, 1987.

Golomb, H., 'Value Structuration in *Three Sisters* with Special Reference to the Roles of Time and Place', *Assaph: Studies in the Theatre* (Tel-Aviv University), Vol. 4, 1988.

Golomb, H., '*В Москву!* (To Moscow!): On Moscow's Role in Controlling Performance and Audience Response in Chekhov's *The Seagull* and *Three Sisters*', *Theatre Perspectives International*, 1994.

Golub, S., 'Arrival and Departures (*The Cherry Orchard*)', in *The Recurrence of Fate: Theatre and Memory in Twentieth-Century Russia*, University of Iowa Press, Iowa, 1994.

Goodliffe, J. D., 'Time in Chekhov's Plays', *New Zealand Slavonic Journal*, Winter 1971.

Gorky, M., 'Anton Chekhov', in Katzer, J., ed., *1860–1960 A. P. Chekhov*, Foreign Languages Publishing House, Moscow, 1960.

Gorky, M., 'Fragment from Reminiscences', in Jackson, R. L., ed., *Chekhov: A Collection of Critical Essays*, Prentice-Hall, New Jersey, 1967.

Gorky, M., 'Anton Chekhov', in *On Literature*, University of Washington Press, Seattle, 1973.

Gottlieb, V., 'Chekhov in Limbo: British Productions of the Plays of Chekhov', in Scolnicov, H. and Holland, P., eds, *The Play Out of Context: Transferring Plays from Culture to Culture*, Cambridge University Press, Cambridge, 1989.

Gottlieb, V., 'Why this Farce?', *New Theatre Quarterly*, Vol. 7, No. 27, August 1991.

Gottlieb, V., 'The Politics of British Chekhov', in Miles, P., *Chekhov on the British Stage*, Cambridge University Pres, Cambridge, 1993.

Gottlieb, V., 'Chekhov's One-Act Plays and the Full-Length Plays' and 'Chekhov's Comedy', in Bloom, H., *Anton Chekhov: Modern Critical Views*, Chelsea House Publishers, Philadelphia, 1999.

Greene, G., Review of *The Cherry Orchard, Spectator*, 5 September 1941.

Grossman, L., 'The Naturalism of Chekhov', in Jackson, R. L., ed., *Chekhov: A Collection of Critical Essays*, Prentice-Hall, New Jersey, 1967.

Gurev, P., 'Summing Up Russian Symbolist Poetry', in Rabinowitz, S., *The Noise of Change: Russian Literature and the Critics (1891–1917)*, Ardis, Ann Arbor, 1986.

Guthrie, T., 'A Director's View of *The Cherry Orchard*', in Guthrie, T. and Kipnis, L., trans., *The Cherry Orchard*, University of Minnesota Press, Minneapolis, 1965.

Hagan, J., 'Chekhov's Fiction and the Ideal of "Objectivity"', *Proceedings of the Modern Language Association*, Vol. 81, October 1966.

Hahn, B., 'Chekhov: *The Three Sisters*', *The Critical Review* (Melbourne), No. 15, 1972.

Hahn, B., 'Chekhov's *The Cherry Orchard*', *The Critical Review* (Melbourne), No. 16, 1973.

Harrop, J., 'Masking Chekhov and Revealing Action: A Rehearsal Process', in Redmond, J., ed., *Drama and the Actor: Themes in Drama 6*, Cambridge University Press, Cambridge, 1984.

Heifetz, L., 'Notes from a Director: *Uncle Vanya*', in Bloom, H., *Anton Chekhov: Modern Critical Views,* Chelsea House Publishers, Philadelphia, 1999.

Heim, M., 'Chekhov and the Moscow Art Theatre', in Barricelli, J-P., ed., *Chekhov's Great Plays: A Critical Anthology*, New York University Press, New York, 1981.

Hewison, R., 'Chekhov with an Irish Lilt (*Three Sisters*)', *Sunday Times*, 29 July 1990.

Hewison, R., Review of *The Seagull*, *Sunday Times*, 17 July 1994.

Hinchliffe, A., 'Chekhov As I See Him', *Soviet Literature*, No. 1, January 1980.

Holland, P., 'Chekhov and the Resistant Symbol', in Redmond, J., *Drama and Symbolism: Themes in Drama 4*, Cambridge University Press, Cambridge, 1982.

Holland, P., 'The Director and the Playwright: Control over the Means of Production', *New Theatre Quarterly*, Vol. 3, No. 11, August 1987.

Hollosi, C., 'Chekhov's Reaction to Two Interpretations of Nina', *Theatre Survey*, Vol. 24, Nos 1 & 2, 1983.

Hollosi, C., 'The Importance of Being Earnest (or Funny) in Adapting Chekhov: The Case of *Platonov*', in Clayton, J. D., ed., *Chekhov Then and Now: The Reception of Chekhov in World Culture,* Peter Lang, New York, 1997.

Hristic, J., 'Time in Chekhov: The Inexorable and the Ironic', *New Theatre Quarterly*, Vol. 1, No. 3, August 1985.

Hristic, J., '"Thinking with Chekhov": The Evidence of Stanislavsky's Notebooks', *New Theatre Quarterly*, Vol. 11, No. 42, 1995.

Hubbs, C. A., 'The Function of Repetition in the Plays of Chekhov', *Modern Drama*, Vol. 22, 1979.

Hubbs, C. A., 'Chekhov and the Contemporary Theatre', *Modern Drama*, Vol. 24, No. 3, 1981.

Hurren, K., Review of *Uncle Vanya*, *Mail on Sunday*, 1 March 1992.

Irvine, St J., Review of *The Seagull*, *Observer*, 29 September 1929, quoted in Miles, P., *Chekhov on the British Stage*, Sam & Sam, England, 1987, p. 21.

Jackson, R. L., 'Introduction: Perspectives on Chekhov', in Jackson, R. L., ed., *Chekhov: A Collection of Critical Essays*, Prentice-Hall, New Jersey, 1967.

Jackson, R. L., 'Chekhov's *Seagull:* The Empty Well, the Dry Lake, and the Cold Cave', in Barricelli, J-P., ed., *Chekhov's Great Plays: A Critical Anthology*, New York University Press, New York, 1981.

Johnsen-Neshati, K., 'A Portrait of *Ivanov* and an Interview', *Theater*, Vol. 22, No. 2, 1991.

Jones, W. G., 'Chekhov's Undercurrent of Time', *Modern Language Review*, Vol. 64, 1969.

de Jongh, N., 'A Frigid Family Occasion (*Three Sisters*)', *Guardian Weekly*, 5 August 1990.

Karlinsky, S., 'Huntsmen, Birds, Forests, and Three Sisters', in Barricelli, J-P., ed., *Chekhov's Great Plays: A Critical Anthology*, New York University Press, New York, 1981.

Karlinsky, S., 'Russian Anti-Chekhovians', *Russian Literature*, Vol. 15, 1984.

Karlinsky, S., 'Chekhov: The Gentle Subversive', in Wellek, R. and N. D., eds, *Chekhov: New Perspectives*, Twentieth Century Views, Prentice-Hall Inc., New Jersey, 1984.

Katayev, V., 'Understanding Chekhov's World', *Soviet Literature*, January 1980.

Katsell, J. H., 'Chekhov's *The Seagull* and Maupassant's *Sur l'eau*', in Barricelli, J-P., ed., *Chekhov's Great Plays: A Critical Anthology*, New York University Press, New York, 1981.

Kelson, J., 'Allegory and Myth in *The Cherry Orchard*', *Western Humanities Review*, Vol. 8, No. 13, 1959.

Kernan, A. B., 'Truth and the Dramatic Mode in the Modern Theater: Chekhov, Pirandello, and Williams', *Modern Drama*, Vol. 1, 1958.

Keyssar, H., 'The Strategy of Drama in Recognition Scenes', *Proceedings of the Modern Language Association*, Vol. 92, 1977.

Kilroy, T., '*The Seagull:* An Adaptation', in Bloom, H., *Anton Chekhov: Modern Critical Views,* Chelsea House Publishers, Philadelphia, 1999.

King, F., Review of *Uncle Vanya, Sunday Telegraph*, quoted in *London Theatre Record*, 15 July–15 August 1982.

King, F., Review of *The Seagull, Sunday Telegraph*, 5 May 1985.

King, F., Review of *The Seagull, Sunday Telegraph*, 11 August 1985.

Kingston, J., Review of *The Seagull, The Times*, 12 July 1991.

Kitchin, L., 'Chekhov Without Inhibitions: The Moscow Art Theatre in London', *Encounter,* Vol. 11, No. 2, August 1958.

Kleber, P., 'The Whole of Italy is Our Orchard: Strehler's *Cherry Orchard', Modern Drama,* Vol. 42, No. 4, 1999.

Knipper-Chekhova, O., 'The Last Years', in Katzer, J., ed., *1860–1960 A. P. Chekhov*, Foreign Languages Publishing House, Moscow, 1960.

Kobatake, M., 'Soliloquy and Modern Drama', *Theatre Annual*, Vol. 18, 1961.

Kovitz, S., 'A Fine Day to Hang Oneself: On Chekhov's Plays', in Barricelli, J-P., ed., *Chekhov's Great Plays: A Critical Anthology*, New York University Press, New York, 1981.

Kozhevnikova, I., 'The Artists of Chekhov's Time', *Soviet Literature,* January 1980.

Kramer, K. D., 'Chekhov at the End of the Eighties: The Question of Identity', *Études Slaves et Est-Européennes*, Vol. 2, 1966.

Kramer, K. D., '*Three Sisters* or Taking a Chance on Love', in Barricelli, J-P., ed., *Chekhov's Great Plays: A Critical Anthology*, New York University Press, New York, 1981.

Kramer, K. D., '"A Subject Worthy of Ayvazovsky's Brush": Vanya's Misdirected Fury', *Modern Drama,* Vol. 42, No. 4, 1999.

Krause, D., 'Freil's Ballybeggared Version of Chekhov', *Modern Drama,* Vol. 42, No. 4, 1999.

Krutch, J. W., *Nation*, 31 October 1928, in Emeljanow, V., op. cit., pp. 338–9.

Kuprin, A., 'Reminiscences of Anton Tchekhov', in Koteliansky, S. S., ed., *Anton Tchekhov: Literary and Theatrical Reminiscences*, Benjamin Blom, New York, 1965; Haskell House Publishers, New York, 1974.

Kuzicheva, A., '"Breaking the Rules": Chekhov and His Contemporaries', in Clayton, J. D., ed., *Chekhov Then and Now: The Reception of Chekhov in World Culture*, Peter Lang, New York, 1997.

Lahr, J., 'Pinter and Chekhov: The Bond of Naturalism', *Tulane Drama Review*, Vol. 13, No. 2 (T 42), Winter 1968.

Landesman, R., 'Comrade Serban in *The Cherry Orchard*', *Yale Theatre*, Vol. 8, Nos 2 & 3, Spring 1977.

Lantz, K. A., 'Chekhov's Cast of Characters', in Clyman, T. W., ed., *A Chekhov Companion*, Greenwood Press, Westport, 1985.

Latham, J. E. M., '*The Cherry Orchard* as Comedy', *Educational Theatre Journal*, Vol. 10, March 1958.

Lawson, M., 'The Mark of Frayn', *Drama*, Vol. 3, No. 169, 1988.

Leblanc, R., 'Liberating Chekhov or Destroying Him? Joel Gershmann's Farcical Production of *The Cherry Orchard*', in Clayton, J. D., ed., *Chekhov Then and Now: The Reception of Chekhov in World Culture*, Peter Lang, New York, 1997.

Leighton, L. G., 'Chekhov in English', in Clyman, T. W., ed., *A Chekhov Companion*, Greenwood Press, Westport, 1985.

Levin, R., 'Performance Critics vs Close Readers in the Study of Renaissance Drama', *Modern Language Review*, Vol. 81, July 1986.

Lieberson, J., 'Chopping up *The Cherry Orchard*', *The New York Review of Books*, Vol. 35, No. 3, 3 March 1988.

Lindheim, R., 'Chekhov's Major Themes', in Clyman, T. W., ed., *A Chekhov Companion*, Greenwood Press, Westport, 1985.

Lindheim, R., 'Introduction' (special issue on Chekhov), *Modern Drama*, Vol. 42, No. 4, 1999.

Lomunov, K., 'Tolstoy–Chekhov–The Moscow Art Theatre', *Soviet Literature*, No. 1, January 1980.

*London Theatre Record* (*The Cherry Orchard*), 15 July–11 August 1982.

*London Theatre Record* (*The Cherry Orchard*), 8–21 October 1983.

*London Theatre Record* (*The Cherry Orchard*), 1–14 January 1986.

*London Theatre Record* (*The Cherry Orchard*), 22 October–4 November 1989.

*London Theatre Record* (*Ivanov*), 9–22 April 1989.

*London Theatre Record* (*Three Sisters*), 26 March–8 April 1986.

*London Theatre Record* (*Three Sisters*), 12–25 March 1987.

*London Theatre Record* (*Three Sisters*), 21 May–3 June 1987.

*London Theatre Record* (*Three Sisters*), 29 July–11 August 1988.

*London Theatre Record* (*Three Sisters*), 16–29 July 1989.

*London Theatre Record* (*Uncle Vanya*), 6–19 May 1982.

*London Theatre Record* (*Uncle Vanya*), 15 July–11 August 1982.

*London Theatre Record* (*Uncle Vanya*), 10–23 September 1989.

*London Theatre Record* (*Uncle Vanya*), 12–25 March 1990.

*London Theatre Record* (*Uncle Vanya*), 5–18 November 1990.

*London Theatre Record* (*Uncle Vanya*), 30 July–26 August 1991.

*London Theatre Record* (*Uncle Vanya*), 12–15 February 1992.

*London Theatre Record* (*Wild Honey*), 2–29 July 1984.

Long, R. E. C., *Fortnightly Review*, July–December 1902, quoted in Emeljanow, V., op. cit., p. 67.

Magarshack, D., '*The Cherry Orchard*', in Wellek, R. and N. D., eds, *Chekhov: New Perspectives*, Twentieth Century Views, Prentice-Hall Inc., New Jersey, 1984.

Majdalany, M., 'Natasha Ivanovna, the Lonely *Bourgeoise*', *Modern Drama*, Vol. 26, 1983.

Mann, T., 'The Stature of Anton Chekhov', *The New Republic,* Vol. 132, May 1955.

Mann, T., 'Anton Chekhov', *Mainstream*, Vol. 12, March 1959.

Marsh, C., 'The Stage Representation of Chekhov's Women', in Bloom, H., *Anton Chekhov: Modern Critical Views,* Chelsea House Publishers, Philadelphia, 1999.

Martin, D., 'Philosophy in Cechov's Major Plays', *Welt Der Slaven*, Vol. 23, 1978.

Mathewson, R. W. Jr, 'Chekhov's Legacy: Icebergs and Epiphanies', in Bloom, H., *Anton Chekhov: Modern Critical Views*, Chelsea House Publishers, Philadelphia, 1999.

May, C. E., 'Chekhov and the Modern Short Story', in Clyman, T. W., ed., *A Chekhov Companion*, Greenwood Press, Westport, 1985.

McFarlane, J., 'Intimate Theatre: Maeterlinck to Strindberg', in Bradbury, M. and McFarlane, J., eds, *Modernism*, Penguin, Harmondsworth, 1981.

McKellen, I., 'Acting Chekhov', in Bloom, H., *Anton Chekhov: Modern Critical Views,* Chelsea House Publishers, Philadelphia, 1999.

Meister, C. W., 'Chekhov's Reception in England and America', *American Slavic Review and East European Review,* Vol. 12, February 1953.

Melnick, B., 'Theatre and Performance: *The Cherry Orchard* and *Henry V*', *Tulane Drama Review*, Vol. 11, No. 4 (T 36), Summer 1967.

Meyerhold, V., 'Naturalistic Theater and the Theater of Mood', in Jackson, R. L., ed., *Chekhov: A Collection of Critical Essays*, Prentice-Hall, New Jersey, 1967.

Miller, J., 'Directing the Classics', ABC broadcast of Adelaide Festival Talk, n.d.

Moravcevich, N., 'Chekhov and Naturalism: From Affinity to Divergence', *Comparative Drama*, Vol. 4, No. 4, Winter 1970–71.

Moravcevich, N., 'Scène-à-faire and the Chekhovian Dramatic Structure', in Debreczeny, P. and Eekman, T., eds, *Chekhov's Art of Writing*, Slavica Publishers, Columbus, 1977.

Moravcevich, N., 'Women in Chekhov's Plays', in Barricelli, J-P., ed., *Chekhov's Great Plays: A Critical Anthology*, New York University Press, New York, 1981.

Moravcevich, N., 'The Dark Side of the Chekhovian Smile', *Drama Survey*, Vol. 5, No. 3, Winter 1996–7.

Morson, G. S., 'Prosaic Chekhov: Metadrama, the Intelligentsia, and *Uncle Vanya*', *Tri-Quarterly*, No. 80, Winter 1990–91.

Moss, H., 'Three Sisters', *The Hudson Review*, Vol. 30, No. 4, 1977.

Mudrick, M., 'Boyish Charmer and Last Mad Genius', *The Hudson Review*, Vol. 27, No. 1, 1974.

Nag, M., 'On the Aspects of Time and Place in Anton Chekhov's Dramaturgy', *Scando-Slavica*, Vol. 16, 1970.

Nathan, D., Review of *Three Sisters*, *Jewish Chronicle*, 11 April 1986.

Neill, H., 'Bleak Comedy of a Changing World', *The Times,* 24 October 1989.

Nichols, J. R., 'Chekhov's *The Cherry Orchard:* The Fallacy of the Bourgeoisie Hero', *Studies in the Twentieth Century*, No. 9, Spring 1972.

Nilsson, N. A., 'Intonation and Rhythm in Cechov's Plays', in Eekman, T., ed., *Anton Cechov, 1860–1960: Some Essays*, E. J. Brill, Leiden, 1960.

Nilsson, N. A., 'Two Chekhovs: Mayakovskiy on Chekhov's "Futurism"', in Barricelli, J-P., ed., *Chekhov's Great Plays: A Critical Anthology*, New York University Press, New York, 1981.

Nordmann, A., 'The Actor's Brief: Experiences with Chekhov', *Theatre Research International,* Vol. 19, No. 2, 1994.

Nunn, T., 'Notes from a Director: *Three Sisters*', in Bloom, H., *Anton Chekhov: Modern Critical Views,* Chelsea House Publishers, Philadelphia, 1999.

O'Connor, F., 'The Slave's Son', *The Kenyon Review,* Vol. 25, No. 1, 1963.

Odesskaya, M., 'Chekhov's *Tatyana Repina:* From Melodrama to Mystery Play', *Modern Drama,* Vol. 42, No. 4, 1999.

Orr, J., 'The Everyday and the Transient in Chekhov's Tragedy', in *Tragic Drama and Modern Society,* The Macmillan Press, London, 1981.

Osborne, C., Review of *The Seagull, Daily Telegraph,* 25 April 1991.

Paperny, Z., 'Truth and Faith: Reading Chekhov's Rough Drafts and Notebooks', *Soviet Literature,* January 1980.

Paul, B., 'Chekhov's "Five Sisters"', *Modern Drama,* February 1972.

Pavis, P., '*Ivanov:* The Invention of a Negative Dramaturgy', in Bloom, H., *Anton Chekhov: Modern Critical Views,* Chelsea House Publishers, Philadelphia, 1999.

Peace, R., 'Chekhov's "Modern Classicism"', *Slavonic and East European Review,* Vol. 65, No. 1, January 1987.

Pearson, A., Review of *Uncle Vanya, Independent on Sunday,* 18 August 1991.

Pearson, A. G., 'The Cabaret Comes to Russia: "Theatre of Small Forms" as Cultural Catalyst', *Theatre Quarterly,* Vol. 9, No. 36, Winter 1980.

Pedrotti, L., 'Chekhov's Major Plays: A Doctor in the House', in Barricelli, J-P., ed., *Chekhov's Great Plays: A Critical Anthology,* New York University Press, New York, 1981.

Pinter, H., 'Writing for the Theatre', in *Pinter Plays,* Vol. 1, Methuen, London, 1976.

Pitcher, H., 'The Chekhov Play', in Wellek, R. and N. D., eds, *Chekhov: New Perspectives,* Twentieth Century Views, Prentice-Hall Inc., New Jersey, 1984.

Pitcher, H., 'Chekhov's Humour', in Clyman, T. W., ed., *A Chekhov Companion,* Greenwood Press, Westport, 1985.

Poggioli, R., 'Realism in Russia', *Comparative Literature,* Vol. 3, 1951.

Polakiewicz, L., 'Selected Bibliography', in Clyman, T. W., ed., *A Chekhov Companion,* Greenwood Press, Westport, 1985.

Polotskaya, E., 'Chekhov and His Russia', in Bloom, H., *Anton Chekhov: Modern Critical Views,* Chelsea House Publishers, Philadelphia, 1999.

Quinn, M. L., 'Reading and Directing the Play', *New Theatre Quarterly,* Vol. 3, No. 11, August 1987.

Rabkin, G., 'The Play of Misreading: Text/Theatre/Deconstruction', *Performing Arts Journal,* Vol. 7, No. 1, 1983.

Rabkin, G., 'Is There a Text on This Stage?: Theatre/Authorship/ Interpretation', *Performing Arts Journal*, Vol. 9, Nos 2 & 3, 1985.

Radin, V., Review of *The Seagull*, *New Statesman*, 9 August 1985.

Ratcliffe, M., Review of *Three Sisters*, *Observer*, 6 April 1986.

Ratcliffe, M., 'Bringers of Light (*Three Sisters*)', *Observer*, 16 July 1989.

Rayfield, D., 'Chekhov: The Evolution of His Art', in Wellek, R. and N. D., eds, *Chekhov: New Perspectives*, Twentieth Century Views, Prentice-Hall Inc., New Jersey, 1984.

Rayfield, D., 'Chekhov and the Literary Tradition', in Clyman, T. W., ed., *A Chekhov Companion*, Greenwood Press, Westport, 1985.

Rayfield, D., 'Chekhov's Stories and the Plays', in Bloom, H., *Anton Chekhov: Modern Critical Views*, Chelsea House Publishers, Philadelphia, 1999.

Rayner, A., 'Soul in the System: On Meaning and Mystique in Stanislavski and A. C. Bradley', *New Theatre Quarterly*, Vol. 1, No. 4, November 1985.

Risso, R. D., 'Chekhov: A View of the Basic Ironic Structures', in Barricelli, J-P., ed., *Chekhov's Great Plays: A Critical Anthology*, New York University Press, New York, 1981.

Robinson, M., 'M. Robinson Replies to the Notion that Chekhov's Characters "Are Forever Conquered by Life"', *Adelphi*, May 1927, in Emeljanow, V., ed., *Chekhov: The Critical Heritage*, Routledge and Kegan Paul, London, 1981.

Rogoff, G., 'The Carpet Orchard: Brook's *The Cherry Orchard* in Brooklyn', *Theater*, Vol. 19, No. 2, 1988.

Rose, H., Review of *Three Sisters*, *Time Out*, 9 April 1986.

Rutherford, M., Review of *Uncle Vanya*, *Financial Times*, 27 February 1992.

Schmitt, N. C., 'Stanislavski, Creativity, and the Unconscious', *New Theatre Quarterly*, Vol. 2, No. 8, November 1988.

Scolnicov, H., 'Chekhov's Reading of *Hamlet*', in Scolnicov, H. and Holland, P., eds, *Reading Plays: Interpretation and Reception*, Cambridge University Press, Cambridge, 1991.

Scott-Norman, F., Review of *Uncle Vanya*, *In Press*, 3 July 1991.

Senderovich, S., '*The Cherry Orchard*: Cechov's Last Testament', *Russian Literature*, Vol. 35, 1994.

Senelick, L., 'Chekhov's Drama, Maeterlinck, and the Russian Symbolists', in Barricelli, J-P., ed., *Chekhov's Great Plays: A Critical Anthology*, New York University Press, New York, 1981.

Senelick, L., 'Chekhov and the Irresistible Symbol: A Response to Peter Holland', in Redmond, J., *Drama and Symbolism: Themes in Drama 4*, Cambridge University Press, Cambridge, 1982.

Senelick, L., 'Chekhov on Stage', in Clyman, T. W., ed., *A Chekhov Companion*, Greenwood Press, Westport, 1985.

Senelick, L., 'Stuffed Seagulls: Parody and the Reception of Chekhov's Plays', *Poetics Today*, Vol. 8, No. 2, 1987.

Senelick, L., 'Offenbach and Chekhov; or, La Belle Yeliena', *Theatre Journal*, Vol. 42, No. 4, December 1990.

Senelick, L., 'The Department of Missing Plays, Chekhov Division', *Theater*, Vol. 22, No. 2, 1991.

Senelick, L., 'Chekhov and the Bubble Reputation', in Clayton, J. D., ed., *Chekhov Then and Now: The Reception of Chekhov in World Culture*, Peter Lang, New York, 1997.

Senelick, L., 'Director's Chekhov', in Bloom, H., *Anton Chekhov: Modern Critical Views*, Chelsea House Publishers, Philadelphia, 1999.

Sevastyanov, V., 'Tribute to Chekhov', *Soviet Literature*, Vol. 1, January 1980.

Seymour, A., 'Summer Seagull, Winter Love', *The London Magazine*, May 1964.

Shakh-Azizova, T., 'A Russian *Hamlet*', *Soviet Literature*, Vol. 1, January 1980.

Shakh-Azizova, T., 'Chekhov on the Russian Stage', in Bloom, H., *Anton Chekhov: Modern Critical Views*, Chelsea House Publishers, Philadelphia, 1999.

Shestov, L., 'Anton Chekhov: (Creation from the Void)', in Bloom, H., *Anton Chekhov: Modern Critical Views*, Chelsea House Publishers, Philadelphia, 1999.

Shorter, E., Review of *Three Sisters*, *Daily Telegraph*, 3 April 1986.

Shulman, M., Review of *The Seagull*, *Standard*, 27 April 1984.

Shulman, M., Review of *The Seagull*, *Standard*, 29 April 1985.

Shulman, M., Review of *Uncle Vanya*, *Evening Standard*, 15 September 1989.

Silverstein, N., 'Chekhov's Comic Spirit and *The Cherry Orchard*', *Modern Drama*, Vol. 1, No. 3, September 1958.

Skaftymov, A., 'Principles of Structure in Chekhov's Plays', in Jackson, R. L., ed., *Chekhov: A Collection of Critical Essays*, Prentice-Hall, New Jersey, 1967.

Smeliansky, A., 'Chekhov at the Moscow Art Theatre', in Bloom, H., *Anton Chekhov: Modern Critical Views*, Chelsea House Publishers, Philadelphia, 1999.

Smith, J. O., 'Chekhov and the "Theatre of the Absurd"', *Bucknell Review*, Vol. 14, December 1966.

Sobolev, Y., 'Tchekhov's Creative Method', in Koteliansky, S. S., ed., *Anton Tchekhov: Literary and Theatrical Reminiscences*, Benjamin Blom, New York, 1965.

Speirs, L., '"I Shall Call the Play a Comedy": *The Cherry Orchard*', *The Oxford Review*, Vol. 5, 1967.

Spencer, C., Review of *Uncle Vanya*, *Daily Telegraph*, 27 February 1992.

Stanislavski, C., 'Memories of Chekhov', in Hapgood, E. R., ed., *Stanislavski's Legacy*, Max Reinhardt, London, 1958.

Stanislavski, C., 'A. P. Chekhov at the Arts Theater', in Turkov, A., ed., *Anton Chekhov and His Times*, University of Arkansas Press, Fayetteville, 1995.

States, B. O., 'Chekhov's Dramatic Strategy', *Yale Review*, Vol. 56, December 1966.

Stein, W., 'Tragedy and the Absurd', *The Dublin Review*, Vol. 233, Winter 1959–60.

Stowell, H. P., 'Chekhov and the *nouveau roman*: Subjective Objectivism', in Debreczeny, P. and Eekman, T., eds, *Chekhov's Art of Writing*, Slavica Publishers, Columbus, 1977.

Stowell, H. P., 'Chekhov into Film', in Clyman, T. W., ed., *A Chekhov Companion*, Greenwood Press, Westport, 1985.

Strindberg, A., 'Author's Foreword to *Miss Julie*', in Sprigge, E., ed., *Six Plays of Strindberg*, Doubleday Anchor Books, New York, 1955.

Stroyeva, N. M., '*The Three Sisters* at the MAT', *Tulane Drama Review*, Vol. 9, No. 1, 1964.

Stroyeva, N. M., 'Everyone Has His Own Chekhov', *Soviet Literature*, No. 2, February 1980.

Styan, J. L., 'The Delicate Balance: Audience Ambivalence in the Comedy of Shakespeare and Chekhov', *Costerus*, Vol. 2, 1972.

Styan, J. L., 'Chekhov's Dramatic Technique', in Clyman, T. W., ed., *A Chekhov Companion*, Greenwood Press, Westport, 1985.

Swinnerton, F., *Nation*, 17 July 1920, quoted in Miles, P., op. cit., p. 9.

Szewcow, M., 'Anatolij Efros Directs Chekhov's *The Cherry Orchard* and Gogol's *The Marriage*', *Theatre Quarterly*, Vol. 7, No. 26, 1977.

Szondi, P., 'The Drama in Crisis', in Bloom, H., *Anton Chekhov: Modern Critical Views*, Chelsea House Publishers, Philadelphia, 1999.

Tait, P., 'The Proposal Reconsidered: A Biography of Love', in Clayton, J. D., ed., *Chekhov Then and Now: The Reception of Chekhov in World Culture*, Peter Lang, New York, 1997.

Taylor, P., Review of *The Seagull, Independent*, 23 February 1990.

Taylor, P., Review of *The Seagull, Independent*, 8 November 1990.

Terras, V., 'Chekhov at Home: Russian Criticism', in Clyman, T. W., ed., *A Chekhov Companion*, Greenwood Press, Westport, 1985.

Timmer, C. B., 'The Bizarre Elements in Chekhov's Art', in Eekman, T., ed., *Anton Cechov 1860–1960: Some Essays*, E. J. Brill, Leiden, 1960.

Tovstonogov, G., 'Chekhov's *Three Sisters* at the Gorky Theatre', *Tulane Drama Review*, Vol. 13, No. 2, 1968.

Tufts, C. F., 'Prisoners of Their Plots: Satiric Drama of Self-Consciousness in Chekhov's *Three Sisters*', *Modern Drama*, Vol. 32, 1989.

Tulloch, J., 'Chekhov Abroad: Western Criticism', in Clyman, T. W., ed., *A Chekhov Companion*, Greenwood Press, Westport, 1985.

Tulloch, J., Burvill, T. and Hood, A., 'Reinhabiting *The Cherry Orchard*: Class and History in Performing Chekhov', *New Theatre Quarterly*, Vol. 13, No. 52, 1997.

Tulloch, J., Burvill, T. and Hood, A., 'Transformations and Transcodifications: *The Cherry Orchard* on Television', in Clayton, J. D., ed., *Chekhov Then and Now: The Reception of Chekhov in World Culture*, Peter Lang, New York, 1997.

Tulloch, J., Burvill, T. and Hood, A., 'Chekhov in Massachusetts: Competing Modernisms at the American Repertory Theatre', *Modern Drama*, Vol. 42, No. 4, 1999.

Turner, C. J. G., 'Time in Chekhov's *Tri Sestry*', *Canadian Slavonic Papers*, Vol. 28, No. 1, 1986.

Valency, M., 'Vershinin', in Barricelli, J-P., ed., *Chekhov's Great Plays: A Critical Anthology*, New York University Press, New York, 1981.

Various Authors, 'The Chekhov Centenary', *World Theatre*, Vol. 9, No. 2, Summer 1960.

Various Authors, 'Reminiscences', *Soviet Literature*, January 1980.

Vilar, J., 'Murder of the Director', in Corrigan, R., *Theatre in the Twentieth Century*, Grove Press, New York, 1963.

Vitins, I., 'Uncle Vanja's Predicament', *Slavic and East European Journal*, Vol. 22, No. 4, 1978.

W—, A. E., Review of *Three Sisters*, *Star*, 17 February 1926, quoted in Emeljanow, V., op. cit., p. 300.

Walker, H., 'Chasing Chekhov', *Drama*, Vol. 3, No. 169, 1988.

Walton, M., '"If Only We Knew"', *New Theatre Magazine*, Vol. 8, No. 1, Autumn 1968.

Weightman, J., 'Chekhov and Chekhovian', *Encounter*, Vol. 41, No. 2, August 1973.

Wesker, A., 'Interpretation: To Impose or Explain', *Performing Arts Journal*, Vol. 11, No. 2, 1988.

Williams, R., 'Anton Chekhov', in Bloom, H., *Anton Chekhov: Modern Critical Views*, Chelsea House Publishers, Philadelphia, 1999.

Wimsatt, W. K., 'The Two Meanings of Symbolism', *Hateful Contraries*, Kentucky University Press, Kentucky, 1965.

Winner, T. G., 'Cechov and Scientism: Observations on the Searching Stories', in Eekman, T., ed., *Anton Cechov 1860–1960: Some Essays*, E. J. Brill, Leiden, 1960.

Winner, T. G., '*The Seagull* and *Hamlet*', in Wellek, R. and N. D., eds, *Chekhov: New Perspectives*, Twentieth Century Views, Prentice-Hall Inc., New Jersey, 1984.

Woolf, V., '*The Cherry Orchard*', in Bloom, H., *Anton Chekhov: Modern Critical Views*, Chelsea House Publishers, Philadelphia, 1999.

Worrall, N., 'Stanislavsky's Production of *Three Sisters*', in Russell, R. and Barratt, A., eds, *Russian Theatre in the Age of Modernism*, Macmillan, London, 1990.

Worrall, N., 'Robert Sturua's Interpretation of Chekhov's *Three Sisters*: An Experiment in Post-modern Theatre', in Clayton, J. D., ed., *Chekhov Then and Now: The Reception of Chekhov in World Culture*, Peter Lang, New York, 1997.

Worrall, N., 'Stanislavsky's Production Score for Chekhov's *The Cherry Orchard* (1904): A Synoptic Overview', *Modern Drama*, Vol. 42, No. 4, 1999.

Yermilov, V., 'A Great Artist and Innovator', in Katzer, J., ed., *1860–1960 A. P. Chekhov*, Foreign Languages Publishing House, Moscow, 1960.

Yermilov, V., '*Uncle Vanya*: The Play's Movement', in Jackson, R. L., ed., *Chekhov: A Collection of Critical Essays*, Prentice-Hall, New Jersey, 1967.

**Other literary works cited**

Beckett, S., *Waiting for Godot*, Faber and Faber, London, 1965.

Borny, G. J., *Petty Sessions,* a verse translation of Racine's *Les Plaideurs*, University of New England Press, Armidale, 1988.

Davison, D., ed., *Andrew Marvell: Selected Poetry and Prose*, Harrap and Company, London, 1952.

Robbins, H., *The Dream Merchants*, New English Library, London, 1980.

Shakespeare, W., *Hamlet*.

Shakespeare, W., *Julius Caesar*.

# Index

*A Dreary Story*, 39, 60, 78
*A Lady with a Dog*, 79
*A Midsummer Night's Dream*, 13, 231
*A Moscow Hamlet*, 38, 110
*A Nervous Breakdown*, 60, 69
*A Streetcar Named Desire*, 203
*A Thousand and One Passions*, 62
*A Tragic Role*, 94
Absurdists, 26, 27, 38
Ackland, Rodney, 13, 14
acting style, 64
actor, privileging of, 231
*Adrienne Lecouvreur*, 63
Aeschylus, 71
Alexandrinsky Theatre, St Petersburgh, 128
Alfreds, Mike, 157, 196, 197, 264
alienation, 78, 189
*An Anonymous Story*, 21, 33, 44
'anaesthesia of the heart', 157, 159, 228
*anagnorisis* (recognition) scene, 254, 255
*Anna Karenina*, 73
*Ariadne*, 78
art as social corrective, 34
artist as 'unbiased witness', 68
Ashton, Basil, 3
aside, the, 127
audience's decoding, 5
  mediated by director/actors, 82
author's intention, 1, 6
  literary playtext, 2, 4, 5, 8, 9, 10, 14, 15, 140
authorial interventions, 67, 68
Avilova, Lydia, 129

Bakhtin, 121 (see also 'postmodernism')
Balukhaty, S., 173
Bannen, Ian, 175
Barthes, 6
Beckerman, Bernard, 11
Beckett, Samuel, 27, 195, 200
Bentley, Eric, 184, 185
Berdnikov, G., 114–115
Bergson, 157, 227

Bernhardt, Sarah, 63, 158, 161
Billington, Michael, 146, 150, 151, 159–160, 197, 198
*Bolvanov*, 111
Bourget, 46
Brecht, 69
British Chekhov, 150, 226–227
Brook, Peter, 3, 13, 208
Brustein, Robert, 38, 207
Burge, Stuart, 187
Butova, I.S., 177–178

Caird, John, 150
casting, importance of, 113
characterisation
  in short stories, 70
  in major plays, 80
Chekhov, A.P.
  artistic credo, 57, 68
    cautious optimist, 135
  attitude towards actors, 1, 3, 7
    towards directors, 1, 3
    towards Stanislavski's work, 3, 22–23, 121
  change, 23
  commitment to realism, 64
  gardening, 23, 24
  God, no belief in, 36, 41, 185
  literary artist, 22
  medical practitioner, 34
  optimism, 46
  playwright, 93
  'poetic-realist', 86
  progress through education, 23, 25, 29, 30, 34, 49, 191, 207, 214
  progress though work, 23, 49, 182, 191, 254
  proto-Absurdist, 42, 43, 195, 265
  proto-Marxist, 43
  psychiatry, 112
  roles, multiplicity of, 22
  'sermonizing', 36
  short-story writer, 93
  social improvement, commitment to, 29
  socio-political goals, 35
  symbolism, parodic use of, 157

theory of drama, 66
Tolstoy and immortality, 36–37
tragic-comic technique, 177, 182
treatise on prison conditions, 25
understatement, 174
vision of reality, 4, **21–55**, 57, 73, 80, 122, 153, 178, 191, 198, 257
    objective correlative of, 51, 66, 77, 93
Chekhov's characters/characterisation
    behaviourist approach to, 115
    fallibility of, 212
    happy martyrs, 204
    (non-)judgement of, 74, 101, 205, 207
    psychology, 116
    refusal to act, 200
    self-deception, 30–31
    self-dramatising, 152, 187, 190
    subjective/objective lives, 77, 98, 237, 246, 248
    view of women, 139
Chekhov's work
    anti-theatricalist approach, 75
    the bizarre in, 81
    content/form distinction, 57
    early plays, 93–126
    form, the search for, 57–91
    synthetic tragi-comedy, 98, 100, 141, 178, 230
Chekhov, Alexander, 70, 102, 105, 106, 115
Chekhov, Mikhail, 99, 131
*Chekhov: A Structuralist Study*, 25
Chitau-Karmina, M., 138, 139
cholera epidemic 1892, 43
chorus, 72
Clark, Anthony, 150
colonial exploitation, 44
comedy
    distancing effect of, 190
    social corrective, 23, 190, 201
comic irony, 144
commedia dell'arte, 96
communication chain, 5
*Complete Collected Works*, 95
Compte, 58

conventions
    clichéd, 103, 127
        parodic use of, 161
    of realism, 67, 68, 75, 101, 116, 119, 174, 255
    theatrical, 72, 139
creativity, 9
*Crocodile Tears*, 62

Darwin, 58
Darwinian viewpoint, 42, 43, 212
Davydov, V.N., 102, 103, 105, 108, 113
de la Tour, Frances, 183
deconstruction, 4, 9
deconstructive theory, 7
Dench, Judi, 160
depression, 40, 41, 113
'determinancy/indeterminancy', 14
Devine, George, 120
Diaghilev, 43
didactic view of art, 74
*Disciple*, 46
*Dishonourable Tragedians and Leprous Dramatists*, 62
director
    'as butler', 3, 14
    function of, vis-à-vis author, 4, 10, 14
    as interpreter/translator, 4, 132
    privileging of, 3, 10
'director's theatre', 7
Dostoevesky, 36, 58
dramatic techniques, 93
*Dreams*, 69
dualism
    'both/and', 48, 229
    'either/or', 48, 257
    externalised/internalised life, 97, 115, 141
    long-term optimism/short-term pessimism, 182
    'tragic/comic', 18, 120, 121, 141, 150, 159, 246
    passive/active, 209
    progressive/nihilistic, 23
    text/subtext, 18, 77, 78, 80, 97, 98, 117

dislocation of, 81, 235
juxtaposing, 87
dualistic balance, 51, 150, 159, 203, 205, 220, 229, 257
dualistic lives, 78

ecology, 182
Ellis-Fermor, Una, 109
Eliot, T.S., 141
endurance, virtue of, 217
English farce, 160
English theatre practitioners, 263
entropy, 151
Elsom, John, 72, 73
Esslin, Martin, 5, 26
Eugene Onegin, 73
evolutionary gradualism, 41, 43, 212, 2155
extremism, 42
Eyre, Richard, 226

'faith', 31, 42, 43, 182, 186
    in the future, 218
Fettes, Christopher, 182
Filmer, Esme, 146, 157
*fin-de-siècle* gloom and despair, 136, 197
fourth wall convention, 116, 122
Frayn, Michael, 128, 151, 204–205, 229
freedom
    artistic, 149
    personal, 50, 149
Furst and Skrine, 47, 48, 58

Gaskell, Ronald, 58
Gershmann, Joel, 228
*Ghost Sonata*, 207–208
*Ghosts*, 72
Gielgud, John, 157
Gillès, David, 130, 135, 203
Gilman, Richhard, 195–197
Goddard, Harold, 8, 9
Gogol, 62
*Gooseberries*, 118
Gorky, Maxim, 23, 24, 37, 174
Gottlieb, Vera, 98–99, 157, 160, 188, 189, 198, 200, 264

Griffiths, Trevor, 226, 227, 250
    on English sensibilities, 263–264
Gross, Roger, 11, 15
Guthrie, Tyrone, 15

*Hamlet*, 9, 11, 12, 241, 250
Hamlet, 70, 151, 157
Hands, Terry, 151
*Happy Days*, 195, 196
Hingley, Ronald, 21, 29, 30, 94, 249
Hollosi, Clara, 132, 139
Hong Kong, 44
Howard, Jean, 15
human activity, 38, 186
human condition, 142
human happiness, 38
human inactivity, 28
human possibility and actuality, gap between, 28
human psychology, 47
humanist faith, 41

Ibsen, 69, 72, 81, 121
*In the Hollow*, 74
intelligentsia, 32, 191, 211, 249, 250
interpretation
    act of, 3
    anarchic view of, 6
    by audience, 5, 82
    by director, 4, 5
    definition of, 7, 8
    patterns of, 9
    polarised, 48, 204, 219, 228
    problems of, 83
    theatrical, 8
*Ivanov*, 66, 70, 86, **93–126**, 127
    Jones' 1976 production, 108–109
    wasted potential in, 110,

*Jane Eyre*, 118
Jones, David, 108
*Julius Caesar*, 80
Jullien, Jean, 70

Karlinsky, Simon, 25, 93, 110, 195, 201

Karpov, E.M., 62, 64, 122
*King Lear*, 208
King, Martin Luther, 205
Knipper, Olga, 16, 59, 60, 136, 173, 175, 201, 217, 250
Kiseleva, M.V., 57
Kommissarzhevskaya, Vera, 130, 131, 132, 138, 139, 202, 219
Komisarjevsky, 146
Korsh, Fyodor, 100, 102, 103, 105, 106
Kosky, Barry, 3
Kotzebue, August, 62
Kuprin, Alexander, 29, 71, 76

*Lady Audley's Secret*, 9
*larmoyante*, 226
laziness, 25
Leontyev-Shcheglov, I.L., 40, 44
*Letters of A.P. Chekhov*, 99
Levin, Richard, 9, 10
Levkeyeva, E.I., 128
Leykin, Nicolai, 106
'life as it is', 37, 46, 57, 63, 65, 67, 75, 77, 80, 87, 101, 127, 154, 191, 211, 217
'life as it should be', 38, 57, 77, 80, 154, 191, 211, 248
'life as it should *not* be', 38, 46, 87, 154
Lilina, Mariya Petrovna, 225
'logic of the lie in the public world', 77
*Lonely Lives*, 59
Long, R.E.C., 76
Luhrmann, Baz, 3

Maeterlinck, Maurice, 119, 148
Magarshack, David, 41, 83, 93, 94, 101, 135, 169, 197, 207, 228, 233, 246, 256
  'direct'/'indirect action', 119–120, 141, 159
Majdalany, Marina, 208–210
Malle, Louis, 187
Maly Theatre, Moscow, 99, 170
Marks, A.F., 95
Marvell, Andrew, 196
Mastantonio, Mary Elizabeth, 175
materialist vision, 58
Mathias, Sean, 173
Maupassant, 142

Medical School of Moscow University, 47
Melikhovo, 40
melodrama, 99, 100, 111, 127, 143, 248
  Chekhov's parodic use of, 143, 144
  nineteenth-century Russia, 62, 63, 86
  Scribean, 118, 233
'messenger element', 83, 84, 85, 86, 236, 238, 240, 241
Meyerhold, 59, 133, 171, 173
military, the, 214
Miller, Hillis, 9
Miller, Jonathan, 2, 3, 10, 13, 14, 208
*Mire*, 34
Mirolubov, Victor, 186
misinterpretations, 18, 266
  as Absurdist, 26, 34, 204
  as tragic fatalist, 26
*Miss Julie*, 105
Mizonova, L.S., 40
Modernism, 58
Molière, 34, 173, 201
'mooing' episode, 239
Morley, Robert, 121
Morson, Gary Saul, 186–187
Moscow Art Theatre, 16, 107, 121, 122, 130, 169, 172, 263
Mosher, Gregory, 175
'museum theatre', 12
*My Life in Art*, 137, 203
*My Life in the Russian Theatre*, 171–172, 199
mythical golden age, 2

'naïve realism', 65
Naturalism, 47–49, 57, 58, 59
Naturalists, 65
naturalistic objectivity, 112
nature/nurture debate, 215
nature, scientific explanation of, 42
Nemirovich-Danchenko, 15, 16, 107, 130, 133, 135, 137, 170, 174, 198, 199, 217, 265
'new forms' of drama, 129, 140
Nicholls, Phoebe, 146
Nilsson, Nils Ake, 83
*Notebooks*, 24, 34, 37, 41, 44, 45, 49, 185
'nothing to be done', 28, 195, 204, 216, 254

*Old Times*, 80
Ophelia's madness, 11, 12
Orlov, I.I., 250

'parameters', 11, 12, 16, 23, 51
performance code, 4
performance text, 4, 5, 9, 15, 140
Physical Events, 12, 65
Pidgeon, Rebecca, 175
Pinter, Harold, 69, 70, 80, 140
Pitcher, Harvey, 82, 188, 202, 208, 209, 232
Pixérécourt, Guilbert de, 62
*Platanov*, 66, 86, 93–126
playwright
    intention, 2
    primacy of, 6
    privileging of, 11
Plescheyev, A.N., 60, 101
polarities, 18
polemical writing, 74
Polonsky, Yakov, 120
postmodern theories, 1, 2, 4, 121
pre-Chekhovian drama, 118
'priority', 14
'privileging', 14, 15
Prowse, Philip, 145
Pryce, Jonathan, 159, 160
Przevalsky, N., 32
Psychic Events, 12, 14, 15, 65, 191
psychic phenomena, 47
purpose, 34, 40
Pushkin, 62

Rabkin, Gerald, 7, 8
Rapaport, I., 97
readings
    absurdist, 17
    gloomy/pessimistic, 17
    plurality of 10, 11
    positive/optimistic, 17, 18
reductionist, 18
realism, 72
    literal, 87
Redgrave, Michael, 187
Redgrave, Vanessa, 159–160

religion, 186
Reminiscences, 177
*Reminiscences of Anton Tchekhov*, 29
representational form, limitations of, 65, 107, 117
Robbins, Harold, 67, 68
Romanticism, 58
Rosanov, Vasili, 186
Roxonova, 132, 133, 135, 139
Russian critics, 17
Russian Revolution, 50, 197, 213
Russian sensibilities, 264

Sakhalin, 24, 25, 32, 33, 44
Sartre, Jean-Paul, 27, 152, 263
Sazonova, Sofya Ivanovna, 22
scientific materialism, 47
scientific method, 34, 46, 57
    application to literature, 65, 178
Scott, Walter, 62
Scribe, 72 (see also 'well-made play' and 'melodrama')
secular faith, 46
Senelick, Laurence, 62, 148, 156
Serban, Andrei, 6
Sevastyanov, Vitali, 50–51
Shakespeare, 8
Shavrova, Yelena, 73, 74
Shawn, Wallace, 187
Shcheglov, Ivan, 61
Sher, Antony, 173–174
short-story techniques, 93
Shulman, Milton, 145, 147, 169
Simmons, Ernest, 96
*Smoking Is Bad for You*, 27, **95–99**
Sobolev, Y., 115
social responsibility, 22
soliloquies, 72, 80, 108, 115, 116, 127, 139
    'disguised', 83, 84, 85, 86, 108, 187, 211, 236, 237, 238, 240, 250, 255
Solomon, 41
Sophocles, 72
sound effects, 82, 118, 136, 239, 256
Stalinist oppression, 218
Stanislavski, Konstantin, 1, 10, 15, 16, 59, 63, 118, 137, 175, 225

system of acting, 64, 80, 83, 97, 117, 134, 263
Stanislavskian overkill, 133, 177
Stanislavskian tradition, 169
States, Bert O., 81
stereotypes, 70, 96, 110, 114
Strindberg, 99, 105, 207
Sturridge, Charles, 146
Sturua, Robert, 121
subtextual inner life, 80, 84, 231, 233, 263
suicide, 38, 39, 70, 114, 118
'superfluous man', 38, 110, 114
   debunking of, 111
Suvorin, A.S., 7, 22, 24, 33, 35, 38, 61, 70, 73, 101, 107, 111, 131
symbolism, 85, 86, 87, 119
   seagull as, 156–157
   Treplev's playlet 153
   Yepihodov's breaking string, 86, 255, 256
Symbolists, 148
symbolist aesthetic, 155

Taganrog, 28, 94, 210–211
'tak zhit nelzna', 264
*Terror*, 21
text
   valid/invalid interpretations of, 11, 16
'texts on legs', 2
'Thaw', the, 218, 219
theatre 'as it is', 61
theatre 'as it should *not* be', 61
theatre, educative function of, 61
theatre, late-nineteenth century, 61, 62
*The Bear*, 94
*The Blind*, 148
*The Cherry Orchard*, 3, 9, 10, 16, 44, 45, 81, 84, 85, **225–261**,
   Eyre's 1977 production, 226
   Fagan's 1928 production, 80, 81,
   Gershmann's 1986 production, 228, 229
   interpretive controversy, 225–230
   Moscow Art Theatre 1958 production, 226
   proposal scene, 240–248
   Serban's 1977 production, 227–228

Stanislavski's production, 11
*The Dream Merchants*, 67
*The Duel*, 29–32, 44, 78, 114
"The Death of the Author", 6
theatre-making, 3
theatricality, old-fashioned, 105
*The Forest Tramp*, 63
*The Horse Stealers*, 68
*The Island: A Journey to Sakhalin*, 33
*The Merchant of Venice*, 13
*The Party*, 60, 77
*The Proposal*, 94
*The Seagull*, 3, 15, 66, 84, 85, **127–168**, 248
   Alfreds' 1991 production, 157
   Caird's 1994 production, 150, 160
   Clark's 1990 production, 150–151
   Filmer's 1925 production, 157
   Filmer's 1929 production, 146
   Hands' 1990 production, 151
   Karpov's 1896 production, 64, 122, 130, 173
   Prowse's 1984 production, 145
   Stanislavski's 1898 production, 122, 132, 133, 144, 145, 170
   Sturridge's 1985 production, 146, 159–160
*The Sneeze*, 50
*The Wood Demon*, 66, 86, 93–126, 127
thesis play (*pièce à thèse*), 72, 73, 161
*Thieves*, 73, 74
*Three Sisters*, 45, 82, 84, 98, **195–224**, 248
   Alfreds' 1986 production, 197–198, 203–204
   comedy/farce, 202
   'culture' and 'vulgarity', 209
   expressions of hope, 217
   Komisarjevski's 1926 production, 13, 14, 195
   Miller's 1976 production, 13, 14
   Nemirovich-Danchenko's 1940 production, 199–200, 219
   Stanislavski's 1901 production, 198, 200, 203
   Sturua's production, 121
   Tolstoy's view of, 75
   Tovstonogov's 1965 production,

218–220
wasted potential in, 206, 210, 256
*Three Years*, 74
Tikhonov, Alexander, 22, 145
'tolerances', 11, 16, 23, 51
Tolstoy, L.N., 37, 38, 58, 75,
  objections to Chekhov's plays, 76, 116
Tovstonogov, Georgii, 218–200
Tsar Nicholas II, 29
Tsarist Russia, 50
Tulloch, John, 25–26, 30
Tynan, Kenneth, 226, 264

*Uncle Vanya*, 6, 45, 81, 98, 99, 103, **169–194**,
  Branagh/Egan's 1991 production, 189
  Burge's 1963 TV production, 187
  Fettes' 1882 production, 183
  Mathias' 1992 production, 173
  Mosher's TV version, 175, 176, 185
  Serban's production of, 12, 13
  Stanislavski's 1899 production, 169, 171, 232
  Unwin's 1990 production, 188
  Yefremov's 1989 production, 169

*Understanding Playscripts: Theory and Method*, 11

Valency, Maurice, 21, 22, 27, 28
*Vanya on Forty-Second Street*, 187
'vaudevilles', 94, 95, 202
'vaunted 60s', 44
virtuosity, 13, 14, 15
Vishnevsky, A.L., 170, 199

*Waiting for Godot*, 27, 195, 196
well-made play, the (*pièce bien faite*), 72, 73, 75, 83, 103, 104, 112, 120, 121, 147, 159, 253, 257
  conventions of, 128, 161, 188
Wesker, Arnold, 6, 7
West, Timothy, 188
Western critics, 17
Williams, Raymond, 71, 119, 140, 249
Williams, Tennessee, 203

"Writing for the Theatre", 70

Yeats, W.B., 69
Yezhov, 102, 136
Young, Stark, 12, 13

Zola, 65

www.ingramcontent.com/pod-product-compliance
Lightning Source LLC
Chambersburg PA
CBHW040310240426
43666CB00022B/2922